The Asbury Theological S̶
Christian Revitaliz̶

This volume is published in collaboration with the Center for the Study of World Christian Revitalization Movements, a cooperative initiative of Asbury Theological Seminary faculty. Building on the work of the previous Wesleyan/Holiness Studies Center at the Seminary, the Center provides a focus for research in the Wesleyan Holiness and other related Christian renewal movements, including Pietism and Pentecostal movements, which have had a world impact. The research seeks to develop analytical models of these movements, including their biblical and theological assessment. Using an interdisciplinary approach, the Center bridges relevant discourses in several areas in order to gain insights for effective Christian mission globally. It recognizes the need for conducting research that combines insights from the history of evangelical renewal and revival movements with anthropological and religious studies literature on revitalization movements. It also networks with similar or related research and study centers around the world, in addition to sponsoring its own research projects.

In this study, Robert Webster offers a fresh perspective on the supernatural as a significant identifying mark of eighteenth century Methodism. He does so from a comprehensive review of Wesley's interaction with this phenomena as reflected in his writings. Webster's concern is to challenge the assumption that, given this emphasis, early Methodism was out of step with the intellectual climate of his day and, furthermore, that Wesley's treatment of the supernatural served to inculcate a distinctive identity for early Methodists. With this focus the author offers insight into the significance of early Methodism as a revitalization movement.

J. Steven O'Malley
Editor, The Pietist and Wesleyan Studies Series in the Asbury
Theological Seminary Studies in Christian Revitalization

Methodism and the Miraculous

John Wesley's Idea of the Supernatural and the Identification of Methodists in the Eighteenth Century

Robert Webster

Asbury Theological Seminary Series:
The Study of World Christian Revitalization Movements in
Pietist/Wesleyan Studies, No. 12

EMETH PRESS
www.emethpress.com

Methodism and the Miraculous John Wesley's Idea of the Supernatural and the Identification of Methodists in the Eighteenth-Century

Library of Congress Cataloging-in-Publication Data

Webster, Robert, 1956-
   Methodism and the miraculous : John Wesley's idea of the supernatural and the identification of Methodists in the eighteenth-century / Robert Webster.
      p. cm. -- (The study of world Christian revitalization movements in Pietist/Wesleyan studies)
   Originally presented as the author's thesis (D. Phil.)--Oxford University, 2006.
   Includes bibliographical references (p.   ).
   ISBN 978-1-60947-048-7 (alk. paper)
   1. Wesley, John, 1703-1791. 2. Supernatural. 3. Methodist Church--History of doctrines--18th century. 4. Methodist Church--History of doctrines--19th century. I. Title.
   BX8495.W5W35 2012
   230'.7092--dc23
                              2012043118

The photo on the cover of John Wesley preaching in Ireland in the open air is from a painting by Marla Spillsbury and is on display in the Museum of Methodism in Great Britain. Used by permission.

In Memoriam

Guy Fytch Lytle, III

Contents

Acknowledgments

This study explores the thesis that belief in the supernatural became a significant identifying mark of Methodists living in the eighteenth-century. Not only did John Wesley believe in the reality of angels and demons but he also reflected on witchcraft, visionary experiences, trances, healings, and providential portents in a way that both affirmed his commitment to the theological strictures of primitive Christianity and developed a religious self-awareness for Methodists living in a changing modern world. Additionally, contrary to previous approaches to the place of the Methodists in Enlightenment culture, this book argues that a belief in the supernatural was far from eclipsed in the minds and hearts of people living in the eighteenth-century. Instead, during the historical period that has often been called "the long eighteenth century," there were many debates about the invisible world and how it affected historical existence. Thus, the research offered here poses an objection to the proposition that John Wesley and his Methodist followers were out of step with the intellectual climate of their day. Rather, it will be demonstrated, that John Wesley was familiar with various wide-ranging debates about miracles, demonic possession and exorcism, visions, dreams and other aspects related to the idea of the supernatural which were occurring in the period and became a contributor in ways that not only asserted a fundamental belief in miraculous and supernatural occurrences but crafted his ideas in a manner that both promoted and inculcated a self-identity for Methodists.

There are a variety of people that I wish to acknowledge and thank in the completion of this project that was first accepted as a D. Phil thesis at Oxford University. First, what seems a long time ago, I entered into the office of Rev Dr Guy Fytch Lytle, III, to inquire about the possibility of graduate study at Oxford. Previously he attended Oxford University as a Marshall scholar and was instrumental in my reception of the first Hartman Scholarship, a three-year award granted to me by the faculty of the School of Theology at the University of the South in Sewanee, Tennessee (USA). I could not have started or completed my research without the considerable assistance this provided. This work is dedicated to him. Second, I would also like to thank the Tennessee Conference of the United Methodist Church (USA) for a grant that provided financial assistance at a critical time in this research. Third, my sincere gratitude is extended to Professor Ernest Nicholson, former Provost of Oriel College, Oxford and Dr. Richard Cross (now of Notre Dame University), who helped and supported me in various ways while I was a graduate research student at Oriel College.

One of the values of being a part of Oxford University is sharing of resources and ideas in the context of an academic community. I owe a great deal of appreciation to Rev Dr Jane Shaw who supervised this work initially as a doctoral thesis. She offered continual support and her commitment and constructive criticism has been helpful and insightful along the way. Shaw's expertise as a scholar of the Enlightenment has proven valuable to the research presented here. Additionally, anyone who has interest in the rise of Methodism in eighteenth-century England cannot lightly pass over the name and scholarship of Dr John Walsh. His interest in the topic and the offering of his knowledge in a free and open manner has been of great assistance. If the work offered here has any merit, it is due to his commitment and care for the project. I would also like to express my sincere thanks to Dr Peter Nockles and Dr Gareth Lloyd who work with the Methodist Archives at the John Rylands University Library in Manchester, UK. They were very helpful not only in securing various materials for my research but exhibited an on-going attention in the concepts and issues that are treated in the following pages. A special word of gratitude also goes to Dr Dorothy Clayton of the Methodist Archives for granting permission to quote and use various sources for the publication of this book. I would also like to thank the librarians at the Bodleian Library for help and assistance in a variety of ways. Their expertise and assistance saved me a lot of time in what has been already a very long process. Additionally, the librarians at Oriel College, Lincoln College, All Souls College, and Corpus Christi College were great help at various points too. The assistance of librarians at Vanderbilt University, in Nashville, Tennessee, have aided in the completion of my research in the United States.

I would be remiss if I did not thank all those in England and North America who have encouraged me while researching and writing this book. Their commitment and support have been felt daily in a multitude of ways. Chief among those are Principal Ralph Waller (Manchester College, Oxford University) and Dr Henry Rack (Emeritus, University of Manchester) who served as examiners for this work when submitted for the Doctor of Philosophy degree at Oxford University. Their judicious comments have proved invaluable in the final stages of this work. Of course, any errors in judgment remain my own. As always, Victoria Webster, my wife, has offered continual love and support to me and her presence in my life has provided encouragement that is valued and appreciated.

Robert Webster
June 28, 2012
Birthday of John Wesley (Gregorian calendar)

Abbreviations

ANF	*Ante Nicene Fathers*, 10 vols.
BEW	The Bicentennial Edition of *The Works of John Wesley*.
DEB	*Dictionary of Evangelical Biography*,
DMBI	*A Dictionary of Methodism in Britain and Ireland.*
DNB	*The Dictionary of National Biography.*
JWJW	*The Works of John Wesley.*
JWJWcd	*The Works of John Wesley on Compact Disc.*
JWW	John Wesley's *Works*.
LJW	*The Letters of the Rev. John Wesley, A. M.,*
MARC	Methodist Church Archives. John Rylands University Library, University of Manchester.
NPNF	*Nicene and Post-Nicene Fathers*, First Series.
ODNB	*The Oxford Dictionary of National Biography.*
PW	*The Poetical Works of John and Charles Wesley.*

Chapter 1

The Supernatural in the Enlightenment: Models for Dialogue

Millions of spiritual Creatures walk the Earth
Unseen, both when we wake, and when we sleep.[1]

What then will your reason do here? How will it pass from things natural to spiritual; from the things that are seen to those that are not seen; from the visible to the invisible world? What a gulf is here! By what art will reason get over the immense chasm? This cannot be till the Almighty come in to your succour, and give you that faith you have hitherto despised. Then upborne, as it were, on eagles' wings, you shall soar away into the regions of eternity; and your enlightened reason shall explore even "the deep things of God;" God himself "revealing them to you by his Spirit."[2]

In 1713, Clement XI (1649-1721) issued a papal bull *Unigenitus Dei Filius*, which condemned Jansenist views on a variety of theological issues like predestination, sin, and irresistible grace.[3] Shortly thereafter a Jansenist in the Saint-Médard seminary witnessed a variety of miracles at the tomb of Abbé Francois de Pâris, which incited debates about the existence of miracles at the beginning of the eighteenth century.[4]

A few years later, in 1731, the French skeptic and Deist—Louis-Basile Carré de Montgeron (1686-1754)—made a pilgrimage to the burial place where he was overwhelmed in a trance that lasted over four hours. Montegron's conversion was followed by his missionary zeal to defend the Pâris miracles and the

1

revelatory nature of divine power. His magnum opus, *La Vérité des Miracles Opérés par l'intercession de M. de Paris et autres appellans démontré*, totaled over nine hundred pages and defended the idea of miracles in the modern world.[5]

In 1750, John Wesley (1703-91) was reading Montgeron and the miraculous events which the skeptic had experienced at Abbé Pâris. Wesley's excitement was mixed with caution when he recorded in his journal on Thursday, 11 January: "I had always looked on the whole affair as a mere legend, as I suppose most Protestants do, but I see no possible way to deny these facts without invalidating all human testimony. I may full as reasonably deny there is such a person as Mr. Montgeron, or such a city as Paris in the world. Indeed in many of these instances I see great superstition as well as strong faith. But the 'times of ignorance God does wink at' still, and bless the faith, notwithstanding the superstition."[6] Thirteen years later, when John Wesley responded to Bishop William Warburton (1698-1779) and his attack on the Methodists, Wesley again utilized the "Abbé Pâris affair" with all of its political overtones. "Meantime I would just observe," wrote Wesley to Warburton, "that if these miracles were real, they strike at the root of the whole papal authority, as having been wrought in direct opposition to the famous Bull *Unigenitus*."[7]

Philosophical Considerations of the Supernatural in the Enlightenment

At the beginning of the Enlightenment Isaac Newton (1642-1727) revolutionized the way people in the seventeenth and eighteenth centuries began to think about the world in which they lived.[8] Born in 1642, Newton went to Cambridge at the age of nineteen and in 1666, became a fellow of Trinity College. In 1703, he was elected president of the Royal Society and two years later was knighted the first scion of science. Newton's thought, however, was not an easy one to trace. Not only was he a man whose ideas were obtuse for the average person, but also many of his writings were held privately under his watchful eye. Newton's ground breaking *Philosophiae Naturalis Principia Mathematica*, was a case in point.[9] Only after Edmund Halley (1656-1742) encouraged Newton to expand his views of universal gravitation did the Cambridge fellow put his ideas into print.[10]

Newton's ideas of the world were revolutionary and influential; most notably because he posited a unified scheme of the created world in the guise of a machine with connected components that functioned congruently with one another. Not only did Newton's model of the world facilitate a new understanding of the universe in which men and women lived but it also played a significant role in sparking the industrial revolution with an emphasis on the machine as a means of improving human existence.[11] Moreover, in regard to the apparent contradictions that existed between Newton's conjectures about the natural world and the theological implications of his thought, there seemed to be more of a conundrum in the minds of some of his followers than for Newton himself. John Hedley Brooke noted in his inaugural lecture at Oxford University that the Cambridge mathematician was "convinced the task of natural philosophy to be the deduction of causes from their effects until one eventually arrived at the first great cause, which in his own words, was certainly not mechanical."[12]

There is little question that Newton and the adherents of mechanical philosophy pushed the horizons of Enlightenment culture into directions that were unexpected.[13] With increasing popularity, Newton's manner of conceptualizing the universe caused a paradigmatic shift in the way individuals perceived the world in which they lived, worked, and prayed. His belief that the world could be investigated and knowledge about that world assimilated, apart from any *a priori* reasoning, radicalized the entire field of natural philosophy. From coffee house discussions to pulpit sermons, Newton and the mechanical philosophy that he espoused became the grid whereby individuals articulated an understanding of the universe.[14]

A tension continued, however, between Newtonian discourse and the traditional beliefs and views embedded in popular culture.[15] Thomas Sprat (1635-1713), Bishop of Rochester and Dean of Westminster, foresaw a conflict between the progress that science was fostering and the primitive values which individuals embraced about the world. In *The History of the Royal-Society of London, for the Improving of Natural Knowledge*, a work that was first published in 1667 and republished until 1764, Sprat maintained an observance and compliance to the laws of the new science did not imply that divine presence was no longer operative in the world as it had been in previous generations. In his defense of the Royal Society, Sprat used language that implied that divine agency continued to have a place in the investigations of the new scientists. He asserted: "To declare against the possibility, that new Prophets may be sent from Heven, is to insinuate that the same infinit Wisdom which once shew'd itself that way, is not at an end."[16] Twenty-five years after the first edition of Sprat's work, however, Newtonian science emerged with daunting epistemological implications; so that, in the words of Alan Gross, the defining mark of the age was one that asserted "experiment bears the full weight of discovery and theory."[17] Within this social and scientific development, individuals modified their ideas about a variety of topics, including the viability of an invisible world, and restated their understandings of order, creation, and the Creator of the universe.

For Newton and the adherents of mechanical philosophy, however, the empirical approach to the natural world did not indicate a deletion of the concept of miracles from their frame of reference.[18] It was Augustine (354-430) who first offered a discussion of miracles for Christian theology but initially fell short of articulating any precise definition and conflated the concept of miracles with nature. "Everything," he wrote in *The City of God*, "is full of marvels and miracles, but they are so common that we regard them as cheap and of no account."[19] Later in that work, Augustine changed his mind and was forced to admit that he was confronted by specific cases and individuals who had undergone miraculous displays of grace and power.[20]

The next significant development to emerge in an attempt to define miracles occurred in the twelfth century with Thomas Aquinas (1224-74) and his theological appropriation of Aristotle (384-22) for western Christianity. While Aquinas, like Augustine before him, contended that there was a sense of wonder in the occurrence of miracles, he believed that miraculous demonstrations of divine power contained signs that confirmed the truth of Christianity. In matters of reason, Aquinas maintained, logical argument provided sufficient demonstration but in matters related to revelation miracles were needed. Miracles were divided into two categories in his discussion: the "working of miracles" and the "discernment of spirits." The latter included prophecy, the knowledge of future contingencies, and an awareness of the inner secrets that sometimes resided in the human heart. The former, Aquinas argued, was such that "the teacher of sacred teaching should do what God alone can do, by performing miracles: this may be for bodily health, and so we have the grace of *healing*; or it may be for the dark, or the waters divided; and here we have the working of miracles."[21] A miracle was an occurrence in the natural world that evidenced a reality that transcended the miracle itself.

Still, for Newton and many that embraced his idea of mechanical philosophy, an understanding of nature was articulated in terms of a world that reflected rather than revealed divine truth. This consensus among the adherents of the new science enabled a coherent and functional framework for the conceptualization of the miraculous while leaving intact an intellectual integrity that made room for new and different discoveries of the world in which individuals lived. Peter Harrison makes a similar point when he writes at the beginning of his article on Newtonian thought that "leading scientists of this era, almost without exception, had a dual commitment on the one hand to a science premised upon a mechanical universe governed by immutable laws of nature and on the other to a omnipotent God who intervened in the natural order from time to time, breaching these 'laws' of nature."[22]

For Newton, the belief in a supernatural deity was essential to his understanding of the natural world. "God made the world," he declared, "and governs it invisibly."[23] A brief consideration of Newton's theological manuscripts suggest that the issues of natural philosophy he investigated included serious discussions about God and the reality of miraculous presence in the world.[24] And those who came after Newton took his theological concerns to heart. William Whiston (1667-1752), Newton's successor at Cambridge, wrote on the existence of an invisible world as the foundational starting point for understanding the natural world. In *A New Theory of the Earth*, Whiston argued that an understanding of gravity depended on "the supernatural and miraculous Influence of the Almighty God."[25] He also wrote books on miracles, demonic possession, and hell in addition to his 1708 Boyle lecture that addressed the role and significance of scriptural prophecy.[26] Like Newton and Whiston, Samuel Clarke (1675-1729) found miracles to be congruous with a view of natural law. Educated at Caius College, Cambridge, Clarke defended one of Newton's principles in his disputation for his Bachelors Degree in 1691.[27] Anon, in his second Boyle lecture in 1705, Clarke gave attention to the concept of miracle in relation to natural law where he argued that the presence of miracles did not imply that the laws of nature had been violated or suspended but only that the matter of the created order had been acted on by God. Clarke surmised: "So that all those things which we commonly say are the effects of the natural powers of matter and laws of motion, of gravitation, attraction, or the like, are indeed . . . the effects of God's acting upon matter continually and every moment either immediately by himself, or mediately by some created intelligent beings (which observation, by the way, furnishes us . . . with an excellent natural demonstration of providence)."[28] Also in a sermon taken from his second Boyle lecture, Clarke articulated his view about divine intervention. "All those things which we commonly say are the Effects of the *Natural Powers of Matter*, and *Laws of Motion* . . . are indeed . . . the Effects of *God's* acting upon Matter continually and every moment."[29] Like Newton before them, many of the Newtonians of the seventeenth and eighteenth centuries considered the belief in the miraculous a category that held a place in their philosophic and scientific investigations.

From a different angle, a more formidable opponent to orthodox Christianity and the belief in miracles during the eighteenth century came from the Scottish philosopher David Hume (1711-76). Robert M. Burns stated in his book on the debate about miracles that "it is possible to count the number of responses to the essay published during Hume's lifetime on the fingers of one's hands."[30] An examination of the documents, however, questions Burn's observation and makes his assessment questionable at the very least.

Undoubtedly there was a significant reaction to Hume's ideas about religion in general and miracles in particular during the period. James Fieser, for example, has collected documents in the eighteenth century consisting of ten volumes and over three thousand pages of essays, tracts, and book reviews responding to Hume's writings, of which a significant portion was metaphysics and religion.[31] Furthermore, there were many in the eighteenth century who had not directly read the writings of Hume but nevertheless reacted negatively to an antimiraculous rhetoric that became closely associated to his thought. John Wesley, for example, twenty years after the publication of Hume's essay recorded that the skeptical philosopher was "the most insolent despiser of truth and virtue that ever appeared in the world" and "an avowed enemy to God and man, and to all that is sacred and valuable in the world."[32] More recently, Isabel Rivers has examined Anglican and Dissenter reactions to Hume and demonstrated that the philosopher's influence was more important than suggested by Burns. She maintains that the pivotal point for discussing Hume rests in a consideration of his concept of ethics and the development of a moral self-identification. "Hume is thus a significant figure in the history of the relationship between religion and ethics," writes Rivers, "not only for his own highly original attempt to undo this relationship, but also for the different ways in which his critics tried to come to terms with the implications or avert the effects of this attempt."[33]

Hume's rhetoric of skepticism, especially in relation to the priority and place of religion, provided continual debate over the validity of miracles in the eighteenth century; a debate which continues in modern scholarship today.[34] At the beginning of section ten of his *An Enquiry Concerning Human Understanding*, entitled "Of Miracles," Hume decried the belief in miracles and suggested that he had formulated an argument that could render superstitious claims conceptually false and pragmatically useless.[35] Hume boasted: "I flatter myself that I have discovered an argument . . . which, if just, will with the wise and learned, be an everlasting check to all kinds of superstitious delusion, and consequently, will be useful as long as the world endures. For so long, I presume, will the accounts of miracles and prodigies be found in all history, sacred and profane."[36] Hume, thereafter, outlined his argument against "superstitious delusion" with a definition of miracles which incorporated an understanding of the laws of nature separated from the idea of divine intervention. According to Hume, all events that surfaced within the boundaries of nature were excluded from the category of miracle. "Nothing is esteemed a miracle," Hume averred, "if it ever happen in the course of nature."[37] Human experience verifies the laws of nature, which by inference, must be seen as a uniform regulation which endures throughout time. As a result, the concept and occurrence of miracles were impossible in Hume's way of thinking. The acceptance of the idea of the miraculous, Hume further argued, necessarily included the possibility of a greater miracle that would in turn render the lesser one normative. Consequently, in a scenario of comparative miraculous events, Hume opted for a reductionism until the idea of miracle was eliminated. Hume asserted: "I pronounce my decision, and always reject the greater miracle."[38]

A more problematical note in Hume's discourse against miracles was his disparagement of the epistemological significance of testimony. A radical empiricist who believed in the priority of experience and observation, he discounted testimony as alien to the cognitive process. At this juncture, Hume's *ad hominem* attack on those who claimed to have witnessed miracles was striking. After disputing that there was a sufficient amount of testimonies from people of "good-sense" who attested to the miraculous, he classified those who claimed such experiences as "ignorant and barbarous." Hume boldly claimed:

> It forms a strong presumption against all supernatural and miraculous relations, that they are observed chiefly to abound among ignorant and barbarous nations; or if a civilized people has ever given admission to any of them that people will be found to have received them from ignorant and barbarous ancestors, who transmitted them with that inviolable sanction and authority, which always attend received opinions.[39]

To add fuel to the fire, Hume added: "But it is nothing strange, I hope, that men should lie in all ages."[40] In other words, testimony can never serve as a reliable source of knowledge, especially in regard to claims about miraculous occurrences. In this way, Hume believed he had eliminated all previous experiences and accounts of the supernatural from his epistemological agenda. "But according to this principle," he wrote, "all popular religions, amounts to an entire annihilation; and therefore we may establish it as a maxim, that no human testimony can have such a force as to prove a miracle, and make it a just foundation for any such system of religion."[41] Therefore, Hume reasoned, religion and the belief in the supernatural must be eclipsed from a discourse that considers empirical investigation normative in the process of acquiring accurate and adequate knowledge of the world. The radical nature of Hume's programme not only offended orthodox theologians of his day but also assaulted the idea of human testimony and its epistemic value. In his philosophical study of testimony,

C. A. J. Coady has cogently argued that Hume not only ambiguously utilized terms like "experience" and "observation" that ultimately caused him to fall prey to a type of question-begging but, in the end, he configured testimony *a priori* so that a bifurcation between testimony and reality was the end result. David Hume, then, committed the cardinal sin in the empirical enterprise.[42]

John Wesley, the Enlightenment, and a Rhetoric of the Supernatural

In recent years there has been a resurgent interest in religious rhetoric and its role in the development of self-identification.[43] At one level, all communication is inclusive of rhetoric and reveals a desire to advance a particular notion of self-understanding. George Kennedy reminds: "Every communication is rhetorical because it uses some technique to affect the beliefs, actions, or emotions of an audience."[44] Historically speaking, rhetorical devices utilized for apologetic purposes have a significant place in the history of Christian thought. Jaroslav Pelikan, for example, aptly demonstrated in his Gifford Lectures that from ancient times religious communities were interested in rhetoric as a tool that would defend and promote a particular type of religious knowledge.[45] Averil Cameron also has addressed this theme in her *Christianity and the Rhetoric of Empire: The Development of Christian Discourse,* and highlights the importance of rhetoric in the development of early Christian communities. In her work, Cameron succinctly gets to the point of the matter when she writes, "Christianity was a religion with a story."[46] The story of redemption and God's love which is central to the Christian religion was communicated with a variety of techniques that were already present in classical culture and incorporated into the faith and work of the early church.

On another plane, it must be noted that there have been significant changes in the historiography of the Enlightenment in contemporary scholarship.[47]

Peter Gay, representative of an older view of the period, sees a clear and distinct marking of the Enlightenment where science and progress were on one side and religion and superstition on the other. Gay was among those who finds in the French *philosophes* a tendency to lean heavily toward paganism as the telling subtitle of the first volume in his history states.[48] In the introduction to his analysis of the era, Gay maintains: "The Enlightenment . . . was a single army with a single banner, with a large central corps, a right and left wing, daring scouts, and lame stragglers . . . The Enlightenment was a volatile mixture of classicism, impiety, and science; the philosophes, in a phrase, were modern pagans."[49] Such an approach, however, passes too quickly over the history of a period that was variegated and Gay's sweeping generalizations are simplistic. More recently, Roy Porter fell prey to this approach too and looked at the development of Enlightenment culture primarily through the lenses of the French *philosophes.*[50] A case in point was Porter's reading of Newton. According to Porter, Newton's discovery of optics pointed to the primary agenda of the Enlightenment; namely, to cast off the darkness of antiquarian customs and embrace a more clear-sighted and realistic understanding of the world. Thus, Newton's significance for eighteenth-century Britain was characterized "crucial to the newly dominant epistemology, as empiricism turned the problem of knowing into a matter of seeing: to know was henceforth to see."[51]

Conversely, Dorinda Outram and Gertrude Himmelfarb have assessed that the Enlightenment in England was an important movement with influences not so neatly compartmentalized.[52] In eighteenth-century England, the push for illumination came not from atheist or agnostic philosophers who opposed the religiosity of their day but from moralists who viewed their primary task in terms of acquiring a knowledge which would benefit society in its pursuit of the common good. Outram in her analysis of the seventeenth and eighteenth centuries sees the Enlightenment not as a period marked by unified assaults on past cultures and antiquarian thoughts but rather a polyvalent configuration that was informed by various intellectual debates and cultural wars that transformed society in a multitude of ways. "This presentation of the Enlightenment," she writes, "sees this movement as a group of capsules or flashpoints where intellectual projects changed society and government on a world-wide basis."[53]

Himmelfarb also contends that the Enlightenment in England was unique because it did not position various debates alongside one another in a universal onslaught against superstitious beliefs. The Enlightenment, accordingly, was a radical departure from traditional views because it turned the prominence of reason on its head. In this vein, the distinctive qualities of the movement in England flowed through the moralists and their pursuit of virtue. Himmelfarb writes:

> To bring the British Enlightenment onto the stage of history, indeed, the center stage, is to redefine the idea of Enlightenment. In the usual litany of traits associated with the Enlightenment—reason, rights, nature, liberty, equality, tolerance, science, progress—reason invariably leads the list. What is conspicuously absent is virtue. Yet it was virtue rather than reason, that took precedence for the British . . . They did not deny reason; they were by no means irrationalists. But they gave reason a secondary, instrumental role, rather than the primary, determinant one that the *philosophes* gave it.[54]

Contrary to a view of the eighteenth century which separated reason from faith and religion from truth, then, many people living in the period lived out their lives within a context where each illuminated the other.

The older view of the Enlightenment also distorted the priority of reason in the life of religion for people living in the eighteenth century. Because of an outlook that sharply divided faith from reason there emerged detrimental problems for Christianity and its reliance on the idea of divine agency, according to this historiographical view, precisely because Christian theologians and philosophers could not satisfy the canons of reason. Theodore Adorno and Max Horkheimer characterized this period of intellectual history, for example, as one that was fearful of myth for the life of reason. They wrote: "The mythic terror feared by the Enlightenment accords with myth . . . The self (which, according to the methodical extirpation of all natural residues because they are mythological, must no longer be either body or blood, or soul, or even the natural I)."[55] However, a picture of the era which segregated faith and reason must now be seen as erroneous and misplaced.[56] For the Enlightenment, as it was later referred to in the nineteenth century, was anything but neatly divided. Throughout the era individuals and groups wove in and out of issues that intersected faith and reason with regularity and often saw no inherent contradiction in doing so.[57] There were many who attempted to clarify both faith and reason as authentic categories that constituted human nature by showing how they intersected and illuminated one another. On this point, William Burns has argued that belief in divine agency and the existence of prodigies continued throughout the eighteenth century. Their influence was felt in the religious, scientific, and political discourses of the day.[58] Jane Shaw, too, sees in the Enlightenment a reluctance to dismiss the belief in the miraculous. Her book opens with an observation that must now be sorted out in eighteenth-century historiography:

> These claims of miracles, over a period of about sixty years, provoked investigation, discussion and debate at all levels of society: amongst fellows of the Royal Society, small-town physicians, nonconformist ministers, Anglican clergy and bishops, printers and booksellers, philosophers and theologians, as well as the neighbours, family members and friends of those who claimed they were cured, raided from the dead and had survived for a prodigiously long time without food.[59]

This social reality that occurred in the intellectual and cultural milieu of the period amounted to a demonstration that an adequate rhetoric was being hammered out which would provide a coherent model for living out faith in a world that was increasingly changing while also satisfying the canons of rationality. Robert Boyle (1627-91) noted that the relationship between knowledge of the natural world and knowledge of God were intricately connected. "The two chief advantages," wrote Boyle, "which a real acquaintance with nature brings to our minds, are, first, by instructing our understandings, and gratifying our curiosities; and next, by exciting and cherishing our devotion."[60] For many in the so-called "Age of Reason" the belief in the supernatural was embraced not only because it was critical to defending a particular historical tradition but because such discourse was a powerful instrument in contouring a self-identification that was comprehensive in its scope.[61]

Coupled with these developments in the intellectual history of the Enlightenment there has been a renewed interest about John Wesley and the rise of Methodism in eighteenth-century England. The American scholar, Richard P. Heitzenrater, noted in 1989 that since John Wesley's death there have been voluminous books written about the architect of the Methodist movement.[62] More recently, the British historian of religion, Jeremy Gregory has noted: "Wesley was arguably the most significant single individual in eighteenth-century religious developments."[63]

If there was anything that set the Methodists at odds with the dominant trends of the Enlightenment, however, it was their commitment to a belief in the existence of an invisible world. For John Wesley, and many of his followers in the eighteenth century, the belief in the existence of the supernatural was a fabric of their religious consciousness that they refused to dismiss.

Early Methodist autobiographies, for example, were filled with various religious experiences that unabashedly associated themselves with the belief in nonmaterial realities. John Haime (1710-84), a soldier and Methodist itinerant preacher who came to be known as the "soldier preacher,"[64] wrote of a time in his life after experiencing justifying grace when a diabolic force affronted him. "With this [preaching justification by faith alone]," wrote Haimes, "Satan was not well pleased; for one day, as I was walking alone, and faintly crying for mercy, suddenly such a hot blast of brimstone flashed in my face as almost took away my breadth. And presently after, as I was walking, an invisible power struck up my heels, and threw me violently upon my face."[65] Phyllis Mack surmises the political dimensions of the commitment to an invisible world among female Methodists, by noting that there was a "fusion of self-transcendence and agency, coupled with new political and social ideologies."[66]

John Wesley's commitment to a world view that maintained the viability of supernatural occurrences hurled him into many intense debates during the eighteenth century. Although the legitimization of preternatural and supernatural occurrences fascinated Wesley throughout his lifetime, Bishop George Lavington's (1684-1762) disparagement of Wesley's zeal for miracles had its stinging effect. "With regard to miracles," wrote Lavington, "Mr. Wesley has got a wolf by the ears, which he cannot safely either hold, or let go."[67]

Certainly Methodists were not alone in the eighteenth century with their adherence to a divine-human intersection of human existence. Even after mechanical philosophy had gained a firm footing in the Enlightenment, there remained in both Catholic and Protestant circles individuals who formulated specific and detailed ideas about the correlations between the phenomenological occurrences of the natural world and the transcendental attributes of a supernatural realm.[68] From a Roman Catholic point of view, for instance, the founding of the Society of the Sacred Heart (Sacré-Coeur) could be authenticated because of various and continual visions received by Marguerite-Marie Alacoque (1647-90) and others like her.[69] On the Protestant side, seventeenth and eighteenth century divines were less than purified from the belief in supernatural experiences, as their Reformation forefathers had been. Despite professions made by theologians in previous centuries, many Protestant writers persisted in the belief of prodigies, portents, and miraculous occurrences.[70]

Additionally, the "extraordinary" as a topic of scientific inquiry, not only secured a place in the philosophical and theological literature of the period but lectures delivered before The Royal Society explained particular and unusual phenomena which corroborated the viability of miracles in the natural world.[71] At the close of "the long eighteenth century,"[72] debates continued over the possibility of encounters with spirits. The Westminster Forum, on 29 December 1798, conducted a debate in London that entertained the question: "Is it true that any ghosts or departed spirits ever appear to a mortal in this world?"[73] Contrary to various figures who maintained that the season of miracles had ceased in the church and been replaced by an emphasis with the written Word of God, a significant number of Protestant figures in Britain utilized the miraculous as a rhetorical trope with apologetic implications.

All this suggests, as I will argue in detail, that John Wesley and the Methodists in the eighteenth century were not out of touch with the times in which they lived but actively engaged in the intellectual climate of their day. In this regard, Henry D. Rack, the noted Methodist historian, has positioned this dimension of Wesley's thought squarely within the Christian religion *and* the Enlightenment, characterizing him as a "cultural mediator."[74] Contrary to sweeping generalizations that dismiss Wesley as a figure engrossed in marginal intellectual issues, Rack maintains that Wesley's commitment to an invisible world was an integral portion of his view of spiritual reality and a dynamic quality of the appeal of Methodists in the eighteenth century. Rack writes: "It is a basic historical error and anachronism to pass over these characteristics as if they were simply contemporary aberrations of otherwise noble minds, for in fact they were an integral part of what Methodism (including Wesley's own teaching) meant and help to explain its peculiar appeal."[75]

The substance of the following examination concurs with Rack's statement and attempts to flesh out Wesley's view of the supernatural in a thorough way. Additionally, the argument presented here maintains that the Methodist movement was in the fray of a wide-ranging debate that was both volatile and vital for the advancement of a religious self-identification that was being fleshed out in the Enlightenment.[76] As will be noted in the following chapters, Wesley's view of the supernatural was not merely based on transcendental categories, but one that fit into a stratification of human experience which, despite objections from various dominant intellectual avenues of the day, was thriving and finding an audience among both the elite and plebeian classes. While there were differences in emphasis among Catholics and Protestants, there is abundant documentation that corroborates the fundamental working proposition of this essay; namely, people who lived in the eighteenth century were reluctant to rescind their belief in supernatural realities. Instead, I will demonstrate that throughout the eighteenth and into the nineteenth centuries individuals both entertained and considered the viability of various aspects of an invisible world. Thus, the place of the Methodist movement and its commitment to the belief in a supernatural realm of existence must be reevaluated.

Methodological and Historiographical Guidelines

The idea of the supernatural permeated John Wesley's thought and life. Not only was it a concern at the beginning of his life but also up until his death in 2 March 1791, he was writing and making commentary on various dimensions of the miraculous as it impinged on the faith and work of the Methodist movement that he founded and sustained during the eighteenth century.[77] Throughout his life Wesley collected various narratives, documents, and testimonies about supernatural occurrences which he in turn utilized in a variety of ways. It will be demonstrated, moreover, that Wesley was convinced that a belief in preternatural and supernatural events was a vital component for the self-identity of Methodists living in a rapidly changing world. In this regard, the analysis offered here stands in direct opposition to those who have dismissed him as a "fundamentalist" with a naïve and extreme fascination for spirits, convulsions, witches, and visions.[78] Additionally, the argument registered here opposes the notion that

Wesley and his views were antiquarian and that he failed to correlate the tenets of primitive Christianity with the discoveries of the world that were emerging in the eighteenth century.[79] The attempt to abort the supernatural from an analysis of Wesley's thought, then, I judge to be short-sighted and fails to understand the cultural ambience in which he lived and disappoints any attempt to understand the man himself. Instead, in the pages that follow, I will examine John Wesley's view of a dimension of Christian existence which was incorporated into a "public sphere" for social, psychological, and theological reasons.[80]

A fundamental implication that permeates the discussion within these pages may now be stated directly: John Wesley throughout his lifetime unabashedly embraced a belief in the supernatural and was convinced that an affirmation of an invisible world was an important component in the mission and ministry of Christianity in general and his Methodist societies in particular.[81] Additionally, a conviction of the reality of an invisible world was a vital component to the Methodist understanding of both divinity and humanity. As Henry Rack observes, it is a grave error to marginalize the place and priority of the supernatural in Wesley's thought. "It is a mistake," writes Rack, "to dismiss this as peripheral to Wesley's teaching and mission. It is fully in line with this general outlook, and could indeed be justified as an aspect of the same design as his histories and science: to show God's presence and action in the world to sceptics. At the same time it illustrates the mental world of Wesley and his people."[82] Building upon Rack's treatment of Wesley's view of the supernatural I will provide for the first time a treatment that examines Wesley's idea of the invisible world in a thorough fashion.

It may be argued, on the one hand, however, that Wesley did not incorporate his views of the supernatural into his larger evangelical agenda in any significant way, but left much to the speculations and sentiments of his followers. Indeed, Wesley was not a systematic theologian in the modern sense of the word and like other early evangelicals resisted attempts towards any systematic analysis of key theological categories.[83] What is more to the point, the absence of any comprehensive attention that has been given by scholars to the manner in which Wesley viewed the identifying marks of the supernatural for members of his societies in connection with his larger evangelical rhetoric may be interpreted as a sign that the miraculous was not as important to his evangelical program as Wesley believed.[84]

Recently, however, there has been an attempt to rediscover John Wesley as a key interlocutor of the period. Isabel Rivers in her study of the language of religion and ethics during the Enlightenment has contended that John Wesley should be considered a formidable voice in a period that was struggling to resolve questions and issues reaching back to the Reformation. She writes at the beginning of her chapter on Wesley: "The most interesting and important of the leaders of the revival is John Wesley . . . especially because of his theology, which constitutes a complex and subtle attempt to resolve the problem that dominated English thought from the time of the Reformation, the relationship between religion and ethics."[85] On another level, rhetoric is an ambiguous term, which at best, has only been vaguely conceptualized. Certainly it is the case that for many the term "rhetoric" has become synonymous with a subjective promotion of individual ideologies which may not always be directly linked to the discovery of truth. Carlo Ginzburg has suggested that most people "almost always consider it inevitable that rhetoric and proof should exclude one another."[86] However, Timothy J. Reiss cogently argues that the transformation of "discovery" in the early modern world had far reaching implications for a rhetoric of science and culture. In his book, *Knowledge, Discovery and Imagination in Early Modern Europe*, Reiss writes:

> It was not a change from oral to visual, from language to spatialization; or at least, not to spatialization in any ordinary sense of the term . . . It was a change in the claims of discovery, from natural language to the "measurable" language of mathematics. It was a change, too, in what was taken to be the nature of discovery: not a finding of something that already existed, but a making of a new rational order for the comprehension of what existed.[87]

Reiss's comments may serve as a springboard for the considerations that I address here. It should be noted, for example, that the ramifications of belief in the supernatural assumed radical dimensions in the face of scientific advances that were emerging in the seventeenth and eighteenth centuries. When a belief in the invisible world was embraced it was often done so with an apologetic flair. One instance was the Puritan pastor and theologian, Richard Baxter (1615-91), who at the end of the seventeenth century penned his final work, *The Certainity of the World of Spirits* (1691), and incorporated narratives that were meant to convince the sceptic and atheist of a supernatural identity which was worthy of empirical and rational considerations. "Therefore I found," wrote Baxter, "that all confirming helps were useful; and among those of the lower sort, Apparitions, and other sensible Manifestations of the certain existence of Spirits of themselves Invisible, was a means that might do much with such as are prone to judge by Sense."[88] Baxter's prefatory remarks revealed that the existence of an invisible world was being used not merely as a device for the construction of an understanding of *another* world but also an innovative instrument for the promotion of a definite and particular view of individual and communal identity in *this* world.

At the beginning of the Enlightenment, therefore, the promotion of an identity that incorporated numerous popular assumptions about the invisible world served an important function. A religious discourse that incorporated the supernatural was utilized in order to make important statements about the validity of a realm of existence that men and women could not necessarily verify within the parameters of the physical senses but excogitated axiomatic for the convergence of divine and human consciousness. In this way, there was a function and appeal for supernatural narratives that related seemingly unexplainable occurrences within an epistemological framework that were resolved by allowing intellectual space for the miraculous. In the minds of awakened believers these narratives convincingly demonstrated a coherent and rational view of the world that was underpinned by an invisible realm. "The stories prove God exists," insists James Hartman, "by presenting undeniable evidence of inexplicable occurrences. They are realistic tales of the supernatural which depict imaginary worlds concretely and convincingly."[89] Concomitantly, the idea of the supernatural surfaced in various contexts which appealed to a vast array of individuals who continued to permit the invisible world to have a vital reference point in understanding their lived out experiences of the sacred.

But, what may be more important, the social receptivity of the supernatural enabled individuals to engage in extended and often complex defences about their experiences and how these encounters should be adjudicated. David Wellbery perceptively observes that the art of rhetoric during the Enlightenment developed from a system of persuasion into a highly portraiture of the human subject. Wellbery writes: "Rhetoric, in short, was naturalized and psychologized, transformed from a highly coded art into a human representational capacity."[90] As noted earlier, there was a strong anti-supernatural rhetoric in the eighteenth century.[91] However, rather than erasing all forms of belief in the supernatural this rhetoric served, especially in the case of John Wesley and the Methodists of the eighteenth century, to secure more pronounced forms of religious discourse which advanced supernatural claims as evidence of a divine presence operative in ways that counterbalanced accusations of irrationalism and fanaticism.

In the context of the Enlightenment, then, the reading of John Wesley I present here reveals a man who was deeply and consciously aware of the power of the supernatural in the course of human history.

John Wesley tirelessly defended the reality of an invisible world against those who he believed had dismissed its existence too neatly and without taking the experiences of thousands into account. In opposition to those who asserted that belief in the supernatural was a denial of the natural and temporal, Wesley registered the strongest objections. Instead, various types of human experiences were revelatory and pointed to a deity that created and sustained humanity on different but connected levels. He further argued that a belief in transcendental realities promoted the idea of a deity who constantly interacted with creation. Even with those opponents who Wesley engaged in vitriolic debate—sometime in his own family—he continued to maintain an unflinching commitment to the idea that supernatural powers were operative in the world. A case in point is his extract of Jonathan Edwards's (1703-58) *A Faithful Narrative of the Surprizing Work of God.*[92] At the end of that work, Edwards commented that the gifts of the Spirit as outlined by Paul in I Corinthians 12 had by and large ceased in modern times. When Wesley published his extract of that influential work, however, he deleted Edwards's caveat. The issue for those familiar with both Edwards's work and Wesley's extract was clear: miraculous powers were present for the contemporary believer.

In the past, treatments of Wesley's life and writings have utilized his sermons, journals, and letter correspondence. Though these sources are valuable in any treatment of Wesley's thought, they do not tell the whole story.

By necessity, then, an adequate treatment of Wesley's idea of the supernatural must go beyond the traditional sources to include less utilized materials. John Wesley collected personal narratives of miraculous occurrences in the Methodist societies, had disputes with members of his own family over the priority of dreams and visions, composed poetry along with his brother Charles about the power of an invisible world, and defended the existence of the miraculous throughout his mission and ministry. In this measure, John Wesley elevated the supernatural to a new level of discourse and proved to be a significant contributor to debates that were occurring in the eighteenth century.[93] In addition to traditional sources, the analysis offered here will also incorporate and examine the *Arminian Magazine*, an extremely influential religious periodical that Wesley edited from 1778 until his death in 1791.[94] The amount of testimonies about an invisible world in this resource was staggering by any estimation. Additionally, an examination of previously unpublished archival materials will confirm that Wesley saw the miraculous not only as an interesting part of the human enterprise but a viable dimension of his mission and ministry.

Therefore, the scholarship and argument I put forward in the following pages makes one noteworthy claim: regardless of how one reacted to supernatural and miraculous claims in the eighteenth century, it was certainly an aspect of a religious identification that could not be ignored. Before we can move into a detailed discussion of some of Wesley's affirmations about the supernatural we must first turn to his idea of religious epistemology and the knowledge of transcendental realities. It is that topic I will now address.

Notes

1. John Milton, "Paradise Lost," iv. ll. 667-68, in Roy Flannagan, ed., *The Riverside Milton* (Boston: Houghton Mifflin Company, 1998), 463.

2. John Wesley, "An Earnest Appeal to Men of Reason and Religion (1743)," in Gerald R. Cragg, ed., *The Appeals to Men of Reason and Religion and Certain Related Open Letters*, *BEW*, (Oxford and Nashville: Oxford University Press and Abingdon Press), 11: 35.

3. Giovanni Francesco Albani (Pope Clement XI), *The Famous Bull Unigenitus, in English. With a Short History of its Rise and Progress* (Portsmouth: W. Horton, 1753).

4. Jeremy Black and Roy Porter, eds., *A Dictionary of Eighteenth Century History* (London: Penguin Books, 1994), "Jansenism." See also, John McManners, *Church and Society in Eighteenth Century France*, 2 vols. (Oxford: Oxford University Press, 1998), 2: 453-55; Jean Robert Armogathe, "A Propos de Miracles de Saint-Médard: les Preuves de Carré de Montgeron et la Positivisme des Lumières," *Revue de L'Histoire des Religions* 180 (1971): 135-60; Ronald A. Knox, *Enthusiasm: A Chapter in the History of Religion with Special Reference to the xvii and xviii Centuries* (Oxford: Clarendon Press, 1950), 372-88; Albert Mousset, *L' étrange histoire des convulsionnaires de St-Médard* (Paris: Les Edition de Minuit, 1953); and Ephraim Radner, *Spirit and Nature: The Saint-Médard Miracles in 18th-Century Jansenism* (New York: The Crossroad Publishing Company, 2002).

5. Carré de Montgeron, *La Vérité des Miracles Opérés par l'intercession de M. de Paris, Demontrée contre M. l' Archevêque de Sens* (Paris: Chez les Libraires de la Compagnie, 1737).

6. 11 January 1750. *BEW* 20: 317-18.

7. John Wesley, "A Letter to the Right Reverend The Lord Bishop of Glouchester. Occasioned by his Tract, On the Office and Operations of the Holy Spirit," *BEW* 11: 479. For a discussion of William Warburton's significance, B. W. Young, *Religion and En-*

lightenment in Eighteenth-Century England: Theological Debate from Locke to Burke (Oxford: Clarendon Press, 1998), 167-213.

8. Leslie Stephen and Sidney Lee, eds., *Dictionary of National Biography*, 22 vols. (1885-1901; repr., Oxford: Oxford University Press, 1998), "Newton, Sir Isaac." See also Betty Jo Teeter Dobbs and Margaret C. Jacobs, *Newton and the Culture of Newtonianism* (Amherst, NY: Promethus Books, 1998) and A. Rupert Hall, *Isaac Newton: Adventure in Thought* (Cambridge: Cambridge University Press, 1992).

9. "His *Principia* . . . was more revered than read." Roy Porter, *Enlightenment: Britain and the Creation of the Modern World* (London: The Penguin Press, 2000), 134.

10. For an opposing viewpoint, Margaret C. Jacob, *Scientific Culture and the Making of the Industrial West* (New York: Oxford University Press, 1997), 68-69.

11. Dobbs and Jacob, *Newton and the Culture of Newtonianism*, 71

12. John Hedley Brooke, *Of Scientists and Their Gods: An Inaugural Lecture Delivered before the University of Oxford on 21 November 2000* (Oxford: Oxford University Press, 2001), 10. See also Isaac Newton's comment where he contended that Atheism was "senseless and odious to mankind" and after a brief consideration of the symmetry of creation asserted that "such like considerations, always have, and ever will prevail with mankind, to believe that there is a Being who made all things, and has all things in his power, and who is therefore to be feared." Isaac Newton, *Isaac Newton: Theological Manuscripts*, ed., Herbert McLachlan (Liverpool: Liverpool University Press, 1950), 48-49.

13. A point that John Hedley Brooke takes up in his *Science and Religion: Some Historical Perspectives* (Cambridge: Cambridge University Press, 1991), 139-51. See also Marie Boas, "The Establishment of Mechanical Philosophy," *Osiris* 10 (1952): 412-541.

14. "The worldview of the Enlightenment, fully shared by most encouraged reverence for Newtonianism, induction, and the argument for God from design in nature." David Bebbington, "Wesley and Science," in David N. Livingston, D. G. Hart, and Mark A. Nolls, eds., *Evangelicals and Science in Historical Perspective* (New York: Oxford University Press, 1999), 128.

15. I have adopted the phrase popular culture within the body of this text in an inclusive manner.

16. Thomas Sprat, *The History of the Royal-Society of London, for the Improving of Natural Knowledge* (London: Printed by Thomas Roycrof, 1667), 359.

17. Alan G. Gross, *The Rhetoric of Science* (Cambridge, MA: Harvard University Press, 1996), 120.

18. See John Harden, "The Concept of Miracle from St. Augustine to Modern Apologetics," *Theological Studies* 15 (1954): 229-57. More recently, Peter Harrison, "Miracles, Modern Science, and Rational Religion," *Church History* 75 (2006): 493-510.

19. Augustine, *The City of God* 10.12 in *NPNF*, 2: 188-89.

20. Augustine, *The City of God* 22.8 in *NPNF* 2: 484-91.

21. Thomas Aquinas *Summae Theologicae* Ia 2æ 111.4.

22. Peter Harrison, "Newtonian Science, Miracles, and the Laws of Nature," *Journal of the History of Ideas* 56 (1995): 531.

23. Newton, *Sir Isaac Newton: Theological Manuscripts*, 54.

24. "As with all matters that he took seriously, the mass of Newton's surviving manuscripts on theology is very large; the portion of the whole sold by Sotheby's in 1936 was catalogued in forty-three lots estimated to contain one and a quarter million words." Hall, *Isaac Newton: Adventurer in Thought*, 238.

25. William Whiston, *A New Theory of the Earth, from its Original to the Consummation of all things, wherein the Creation of the World in six days, the Universal Deluge,*

and the general Conflagration, as laid down in the Holy Scriptures, are shewn to be perfectly agreeaqable to Reason and Philosophy, 5th ed. (London: for John Whiston, 1737),
218.

26. Whiston, *Mr. Whiston's Account of the Exact Time when Miraculous Gifts Ceas'd in the Church* (London: Printed for the Author, 1749); *An Account of the Daemoniacks, and of the Power of Casting our Demons, Both in the New Testament, and in the
Four First Centuries. Occasioned by a Late Pamphlet Intituled, An Enquiry into the
Meaning of Daemonics in the New Testament. To which is added, An Appendix, concerning the Tythes and Oblations paid by Christians, during the same Four Centuries* (London: Printed for John Whiston, 1737); *The Eternity of Hell Torments Considered or, A
Collection of Texts of Scripture, and Testimonies of the Three first Centuries relating to
them. Together with Notes through the Whole, and Observations at the End* (London:
Printed for John Whiston and Ben White, 1740); and *The Accomplishment of Scriptural
Prophecies* (Cambridge: Printed at the University-Press for Benjamin Tooke, 1708). Also, like Newton before him, Whiston wrote meditations on the book of Revelation. Cf.
Newton, *Observations on the Prophecies of Daniel and the Apocalypse of St. John* (London: Printed by J. Darby and T. Browne, 1733) and Whiston, *Essay on the Revelation of
St. John, so far as concerns the Past and Present Times* (London: Printed for the Author,
1706).

27. *DNB*, "Clarke, Samuel (1675-1729)."

28. Samuel Clarke, "*A Discourse Concerning the Unchangeable Obligations of Natural Religion and the Truth and Certainty of the Christian Religion*," in *A Demonstration
of the Being and Attributes of God and Other Writings*, ed., Ezio Vailati (Cambridge:
Cambridge University Press, 1998), 149.

29. Clarke, *The Works of the Honourable Samuel Clarke*, 4 vols. (London: Printed
for John and Paul Knapton, 1738), 2: 697-98. Also note where Clarke maintained to
Leibnitz that the distinction between natural and supernatural were "distinctions merely
in our conceptions of things." H. G. Alexander, ed., *The Leibnitz-Clarke Correspondence*
(Manchester: Manchester University Press, 1956), 24.

30. Robert M. Burns, *The Great Debate on Miracles: From Joseph Glanvill to David
Hume* (London: Associated University Presses, 1981), 10.

31. James Fieser, ed., *Early Responses to Hume*, 2nd rev. ed., 10 vols. (Bristol: Thoemmes Press, 1999-2003). See also, Stanley Tweyman, ed. and introduction, *Hume on
Natural Religion* (Bristol: Thoemmes Press, 1996) and *Hume on Miracles* (Bristol: Thoemmes Press, 1996).

32. 5 May 1772. *BEW* 22: 321.

33. Isabel Rivers, "Responses to Hume on Religion by Anglicans and Dissenters,"
Journal of Ecclesiastical History 52 (2001): 677. Rivers lists among Hume's opponents
William Warburton, Richard Hurd, John Brown, Thomas Balguy, George Horne, Hugh
Hamilton, John Hey, Robert Morehead, Joseph Milner, William Rose, Richard Price, and
Joseph Priestley. Rivers's article confines itself to English reactions against Hume and
does not deal with his Scottish opponents.

34. "*The* Essay on Miracles *deserves to be considered, as one of the most dangerous
attacks that have been made on our religion.*" George Campbell, *A Dissertation on Miracles: Containing an Examination of the Principles Advanced by David Hume, Esq; in an
Essay on Miracles* (Edinburgh: Printed for A. Kincaid and J. Bell, 1762), v-vi. The
Humean debate about miracles continues in contemporary philosophical and theological
circles. Among those who contend that Hume was correct in his sceptical speculations
against miracles are Colin Howson, *Hume's Problem: Induction and the Justification of
Belief* (Oxford: Clarendon Press, 2000); Terrence Penelhum, *Themes in Hume: The Self,
The Will, and Religion* (Oxford: Clarendon Press, 2000); and Stephen Buckle, *Hume's*

Enlightenment Tract: The Unity and Purpose of An Enquiry Concerning Human Under-standing (Oxford: Clarendon Press, 2001). Conversely, among those who contend that Hume's argument concerning miracles were fundamentally flawed are David Johnson, *Hume, Holism, and Miracles* (Ithaca, NY: Cornell University Press, 1999); John Earman, *Hume's Abject Failure: The Argument Against Miracles* (Oxford: Oxford University Press, 2000); and J. H. Houston, *Reported Miracles* (Cambridge: Cambridge University Press, 1994).

35. For key historical documents relating to David Hume's theory of miracles, see Earman's *Hume's Abject Failure*, 95-212 and Tweyman, ed., *Hume on Miracles*.

36. David Hume, *An Enquiry Concerning Human Understanding* (Chicago: Encyclopaedia Britannica, 1952), 489.

37. Hume, *Enquiry Concerning Human Understanding*, 490. For a discussion which calls into question Hume's definition that all miracles are a violation of the laws of nature, see Robert A. Larmer, *Water into Wine?: An Investigation of the Concept of Miracle* (Kingston: McGill-Queen University Press, 1988) and T. W. Mawson, "Miracles and laws of nature," *Religious Studies* 37 (2001): 33-58.

38. Hume, *Enquiry Concerning Human Understanding*, 491.

39. Hume, *Enquiry Concerning Human Understanding*, 491-92.

40. Hume, *Enquiry Concerning Human Understanding*, 493-95.

41. Hume, *Enquiry Concerning Human Understanding*, 495.

42. C. A. J. Coady, *Testimony: A Philosophical Study* (Oxford: Clarendon Press, 1992), 79-100, esp. 79-81, 93-100. Also Jennifer Lackey and Ernest Sosa, eds., *The Epistemology of Testimony* (Oxford: Clarendon Press, 2005).

43. See Walter Jost and Wendy Olmsted, eds., *Rhetorical Invention & Religious Inquiry: New Perspectives* (New Haven: Yale University Press, 2000). Also, Don H. Compier, *What is Rhetorical Theology? Textual Practice and Public Discourse* (Harrisburg, PA: Trinity Press International, 1999) and Dror Wahrman, *The Making of the Modern Self: Identity and Culture in Eighteenth-Century England* (New Haven: Yale University Press, 2004).

44. George A. Kennedy, *Classical Rhetoric & Its Christian and Secular Tradition from Ancient to Modern Times*, 2nd rev. ed. (Chapel Hill, NC: The University of North Carolina Press, 1999), 2.

45. Jaroslav Pelikan, *Christianity and Classical Culture: The Metamorphosis of Natural Theology in the Christian Encounter with Hellenism* (New Haven: Yale University Press, 1993), 15-18. Also, Kennedy, *New Testament Interpretation Through Rhetorical Criticism* (Chapel Hill, NC: The University of North Carolina Press, 1984) and C. Clifton Black and Duane F. Watson, eds., *Words Well Spoken: George Kennedy's Rhetoric of the New Testament* (Waco, TX: Baylor University Press, 2008).

46. Averil Cameron, *Christianity and the Rhetoric of Empire: The Development of Christian Discourse* (Berkley, CA: University of California Press, 1994), 89.

47. Michael Schaich, "A War of Words? Old and New Perspectives on the Enlightenment," *German Historical Institute London Bulletin* 24 (2002): 29-56, for an evaluation of contemporary discussions of the Enlightenment. I am indebted to John Walsh for directing me to this article.

48. Peter Gay, *The Enlightenment: An Interpretation*, 2 vols. (New York: W.W. Norton & Company, 1966).

49. Gay, *The Enlightenment*, 1: 8.

50. Porter, *Enlightenment: Britain and the Creation of the Modern World* and *The Enlightenment*, 2nd ed. (Houndmills: Palgrave, 2001).

51. Porter, *Enlightenment: Britain and the Creation of the Modern World*, 46.

52. In opposition to this approach, see Jonathan Israel, "Enlightenment! Which Enlightenments?" *Journal of the History of Ideas* 67 (2006): 523-45.

53. Dorinda Outram, *The Enlightenment*, 2nd ed. (2005; repr., Cambridge: Cambridge University Press, 2006), 2.

54. Gertrude Himmelfarb, *The Roads to Modernity: The British, French, and American Enlightenment* (New York: Alfred A. Knopf, 2004), 5-6.

55. Theodore W. Adorno and Max Horkheimer, *Dialectic of Enlightenment*, trans. John Cumming (1972; repr., New York: Verso, 1999), 29.

56. Thus, I resist the suggestion of J. C. D. Clark that the Enlightenment was not a phenomenon of human history. "It is taken as axiomatic in this article that 'the Enlightenment' is a polemical term devised in the nineteenth century to place interpretations on what had happened in the eighteenth: the term did not therefore correspond to any clearly-demarcated eighteenth-century phenomena, and could be made to mean whatever its nineteenth- and twentieth-century users wished." J. C. D. Clark, "Providence, Predestination and Progress: or, did the Enlightenment Fail?' *Albion* 35 (2004): 559n2.

57. Young, *Religion and Enlightenment*.

58. William Burns, *An Age of Wonders: Prodigies, Politics and Providence in England 1657-1727* (Manchester: Manchester University Press, 2002), 1-11.

59. Jane Shaw, *Miracles in Enlightenment England* (London: Yale University Press, 2006), 1.

60. Robert Boyle, "Some Considerations Touching the Usefulness of Experimental Natural Philosophy. Proposed in a familiar DISCOURSE to a FRIEND, by Way of Invitation to the Study of It," in The *Works of the Honourable Robert Boyle*, 6 vols. (London: Printed for J. and F. Rivington, 1772), 2: 6.

61. Contemporary studies in neuroscience have returned to the topic of the supernatural as a point for understanding human nature. See Mario Beauregard and Denyse O'Leary, *The Supernatural Brain: A Neuroscientsist's Case for the Existence of the Soul* (New York: Harper Collins Publishers, 2007) and Bruce M. Hood, *Supersense: Why We Believe in the Unbelieveable* (New York: Harper Collins Publishers, 2008).

62. "Since Wesley's Death, nearly two thousand books have been written about him." Richard P. Heitzenrater, *Mirror and Memory: Reflections on Early Methodism* (Nashville, TN: Kingswood Books, 1989), 205. Heitzenrater's statement is misleading, however. He has based his findings on the number of entries in Betty Jarboe, *John and Charles Wesley: A Bibliography* (Metuchen, NJ: The American Theological Library Association and The Scarecrow Press,1987). The number of entries in Jarboe includes essays in books. There have certainly not been two thousand books written about John Wesley in the last two or three hundred years.

63. Jeremy Gregory, "'In the Church I will live and die': John Wesley, the Church of England, and Methodism," in William Gibson and Robert G. Ingram, eds., *Religious Identities in Britain, 1660-1832* (Aldershot: Ashgate, 2005), 149. Further indication of the influence of John Wesley's life and thought for contemporary scholarship is attested by the critical edition of his works which began in 1980 by Oxford University Press and had been continued by Abingdon Press in the United States. The projected thirty-four volumes is over fifty per cent complete with eighteen published volumes.

64. John Vickers, ed., *A Dictionary of Methodism in Britain and Ireland* (London: Epworth Press, 2000), "Haime, John (1710-84)."

65. See John Haimes's autobiographical account, for example, first collected for John Wesley's *Arminian Magazine*, and latter collected along with other Methodist narratives in John Telford, ed., *Wesley's Veterans: Lives of Early Methodist Preachers Told By Themselves*, 7 vols. (1909-1914; repr., Salem, OH: Schmul Publishers, nd), 1: 41.

66. Phyllis Mack, "Religious Dissenters in Enlightenment England," *History Workshop Journal* 49 (2000): 20. See also Mack's "Methodism and Motherhood," in Jane Shaw and Alan Kreider, eds., *Culture and the Nonconformist Tradition* (Cardiff: University of Wales Press, 1999), 26-41 and *Heart Religion in the British Enlightenment: Gender and Emotion in Early Methodism* (Cambridge: Cambridge University Press, 2007).

67. George Lavington, *The Enthusiasm of Methodists and Papists Compar'd*, 3 vols. (London: Printed for J. and P. Knapton, 1749), 1: 191.

68. Dobbs and Jacobs, *Newton and the Culture of Newtonianism*, 61-124.

69. Raymond Jonas, *France and the Cult of the Sacred Heart: An Epic Tale for Modern Times* (Berkeley, CA: University of California Press, 2000), 9-33.

70. For the seventeenth century, Alexandra Walsham's *Providence in Early Modern England* (Oxford: Oxford University Press, 1999); for eighteenth century, Shaw's *Miracles in Enlightenment England*.

71. Note the various articles on convulsions that were delivered in London during this time as documented by *The Royal Society of London Philosophical Transactions General Index for Volumes 1-70 (1665-1780)* (1787; repr. New York: Johnson Reprint Corp., 1963), 117. Compare also Burns, *An Age of Wonders*, 57-97 and Terry Castle, *The Female Thermometer: Eighteenth-Century Culture and the Invention of the Uncanny* (New York: Oxford University Press, 1995), 168-89.

72. For discussion of the long eighteenth century which spans the years 1660-1832, see J. C. D. Clark's *English Society 1660-1832: Religion, Ideology and Politics during the Ancient Regime*, 2nd ed. (Cambridge: Cambridge University Press, 2000).

73. Donna Andrew, ed., *London Debating Societies, 1776-1799* (London: London Record Society, 1994), 384.

74. Henry D. Rack, *Reasonable Enthusiast: John Wesley and the Rise of Methodism*, 3rd ed. (London: Epworth Press, 2003), 435.

75. Rack, *Reasonable Enthusiast*, 432.

76. "The style of argument, the reliance on what had so long possessed authority, the habitual disregard for the growing practice of historical criticism, vividly illustrated his intellectual limitations as a leader, his lack of sympathy for anything which he had not been taught when he was young, the difficulties confronting any attempt to present him as influenced by the Enlightenment." John Kent, *Wesley and the Wesleyans: Religion in Eighteenth-Century Britain* (Cambridge: Cambridge University Press, 2002), 56, for a recent example that attempts to dismiss John Wesley's relevance on this point.

77. As in John Wesley's writings, the terms "miraculous," "supernatural" and "invisible world" are interchangeably throughout this work.

78. "John Wesley's commitment to witchcraft belief has to be seen in the context of his Tory upbringing and nonjuring affections, as well as his biblical fundamentalism." Ian Bostridge, *Witchcraft and its Transformations c. 1650-c. 1750* (Oxford: Clarendon Press, 1997), 158. See also, Kent, *Wesley and the Wesleyans*, whose work can be read along with that of Bostridge as a renewed formulation of William Lecky's characterization of Wesley and eighteenth-century Methodism as "an extraordinary revival of the grossest superstition." See, William Lecky, *A History of England in the Eighteenth Century*, 7 vols. (1878-90; repr., London: Longmans, Green and Company, 1910), 3: 88.

79. Robert Schofield, "John Wesley and Science in 18th Century England," *Isis* 44 (1953): 331-40; Sara Schechner, *Comets, Popular Culture, and the Birth of Modern Cosmology* (Princeton: Princeton University Press, 1997), 167-8; Leslie Stephen, *English Thought in the Eighteenth Century*, 2 vols. (1876; repr. Bristol: Thoemmes Press, 1991), 2: 412-13. For a more charitable view of John Wesley's thought in relation to science, see J. W. Haas, Jr., "John Wesley's Views on Science and Christianity: An Examination of the Charge of Antiscience," *Church History* 63 (1994): 378-92.

80. See Jürgen Habermas, *The Structural Transformation of the Public Sphere: An Inquiry into a Category of Bourgeois Society*, trans. Thomas Burger with the assistance of Frederick Lawrence (1989; repr. Cambridge: Polity Press, 1999).

81. Henry D. Rack has written on Wesley's view of the supernatural in several articles and in his *Reasonable Enthusiast*. As will be apparent, I am much indebted to Rack's scholarship. Additionally, other Wesleyan and non-Wesleyan scholars have given attention to this aspect of Wesley's life and thought. Most notably, W. Stephen Gunter, *The Limits of "Love Divine": John Wesley's Response to Antinomianism and Enthusiasm* (Nashville: Kingswood Books, 1989) and Ann Taves, *Fits, Trances, & Visions: Experiencing Religion and Explaining Experience from Wesley to James* (Princeton: Princeton University Press, 1999), 3-117.

82. Rack, *Reasonable Enthusiast*, 350.

83. See W. R. Ward, *Early Evangelicalism: A Global Intellectual History, 1670-1789* (Cambridge: Cambridge University Press, 2006), 119-39.

84. Frederick Gill, *The Romantic Movement and Methodism: A Study of English Romanticism and the Evangelical Revival* (London: Epworth Press, 1937); James Golden, "John Wesley On Rhetoric and Belles Lettres," *Speech Monographs* 28 (1961): 250-64; William Hansen, *John Wesley and the Rhetoric of Reform* (Ph.D. thesis, University of Oregon, 1972); George Lawton, *John Wesley's English: A Study of his Literary Style* (London: George Allen & Unwin Ltd., 1962). Evelyn Jenson, "John Wesley's Use of Three Types of Classical Oratory—'Forensic,' 'Epideictic,' and 'Deliberative'—in His Journal" (Ed.D. Thesis, Ball State University, 1980); Rivers, *Reason, Grace, and Sentiment*, 1: 205-53; T. B. Shepherd, *Methodism and the Literature of the Eighteenth Century* (London: Epworth Press, 1940) and Jean-Pierre van Noppen, *Transforming Words: The Early Methodist Revival from a Discourse Perspective* (Bern: Peter Lang, 1999).

85. Rivers, *Reason, Grace, and Sentiment*, 1: 207. Mary Thale too has analyzed the Methodist presence in the debating societies of eighteenth-century London, drawing attention to their oratorical success in defence of the Methodist vision in her "Deists, Papists and Methodists at London Debating Societies, 1746-1799," *History* 86 (2001): 328-47.

86. Carlo Ginzburg, *History, Rheotoric, and Proof* (Hanover, NE: University Press of New England, 1999), 1.

87. Timothy J. Reiss, *Knowledge, Discovery and Imagination in Early Modern Europe: The Rise of Aesthetic Rationalism* (Cambridge: Cambridge University Press, 1997), 12.

88. Richard Baxter, *The Certainty of the World of Spirits, Fully Evinced by Unquestionable Histories of APPARITIONS and WITCHCRAFTS, Operations, Voices, &c. Proving the Immortality of Souls, the Malice of the Devils and the Damned, and the Blessedness of the Justified. Written for the Conviction of Sadducees & Infidels* (London: Printed for T. Parkhurst and J. Salisbury, 1691), A4.

89. James Hartman, *Providence Tales and the Birth of American Literature* (Baltimore: The John Hopkins University Press, 1999), 17. The epistemology of the miraculous, then, must be seen as opposed to an understanding that seeks to comprehend the world in terms of natural categories. See Jane Shaw, "The Late Seventeenth and Eighteenth Centuries," in Richard Harries and Henry Mayr-Harting, eds., *Christianity: Two Thousand Years* (Oxford: Oxford University Press, 2001), 162-91, who calls attention to the "undersides" of the Enlightenment.

90. David Wellbery, "The Transformation of Rhetoric" in Marshal Brown, ed., *The Cambridge History of Literary Criticism*, 7 vols. (Cambridge: Cambridge University Press, 1989-2001), 5:189.

91. Hans Frei, *The Eclipse of Biblical Narrative: A Study in Eighteenth and Nine-teenth Century Hermeneutics* (New Haven: Yale University Press, 1974), 1-164. Also, Jonathan Israel's *Radical Enligthenment: Philosophy and the Making of Modernity 1650-1750* (Oxford: Oxford University Press, 2001) and *Enlightenment Contested: Philosophy, Modernity, and the Emancipation of Man 1670-1752* (Oxford: Oxford University Press, 2006) who traces the influence of Benedict de Spinoza for the history of the radical En-lightenment.

92. Jonathan Edwards, *A Faithful Narrative of the Surprizing Work of God in the Conversion of many hundred Souls in Northampton, and the Neighbouring Towns and Villages of New-Hampshire in New-England* (London: Printed for John Oswald, 1737), 22.

93. "John Wesley and George Whitefield revolutionized religious rhetoric." Elie Halevy, *The Birth of Methodism in England*, trans. and ed., Bernard Semmel (Chicago: University of Chicago Press, 1971), 37.

94. Though previous generations of historians and theologians have been aware of Wesley's influential periodical, renewed interest has emerged into the contents of the magazine and the fresh insights it offers into Wesley's intent for and understanding of the Methodists. See, for example, Vicki Tolar Burton, *Spiritual Literacy in John Wesley's Methodism: Reading, Writing, & Speaking to Believe* (Waco: Baylor University Press, 2008). I will argue in detail in chapters 3 and 4 that Wesley's editorship of the *Arminian Magazine* was significant and that a consideration of this facet of Wesley's development dislodges several assumptions that have been erroneously made about Wesley's own commitment to the supernatural.

Chapter 2

The Senses and the Supernatural:
John Wesley's Empirical Epistemology and
the Knowledge of the Lord[1]

> The Laws and Affairs of the other world . . . are vastly differing, from those of our Regions, and therefore 'tis no wonder we cannot judge of their *designs*, when we know nothing of their *ménages*, and so *little* of their *natures* . . . We are in the dark to *one anothers* purposes and intendments; and there are a thousand intrigues in our little matters, which will not presently confess their design even to *sagacious inquisitors*. And therefore 'tis folly and incogitancy to argue any thing one or other from the designs of a sort of Beings, with whom we so little communicate.[2]

> All men naturally desire knowledge. An indication of this is our esteem for the senses; for apart from their use we esteem them for their own sake, and most of all the sense of sight. Not only with a view of action, but even when no action is contemplated, we prefer sight, generally speaking, to all the other senses. The reason of this is that of all the senses sight best helps us to know things, and reveals many distinctions.[3]

John Wesley wrestled with issues relating to religious epistemology throughout his life which spanned the eighteenth century.[4] From his undergraduate days at Christ Church until the end of his life in 1791, Wesley was thinking, writing, and preaching on themes of epistemic value. A cursory reading of his sermons, for example, reveals a consistent and continual concern with issues about the nature, limits, and ramifications of reason and human understanding. Additionally, his letters, tracts, and theological essays treat various epistemological issues. In 1730, when the young Wesley returned to Oxford from Epworth, the human thirst for knowledge was at the forefront of his mind when he preached a sermon in *All Saints* at Oxford. In his homily, *The Promise of Understanding*, Wesley highlighted the pursuit of knowledge as one of the central aspects of human nature. "It is easy," proclaimed Wesley,

> to observe that one of the earliest principles in the soul of man is a desire of knowledge . . . . So long as this is contained within proper bounds and directed to proper objects, there is scarce in the mind of man a more delightful or more useful inclination. The pleasures it yields are without number; the field of knowledge hath no end; and in almost every part of it springs up some plant not only pleasing to the eyes and rejoicing to the heart, but of use to make one wise, to give the true wisdom, to enlighten the eyes, to enlarge the heart, to make us see the all-wise, the all-merciful God in every one even of these his lowest works.[5]

The imagery John Wesley used of knowledge as a "plant" that yields many benefits, both natural and eternal, portrayed a significant characteristic in his epistemology; namely, the ability to recognize the presence of God in the natural world. It is a subject that permeated Wesley's idea of creation and one that also emerged at the end of his life when he considered the eschatological redemption of the world. Throughout his life Wesley attempted to outline his understanding of the world and the possibility of acquiring knowledge of the divine. Like many in the eighteenth century, he saw nature as intricately diverse in its appearance but unified in its essence. As a result, nature served as a critical starting point for his view of knowledge in general and the place and priority of human understanding in particular. So it is essential that the priority of reason and the possibility of transcendental knowledge in Wesley's thought be examined. It is to that task that I now turn.

The Created Order and the Tension of Knowledge

In 1763, Wesley published *A Survey of the Wisdom of God in the Creation: Or A Compendium of Natural Philosophy.*[6] Repeatedly he returned to this work and expanded its material for a total of four editions, which indicates that knowledge of the natural world was both vital for his concept of creation and a significant dimension in his view of the multiplicity of knowledge.[7]

Like many of Wesley's works, the *Survey of the Wisdom of God* was an extract of previous authorities who had written on the subject at hand (in this case natural philosophy) coupled with his own additions to the topic. In the 1763 edition, for instance, Wesley incorporated selections from John Ray's (1627-1705) *The Wisdom of God in the Works of Creation,* William Derham's (1657-1735) *Physcio and Astro-Theology,* Bernard Niewentyt's (1654-1718) *The Religious Philosopher,* Cotton Mather's (1663-1728) *The Christian Philosopher,* and William Wollaston's (1660-1724) *The Religion of Nature Delineated.*[8] Also consistent with his editorial methods, Wesley intended to make the subject matter accessible for the comprehension of readers unfamiliar or untrained in natural philosophy. On the first page of his preface, he identified two crucial issues that were found throughout his writings; one relating to literary style and the other theological discrimination:

> And this [*A Compendium of Natural Philosophy*] I wanted to see . . . in the plainest Dress, simply and nakedly exprest, in the most clear, easy and intelligible manner, that the Nature of the things would allow: Particularly free from all the Jargon of *Mathematics*, which is mere *Heathen Greek* to common Readers. At the same time I wished to see this short, full, plain Account of the visible Creation, directed to its right End: Not barely to entertain an idle, barren Curiosity, but to display the *invisible things* of GOD, his Power, Wisdom and Goodness.[9]

In the eighteenth century, physical science or natural philosophy as it was more commonly called, was concerned with an examination of the created universe and the evidence it referenced was often elaborated in the context of teleological presuppositions. "Natural Philosophy," for Wesley, "treats both of God Himself, and of his Creatures, visible and invisible."[10] In both the complicated and simple alike, he found traces of a structure that led to an undeniable conclusion for the disciplined observer. Divine presence, Wesley maintained, was present in the order and fabric of creation and an objective view of the rudiments of nature revealed an invisible origin for its genesis. At the conclusion of the second part of his work entitled "General Conclusions and Observations," Wesley delineated his teleological hermeneutic: "Proofs of a wise, a good and powerful Being are indeed deducible from every thing around us: But the extremely Great and the extremely Small seem to furnish us with those that are most convincing . . . In short, the World around us is the mighty Volume wherein God hath declared himself."[11]

Creation, like its Creator, was beyond any exhaustive comprehension by the human observer. The vast amount of data that made up the constitution of the world was both a sign of nature's mystery and a reminder of the limitation of human reason. Indeed, even the simplest creature was beyond the comprehension of the human mind. Wesley was quick to remind his readers of the limitation of the mind when stacked up against the complexity of creation: "The Eye of a little Worm is a subject capable of exhausting all our boasted speculations."[12] Additionally, in his sermons, Wesley noted the insurmountable challenge that confronted human reason and the task of acquiring and assimilating a comprehensive knowledge of the universe. As early as 1741, he took his text from Philippians 3.12 and preached a sermon on Christian perfection. In that homily, he declared that human nature was fundamentally characterized by an inability to know the world in any type of absolute manner.[13] This analysis indicates a fundamental starting point in Wesley's epistemology. Creation presents humanity with an overwhelming amount of data. The diversity, unity, and extent of the created order can be seen in every corner of the universe, causing wonder, excitement, and adoration for the observer. Its essential nature, however, is beyond the scope of human reason. At the outset of his *Survey of the Wisdom of God*, John Wesley reminded his readers: "*we cannot search them* [the causes] out *to perfection*."[14]

This starting point in Wesley's epistemology also played out a tension in his thought. On the one hand, humanity has a thirst for knowledge that cannot be ignored or suppressed. Wesley himself epitomised this, being a man of almost boundless curiosity. In this regard, he was a man of his century, an exemplar of the desire for knowledge and the acquisition of information which permeated the Enlightenment. The overwhelming volume of physical data which surfaced in the seventeenth and eighteenth centuries compelled the natural philosopher to take the primary task of "description" seriously. Furthermore, as a flood of literature emerged that described the multi-faceted nature of creation, a revolution in classification and measurement surfaced too.[15] This was the age of de Buffon's (1707-88) forty-four volume *Natural History,* d'Alembert (1717-83) and Diderot's (1713-84) seventeen volume *Encyclopedie of Arts and Sciences*, and the three volume and later expanded into eighteen volume *Encyclopædia Britannica*.[16] The multiplying of knowledge seemed endless as individuals increasingly discovered the world and the environment they inhabited.

On the other hand, Wesley was not willing to place his epistemological confidence in reason alone. Although he was thoroughly empirical in his epistemology, his view of cognitive activity did not exclude metaphysics from the theatre of knowledge. Quite the opposite, inspired by John Locke and others in the seventeenth and eighteenth centuries, his observations of the connected quality of the natural world enabled Wesley to posit a nexus that supported and maintained the possibility of knowledge in both temporal and transcendental dimensions. There existed, in other words, an eternal principle that permeated the created universe; a form of reason which sustained not only all empirical discoveries and the advancement of data about the natural world but also served as a bridge for knowledge of the supernatural. Pondering planetary position and motion, Wesley suggested that the world was so clearly sustained by God that the Atheist should be shamed. "Certainly could Argument avail," Wesley reasoned, "Atheism would not be utterly ashamed to shew its Head, and forced to acknowledge, that it was an eternal and Almighty Being, it was God alone, who gave to each of the celestial Bodies, its proper Magnitude and measure of Heat, its Dueness of Distance, and Regularity of Motion."[17] Like most cosmological proofs, the denial of God—for Wesley—was inseparably linked to the abdication of reason and the pursuit of knowledge.

The Nature of Reason:
John Wesley's Idea of Human Understanding

Any discussion that examines the relationship of reason and faith in the thought of John Wesley must admit that he was never one to demean or vilify the use of reason. He continually embraced reason as a principle of value and in one sense Wesley's biography can be read as a pursuit of the life of the mind. In correspondence with Joseph Benson (1749-1821) on 5 October 1770, Wesley wrote: "Passion and prejudice govern the world, only under the name of reason. It is our part, by religion and reason joined, to counteract them all we can."[18] Throughout his life, Wesley addressed the subject of reason and the viability of its relationship to religious issues. Always under attack as an "enthusiast," he continued to make the case for the priority of reason for the Methodist movement which he organized and sustained. In 1742, Josiah Tucker (1712-99), an economist and divine who became curate of St. Stephen's (1737) and later rector of All Saints (1739) in Bristol, released his *Brief History of the Principles of Methodism* in which he zealously attempted to link John Wesley and his Methodist followers to the mysticism of William Law (1686-1761).[19]

Wesley countered Tucker's attack with the publication of his own *The Principles of a Methodist*.[20] The same year Wesley published *An Earnest Appeal to Men of Reason and Religion* followed in 1744 by *A Farther Appeal to Men of Reason and Religion*.[21] In those works, Wesley made an argument for both the Methodist movement and the import of reason in the believer's life. "We therefore not only allow," wrote Wesley, "but earnestly exhort, all who seek after true religion, to use all the reason which God hath given them, in searching out the things of God."[22] Reason, for Wesley, was not merely a primer for an apologetic defence of the Christian faith, however. From his early days at Oxford, he found a great amount of professional and personal satisfaction in the life of the mind.[23] Particularly gratifying for him was the discipline of logic and the disputations that he moderated at Lincoln College.[24] Lucy Sutherland described the University disputations that, if taken seriously, which by no means was always the case, was an onerous task. After a student had fulfilled at least two years of residency he was expected to dispute in the areas of grammar and logic. The disputations were held three days during the week under the direction of regent masters and proctors. Sutherland explained the process:

> When a candidate took part in them in the course of qualifying himself, he was said to do so *pro forma,* and when he had successfully completed the exercise, he was created a "general Sophister." In the eighteenth century the process was usually described as "doing Generals." Thereafter he was supposed to take part in the same disputations at least once a term until he graduated—though even in the earlier years of the century he was held to have fulfilled this obligation when he had taken part in three of them; it was called "doing Juraments" and by 1773 attendance at such disputations had died out. Finally he had to "answer under Bachelor" in the elaborate Lenten disputations in which those who had recently graduated were said to "determine," an exercise necessary to make the BA degree more than a courtesy title, and which was essential for those who wished to proceed to the MA. The undergraduate "answering under Bachelor" had to respond twice to a BA (known as his "father") in logic and rhetoric.[25]

John Wesley was unusually conscientious about his tutorial experiences at Lincoln College and wrote of them in 1766: "For several years I was Moderator in the disputations which were held six times a week at Lincoln College, in Oxford. I could not avoid acquiring hereby some degree of expertness in arguing; and especially in discerning and pointing out well-covered and plausible fallacies."[26] While this remark tells of Wesley's enjoyment in the disputations, it still leaves uncovered the origin of his view of the priority of reason for human nature.

The sources of Wesley's training in logic and disputation, however, are fairly easy to trace through his journal entries and letter correspondence. High on the list of his mentors was Henry Aldrich (1647-1710), Dean of Christ Church from 1689 until his death in 1710 and also served as Vice-Chancellor of Oxford University from 1692 to 1695. Aldrich had reacted against the Port-Royal logicians and defined the syllogism as a chief characteristic of the logical system. In 1691, he published his *Artis Logicae Compendium* which replaced Robert Sanderson's (1587-1663) *Logicae Artis Compendium* (1615) as the standard text at Oxford.[27]

By the time Wesley arrived in Oxford to read for his Bachelor's degree, Aldrich's *Compendium* was firmly established as required reading for undergraduates. According to V. H. H. Green, Wesley read Aldrich's book in 1729 and like others at Oxford, regarded it "with profound reverence."[28] On one occasion, Wesley translated Aldrich's Latin text in approximately three or four hours, while he waited for better travelling weather at Tan-y-bwich.[29] Wesley's translation, *A Compendium of Logick* first appeared in 1750 and during his lifetime went through two other editions in 1756 and 1790.[30] Repeatedly, in his letter correspondence and published journals, Wesley recommended reading and practicing Aldrich's principles of logic for the Methodist societies and schools. On 23 February 1749, for example, he explained in his journal: "My design was to have as many of our assistants here [Kingswood], during the Lent, as could possibly be spared, and to read lectures to them every day, as I did to my pupils in Oxford. I have seventeen of them in all. These I divided into two classes, and read to one Bishop Pearson on the Creed, to the other Aldrich's Logic, and to both Rules for Action and Utterance."[31] Much of Wesley's logical prowess was due to his commitment to Aldrich and the standard of Aristotelian logic which he made famous at Oxford.[32]

Wesley's idea of reason found its fundamental starting point, then, from his understanding of Aristotelian logic. Wesley's own translation of Aldrich followed the *Compendium* faithfully when he defined the function of the mind: "The Operations of the Mind are three, *Simple Apprehension, Judgment, Discourse.*"[33]

In Wesley's determination, a theory of knowledge must first *apprehend* the object available for cognition. It was "the first and most simple act of understanding."[34] Following John Locke, Wesley conceived knowledge not as a process for the formulation of innate ideas that are pre-infused onto the mind but the actualization of an encounter between subject and object.[35] In his influential *An Essay Concerning Human Understanding,* Locke had maintained, "it seeming to me near a Contradiction, to say, that there are Truths imprinted on the Soul, which it perceives or understand not; imprinting, if it signify anything, being nothing else, but the making certain Truths to be perceived."[36] Locke maintained that when a child was born his or her mind should be viewed as white paper or a blank slate [*tabula rasa*]. The experiences, which the mind of an individual encountered, resulted in particular impressions or sensations being formed.[37] Wesley agreed with Locke that the notion of innate ideas which stipulated that thinking was possible simply by giving expression to certain ideas which were already stamped onto the mind was incongruous with human experience. In his sermon entitled *On the Discoveries of Faith*, written and perhaps preached at Yarm during a Northern tour in 1788, Wesley constructed a treatment of the epistemic dimensions of faith, and offered a concise account of his understanding of the cognitive process. Wesley asserted:

> For many ages it has been allowed by sensible men, *Nihil est in intellectu quod non fait prius in sensu:* that is, "There is nothing in the understanding which was not first perceived by some of the senses." All the knowledge which we naturally have is originally derived from our senses. And therefore those who want any sense, cannot have the least knowledge or idea of the objects of that sense—as they that never had sight, have not the least knowledge or conception of light or colours. Some indeed have, of late years, endeavoured to prove that we have *innate ideas,* not derived from any of the senses, but coeval with the understanding. But this point has been now thoroughly discussed by men of the most eminent sense and learning. And it is agreed by all impartial persons, that although some things are so plain and obvious, that we can very hardly avoid knowing them as soon as we come to the use of our understanding, yet the knowledge even of those is not innate, but derived from some of our senses.[38]

Twenty-five years earlier, in 1763, Wesley was more down-to-earth when, in his *Survey of the Wisdom of God,* he gave a simple definition of an idea. "If any one asks, what an Idea is," instructed Wesley, "let him look upon a Tree, and then immediately shutting his Eyes, try if he retains any Resemblance of what he saw, and that is an Idea."[39] Wesley was convinced that knowledge of an object was based upon its experience in the sense and verification in the mind.[40] For both Locke and Wesley, this was the process that everyone passed through in the accumulation and formation of knowledge.

The second stage that Wesley recognized in the cognitive process, following Aldrich, was what he termed *Judgment*. The nature of judgment discerned the representational ideas and distinguished them from fabrications and deceptions. From Wesley's perspective, there were many instances in which those who adjudicated human experiences, especially religious ones, tended to move into one extreme or another. The operation of judgment, however, allowed for the determination of the apprehended object and showed how it fit within previous considered judgments of the object being investigated. Without the category and function of judgment, the concept of "reasonable" was disputable which, in turn, would sever the possibility of determining the claims of extremists, such as in the case of "enthusiasm" and "scepticism." In Wesley's understanding of cognition, it was in judgment where apprehensions are filtered and ultimately sorted out in the mind and articulated in the formation of discourse.

This activity of judgment was demonstrated easily in Wesley's way of thinking. At one juncture, there were those "enthusiasts" who decried the presence of reason in their practice of faith, and asserted that reason was an offence to piety and devotion. Such individuals, observed Wesley, always supposed "the dreams of their own imagination to be revelations from God."[41] The French Prophets, for the most part, fell into this category and, for many in the early eighteenth century served as a vivid example of a group that neglected reason in their life of faith. For those who were attracted to their defence of immediate inspiration, initiation into their close-knit group replaced the need for empirical knowledge and epistemological verification. In his study of the French Prophets and the miracles they claimed to perform, Hillel Schwartz writes:

> Physical healing had spiritual reverberations, and those miraculously cured often became believers . . . It was not simply the powers of the prophets or the relief of illness that brought these healed men into the group; it was also the spiritual drama of the cure. The experience of physical disruption and restoration could contribute positively to an awareness of the spiritual side of life. Prophecy and miracle promised to meet the desire for an understanding of that providence through which one had been so singularly blessed.[42]

At the dawn of the Methodist movement the French Prophets attracted the attention of John Wesley.[43] On 28 January 1739, long after the heyday of the French Prophets, he recorded in his journal an encounter with a prophetess. It was an interesting meeting and Wesley's description of the encounter detailed the ecstatic experience of the woman and his own process of evaluating her authenticity. Wesley related:

> I went (having been long importuned thereto,) about five in the evening, with four or five of my friends, to a house where was one of those commonly called French prophets. After a time, she came in. She seemed about four or five and twenty, of an agreeable speech and behaviour. She asked, why we came. I said, "To try the spirits, whether they be of God." Presently after she leaned back in her chair, and seemed to have strong workings in her breast, with deep sighings intermixed. Her head and hands, and by turns, every part of her body, seemed also to be in a kind of convulsive motion. This continued about ten minutes, till, at six, she began to speak (though the workings, sighings, and contortions of her body were so intermixed with her words, that she seldom spoke half a sentence together) with a clear, strong voice . . . She spoke much (all as in the person of God, and mostly in Scripture words) of the fulfilling of the prophecies, the coming of Christ now at hand, and the spreading of the Gospel over all the earth . . . Two or three of our company were much affected, and believed she spoke by the Spirit of God. But this was in no wise clear to me. The motion might be either hysterical or artificial. And the same words, any person of a good understanding and well versed in the Scriptures might have spoken. But I let the matter alone; knowing this, that "if it be not of God, it will come to nought."[44]

It seemed, though, by the summer of 1739, Wesley had made up his mind that the French Prophets were not "sent by God" and instead were a source of confusion and distraction. In a journal entry Wesley stated with disappointment, "I called on one who 'did run well,' till he was hindered by some of those called French prophets. 'Woe unto the prophets, saith the Lord, who prophesy in my name, and I have not sent them.' At Weaver's Hall, I endeavoured to point them out; and earnestly exhorted all that followed after holiness, to avoid, as fire, all who do not speak according 'to the Law and Testimony.'"[45] There is little doubt that the French Prophet's extreme views of inspiration, which eschewed mediated knowledge, coupled with the disrepute into which they brought these concepts informed Wesley's evaluation.

Obversely, Wesley criticized those "sceptics" who had leaned too far to the other end of the spectrum and relied heavily on reason. They, in his view, had diluted the life of faith with a heavy element of rationalism which had become prevalent in eighteenth-century England. This point of view did not monopolize eighteenth-century culture, however, and those who exalted the life of reason and sought to eclipse the supernatural from human consciousness did not go unchallenged, but provoked a variety of responses that challenged their funda-mental presuppositions. B. W. Young observes, "far from being a rationalistic monopoly, religious debate in eighteenth-century England contained significant mystical, visionary, and essentially biblical elements."[46] There were many cote-ries that espoused the mystical way to religious knowledge, not least those who admired Jacob Boehme (1575-1624), like William Law (1686-1761) and some of Wesley's own followers.[47] John Wesley was not a Rationalist in the strict sense of the term but did endorse the pursuit of philosophical and practical rea-son. A brief look at his reading habits and the recommendations which he gave to the societies, for example, illustrate that Wesley entertained and enjoyed a vigorous pursuit of knowledge at various levels.[48] In addition to his own life of study, Wesley expected the Methodist people, to be avid readers too. So in a letter to Richard Boardman (1738-82), an itinerant preacher, John Wesley ap-prised: "Our little books you should spread wherever you go. Reading Christians will be knowing Christians."[49] Scattered throughout his correspondence of sev-enty years were recommendations of books and subjects that assisted Methodists in their pursuit of religious knowledge and spiritual perfection.[50]

The third aspect of reason was what Wesley termed *discourse*. Simply put, discourse was the "progress of mind from one judgment to another."[51] Discourse differed from judgment in that the latter makes determinations related to the coherent construction of ideas and the former assesses judgment and builds an argument which convinces others of its validity. In various and repeated ways, Wesley was forced to defend the Methodist mission against the false assump-tions and arguments of his opponents. At this juncture, Wesley's joining of rea-son and rhetoric faced its most stringent test in the battle for legitimacy. In many instances, Wesley's answers to his opponents were not only exercises in self-defence but opportunities for the recommendation of a way of life which "Meth-odism" urged all Christians to embrace. For the accomplishment of this task, he dismantled the arguments of his adversaries with logical precision and suggested that the actions, words, and manners of the Methodists were closer to the reali-ties of spiritual truth than they would allow. John Wesley's disputes with Bishop George Lavington, Edmund Gibson (1669-1748), and William Warburton, each in their own way, demonstrated a *modus operandi* that embraced both religion and reason and incorporated the significance of both. The motive for Wesley's intensity in controversies like these was, that for him, there was so much at stake for the renewal that he was directing within the Methodist societies. It was not, however, merely the acceptance of the Methodist way of life. Throughout the eighteenth century, Wesley was aware that there were many outside the Method-ist connexion who were already doing the will of God. The issue was whether the church would recognize its own fulfilment. The lack of understanding, in this regard, Wesley considered a lacuna in the life and spirituality of the ecclesial community which had ordained him to the priesthood.[52]

Though Wesley was enamoured with the discipline of logic, he could not hand over an undivided commitment to reason alone. As Wesley saw it, reason was fundamentally flawed and the idea that it was sufficient in itself for the achievement of happiness and truth was a distraction from the important issues that required immediate attention. In *A Compendium of Logick*, Wesley had noted the limitations of human reason in all of its operations: "Our Apprehension is apt to be Indistinct, our Judgment False, our Discourse Inconclusive."[53]

In this matter, therefore, Wesley could not simply agree with Locke that the mind was a piece of white paper which had only to be marked and imprinted by the experiences of life. From a reading of the biblical documents, the sin of Adam and Eve in the Garden of Eden had altered the nature of humanity and all creation. Therefore, in a very precise and logical manner, Wesley calculated that the mind was already marked with original sin which was visible throughout human history. An objective observation of human nature revealed the effects of sin and the reality of evil. Certainly Wesley allowed that reason had great power to enlighten human life and make its burden light. It could aid men and women in the performance of the most difficult tasks of life, but it was not able to remove the mark of sin that had dislodged its original purity. There were also times when Wesley noted that the interaction of sin with human reason was due to diabolical agency. For example, in one of his letters addressed to Mary Bishop (1725-90), who found herself entangled in the Antinomian controversy, Wesley advised: "Although I am thoroughly persuaded that those reasonings are in a great measure from a preternatural cause, and therefore chiefly to be resisted by continuing instant in prayer, yet I think Christian prudence not only permits but requires you to add other means to this."[54]

In this and other letters one can see Wesley as a pastoral leader who was engaged in the cure of souls, but he also emphasized the ways in which sin had marked the human understanding and imposed limitations on human reason. Nowhere could the limitations of human reason be more transparent than in its inability to commune with God and exhibit a knowledge of the supernatural for human existence. Such communion required an additional feature in John Wesley's epistemology.

Spiritual Sensorium: John Wesley's Concept of Faith

Laurence Wood remarks that the key to Wesley's epistemology was his view of faith: "Here is where all the great metaphysical problems are resolved."[55] In the previous section, Wesley's idea of the benefits and limitations of reason was examined. Wesley, however, was not ambiguous about the value of reason. On the contrary, he believed and asserted that human beings had not been abandoned in the world to wander aimlessly, epistemologically speaking. Nevertheless, the pathos of the human situation was illustrated for Wesley in the deathbed scene of Thomas Hobbes (1588-1679). According to tradition, when Hobbes was asked at the end of his life about existence beyond the grave, he only replied

"I am taking a leap in the dark."[56] The philosopher, according to Wesley, should have known better, and used his intellect to realize that the darkness of a life separated from God could be avoided.

The connection that faith demonstrated in the quest for transcendental knowledge revolved around the issue of testimony for John Wesley. On 2 January 1749, he recorded in a journal entry that he had intended to travel to Rotterdam, but changed his plans when a book written by the Cambridge scholar, Conyers Middleton (1683-1750), came to his attention. "But being much pressed to answer Dr. Middleton's book against the Fathers, I postponed my voyage and spent almost twenty days in that unpleasant employment."[57] Middleton had been educated at Trinity College, Cambridge, the college of Newton. In 1706, he had been made a Fellow of the college and had made his mark in the academic community as a classical scholar, writing essays on Roman rhetoric and a life of Cicero.[58] At the same time David Hume published his *An Enquiry Concerning Human Understanding,* Conyers Middleton was working on his *A Free Inquiry into the Miraculous Powers, which are Supposed to have Subsisted in the Christian Church*, which was published a few months later.[59]

Middleton's work, like Hume's, was seen as an attack upon orthodox Christianity and its idea that the supernatural power of the Spirit was a key factor in the formation of the Christian community. His essay had been preceded two years earlier by *An Introductory Discourse*, in which he initially formulated his presuppositions and promised an extended treatise that would lay out in full detail his views about the miraculous in the post-Apostolic era.[60] Whenever John Wesley interrupted travelling from his pre-arranged preaching tours, it was for something which he considered crucial for his evangelical cause. In this case, it was the implications of Middleton's argument against a belief in the invisible world, a challenge that Wesley considered detrimental both to the Methodist agenda and the entire mission of Christianity itself.[61]

Middleton's attack against the idea of miracles in the early church, and Wesley's response to Middleton, irradiate Wesley's religious epistemology and his understanding of the nature of faith. Middleton had utilized two fundamental approaches in his *Free Enquiry*, which he thought were sufficient for any reasonable individual who would look at the historical development of primitive Christianity.[62] In the preface to that work he suggested that the whole question that related testimony to the occurrences of supernatural episodes in the church depended "on the joint credibility of the facts, pretended to have been produced by those powers, and of the witnesses, who attest them."[63] An affirmation of the early church's narrative accounts, which Middleton believed had been bolstered with a world-view that relied heavily on the notion of the supernatural, was historically and morally untenable. Instead, in the list of spiritual gifts (χαρίσματα) found in the New Testament, Middleton contended that at the close of the apostolic age there was an absence of particular gifts found to be active in the community of faith.[64] Consequently, he posed a fundamental problem for his readers. How is it, Middleton cynically pondered, that in the post-apostolic church there were witnesses to various gifts except one; namely, tongues (γλώσσαις)? Middleton refused to adopt a modified position and maintained that the gifts in their totality must either continue or cease throughout history. Middleton further enraged his orthodox opponents by suggesting that if the gift of tongues had ceased, as he argued it had, then one must logically infer that the remaining gifts were either fabrications of religious impostors or an attempt by the primitive Church to defend the integrity of its faith against social and intellectual odds. Middleton's conclusion was akin to Hume's:

> If this then appears to have been the case of this particular gift [γλώσσαιs]; that false claim to it was made by the early Fathers, and held up for a while, till it could no longer be supported; it is sufficient, one would think, of itself, to blast the general credit of all the rest, tho' no particular mark of fraud could have been fixed on each of them separately: but when there is not a single one among them all, which, either from it's nature, or end, or manner of exertion, or the character of it's witness, does not furnish just ground to suspect it as fictitious, it must needs persuade every rational inquirer, that they were all derived from the same source of craft and imposture.[65]

It was this argument from suspicion, which questioned the reliability of the primitive church's testimony that infuriated Wesley. As a consequence, Wesley's letter constructed an argument that was designed to dismantle Middleton's presuppositions about the miraculous while also establishing his own views of faith and religious epistemology.[66]

The letter sent to Middleton was the longest one that Wesley composed in his lifetime, surpassing two hundred pages in its original folio edition.[67] From the very outset, John Wesley registered his disagreement with Conyers Middleton and his accusation against primitive Christianity. It was Middleton's accusation that the early Church had intentionally fabricated stories that idealized the notion of supernatural occurrences that concerned Wesley. He conceded, with Middleton, that after the third century impurities had arisen in the church; and as a result he had "no more to do with the writers or miracles of the fourth than with those of the fourteenth century."[68]

Nevertheless Wesley was not prepared to accept Middleton's blanket generalizations and at one point extended an invitation to the Cambridge don: "I should desire you to prove that the miracles of the fourth century were all forged, but that it is not material to our question."[69] Wesley's identification with primitive Christianity has been a point of discussion in recent scholarship.[70] One of the interesting elements in the Methodist leader's writings was his treatment of tradition and in his letter to Middleton; Wesley unabashedly identified himself with the theological and spiritual affirmations of the early Christians. For Middleton's charge that spiritual gifts had ceased in the early church, Wesley, the adept logician, asserted: "I want the proof. Though I am but one of the vulgar, yet I am not half so credulous as you apprehend the first Christians to have been. *Ipse dixi* will not satisfy me: I want plain, clear, logical proof; especially when I consider how much you build upon this, that it is the main foundation whereon your hypothesis stands."[71]

At one level, then, Wesley's letter can be viewed as a rhetorical exercise which attempted to expose the logical fallacies of his opponent's argument while aligning himself and his Methodist movement the accumulated wisdom of

Christian tradition. In this way, this reading of the letter reveals that Wesley, with his great learning of history, saw himself in a long line of apologists who defended the belief in miracles and the existence of an invisible world. At the core of his argument was a view of testimony and its validity for the establishment of knowledge that could be sustained by history and reason. One example can be cited. "I must take notice here," wrote Wesley to Middleton, "of another of your postulatums which leads you into many mistakes. With regard to past ages, you continually take this for granted: 'What is not recorded was not done.'"[72] Then, a few pages later Wesley jibes Middleton with an accusation that gets at the root of his dismay: "Surely there is something very peculiar in this—something extraordinary, though not miraculous—that a man who is too wise to believe the Bible should believe everything but the Bible! Should swallow any tale, so God be out of the question, though ever improbable, ever so impossible."[73] Wesley went on and maintained that God has different ways of executing his will and is not limited by space or time to a uniform method. Though the early Christian community had not recorded every event in its history that certainly did not invalidate the things that *were* recorded.

As the controversy with Middleton demonstrated, Wesley's idea of knowledge could not be clearly articulated apart from a consideration of faith. The idea of testimony holds tightly to the notion that the veracity of sources may be relied on in light of one's absence from direct sensory experience. As such, testimony incorporates the concept of reliable witnesses as a part of its essential structure.[74] If such a process has no validity, epistemologically speaking, then scepticism is the end result.[75]

For natural philosophers during the Enlightenment, there was an overwhelming consensus, as Steven Shapin has argued, for the primacy of testimony in the articulation of knowledge. Shapin has outlined in great detail that during the Enlightenment testimony was conceived within a framework that satisfied the canons of rationality. Not only was it impossible for one individual to experience all of the data that went into making up a body of knowledge but to suggest that testimony and knowledge were mutually exclusive generated a solipsism that eclipsed the experiences of the self from external and internal reference points. Conversely, maintains Shapin: "Knowledge we had by way of testimony might be only probable, but there were degrees of probability which effectively mimicked the certainty of demonstration and eye-witness and which were wholly adequate as bases for conducting the affairs of everyday life."[76] This became particularly important when one approached the testimony of biblical writers and the moral direction that Scripture offered. The Christian witness of scripture had a long historical continuum and to question its veracity was to attack the moral integrity of religious knowledge and the Christian faith that had emerged throughout each succeeding generation.[77] In this matter, therefore, the word "faith" for Wesley became a crucial term that carried the strongest overtones in his understanding of the biblical writers and their affirmation of the order of salvation (*ordo salutis*). After 1740, Wesley never preached on faith without quoting from the letter to the Hebrews and it was to this epistle and its definition of faith that he returned many times in his sermons, journals, letters, and theological essays. For example, in his sermon *On Faith*, Wesley preached from Hebrews 11.6 (*"Without faith it is impossible to please him"*) and reiterated Hebrews 11.1 (*"For faith is the substance of things hoped for, the evidence of things not seen"*) and formulated what would become his working definition: "Particularly, it is a divine evidence and conviction of God and the things of God. This is the most comprehensive definition of faith that ever was or can be given, as including every species of faith, from the lowest to the highest."[78] But, in other places, Wesley expanded his concept of faith and included the existence of a nonmaterial realm too. In his last written sermon, dated 17 January 1791, and composed in London, Wesley expounded his definition characterizing faith "in one sense of the word, a divine conviction of God and of the things of God; in another (nearly related to, yet not altogether the same) it is a divine conviction of the invisible and eternal world."[79]

John Wesley's doctrine of faith, then, was quite different from the transcendental idealism of Immanuel Kant (1724-1804), who made a profound impact on the continental Enlightenment.[80] A close analysis of Wesley's understanding of faith specified definite epistemological presuppositions. From a very early phase in his odyssey in which, after debate with his mother, he abandoned the view that faith was merely an activity of the mind that assented to certain propositional truths, he became intensely interested in the viability of a transcendental knowledge, not simply a transcendental ideal.[81]

Consonant with Wesley's commitment to a knowledge derived from the senses coupled with his interests in cognition, he conjectured that every human being possessed spiritual senses. In his sermon, *On the Discoveries of Faith*, preached on Hebrews 11.1 in 1788, Wesley further outlined his religious epistemology. If the notion of "innate ideas" was abandoned in favour of a quasi-Lockean sensationalism; namely, the principle, "There is nothing in the understanding which was not first perceived by some of the senses" (*"Nihil est in intellectu quod non fuit prius in sensu"*), then all data, which was not available to the senses cannot exist in the mind. "All the knowledge which we naturally have is originally derived from our senses. And therefore those who want any sense cannot have the least knowledge or idea of the objects of that sense—as they that never had seen have not the least knowledge or conception of light or colours."[82] Wesley reminisced that the human senses played an important role in the accumulation of knowledge in various ways: Hearing related to the acquisition of sounds, touch to texture, and sight to vision. Furthermore, he understood that no physical sense could transcend the world of nature. But, here again, as in his understanding of biblical revelation, God had not left humanity in a dark place. From divine wisdom, God had provided humanity with the gift of faith that could register the objects and experiences of the invisible world by means of sensations which were analogous to those of the physical world. God "hath appointed faith to supply the defect of sense; to take us up where sense sets us down, and help us over the great gulf. Its office begins where that of sense ends."[83] Apart from this faith, human nature cannot see, feel, or touch the invisible world. Faith was, in Wesley's way of thinking, the extra sense requisite for the perception of the supernatural and its effects on the natural order.

At this point, however, Wesley found Locke inadequate for his own epistemological undertaking. It has been noted that when Wesley came to provide an abridgement of Locke's *Essay* in his *Arminian Magazine* he omitted Books III and IV for specific and consistent reasons. The fourth part of Locke's *Essay* entitled "Knowledge and Probability" located the empirical process as one that must, in some areas, resign itself to probability. For Locke, "we must in many things content ourselves with faith and probability."[84] While Wesley believed with Locke that one could never comprehend the data of knowledge exhaustively, he could not accept that human knowledge was relegated to probability.

Instead of Locke, Wesley found a more congenial partner in Peter Browne (1665?-1735), Bishop of Cork.[85] Browne had found it necessary to confront the Deists, especially John Toland (1670-1722), in several of his theological essays. Two of those were *The Procedure, Extent, and Limit of Human Understanding* and *Things Divine and Supernatural Conceived By Analogy with Things Natural and Human.*[86] John Wesley had read Browne's *Procedure* a year after it was published while he was at Oxford in 1729.[87] Throughout his life Wesley recommended Browne to those who wanted a correct grounding in epistemology, especially on the issues that related to religion.[88] In those important essays, Browne placed his theory of knowledge in line with the empiricists who contended that human beings have no innate knowledge of objects. Where he differed from others, though, was in his insistence that human knowledge was obtained through analogy. Metaphor was not to be confused with analogy in Browne's thought and at the beginning of *Things Divine and Supernatural,* he made the distinction between the terms:

> METAPHOR in general, is a *Substitution* of the *Idea* or *Conception* of one Thing, with the Term belonging to it, to *Stand for* another Thing, on Account of an *Appearing* Similitude only, *Without any real Resemblance, and true correspondency between the Things compared* . . . ANALOGY in general, is the *Substituting* the *Idea* or *Conception* of one Thing to *Stand for* and *Represent* another, on Account of a *True Resemblance, and Correspondent Reality in the very Nature of the Things compared.*[89]

In Browne's view, it was analogy that provided certainty in the face of the incompleteness of human knowledge. Furthermore, according to the Irish Bishop, revelation in a finite and contingent world often occurred through analogy. Though all human knowledge was incomplete, God uses human ideas that are consistent with the realities of the supernatural world.[90] This seemed to Wesley more in harmony for an agenda of divine knowledge than straight Lockeanism and was compatible with his ideas of faith as a necessary component for knowledge of the invisible world, which rested on the reliability of human testimony. This idea was portrayed vividly in a sermon written in 1788. The homily, *Walking by Sight and Walking by Faith*, amounted to a mini-treatise on faith. As in his other sermons, which broached the topic, it carried significant epistemological overtones. At its conclusion, Wesley defined faith as that element whereby the believer who had been touched by God could perceive divine presence and the rudiments of an invisible world. "How different is the case," Wesley wrote, "how vast the pre-eminence of them that 'walk by faith'! God, having 'opened the eyes of their understanding,' to see God and the things of God."[91]

At the same time, Wesley was more than aware that original sin and human fragility enabled self-deception in matters of personal religious experience. How, then, could one discern the difference between the inspiration of the Holy Spirit and demonic or self-imagined impressions? Standing in the lineage of the Reformation Wesley answered: "The Holy Scriptures abound with marks whereby the one may be distinguished from the other. They describe in the plainest manner the circumstances which go before, which accompany, and which follow, the true, genuine testimony of the Spirit of God with the spirit of a believer. Whoever carefully weighs and attends to these will not need to put darkness for light."[92] In short, the Bible offered for Wesley a template by which a measurement of the varied sensations visible in the *ordo salutis* were adjudicated. Thus, marks not only served to confirm the authentic saint but judge the vilest sinner as well. "Discover thyself," proclaimed Wesley,

> Thou poor self-deceiver! Thou who art confident of being a child of God; thou who sayest, "I have the witness in myself," and therefore defiest all thy enemies. Thou are weighed in the balance and found wanting, even in the valance of the sanctuary. The Word of the Lord hath tried thy soul, and proved thee to be reprobate silver. Thou art not lowly of heart; therefore thou has not received the Spirit of Jesus unto this day. Thou are not gentle and meek; therefore thy joy is nothing worth: it is not joy in the Lord. Thou dost not keep his commandments; therefore thou lovest him not, neither art thou partaker of the Holy Ghost. It is consequently as certain and as evident as the oracles of God can make it, his Spirit doth not bear witness with thy spirit that thou are a child of God.[93]

The issue of perception was also the topic of an exchange of correspondence between Wesley and an unknown clergyman in the eighteenth century. Over the course of a three year span in the mid 1740s, Wesley corresponded with a clergyman about an idea that further solidified his belief in the authenticity of the miraculous; namely, "perceptible inspiration."[94]

Throughout the eighteenth century Methodists were accused of embracing a lifestyle that focused on the supernatural to the detriment of reason. Certainly, in the lives of Methodist "enthusiasts," like the preacher Thomas Maxfield (?-1784) and the ex-lifeguard George Bell, (?-1807) John Wesley became all too familiar with the perils of self-deception and a spirituality that was uncontrolled and self-indulgent.[95] Authentic spiritual knowledge, for Wesley, was not the result of gusts of emotion but solidified in a long continuum that received and appropriated testimonies that witnessed to the power of the Spirit in the church. In Wesley's estimation it was not a matter of immediate inspiration but testimonies of mediated knowledge, which were verified across time, which formulated the network of knowledge of the invisible world.

Supernatural occurrences were apprehended through the "means of grace"—the reading of Scripture, the Sacraments, and godly fellowship. In correspondence with Smith, Wesley affirmed both his belief in the continuum of grace that was manifested in the Apostolic era and the means of grace that God had established for the communication of supernatural manifestations. Faith, for Wesley, "as every Christian grace, is properly supernatural, is an immediate gift of God, which he commonly gives in the use of such means as he hath ordained."[96] Wesley further reasoned that this grace, for some, came through long periods where assurance would be realized in incremental moments but in others it happened instantaneously, but nevertheless "easily discernable from bare reason or fancy."[97] This, Wesley maintained, was not merely a theoretical presupposition but, as indicated in his letter to Smith, a matter that he empirically verified by examining the testimonies of more than thirteen-hundred individuals who had related to him that they were able to pinpoint the movement of grace in their lives.[98] Furthermore, Wesley advocated to Smith at the end of 1745 that immediate inspiration was not only a tenet of Methodism but of Christianity itself. On the eve of a new year, in a letter written on 30 December 1745, Wesley wrote:

> We mean that inspiration of God's Holy Spirit whereby he fills us with righteousness, peace, and joy, with love to him and to all mankind. And we believe it cannot be, in the nature of things, that a man should be filled with this peace and joy and love by the inspiration of the Holy Ghost without perceiving it, as clearly as he does the light of the sun . . . . I know the proposition I have to prove, and I will not move an hair's breadth from it. It is this: "No man can be a *true Christian* without such an inspiration of the Holy Ghost as fills his heart with peace and joy and love; which he who perceives not, has it not." This is the point for which alone I contend. And this I take to be the very foundation of Christianity.[99]

The correspondence revealed, among other things, John Wesley's commitment to the experience of the supernatural in the realm of the natural world and his adherence to the idea of the empirical quality of human testimony that referenced transcendental knowledge.

Aldersgate: The Socio-Rhetorical Significance of Divine Knowledge

At the beginning of his sociology of the Enlightenment, Piet Strydom has emphasized the role of the early modern communication revolution in laying the base for modernisation. "Not only everything," writes Strydom, "but everybody became connected with one another through communication, and it became possible to change virtually anything, as long as there was an opportunity to communicate about it."[100] The leaders of the Methodist movement constructed and built their program of religious knowledge on the foundation of communicating a particular type of discourse. For Wesley, and many of his followers, the supernatural element in their conversions and the communication of their experiences to others was an essential feature of the formation of a self-identification that permeated their faith and work.

Though John Wesley was remarkably reticent about his own personal life, the Aldersgate experience of "a heart strangely warmed" became a signal event in the definition of Methodism and directed his followers to the idea of a relationship with a supernatural God. Concerning the events of 24 May 1738, Wesley wrote in his journal that there might be some that could not understand or comprehend such an experience. He then urged his readers: "Let him that cannot receive it ask of the Father of lights that he would give more light to him and me."[101] With other leaders of the Evangelical Revival, not least his brother Charles who had undergone a psychic "palpitation of heart," John Wesley communicated a religion of the heart that highlighted feeling and the experience of God's redeeming love.[102] Methodist autobiographies were filled with examples of people from varied walks of life that were overcome by the sense of sin and the subsequent deliverance of God's forgiveness. At the centre of these writings, as with John Wesley's own account of his Aldersgate experience, was the knowledge of the supernatural. Wesley's account of that evening on Aldersgate street and his chronicling of the days following it indicated that he was convinced that something had happened in his life that was not limited by time or space; an experience which by the influence of the Holy Spirit could be replicated in other people too.[103] The Aldersgate experience, for Wesley, was an event about religious epistemology and how one could be aware of a presence that transcended the natural world. As Heitzenrater comments, "The problem that confronted Wesley at Aldersgate was the question, how do I know I am a Christian."[104] As I have demonstrated, the issue of religious epistemology became central to understanding Wesley's agenda. With his ideas of faith and reason, Wesley sought to address both issues that had already a long philosophical and theological history but also added to the discourse by moving the discussion into a realm that defended the integrity of orthodox Christianity in the face of an every changing scientific environment. The end result was a Methodist movement that took the supernatural dimension of life seriously and sought to understand that dimension in the context of its mission and ministry.

Notes

1. A different version of this chapter appears in my article entitled "Sensing the Supernatural: John Wesley's Empirical Epistemology and the Pursuit of Divine Knowledge," *Sewanee Theological Review* 54 (2011): 254-81.

2. Joseph Glanvil, *Saducimus Triumphatus: or, Full and Plain Evidence Concerning Witches and Apparitions. In Two Parts. The First Treating of their Possibility, The Second of their Real Existence* (London: Printed for J. Collins and S. Lownds, 1681), 35.

3. Aristotle, *Metaphysics*. Trans. Hugh Tredennick. The Loeb Classic Library, 271: I.1.i.

4. Two opposing views of Wesley's epistemology may be found in Yoship Noro, "Wesley's Theological Epistemology," *Iliff Review* 28 (1971): 59-76, who suggests that Wesley's epistemology should be viewed through the lens of existentialism and Laurence Willard Wood, "Wesley's Epistemology," *Wesleyan Theological Journal* 10 (1975): 48-59, who contends that Wesley's epistemology was an application of Reformation theology. See also Noro's former student, Shimizu Mitsuo, *Epistemology in the Thought of John Wesley* (Ph. D. Thesis, Drew University, 1980), who strikes a more balanced view locating Wesley's theory of knowledge within his Anglican heritage.

5. John Wesley, "The Promise of Understanding," *BEW* 4: 281.

6. John Wesley, *A Survey of the Wisdom of God in the Creation: Or A Compendium of Natural Philosophy*, 2 vols. (Bristol: William Pine, 1763).

7. In addition to the first edition of the *Survey of the Wisdom of God* in 1763, which consisted of two volumes, Wesley added a third volume in 1770, and a total of five volumes in the 1776 and 1784 editions.

8. William Derham, *Physico-Theology: or, a Demonstration of the Being and Attributes of God, from His Work of Creation. Being the Substance of XVI Sermons* (London: Printed for W. Innys, 1713); William Derham, *Astro-Theology: or a Demonstration of the Being and Attributes of God, from a Survey of the Heavens. Illustrated with Copper-Plates* (London: Printed for W. Innys, 1715); Cotton Mather, *The Christian Philosopher: A Collection of the Best Discoveries in Nature with Religious Improvements* (London: Printed for Emmanuel Matthews, 1721); Bernard Niewentyt, *The Religious Philosopher: or, the Right Use of the Contemplation of the World,* trans. J. Chamberlayne, 3 vols. (London: n.p., 1718-19); John Ray, *The Wisdom of God in the Works of Creation: in Two Parts, viz., Manifested in the Hevenly Bodies, Elements, Metors,* 3rd ed. (London: Printed for Sam Smith and Benjamin Walford, 1701); and William Wollaston, *The Religion of Nature Delineated* (n. p.: n. p., 1722).

9. Wesley, *Survey of the Wisdom of God,* 1: iii.

10. Wesley, *Survey of the Wisdom of God,* 1: 8.

11. Wesley, *Survey of the Wisdom of God,* 1: 229. Wesley, *Explanatory Notes,* 4: 586 (Hebrews 11.3).

12. Wesley, *Survey of the Wisdom of God,* 1: 285-86.

13. John Wesley, "Christian Perfection," *BEW* 2: 100.

14. Wesley, *Survey of the Wisdom of God,* 1: v.

15. Daniel R. Headrick, *When Information Came of Age: Technologies of Knowledge in the Age of Reason and Revolution 1700-1850* (Oxford: Oxford University Press, 2000), 15-58.

16. Georges Louis Leclerc Buffon, *Histoire Naturelle,* 44 vols. (Paris: De l' Imprimerie Royale, 1749-1766); Jean Le Rond d'Alembert and Denis Diderot, *Encyclopedie, ou, Dictionnaire Raisonne des Sciences, des Arts, et des Metiers, mis en Ordre, par une Societe De Gens De Lettres,* 17 vols. (Paris: Antoine-Claude Briasson 1751-80); Colin Macfarquhar and George Gleig, eds., *Encyclopædia Britannica: or, A Dictionary of Arts and Sciences Compiled upon a New Plan,* 3rd ed., 18 vols. (London: Colin Macfarquhar and George Gleig, 1788-97).

17. Wesley, *Survey of the Wisdom of God,* 2: 193-94.

18. John Wesley to Joseph Benson, 5 October 1770. *LJW* 5: 202. See also, Rex Matthews, *"Religion and Reason Joined": A Study in the Theology of John Wesley* (Ph. D. thesis, Harvard University, 1986), who constructs an understanding of Wesley's epistemology around this particular quotation.

19. Josiah Tucker, *A Brief History of the Principles of Methodism, wherein the Rise and Progress, together with the Causes of Several Variations, Divisions, and Present Inconsistencies of this Sect are Attempted to be Traced out, and Accounted for* (Oxford: James Fletcher, 1742).

20. John Wesley, "The Methodist Societies: History, Nature and Design," *BEW* 9: 45-66 45-66.

21. John Wesley, "The Appeals to Men of Reason and Religion and Certain Related Open Letters," *BEW* 11: 43-94 and 103-325 respectively. See also Richard P. Heitzenrater, *Wesley and the People Called Methodist* (Nashville, TN: Abingdon Press, 1995), 128-31.

22. Wesley, "The Appeals to Men of Reason and Religion and Certain Related Open Letters," *BEW* 11: 56.

23. V. H. H. Green, *The Young Mr. Wesley* (London: Edward Arnold Publishers Ltd., 1961), 61-144. See also Green's "Appendix I: Wesley's Reading, 1725-34," 305-19.

24. V. H. H. Green, *The Commonwealth of Lincoln College 1427-1977* (Oxford: Oxford University Press, 1979), 334-35.

25. Lucy S. Sutherland, "The Curriculum," in Lucy S. Sutherland and Leslie G. Mitchell, eds., *The History of the University of Oxford*, 8 vols. (Oxford: Clarendon Press, 1984-2001), 5: 470-71.

26. John Wesley, "Some Remarks on 'A Defence of the Preface to the Edinburgh Edition of Aspasio Vindicated,'" in Thomas Jackson, ed., *The Works of John Wesley*, 14 vols. (London: Wesleyan Methodist Book Room, 1866), *WJW* 10: 353.

27. Henry Aldrich, *Artis Logicae Compendium* (Oxoford: Theatro Sheldoniano, 1691); Robert Sanderson, *Logicae Artis Compendium*, 2nd ed. (Oxford: Excudebant Iohannes Lichfield & Iacobus Short, 1618). See also Paul Quarrie, "The Christ Church Collection Books," in *History of Oxford University* 5:504.

28. Green, *The Young Mr. Wesley*, 130.

29. 24 March 1750. *BEW 20:* 325.

30. John Wesley, *A Compendium of Logick* (Bristol: Felix Farley, 1750). An unidentified copy of the first edition was found in a volume entitled "Pamphlets" in the Bodleian library, shelfmark 1419f. 1794 (2). See my "Copy of A Compendium of Logick Found," *Proceedings of the Wesley Historical Society* 53 (2002): 215.

31. 23 February 1749. *BEW* 20:263. "If your French book is *The Art of Thinking*, the author is a very poor tool. But there is none like Aldrich. I scarce know one Latin writer who says so much in so few words." John Wesley to Samuel Furley, 14 March 1756. *LJW* 3: 173.

32. Barry Bryant, *John Wesley's Doctrine of Sin* (Ph.D. Thesis., University of London, 1992), 28-29, suggests that Wesley's logical influence can be traced to Peter of Spain (1205-77), Pope John XXI from 1276-77. However, a search in *WJWcd* has no citations for "Pope John XXI," "Peter of Spain," or "*Summa Logicales*" which was Peter of Spain's medieval textbook of logic. It seems more reasonable, therefore, to locate Wesley's primary influence with Aldrich.

33. Wesley, *A Compendium of Logick*, 3. The same definition appeared in Wesley's sermon, "The Case of Reason Impartially Considered," *BEW* 2: 590.

34. John Wesley, "The Case of Reason Impartially Considered," *BEW* 2:590. This sermon by John Wesley was preached on 6 July 1781, and initially included in the *Arminian Magazine* 4 (1781): 574-80, 630-36. "'The Imperfection of Human Knowledge" emphasized 'the practical implications for Christian living of an intellectual modesty deeply grounded in a religious understanding of transcendence,'" in Albert Outler's introductory comment to Wesley's sermon, *BEW* 2: 567.

35. John Wesley's extract of Locke's *Essay Concerning Human Understanding* is found in the *Arminian Magazine* 5 (1782): 27-30, 85-88, 144-46, 190-95, 247-49, 307-10, 361-63, 413-17, 476-78, 528-37, 585-87, 646-48 and 6 (1783): 30-31, 86-89, 136-38, 197-99, 245 [sic]-56, 310-312, 366-68, 418-20, 480-84, 534-36, 590-94.

36. John Locke, *An Essay Concerning Human Understanding*, ed., Peter H. Nidditch (Oxford: Clarendon Press, 1975), I. 2. v. There are numerous works examining Locke's epistemology. See, Vere Chappell, ed., *The Cambridge Companion to Locke* (Cambridge: Cambridge University Press, 1994), 26-55; Michael Ayers, *Locke: Epistemology & Ontology* (1991; repr. London: Routledge, 2001); John L. Mackie, *Problems from Locke* (Oxford: Clarendon Press, 1976); and Raymond Martin and John Barresi, *Naturalization of the Soul: Self and Personal Identity in the Eighteenth Century* (London: Routledge, 2000).

37. "Whence has it [the Mind] all the materials of Reason and Knowledge? To this I answer, in one word, from *Experience*: In that, all our Knowledge is founded; and from

that it ultimately derives it self." Locke, *An Essay Concerning Human Understanding*, II. 1. ii, 104.

38. John Wesley, "On the Discoveries of Faith," *BEW* 4: 29. The maxim, *nihil est in intellectu quod non fait prius in sensu,* is found in Aristotle, *On the Soul*, trans. W.S. Hett. Loeb Classical Library, 288, III.7 and discussed by Thomas Aquinas, *Summa Theologica*, ed., Thomas Gilby, O.P., 61 vols. (London: Blackfriars in conjunction with Eyre & Spottiswoode,1964-81), Part I, Q. 84, Arts. 1-8.

39. Wesley, *Survey of the Wisdom of God*, 2: 204.

40. "Can another man perceive that I am conscious of anything, when I perceive it not myself? No man's knowledge here can go beyond his experience." Locke, *Essay Concerning Human Understanding*, 2.1.19.

41. Wesley, "The Case of Reason Impartially Considered," *BEW* 2: 587.

42. Hillel Schwartz, *The French Prophets: The History of a Millenarian Group in Eighteenth-Century England* (Berkley, CA: University of California Press, 1980), 219. For a sampling of some of the primary documents of the French Prophets one should also consult John Mullan and Christopher Reid, eds., *Eighteenth-Century Popular Culture: A Selection* (Oxford: Oxford University Press, 2000), 86-114.

43. See Henry D. Rack's "Doctors, Demons, and Early Methodist Healings," in W. J. Sheils, ed., *The Church and Healing* (Oxford: Blackwell, 1982), 137-52 and Kenneth G. C. Newport, "The French Prophets and Early Methodism: Some New Evidence," *Proceedings of the Wesley Historical Society* 50 (1996): 127-40.

44. 28 January 1739. *BEW* 19: 32-4.

45. 22 June 1739. *BEW* 19: 72.

46. Young, *Religion and Enlightenment in Eighteenth-Century England*, 121.

47. See John Walsh, "The Cambridge Methodists," in Peter Brooks, ed., *Christian Spirituality: Essays in Honor of Gordon Rupp* (London: SCM Press, 1975), 251-83.

48. Green, *The Young Mr. Wesley*, 305-19. "He was a voracious and widely eclectic reader, and it was his custom to write down in his Journal a short description, critical estimate, recommendation, or condemnation of each book as he completed it." Thomas Herbert, *John Wesley as Editor and Author* (Princeton: Princeton University Press, 1940), 12.

49. John Wesley to Richard Boardman, 12 January 1776. *LJW* 6: 201.

50. For example, to his niece, Sarah Wesley, John Wesley wrote on 8 September 1781 with a regimented study and reading program: The Bible, *Explanatory Notes,* History, Poetry, Grammar, Arithmetic, Geography, *Survey of the Wisdom of God,* Metaphysics, and Divinity. And, then, at the end of the letter Wesley stated: "By this course of study you may gain all the knowledge which any reasonable Christian needs." See John Wesley to Sarah Wesley, 8 September 1781. *LJW* 8: 81-83.

51. Wesley, *A Compendium of Logick*, 3.

52. "Unlike many of their predecessors and successors eighteenth-century English clerics were sufficiently relaxed in their churchmanship to feel little need to defend the integrity of their Church or to define its identity." John Walsh and Stephen Taylor, "Introduction: the Church and Anglicanism in the 'long' eighteenth-century," in John Walsh, Colin Hayden, and Stephen Taylor, eds., *The Church of England c. 1689-c. 1833: From Toleration to Tractarianism* (Cambridge: Cambridge University Press, 1993), 58. For a more positive view of *ecclesia anglicana* in the eighteenth-century see Norman Sykes, *Church and State in England in the XVIIIth Century* (Cambridge: Cambridge University Press, 1934). Also, Jeremy Gregory and Jeffrey Chamberlain, eds., *The National Church in Local Perspective: The Church of England and the Regions, 1660-1800* (Woodbridge: The Boydell Press, 2003).

53. Wesley, *A Compendium of Logick*, 3.

54. John Wesley to Mary Bishop, 4 February 1776. *LJW* 6: 205. See Matthews, *Religion and Reason Joined*, 175-83.

55. Laurence Wood, "Wesley's Epistemology," *Wesleyan Theological Journal* 10 (1975): 53.

56. Wesley reminded that these "dying words ought never to be forgotten . . . Just such an evidence of the invisible world can bare reason give to the wisest of men!" Wesley, "The Case of Reason Impartially Considered," *BEW* 2: 595. Also, Quentin Skinner, *Reason and Rhetoric in the Philosophy of Hobbes* (Cambridge: Cambridge University Press, 1996), 347, who maintains that there was a radical shift in Hobbes thinking and by the time he moved from *De Cive* to *Leviathan* he was fully aware of the limitations of human reason. Wesley's citation, therefore, may be read as a heart-felt sympathy for those who come to their deathbeds without the vision that is given by faith.

57. 2 January 1749. *BEW* 20: 262.

58. "Middleton was born at Richmond, in Yorkshire, in 1683, and died the year after Wesley wrote his letter. He was a favourite of George I; was hated by Dr. Bentley, the master of his college: had three wives; was Woodwardian professor, and the university librarian; a writer of great powers, but more than one of whose productions are debased by the leaven of infidelity. Of an irritable temper, was always creating antagonists instead of friends," pejoratively described by Luke Tyerman, *The Life and Times of the Rev. John Wesley, M. A.: Founder of the Methodists*, 3 vols. (London: Hodder & Houghton, 1870), 2: 61.

59. Conyers Middleton, *A Free Inquiry into the Miraculous Powers, which are Supposed to have Subsisted in the Christian Church, from the Earliest Ages through Several Successive Centuries. By Which is Shewn, that we have no Sufficient Reason to Believe, upon the Authority of the Primitive Fathers, that any such Powers were Continued to the Church, after the Days of the Apostles* (London: Printed for R. Manby and H. S. Cox, 1749).

60. Conyers Middleton, *An Introductory Discourse to a Larger Work, Designed Hereafter to be Published, Concerning the Miraculous Powers which are Supposed to have subsisted in the CHRISTIAN CHURCH, from the Earliest Ages, through Several Successive Centuries: Tending to Shew, that we have no Sufficient Reason to Believe, upon the Authority of the PRIMITIVE FATHERS, that any such Power were Continued to the CHURCH, after the Days of the Apostles. With a POSTSCRIPT, Containing Some REMARKS on an Archidiaconal Charge, Delivered the last Summer by the Rev. Dr. Chapman, to the Clergy of the Archdeaconery of Sudbury* (London: Printed for R. Manby and H. S. Cox, 1747).

61. "Wesley's swift reading and response to Middleton's work indicate the seriousness with which Wesley regarded Middleton's argument." Ted Campbell, "John Wesley and Conyers Middleton on Divine Intervention in History," *Church History* 55 (1986): 43.

62. "Plain reasoning grounded on plain facts." Middleton's self-description of his work in *Free Enquiry*, xxxi.

63. Middleton, *Free Enquiry*, ix.

64. According to I Corinthians 12.4-8, the spiritual gifts consist of the word of wisdom, the word of knowledge, faith, healing, miracles, prophecy, discerning of spirits, tongues, and interpretation of tongues. Romans 6.7-8 adds serving, teaching, exhortation, and giving to the list. Ephesians 4.8-11 also adds apostles, evangelists, and pastors.

65. Middleton, *Free Enquiry*, 121-22.

66. In this way, Wesley was engaging in the three goals of an orator: to prove or disprove the allegations of the argument, to arouse the passions of the audience, and to in-

fluence or win over the audience's favor. See Brian Vickers, *In Defence of Rhetoric* (1998; repr., Oxford: Oxford University Press, 2002), 72-80.

67. John Wesley to Conyers Middleton, 4 January 1749. *LJW* 2: 312-88.

68. John Wesley to Conyers Middleton, 4 January 1749. *LJW* 2: 313.

69. John Wesley to Conyers Middleton, 4 January 1749. *LJW* 2: 321.

70. Ted Campbell, *John Wesley and Christian Antiquity: Religious Vision and Cultural Change* (Nashville, TN: Kingswood Books, 1991). See also, Gunther Gassmann, "Toward a Common Expression of the Apostolic Faith Today," and Geoffrey Wainwright, "Methodism and the Apostolic Faith," in M. Douglas Meeks, ed., *What Should Methodists Teach? Wesleyan Tradition and Modern Diversity* (Nashville, TN: Kingswood Books, 1990), 93-100 and 101-17 respectively.

71. John Wesley to Conyers Middleton, 4 January 1749. *LJW 2:* 328.

72. John Wesley to Conyers Middleton, 4 January 1749. *LJW* 2: 364.

73. John Wesley to Conyers Middleton, 4 January 1749. *LJW* 2: 368.

74. Steven Shapin, *A Social History of Truth: Civility and Science in Seventeenth-Century England* (Chicago: University of Chicago Press, 1994), 65-125.

75. "That we 'carve' the world as we do is partly a matter of inevitable genetic disposition but, to a very considerable extent, it is also a matter of communal orientations and interests which each of us discovers by trusting the judgments, reactions, and trainings of others." Coady, *Testimony*, 170. For Coady, this "trusting" is most visible in the language that human beings use and don't use. Certainly, for Wesley, and his Methodist societies, the language of the supernatural conveyed a particular epistemological paradigm which they believed corroborated their human experiences of the divine.

76. Shapin, *A Social History of Truth*, 208-09.

77. Shapin, *A Social History of Truth*, 211.

78. John Wesley, "On Faith," *BEW* 3: 492.

79. John Wesley, "The Important Question," *BEW* 3:188. "As for the text of 'Our Faith,' Heb. 11:1 is the only scripture expounded more than once among the 141 sermons." Richard Brantly, *Locke, Wesley, and the Method of English Romanticism* (Gainsville, FL: University of Florida Press, 1984), 87.

80. Wood, "Wesley's Epistemology," 55.

81. John Wesley to Susanna Wesley, 29 July 1725. *BEW* 25: 173-76, 178-80, and 186-89.

82. John Wesley, "On the Discoveries of Faith," *BEW* 4: 29.

83. Wesley, "On the Discoveries of Faith," *BEW* 4: 30. For a focused examination on this aspect of Wesley's thought see Mark Thomas Mealey, *"Taste and See that the Lord is Good": John Wesley in the Christian Tradition of Spiritual Sensation* (Ph.D. thesis, University of Toronto, 2006).

84. Locke, *Essay Concerning Human Understanding*, 4.2.6. "The most important ingredient of the new philosophical style was an acute sense of human fallibility . . . which had so recently undercut the foundations of all knowledge." Barbara Shapiro, *Probability and Certainty in Seventeenth-Century England: A Study of the Relationships Between Natural Science, Religion, History, Law, and Literature* (Princeton, NJ: Princeton University Press, 1983), 61.

85. *DNB*, "Browne, Peter."

86. Peter Browne, *The Procedure, Extent, and Limit of Human Understanding* (London: Printed by James Bettenham, 1728). Also, Peter Browne's *Things Divine and Supernatural Conceived By Analogy with Things Natural and Human* (1733; repr., Bristol: Thoemmes Antiquarian Books Ltd., 1990). The work that set Bishop Browne on his polemical heels was John Toland, *Christianity Not Mysterious* (London: Printed for Sam Buckley, 1696).

87. Green, *The Young Mr. Wesley*, 309.

88. John Wesley to Mary Pendarves, 3 October 1770. *LJW* 1: 56, 58, 76; John Wesley to Miss J.C. March, 3 August, 1771. *LJW* 5: 270; and 6: 113.

89. Browne, *Things Divine and Supernatural*, 2.

90. Browne, *Procedure, Extent, and Limit of Human Understanding*, 137.

91. John Wesley, "Walking by Sight and Walking by Faith," *BEW* 4: 54.

92. John Wesley, "The Witness of the Spirit, I," *BEW* 1: 277-78.

93. John Wesley, "The Promise of Understanding," *BEW* 4: 281-82.

94. John Wesley and [John Smith] correspondence, May 1745 to 22 March 1748. *BEW* 26: 138-46, 153-61, 164-72, 175-83, 184-90, 197-207, 209-15, 229-37, 238-42, 244-52, 258-61, 287-94. The identity of Wesley's correspondent, "John Smith," remains a mystery. According to Frank Baker the supposition that it may have been Thomas Secker is untenable. For more on the identity of this correspondent see *BEW* 26: 138n18.

95. I will revisit the Perfectionist controversies which Maxfield and Bell played a prominent role in chapter 5.

96. John Wesley to [John Smith], 28 September 1745. *BEW* 26: 157.

97. John Wesley to [John Smith], 28 September 1745. *BEW* 26: 157.

98. "I am acquainted with more than twelve hundred or thirteen hundred persons whom I believe to be truly pious, and not on slight grounds, and who have severally testified to me with their own mouths that they do know the day when the love of God was first shed abroad in their hearts, and when his Spirit first witnessed with their spirits that they were the children of God." John Wesley to [John Smith], 28 September, 1745. *BEW* 26: 158.

99. John Wesley to [John Smith], 30 December 1745. *BEW* 26: 181-82.

100. Piet Strydom, *Discourse and Knowledge: The Making of Enlightenment Sociology* (Liverpool: Liverpool University Press, 2000), 10.

101. 24 May 1738. *BEW* 18: 242.

102. Ted Campbell's *The Religion of the Heart: A Study of European Life in the Seventeenth and Eighteenth Centuries* (Charleston: University of South Carolina Press, 1991) examines this aspect of religious experience in the Enlightenment.

103. This idea will be examined in detail with regard to dreams and visions in chapter 4.

104. Heitzenrater, *Mirror and Memory*, 108.

Chapter 3

"Those Distracting Terrors of the Enemy": John Wesley's Understanding of Evil

> Devils strive to lead human beings to lies by means of the very truths devils manifest.[1]

> O ye fools, did ye suppose the devil was dead? Or that he would not fight for his kingdom? And what weapons shall he fight with, if not with lies? Is he not a liar, and the father of it? Suffer ye then thus far. Let the devil and his children say all manner of evil of us. And let them go on deceiving each other and being deceived. But *ye* need not be deceived also—or if you are, if you *will* believe all they say, be it so, that we are weak, silly, wicked men, without sense, without learning, without even a desire or design of doing good.[2]

Epicurus (341-271), the ancient philosopher, had reflected on God's culpability in relation to the existence of evil in the world and developed four different options for the philosophical problem of theodicy:

- God wishes to take away the evil of the world but is unable to do so.
- God does not wish to take away the evil of the world even though God is able.
- God neither wishes nor is able to take away the evil of the world.
- God wishes and is able to take away the evil of the world.

The explanation which appeared suitable for a coherent view of deity, according to the ancient philosopher, was the final one. In any case, he reasoned, "from what source then are evils? Or why does He [God] not remove them?"[3] The question of *unde malum* [where does evil come from] which Epicurus raised resonated widely throughout eighteenth-century society and tempered the optimism of the Enlightenment. "Unde Malum," wrote Humphrey Ditton (1675-1715) at the beginning of the eighteenth century, "has been a mighty Question."[4] For many, the presence of evil was more than a point of theoretical debate but was one that caused individuals to unite their attempts to provide practical explanations to such ideas as progress, disease, and poverty.

For John Wesley, Epicurus became a representation of an erroneous approach that misunderstood the nature of evil, *vis-à-vis* divine presence, and failed in formulating a significant appraisal of the problem of evil with a spiritual and intellectual resolution.[5] Though Wesley was in some respects an optimist, the presence of evil caused him great concern and he gave attention to it in his writings throughout the eighteenth century. From his early student days at Christ Church, he read and discussed essays that related to the *unde malum* question. In a letter dated 19 December 1729, he wrote home to Samuel Wesley senior (1662-1735) and quoted at length the non-Conformist preacher turned mathematician, Humphrey Ditton, and his "mighty question" statement.[6] A year later Wesley wrote to his father again and commented on William King's (1650-1729) *De Origine Male*. Critical of King, Wesley wrote: "But on looking farther into it I was strangely disappointed, finding it the least satisfactory account of any given by any author whom I ever read in my life."[7] The reason for young Wesley's disappointment with King's answer to the problem of evil was, like the Stoic philosophers, King had failed to articulate a power that satisfactorily addressed the existence of evil. The issues raised by young John in the early correspondence with his father were some that the mature Wesley repeatedly returned to throughout his life, as he formulated his own ideas about the subject.[8]

At a latter stage of his life, Wesley attempted to address the concept of evil and how it could be understood in light of the Christian doctrines of providence and the eschatological hope of Christ's second coming. In 1781, in a sermon he preached from one of his favourite New Testament passages, I John 3.8, Wesley maintained that human beings were incapable of a defence against the assault of evil. The Roman philosophers failed at this point because "they sought for it where it never will be found, namely in themselves—in reason, in philosophy. Broken reeds! Bubbles! Smoke! They did not seek it in God, in whom alone it is possible to find it."[9] In Wesley's view, the ubiquity of evil was not an insurmountable obstacle to a belief in God.[10] On the contrary, the multi-faceted dimensions of evil had a long continuum which must be considered within the context of sinful humanity and the activity of divine grace which was working out redemption in the world. Like others in the eighteenth century, Wesley saw evil in a polyvalent grid where humanity was affected and effected on several different levels. In this chapter I will examine three distinct issues that Wesley addressed in regard to the presence of evil in the world: 1) Original Sin,

2) Earthquakes, and 3) Demonic Possession. Each one them was substantiated by a volatile debate in the Enlightenment and I will show through an examination of Wesley's writings how he became a significant contributor to the discussions that were taking shape in eighteenth-century culture.

John Wesley, Original Sin, and a Discourse of Evil

Figure 1. "A Map of the Garden of Eden, before God Destroy'd it with the Flood," *The Gentleman's Magazine* 8 (1738): 66

An enduring feature of the Enlightenment was the intense discussions that ensued over the concept of Original Sin that in many ways collided with optimistic views of human nature current in the eighteenth century. As Clyde Holbrook has observed: "The controversy over human depravity in the eighteenth century was no mere intramural squabble among theologians. It was an important phase of a revolution that was occurring in Western man's estimate of his nature and potentialities." [11] The Deists had suggested when humanity liberated itself from foolish stories like Adam and Eve in the garden of Eden and superstitious ideas like Original Sin virtue in human society would be put on a better foundation. Anthony Ashley Cooper (1671-1713), the third Earl of Shaftesbury, remarked that "by means of corrupt religion or superstition, many things the most horridly unnatural and inhuman come to be received as excellent, good and laudable in themselves."[12]

From the dawn of the Enlightenment and well into the eighteenth century, those who viewed human nature under the umbrella of natural law asserted that human life should be conceptualized within material boundaries and that the doctrine of Original Sin made little sense; promoting a discourse which was unable to be sustained by empirical argumentation.[13] A decreasing number of literati accepted the authority of a map of the Garden of Eden before God destroyed it with the flood and defence of biblical geography of Genesis 2-3 depicted in the *Gentleman's Magazine* for the year 1738.[14]

With the increasing acceptance of rationalism and materialism by intellectuals in society, people in the eighteenth century became sceptical of the literal interpretation of the Genesis account that appeared incredulous for the modern individual, who sought to maintain an intellectual integrity that was sensitive to the discoveries of modern science. For those defending orthodox expressions of the Christian faith, however, the renunciation of Original Sin was a denial of biblical authority and spiritual reality. William Hammond (1719-83), a Cambridge Methodist who later joined the Moravians, was representative of this orthodox view when he confessed that although he did not understand all aspects of the church's teaching regarding the doctrine was nevertheless disinclined to renounce its truth.[15] In his *Medulla Ecclesiae,* Hammond emphasized his opposition to abandoning the doctrine and invited his readers to consider the state of the world as corroboration:

> But as Serpents produce Serpents, and Vipers beget Vipers, and all manner of wild and venomous Creatures bring forth Creatures as wild and venomous as themselves, so carnal and impure Parents beget Children as carnal and impure as themselves. This follows upon the establish'd Laws of Generation. As to the *Modus,* how this spiritual Contagion is conveyed to us, I do not pretend to determine it: That we are polluted Creatures from the Womb is plain; the Fact is too visible to be denied. We are not therefore so much concerned to know how we came by the Disease, as how or where we may procure a Remedy.[16]

Like Hammond, many adherents of an espoused orthodoxy in eighteenth-century England believed the doctrine of Original Sin served a dual function. First, the teaching of the church sufficiently offered an explanation for the existence and origin of evil. While the particulars of the Genesis account could be debated, there continued to be individuals who relied on its trustworthiness as a model myth which suitably addressed the question of the origin of evil. Second, and more important, the doctrine affirmed the historicity of sin, which was reasoned, underpinned the necessity of the Christian message of redemption. Isaac Watts (1674-1748), in the preface to the second edition of *The Ruin and Recovery of Mankind,* remarked that the rejection of the idea of Original Sin was commensurate with the dismissal of the gospel. Watts concluded:

> Whenever I see this doctrine of *Original Sin* rejected and renounced, there is sufficient Reason from many Observations to expect the Glories of the Gospel will in the same proportion be depreciated, neglected and despised: If we are all born still in our original State of *Nature* and *Innocency,* the abounding Grace and Salvation of *Christ Jesus* does not seem so very necessary for us; if it was but a little Bruise we suffer'd by the Fall of *Adam,* a little Grace may heal us.[17]

For those engaged in the ministry of the church in eighteenth-century England, the idea of individuals fallen from a position of favor with God provided a *raison d'être* for its ongoing work of reformation. Jeremy Gregory makes a similar point when he suggests in the late seventeenth and early eighteenth centuries that priests in the Church of England conceived of their work as an episode of a continual Reformation which was far from complete. "We will have an improved understanding", writes Gregory, "of what the Reformation implied, and its broad social consequences, if we track its influence and its ideology well into the eighteenth century."[18] In this light, the Reformation agenda was intricately linked to the acceptance of Original Sin and the universal depravity of humanity as an accurate description of the human condition.

A conservative view of the doctrine of the Fall and the depravity of humanity was clearly marked out, moreover, in the Articles and Liturgy of the Church of England. The ninth article of religion stated that the misery and sufferings that men and women encountered in the world was an "infection of nature" and a visible sign that humanity "is very far gone from original righteousness, and is of his own nature inclined to evil, so that the Flesh lusteth always contrary to the Spirit."[19] The homily on the *Misery of all Mankind, and of his Condemnation to Death Everlasting, by his own Sin* described humanity as desolate and isolated from true holiness and righteousness. "For of ourselves," stated the homily,

> we be crab-trees, that can bring forth no apples. We be of ourselves of such earth, as can bring forth but weeds, nettles, brambles, briers, cockle, and darnel. Our fruits be declared in the fifth chapter to the Galatians. We have neither faith, charity, hope, patience, chastity, nor any thing else that good is, but of God; and therefore these virtues be called there the fruits of the Holy Ghost, and not the fruits of man. [20]

It was then against this social and theological background during the eighteenth century that John Wesley and the adherents of the Evangelical Revival embraced the concept of Original Sin and the universal depravity of humanity. Charles Wesley (1707-88) is illustrative at this point. Three times in 1739, he preached a sermon using Romans 3:23-24 for his text. After introducing his topic with a direct reference to the *Homily on the Misery of Mankind*, he depicted the condition of humanity in terms of sickness and disease and explained: "We have heard how evil we be of ourselves, how of ourselves and by ourselves we have no goodness, help or salvation; but contrariwise, sin, damnable; not able either to think a good thought, or work a good dead, so that we can find in ourselves no hope of salvation, but rather whatsoever maketh unto our destruction."[21] John Wesley too, in his published sermon on *Original Sin*, painted a bleak picture of humanity before the deluge described in Genesis 6. "For God," declared Wesley, "who 'saw the whole imagination of the thoughts of his heart to be *only* evil,' saw likewise that it was always the same, that it 'was only evil *continually*'—every year, every day, every hour, every moment. He never deviated into good."[22]

The consideration of human depravity, then, is essential to a proper understanding of John Wesley and his view of evil; not the least, because it entailed a cautious refutation of Lockean psychology which, as we have seen in the previous chapter, Wesley both appreciated and regarded with some suspicion. Wesley had provided extracts of Locke's *Essay* along with brief remarks in his *Arminian Magazine* from 1782 to 1784. Among his accolades for Locke's influential work was the comment in the January issue for 1782: "A deep fear of God and reverence for his Word, are discernable throughout the whole. And though there are some mistakes, yet these are abundantly compensated, by many curious and useful Reflections."[23]

However, despite his professed admiration for Locke's creative genius, Wesley's commitment to the doctrine of Original Sin brought him into a sharp divergence with the respected philosopher. At the beginning of Book Two of Locke's treatise, the philosopher had delineated his concept of the mind and its discovery of ideas. Contrary to the notion of innate ideas, Locke framed an argument which contended that the experiences of life were inscribed onto the mind of an individual.[24] This epistemological principle which was present in Locke's early writings was consistently manifested throughout his political, philosophical, and theological essays too. However, early in the 1660s, a tension developed within Locke's thought. In his provocative *Essays on the Law of Nature*, he wrote of the Fall and challenged the belief that the sin of Adam and Eve in the Garden of Eden had qualitatively changed the fabric of the human psyche. Instead he asked his implied interlocutor: "But if it is asserted that this law originally impressed is altogether effaced, where, pray, will be that law of nature for which we search? Surely on this admission it will be nothing, unless we can find a way of knowledge other than by inscription."[25] In *The Reasonableness of Christianity*, Locke affirmed that immortality had been lost in the Fall without encroaching on his commitment to the idea of *tabula rasa* and its fundamental starting point in the study of human nature.[26] Here, however, Locke's assiduous treatment of human nature went awry in the opinion of Wesley. Not only had Locke failed to consider the empirical ramifications of the Fall but had read a view of human nature back into the biblical text.

For John Wesley, however, a fundamental feature of the human condition was its inability to escape from the idea that the sin of its primal parents had affected its constitution. Lockean psychology, Wesley maintained, with its idea of *tabula rasa,* was an inaccurate description of the human condition and must be jettisoned in favour of one that accurately reflected the lives of human beings in the world. Moreover, Wesley held to an understanding of the church's teaching that sought to illuminate the meaning of Original Sin with transbiological and transhistorical categories instead of labelling it as antiquarian and useless for modern discourse. In his treatise against John Taylor, which I will consider shortly, Wesley drew upon Paul's opening chapter in his letter to the church at Rome and developed his argument from the observation of actual sin: "The Apostle's Method is clear and natural. He begins with that which is most obvious, even actual Sin; and then proceeds to speak of Original Sin, as the Cause of the Necessity of Redemption for all Men."[27] Contrary to a strict Lockean psychology, Wesley contended that from its early existence in the womb an individual had been indelibly marked by the stain of sin, which has separated its peace and health from God, nature, and society. Furthermore, on the subject of the origin of sin, Wesley found the idea of a transcendental will, which the biblical writers referred to as "Satan," remarkably congruent for his purposes. This transcendental will had been impressed on everyone who lives in the world. "Satan," Wesley contended,

> has stamped his own image on our heart in *self-will* also. "I will," said he, before he was cast out of heaven, "I will sit upon the sides of the north." I will do my own will and pleasure, independently of that of my Creator. The same does every man born into the world say, and that in a thousand instances. Nay, and avow it, too, without ever blushing upon the account, without either fear or shame. Ask

the man, "Why did you do this?" He answers, "Because I had a mind to it." What is this but, "Because it was my will;" that is, in effect, because the devil and I are agreed; because Satan and I govern our actions by one and the same principle.[28]

The above quotation illustrates that fallen humanity, in Wesley's mind, was already stained at its inception. The disobedient act of Adam and Eve in Genesis 3 marked the emergence of "a disorder in their own spirits, which they had never before been conscious."[29] As a result, any framework of human nature must take the demise of Adam and Eve into account. This was something that Locke failed to do and one that Wesley insisted on.

One of the most important works on Original Sin in the eighteenth century was John Taylor's (1694-1761) *The Scripture-Doctrine of Original Sin Proposed to Free and Candid Examination.*[30] The first edition, in 1740, was followed by two more editions in the author's lifetime and a fourth posthumously in 1767, which included rebutted answers to John Wesley's accusations against him. A dissenting minister who lived in Norwich, Taylor was a scholar of the Hebrew language and had become concerned about the presence of evil in the world and how to account for it theologically.[31] After a consideration of the relevant passages in the Bible, Taylor was convinced that the manner with which the church had traditionally dealt with the presence of sin was both unfounded in the biblical text and fallacious in its argumentation. His published work examined the concept of Original Sin and noted that there were very few places in scripture that concentrated on Adam and Eve, the transgression in the garden of Eden, and its abiding consequence in considering human nature.[32] In his comment on the Adamic covenant and its significance for future descendants, Taylor wrote: "But if it is designed to prove, that the Covenant was so made with *Adam as a public Person, not only for himself, but for his Posterity*; that he sinning, they also should *sin in him*; I must leave it to every Man to make out as he can; and shall only declare for my own Part, I see nothing in the Text that intimateth any such thing."[33] If Taylor's orthodox readers had been uneasy at the beginning of his treatise, with his ideas about the generational transferral of sin, they were certainly alarmed at the conclusion of his essay where he suggested that individuals born into the world were not fundamentally tainted by sin but rather moral agents who were capable of either virtue or vice. He unabashedly maintained:

> This [Adam's fall being a *falling short* rather than a *falling from* Holiness] explains to us the Dispensation we are under, and the Reason why we ought to be born again. Not because we are born wicked; or are by *Nature corrupt, quite disabled, indisposed, and made opposite to all that is spiritually good, and wholly inclined to all Evil.* For in plain Truth this would be a good Reason why we should not be born again, because then we should be uncapable of it, as being no moral Agents.[34]

Immediately after the publication of *The Scriptural Doctrine of Original Sin* there emerged a plethora of reactions against Taylor and his denial of the dogma. Isaac Watts, Jonathan Edwards, and David Jennings (1691-1762), were among many who wrote theological treatises and sermons which attempted to answer John Taylor and his denial of the legitimacy of Original Sin for the canon of Christian theology.[35] An indication of Taylor's impact was furthermore evidenced by the fact that in one of the most heated disputes over the doctrine in North America between Peter Clark (1694-1768) and Samuel Webster (1718-96) the latter was found to be "virtually parroting the opinions of Taylor's *Scripture-Doctrine*."[36] John Taylor, then, represented a voice that many felt compelled to combat. This was easier said than done, however, because Taylor was both intellectually astute and his surmounted attack which asserted that the veracity of the church's teaching could not be located in either scripture, tradition, and experience seemed to not only strike down the accumulated wisdom of the faithful but contradict the notion that the doctrine could be empirically verified in the religious experiences of votaries.

For Wesley's part, Taylor's essay provided a threat to the *fides historica* which he believed should not be passed over lightly. In 1757, he published his reaction to Taylor in *The Doctrine of Original Sin: According to Scripture, Reason, and Experience*.[37] It was the only theological treatise which Wesley wrote during his life and totalled over five hundred pages. In the preface, Wesley identified Taylor as his theological opponent and the peril that he believed Taylor's scepticism led to with regard to the article of faith. In Wesley's judgment, the seriousness of Taylor's error cut at the very root of revealed religion. With rhetorical flair Wesley remarked, "*On the contrary, it may be doubted Whether the Scheme before us, be not far more dangerous than open Deism itself . . . For I cannot look on this Scheme as any other than old Deism in a new Dress: Seeing it saps the very Foundation of all Revealed Religion, whether Jewish or Christian.*"[38] Those who remained faithful to traditional Christian teaching would naturally be guarded against the Deists and their attacks on orthodox Christianity. But, Wesley feared, one could be led astray by Taylor's "*smooth, decent Writings.*"[39] Taylor had, in Wesley's estimation, neglected essential truths concerning the concepts of sin, human existence, and the natural order of the world. These preteritions not only failed to consider the human constitution and its proclivity to fall prey to the temptation of sin but positioned Taylor against the affirmation of the Christian tradition itself.

John Taylor had insisted that sin was manifested in the world because one man had inappropriately used his God-given freedom. By inference, each and every descendant of Adam repeated the act of the progenitor of the human race when he or she consciously determined to misuse the liberty that God granted to every individual. At the conclusion of his treatise, Taylor claimed that human beings needed a "born again" experience not because of a depraved nature but because "without a right Use and Application of our Powers, were they naturally ever so perfect, we could not be judged fit to enter into the Kingdom of God."[40] Furthermore, added Taylor, the experience of temptation exercised the human mind, mature its virtue, and made it fit for God's Kingdom, for which "we cannot be qualified, but by overcoming our present Temptations."[41] In John Wesley's opinion, this was far off the mark. An observation of human nature could never corroborate Taylor's assumptions; fundamentally, that natural inclinations reasonably led not toward shame but glory.[42] All Wesley felt he needed to do was point out particular vices that people were exhibiting in their daily lives in order to refute Taylor's presuppositions. From various types of crimes, oppressions, and addictions, Wesley believed he had highlighted the empirical evidence which showed that human nature was not approaching glory, as Taylor supposed, but was increasingly moving in the direction of ignominy and humiliation. Likewise, an observation of wicked acts committed by individuals coupled with a theological conception of sin gave the inquiry into the origin of evil and its affective qualities a logical link for the rhetoric of evil in Wesley's thought.

In regard to the question of origin, Wesley opted for the traditional teaching of the church, connecting sin and evil to Adam and Eve and their disobedience to God's commandment in the garden, not only because he saw it as a credible explanation of human existence but believed it was substantiated in the Bible. Furthermore Wesley denied that human sinfulness spontaneously clouded human consciousness as a result of successive acts of disobedience, a point Taylor continually maintained. On the contrary, the tendency of humanity was not receptive but rebellious to God. Indeed, it was one of the primary consequences of the soul's "awakening" that it realized the "conviction of sin." "We see, when God opens our eyes," declared Wesley, "that we were before αθεοι εν [τω] κοσμω 'without God,' or rather, 'atheists in the world.'"[43]

What surfaced in Wesley's examination was his contention that Taylor had missed a fundamental precept of the Christian faith when he erased all references to a belief in the doctrine of Original Sin. There was nothing unusual in this as others had criticized Taylor in this fashion. For Wesley, however, the fundamental assertion of Original Sin meant that Adam and Eve had failed to actualize what God intended for them; and by genetic delineation, men and women living contemporaneously with Wesley were not living according to a self-identification that found its reference point in God. From his early student days at Oxford, Wesley had been interested in the nature and identification of the soul, when he read his lecture "The Souls of Animals" (*De Anima Brutorum*) for his disputation in 1726.[44] Regarding the human soul, he believed that God had intended it for greatness. In his original pre-fallen state, Adam was a man with "unerring understanding, an uncorrupt will, and perfect freedom."[45] However, when he ate of the tree of the fruit of the knowledge of good and evil (Genesis 3), Adam was marred physically, volitionally, and spiritually; blemishing the image of God in creation. In Wesley's view, the truth of the temptation narrative conveyed a disobedience by Adam and Eve which initiated a dysfunctional condition for humanity in its relationship to God and the world. Barry Bryant notes:

> They [Adam and Eve] no longer loved God because they no longer trusted God, or believed God to be true. The disintegration of their relationship with the Divine quickly resulted in the experiences of guilt, sorrow, fear, and despair. The estranged relationship between the human and Divine eventually resulted in dysfunctional relationships. The cause of this dysfunction was they no longer loved their neighbour as themselves. More than anything else, the loss of the moral image meant the loss of communion with God, and the beginning of a dysfunctional relationship between Adam and Eve.[46]

Highly sensitive to the dreadful sufferings he witnessed in his journeys, John Wesley nevertheless saw them as positive proofs of the disequilibrium brought about by the Fall. One of the most vivid demonstrations of human sin that disturbed him was the existence of war among nations and individuals. Reflecting on warfare, Wesley wrote at the beginning of his work on Original Sin: "So long as this Monster stalks uncontroll'd, where is Reason, Virtue, Humanity? They are utterly excluded; they have no Place; they are a Name, and nothing more."[47]

The existence of evil in its various forms led to a perplexing problem for Wesley and those who attempted to defend the doctrine against its antagonists in the Enlightenment. Simply stated, how was the sin of Adam and Eve transmitted across time and generations? There was consensus in the seventeenth century that Adam and Eve and their demise in the garden had damaged the cognitive abilities of individuals in successive generations but how that corruption was trans-generationally communicated was more often assumed than proven.[48] One of the primary objections that sceptics levelled against the doctrine was the lack of reasonable explanation among its adherents as to how the sin of Adam and Eve was imputed to their offspring, regardless of location and time.

For many individuals living in the eighteenth century the existence of evil was overshadowed by the belief that men and women retained the ability to manage their human imperfections.[49] Obviously there were those who wanted the doctrine laid aside on the table of superstition; and, what is more, found it imperative to cast shadows of suspicion and disbelief over the concept of human depravity as antiquarian, inappropriate, and inconsequential for the concept of human nature. These criticisms of the doctrine hinged not only on the emergence of higher criticism which questioned the historicity of Adam and Eve, which eventually grew into a full-blown liberalism in the nineteenth century, but also rested on empirical argumentation that asserted the progenitors of the human race and their disobedience in the garden of Eden could not be coherently spelled out. The latter point was made forcefully by John Taylor who stated that the reality of evil in the modern world could not be empirically explained or associated with the transgression of Adam and Eve. In the second edition of his work, Taylor revisited this issue and in a section of questions and answers about the doctrine he began by asking whether the teaching of Original Sin was "necessary" for a coherent understanding of evil? In other words, to the traditionalists and their insistence that the reality of evil was linked to the concept of Original Sin, Taylor answered:

> *Adam's* Nature, it is allowed, was very far from being sinful, and yet he sinned. And therefore the common Doctrine of *Original Sin* is no more necessary to account for the Sin that hath been, or is in the World, than it is to account for *Adam's* Sin. His Sin was not from a depraved Nature, but from his own disobedient Will: And so *must* every Man's Sin, and all the Sin in the World, how much soever, be, as well as his. And to this Cause alone the Scriptures constantly assign the Wickedness of all Men.[50]

For John Wesley, however, the sin of Adam and Eve had been transferred to each individual in the womb before birth. It was clear that Taylor had missed the gravity of the church's teaching and had failed to sufficiently probe the possibilities of its truth. One could not account for the collective expression of wickedness in the world merely by the assertion that it was the result of an accumulation of individual human acts. That was too simplistic for Wesley. Instead he invited his readers to consider the condition of the world: "Look out of your own Doors: Is there any Evil in the City, and Sin hath not done it? Is there any Misfortune or Misery to be named, whereof it is not wither the direct or remove Occasion?"[51] And then a few pages later, Wesley sarcastically jabbed Taylor when he wrote, "if this Fall did not bring them [humanity] into that State [Sin], I would be glad to know, what did?"[52] Fifteen years later, Wesley had not changed his mind and claimed in his sermon entitled *On the Fall of Man* that the acceptance of the idea of Original Sin was the key element in the resolution of the *unde malum* problem. At the beginning of his homily, Wesley commented on Adam's sin as "the clear, intelligible answer to that question, how came evil into the world?"[53]

Still, when it came to the question of how sin was transmitted, Wesley was, like many adherents of the doctrine in the eighteenth century, content with a reverent agnosticism. At the end of his treatise on the subject, he addressed the issue of the imputation of depravity with disinclination: "And if you ask me, How, in what determinate Manner Sin is propagated? How it is transmitted from Father to Son? I answer plainly, I cannot. No more than I can tell, How Man is propagated? How a Body is transmitted from Father to Son? I know both the One and the Other Fact. But I can account for neither."[54] John Wesley's theological development at this point may be traced in part by a consideration of the French philosopher, Nicholas Malebranche (1638-1715); particularly noting how Wesley read the philosopher and used his writings in the Methodist societies.

Nicholas Malebranche, in his *Treatise Concerning the Search After Truth*, contended that a marked impression on the mind and soul of Adam and Eve had occurred after their rebellious act—eating the fruit of the tree of the knowledge of good and evil.[55] It was the disobedience against God's strict commandment which fixed an explicit disruption in the mind of Eden's first inhabitants which in turn has been transmitted to every human being living in the world. The issue of genetic transmission was addressed by Malebranche in Book 2, Chapter 7:

> But that which I would above all have observ'd upon this Subject is, that there are all appearances imaginable of Men's preserving to this day in their Brain the Traces and Impressions of their first Parents. For as Animals produce others that are like them, and with the same Sympathies and Antipathies, and perform the same Actions, at the same junctures, . . . so our First Parents after their Sin, receiv'd such great Prints and deep Traces in their Brain, through the Impression of sensible Objects, as might easily have been communicated to their Children. In so much that the great Adhesion which is found in us, from our Mother's Womb, to sensible Objects, and the great Distance betwixt us and *GOD*, in this our Imperfect State, may in some measure be accounted for, by what we have been saying.[56]

There is no direct evidence that Wesley transcribed or extracted this passage from Malebranche. However, there is support for the idea that Malebranche's ideas about genetic transmission and Original Sin influenced Wesley. It is known through Wesley's correspondence that, on a number of occasions, he wrote to various Methodist societies and recommended Malebranche's *Search After Truth*. On at least one occasion Wesley wrote a short defence of the philosopher too.[57] What has not been recognized, however, was the role that Ephraim Chambers (1680?-1740) played in this aspect of Wesley's development. Albert Outler has noted Chambers' *Cyclopaedia* was Wesley's favourite reference work.[58] In the second edition of Chambers' monumental work, under the definition for "Original Sin," he referenced Malebranche and his idea of humanity's progenitor and transgression; detailing the consequential effects on human nature. After the definition of Original Sin as a "crime that we become guilty of at birth," Chambers proceeded to cite Malebranche as his sole authority in the discussion of sin's transmission. "Now, as it is necessary, according to the order established by nature," commented Chambers,

> that the thoughts of the soul be conformable to the traces in the brain; it may be said that as soon as we are formed in the womb, we are infected with the corruption of our parents: For having traces in the brain like those of the persons who gave us being; it is necessary we have the same thoughts, and the same inclinations with regard to sensible objects. Thus, of course, we must be born with concupiscence, if that be nothing but the natural effort the traces of the brain make on the mind to attach it to sensible things; and with *original* sin, if that be nothing but the prevalency of concupiscence; nothing in effect, but these effects considered as victorious, and as masters of the mind and heart of the child.[59]

As we noted earlier, Wesley was convinced that pre-fallen Adam possessed capabilities far superior to those that human beings possessed after the transgression. *Pace* Taylor, Wesley also maintained that after the fall human epistemic faculties became damaged and were incapable of cognizing as its progenitor once did. Wesley wrote: "But there are essential Defects in mine and your's [reasoning faculties], and every Man's whom we know—Our *Apprehension* is indistinct, our *Judgment* false, our *Reasoning* wrong, in a thousand Instances. So it always was: And so it is still, after the Care we can possibly take."[60] Later, in 1784, when Wesley published his extract of Thomas Boston's *Human Nature in its Fourfold State* under the title of *The Doctrine of Original Sin Extracted From a Late Author,* Wesley wrote again of Adam's sin that was transmitted to all humanity. "And so he [Adam] begat a son in his own likeness: sinful, and therefore mortal; and so sin and death passed on all."[61] Even though Wesley could not explain the idea of the imputation of sin from one generation to another he could not deny the manifestations of sin in each and every generation.

John Wesley's concept and use of Original Sin had interesting implications for his view of evil too. First, despite the fact that many thought Taylor had argued his case against Original Sin better than Wesley defended the doctrine, Wesley made significant advances in his use of the teaching for shaping a particular identity in the Methodist societies; and, on a wider scale, the Evangelical Revival in eighteenth-century Britain.[62] The open air sermons of Methodist preachers, especially Whitefield and Wesley, found their success, in part, because of the reception of human depravity as a viable conceptual framework for understanding human nature and the immediate need for salvation. Second, the doctrine of Original Sin and its validity, firmly placed Wesley within a historical tradition that viewed the teaching both as a coherent paradigm for grading the presence of evil in the world and forecasted an element of hope for restoration and renewal: The *imago dei* had been damaged but it had not been lost in Wesley's view. God was present in the midst of a fragmented world and for a human race which had been molested by sin. It is now, however, to another example which Wesley addressed that I shall turn.

Earth-Shattering Evil and the Punishment of God: The Lisbon Earthquake and John Wesley's Tenuous Solution

On 1 November 1755, in one of the greatest natural disasters in modern Europe, an earthquake shattered much of Lisbon, killing thousands of men, women, and children. T. D. Kendrick's history of the catastrophe noted that "no one will ever know the number of people who lost their lives in the Lisbon earthquake."[63] A catastrophe of this scale received international publicity and, as various scholars have shown, precipitated something approaching a seismological shock in the intellectual life of modern society, forcing a reconsideration of optimistic strands in Enlightenment ideology. The sheer size of the disaster opened various debates about the devastation that swept through Portugal in the eighteenth century.

Of course, Lisbon was not the only place where devastation occurred through climatic storms and earthquakes in the eighteenth century. London was the scene of several alarming earth tremors in the winter of 1750; the first occurred in early February and the second, which was more serious, on 5 March. In his journal entry for the February incident, Wesley recorded his observations of the storm:

> It was about a quarter after twelve that the earthquake began at the skirts of the town. It began in the south-east, went through Southwark, under the river, and then from one end of London to the other . . . There were three distinct shakes, or wavings to and fro, attended with an hoarse, rumbling noise, like thunder. How greatly does God deal with this nation! O that our repentance may prevent heavier marks of his displeasure.[64]

Ten days later unusually intense storms passed through Gosport, Portsmouth, and the Isle of Wight. The result was a remarkable outbreak of group hysteria, particularly in London. Huge thunderstorms and earthquakes periodically precipitated local panics of an impending day of judgment, but the alarm in 1750 was exceptionally heightened. Luke Tyerman was pardonably dramatic when he described the scene: "Multitudes ran about the streets in frantic consternation, quite certain that the final judgment was about to open; and that, before the dawn of another day, all would hear the blast of the archangel's trumpet."[65]

Though John Wesley demonstrated no sign of anxiety in his journal, he was sufficiently moved by the event when he brooded on his own mortality, and wrote in a letter to Grace Bennett (1715-1803) the day after the tremor on 8 February 1750: "This morning my eyes were filled with tears of joy, from a hope that my time here is short."[66] Horace Walpole (1717-97) wrote of the aftermaths of the earthquakes in a letter to Horace Mann (1701-86) and described women who made "earthquake gowns," which enabled those made homeless by the natural catastrophes to wrap themselves and stay safely out of doors until they were transported by coach from the city to the country for relief and assistance.[67]

After the panic subsided, people searched in the face of ruin and despair for intellectual solutions that would sustain their belief in a compassionate deity. Daniel Defoe (1660-1731) had written earlier about the human quest for answers in the midst of tragic storms. His treatise, entitled *The Storm: Or, A Collection of the Most Remarkable Casualties and Disasters which Happen'd in the Late Dreadful Tempest, Both by Sea and Land,* depicted the Atheist as a rhetorical trope, which was common in the era. At one point, Defoe addressed the atheist's mistaken opinions about the existence of God and providential judgments: "*I cannot doubt but the Atheist's hard'ned Soul trembl'ed a little as well as his House, and he felt some Nature asking him some little Questions: as these*—Am not I mistaken? Certainly there is some such thing as a God—What can all this be? What is the matter in the World?"[68] By the middle of the eighteenth century, however, earthquakes forced many to wraxle with the idea of evil.

A review of Sampson Letsome's and John Cooke's *The Preacher's Assistant* indicates a variety of sermons which dealt with storms, earthquakes, and natural disasters.[69] Sermons like Nathaniel Dodge's *God's Voice in the Earthquake: Or a Serious Admonition to a Sinful World,* attempted to link geological eruptions with an apocalyptic hermeneutic that understood earthquakes as ominous signs of God's judicial decree against the universal sinfulness of humanity.[70] Dodge saw parallels between the natural and supernatural worlds and allowed for disruptions in both realms which could be traced to the reality of sin and its consequences. After the London earthquake of 1750, the Bishop of London, Thomas Sherlock (1678-1761), wrote an open letter where he remarked that the inhabitants of London had scorned the gospel and warned unless they repented similar forms of devastation would arise.[71] The literary genre of the jeremiad had a long ancestry that Sherlock and others like him found compatible for their theological agenda. "We have reason to fear," declared Sherlock, "when we see the Beginning of Sorrows, and the Displeasure of the Almighty manifested in the Calamities we suffer under, and in the Signs and Tokens given us to expect a far more dreadful Judgment."[72] The Bishop's letter was significant because it caused a furore of arguments for and against the idea of divine judgment.[73] On the one hand, Sherlock's comments struck a nerve with many who supposed that another earthquake would be a sign of divine wrath and claim their lives. Their anxiety was intense and their reactions were sometimes chaotic. On the other hand, those who maintained that the passionate prognostications of the religious had fallen into superstitious melodrama called into question not only the integrity of the leadership of the church but of the faith they were promoting. The inflamed rhetoric of the two groups showed, at one level, how the reality of earthquakes summoned diverse ideas and discussions about the nature of the physical world and highlighted a discourse of the supernatural that was far from dormant in the consciousness of individuals living in a neoteric world.

John Wesley has been ample criticised with regard to his understanding of God's supernatural intervention and natural catastrophes. Sara Schechner, for example, dismisses Wesley and his view of cosmology as fundamentally anti-quarian.[74] However, Wesley's knowledge of geology and astronomy was considerable and charges of ignorance about the natural world that have been levelled against him are unjustified. Wesley was familiar with current geological theory such as Thomas Burnet's (1635-1715) *Sacred Theory of the Earth* [75] and John Keill's (1671-1721) critique of Burnet in his *An Examination of Dr. Burnet's Theory.*[76] His reading also included the controversial *A New Theory of the Earth* by William Whiston (1667-1752)[77] and John Woodward's (1665-1728) *Natural History of the Earth.*[78]

Additionally, Wesley was interested in current cosmological theories of the universe and was familiar with ideas in astronomy that were moving the modern mind away from ancient views of the earth's central place in the universe.[79] With this knowledge in hand, Wesley sought to accomplish within his agenda of evangelical renewal, a middle ground between the idea that God was fundamentally involved in human history and the notion that religious speculations had waxed too fanatical, and thus, unreasonable.

John Wesley's ideas about earthquakes were easily summarized in a short work entitled *Serious Thoughts Occasioned by the Late Earthquake at Lisbon* and his sermon entitled *The Great Assize* published three years later in 1758.[80] In the latter, he depicted humanity ushered into the final judgment by a mighty and terrible earthquake in which,

> all the waters of the terraqueous globe will feel the violence of those concussions: "the sea and waves roaring," with such an agitation as had never been known before since the hour that "the fountains of the great deep were broken up," to destroy the earth which then "stood out of the water and in the water." The air will be all storm and tempest, full of dark "vapours and pillars of smoke;" resounding with thunder from pole to pole, and torn with ten thousand lightnings. But the commotion will not stop in the region of the air: "The powers of heaven also shall be shaken." "There shall be signs in the sun and in the moon and in the stars"— those fixed as well as those that move round them. "The sun shall be turned into darkness and the moon into blood, before the great and terrible day of the Lord come."[81]

For John, like his brother Charles, earthquakes were a visible indication that the earth was experiencing a level of moral corruption and divine judgment was on the horizon.[82] The observation that Methodists and their use of "nature" for the support of their own theological purpose revealed that they, at one level, retreated from the penetration of scientific knowledge in the Enlightenment. Wesley's allegation that the cause of the Lisbon earthquake could be traced to the injustices of the Inquisition was a case in point. "And is he [God]," wrote Wesley, "now making Inquisition for Blood? If so, it is not surprising, he should begin there, where so much Blood has been poured on the Ground like Water?"[83] The ease by which Wesley and many in the eighteenth-century interpreted physical and natural tragedies as portents that revealed God's displeasure and judgment struck many educated Christians as disturbingly irrational. Archbishop Herring (1693-1757) wrote a letter to William Duncombe (1690-1769) and characterized Wesley as "a most dark and Saturnine creature."[84]

Nevertheless, it must be remembered that Wesley was not alone in the assertion that God possessed the power for radical and unusual judgment. Many people in the eighteenth century were all too ready to see God's hand at work punishing humanity for its rebellion and sin.[85] The whole issue of providence and the belief in judgment was affirmed in the continued practice of Fast Day sermons after national defeats and disasters. In John Wesley's extended confrontation with John Taylor, Wesley had appeared crassly insensitive when he declared that all suffering comes upon the earth because of Adam's sin. "By *Punishment*," Wesley maintained, "I mean *Suffering* consequent upon *Sin* or *Pain* inflicted because of *Sin* preceding."[86] The ultimate form of God's punishment for sin was the universal experience of death for post-Adamic humanity; a justification verified by the belief that God was continually "appointing all Men to die, because Adam sinned."[87] What seems insensitive for the contemporary observer, and far off from a biblical understanding of the love of God, was for the eighteenth-century mind an idea that sustained a belief in God's justice in light of the sinful inclination of the human heart.

Another aspect of Wesley's social environment that must be considered is that a primal fear of storms as portents of divine judgment was deeply embedded in English folk religion and Methodist preachers made good use of it. Thus, as Charles Goodwin notes, "as many as seven-hundred people were added in 1778 to the Birstal circuit in Yorkshire by 'simple means;' of which one was an extraordinary outbreak of thunder and lightening."[88]

Repeatedly eighteenth-century Methodists found supernatural traces in natural phenomena which caused them to see and feel God's providential presence in the face of judgment. Sarcastically Wesley poked at sceptics who contended that God has nothing to do with earthquakes: "If thou prayest then . . . it must be to some of these. Begin 'O Earth, Earth, Earth, hear the Voice of thy Children. Hear, O Air, Water, Fire!'"[89] What Wesley found appealing about natural disasters was their inclusive scope and man's inability to escape their consequences, whatever an individual's wealth or place in society. In a sense, then, an earthquake, or similar disaster, was an egalitarian event that placed all humanity on the same level. At the age of seventy-four, Wesley wrote to Christopher Hopper (1722-1802)[90]: "There is no divine visitation which is likely to have so general an influence upon sinners as an earthquake. The rich can no more guard against it than the poor. Therefore I have often thought this would be no undesirable event."[91] Within this scheme, all human beings were reduced to the same level of helplessness before God. Throughout his life, Wesley always viewed the actualization of grace and salvation a primary goal, by whatever means it was brought about. Ironically here was proof to the world's inhabitants that God was present and not aloof from His created order as Deists and some Anglicans imagined.[92]

Thus far John Wesley's involvement in two crucial dialogues in eighteenth-century culture has indicated how he addressed the problem of the presence of evil. Neither Original Sin nor Earthquakes, however, could match the heated dispute that he entered over the issue of evil spirits and their malicious presence for people living in the modern world.

Devilish Disorder: A Sketch Of Diabolical Evil

"Witches," writes Robin Briggs, "have haunted the human imagination with remarkable persistence."[93] From the beginning of early Christianity, the idea of diabolical evil attracted and confused believer and non-believer alike. For centuries the question of evil and the justification of God's providential care were synchronous with the concept of the Devil, who disrupted and disfigured the peace and harmony of the created order.[94] The affirmation of the existence of Satan posed specific and detailed problems on various accounts. If one posited, for example, the existence of a diabolical cabal of agents that intentionally exhibited malicious acts toward humanity, then to what extent could God's providential love and care be professed? Elaborate explanations were offered in an attempt to resolve issues of theodicy as well as other matters, like pain and suffering, in the human experience of individuals.[95]

Scholars like Keith Thomas, D. P. Walker, James Sharpe, and Stuart Clarke have written on the idea of personified evil and recognize its enduring symbolic potency in the history of social behaviour. Particularly insightful is Stuart Clark and his ground-breaking *Thinking With Demons: The Idea of Witchcraft in Early Modern Europe*. In Clark's analysis, demonology and witchcraft have been defined throughout history as a singular movement in western culture by what they signified about physical and metaphysical realities. Thus, at the dawn of modern European society, "close analogies existed between the logical and rhetorical structures for expressing demonology and the (alleged) behaviour of witches."[96]

A central element of Clark's understanding of demonology in the modern world is what he labels a "rhetoric of disorder" which permeated society with a self-referential approach for interpreting the world.[97] This hermeneutical insight dominated the modern imagination, suggest Clark, and was best exemplified by the "evil woman" and her "supposed aim to overturn the natural order of things and end up on top."[98] The turning of the world's nature, *mundus inversus,* revealed the underlying intentions of the Devil at a fundamental level. "In effect," Clark argues, "the Devil's regimen was a compendium of the paradoxes of misrule: a hierarchy governed from the lowest point of excellence, a society in which dishonour was the badge of status and a *speculum* imitable only by the politically vicious. This was worse than mere anarchy. Moreover there was a specific sense in which demonic allegiance was necessarily associated with disobedience and its consequences."[99]

For men and women living in the modern world, the crux of demonic presence rested on a system of manipulation that sought malignant power for itself and generated injury to individuals and society.[100] Keith Thomas observes that the fear of *maleficium*, whether real or imagined, was the controlling influence behind the witch trials of the sixteenth and seventeenth centuries.[101]

Jacobus Sprenger (1436?-94) and Heinrich Kramer (1430?-1505), two Dominican monks, compiled what has become the *locus classicus* for the *malificum* debate; the *Malleus Maleficarum,* published in 1487. Published in many editions it became influential not only in the fifteenth century but also generations to follow.[102] Within its pages the authors described demonological hierarchy, erotic subversion, and satanic wonders but also constructed ideas of malevolent evil which inspired theories of possession, manipulation, and control. One lively example was the erotic dysfunction of a man who was bewitched into abnormal sexual hysteria because he believed he had offended a woman whom he suspected was a witch. The detail of his possession was demonstrated by an act of self-sex:

> In the presence of his wife he is in the habit of acting after the manner of men with women, that is to say, of practicing coition, as it were, and he continues to do this repeatedly, nor have the cries and urgent appeals of his wife any effect in making him desist. And after he has fornicated thus two or three times, he bawls out, "We are going to start all over again;" when actually there is no person visible to mortal sight lying with him. And after an incredible number of such bouts, the poor man at last sinks to the floor utterly exhausted. When he has recovered his strength a little and is asked how this has happened to him, and whether he has had any woman with him, he answers that he saw nothing, but that his mind is in some way possessed so that he can by no means refrain from such priapism.[103]

This citation offers interesting items for consideration. First, and foremost, it attributed the man's behaviour as bewitched and under the possession of an evil spirit. As such, he was disarranged from normal physical and psychological actions that could enable him to cease from the sexual act by an exercise of his free will. Second, the writers of the *Malleus Maleficarum* not only considered the act dysfunctional but others in the narrative consider it abnormal too. The man's wife unsuccessfully entreated him with "cries and urgent appeals." The narrative corroborated, from Sprenger's and Kramer's point of view, the reality of diabolical agents that were able to prevent the rational control of the possessed as well as the assistance of various individuals who would aid in liberation. Third, at the end of the narrative, the man was exhausted physically, emotionally, and spiritually; unmindful of the act or cause that had dominated his behavior and distressed his wife. The concept of maleficent impressions on the human psyche was an underlying feature in the *Malleus Maleficarum* and throughout its pages the notion of the satanic loomed large.[104] Whatever post-Enlightenment culture might think about such an idea, it was one that took shape in many ways and had a long and detailed history in the witchcraft persecutions of innocent women, men, and children in the fifteenth, sixteenth, and seventeenth centuries.[105] In England, *An Act against Conjuration, Witchcraft, and Dealing with Evil and Wicked Spirits* (1604), for example, had abolished immediate punishment of witches and acts of sorcery, but nevertheless decreed that persons accused and convicted of acts of "Witchcraft, Inchantment, Charme, or Sorcery" should on the first account be imprisoned for one year and as a part of their punishment stand, at least four times during the felons imprisonment, in front of the Market Towne and "for a space of six hours, and there shall openly confess his or her error or offence."[106] Upon a second offence, the offender lost the privilege of sanctuary and was executed. Admittedly, witchcraft was a multifarious phenomenon in the modern world and carried with it polymorphic qualities of meaning depending on geographical, social, and religious location.[107] However, it was the idea of malevolent evil which was most disturbing for modern society.

By the time of John Wesley's birth in 1703, the hegemony of belief in the occult was receding rapidly among the intelligentsia.[108] It was becoming widely accepted that many ideas about agency and causation in the invisible world were empirically unfounded and could not be maintained by scientific verification.[109] In regard to demonology and witchcraft, the elite became particularly sceptical, as a world inhabited by evil spirits was becoming hard to sustain in light of the empirical findings of the new science. A landmark in the growth of this scepticism dated back to the sixteenth century with Johann Weyer (1515-88) and his work, *De Praestigiis Daemonum,* first published in 1563, and followed twenty years later by Reignald Scott's (1538-99) *Discoverie of Witchcraft.*[110] On the first page of his treatise, Scott lampooned those who thought there was demonic influence behind every misfortune in their lives: "Such faithless people (I say) are also persuaded, that neither hail or snow, thunder nor lightening, rain nor tempestuous winds, come from the Heavens at the commandment out to burn Witches; of God; but are raised by the cunning and power of Witches and Conjurers."[111] The Dutch theologian Balthasaar Beeker (1634-98) carried the argument a stage further in his controversial *Betoverde Weereld (The World Bewitched),* which suggested demonology, ghosts, witches, and phantasms originated not in orthodox Christian doctrine but in pagan rituals and beliefs.[112] Bekker was outspoken in his criticism of Christianity's traditional belief in demons and witches, and candidly professed:

> I am Confident, and I hope, that the Reader will more plainly perceive it hereafter, that no point of the Christian Religion is more important than this; and that no certain and sufficient proofs may be had of all the others, than by rejecting the Opinion commonly receiv'd amongst the Vulgar, concerning the Crafts and Power of the Devil. Can it be imagin'd a small Matter to know whether the Devil has a Kingdom upon Earth; and what are the Limits that separate his Dominions from that of God Almighty?[113]

Step by step a sceptical world-view gained ground against the belief in an invisible world, which had existed in various forms dating from primitive Christianity. Still, the momentum of progress did not extinguish the belief in an invisible world—either among the elite or the plebeian populations. It has been an assumption of an older historiographical view of the eighteenth century that after the close of the witch trials in Europe and the repeal in England of the Witchcraft Act (1736), a general unwillingness to credit the occult, witchcraft in particular, emerged among the elite and learned.[114] More recently, other scholars have been added to the list.[115]

Contrary to this trend, however, there has surfaced an increasing amount of scholarly work by historians, social-scientists and theologians that question the assumption that the dominant trends of the Enlightenment eliminated the idea of diabolical agency from the religious consciousness of individuals living in the age.[116] The claim that the empirical sciences caused the plebeian and elite populations of the Enlightenment to embrace an attitude of incredulity towards otherworldly phenomena is not supported by recent scholarship or the primary textual documents of the period.[117]

The Royal Society, it must be remembered, endeavoured to investigate all aspects of reality, physical and metaphysical. One of its first members, Joseph Glanvill, who remained influential in the eighteenth century wrote a treatise on ghosts and apparitions subtitled, *Full and Plain Evidence Concerning Witches and Apparitions. In Two Parts, The First Treating of their Possibility, The Second of their Real Existence.*[118] Glanvill approached the topic through an analogical hermeneutic and noted that because the natural world was voluminously populated with creatures, animate and inanimate, it was logically consistent to infer that the invisible world was inhabited with rational and intellectual beings that had the ability to interact and influence the natural world. Both good and evil spirits had access to the human mind and could at will "move the *instruments* of *sense* in the *brain,* as to awake such *imaginations,* as they have a mind to *excite*; and the imagination having a mighty *influence* upon the *affections*, and they upon the *will* and *external actions.*"[119]

Glanvill resisted, however, propping up his argument by the citation of exotic or unlikely fables. A member of the Royal Society, he was adamant that *scepsis scientifica* was the means of achieving natural and supernatural knowledge in the modern world.[120] What he demonstrated was that both visible and invisible worlds held a fascination for natural philosophers during the seventeenth and eighteenth centuries and adherence to the idea of malicious spirits proposed little difficulty for the leaders of the new science in their experiments and inquiries. Moody Prior made the point long ago, in his article, "Joseph Glanvill, Witchcraft, and Seventeenth-Century Science":

> In spite of their "official" dictum that their concern was only with mechanical causes and with the phenomena of matter and motion, most of the scientific philosophers were reluctant to restrict the field to their interest and study too closely, since they also felt that anything whatever which provided them with material for observation and investigation was not unworthy of their attention. Moreover, however guardedly they tried to concentrate on matter, they found themselves unable, . . . to avoid the subject of spiritual and immaterial forces.[121]

And, more recently, Owen Davies has argued that "as the years passed . . . the belief in witchcraft remained pervasive, occasional voices could be heard reminding the reading public that the popular belief in witchcraft had not died with the Witchcraft Act, and that the rapid progress of human knowledge in their 'enlightened age' was not necessarily an antidote to such beliefs."[122]

An additional point worthy of consideration is that the chasm between primitive and modern mentalities was not as neat and compartmentalized as some historians have asserted. There was, to be sure, a stream of thought in the Enlightenment that challenged the assumptions of previous generations in regard to physics and metaphysics.[123] Jonathan Swift (1667-1745), for one, wrote of the apparent demise of ghosts in the modern world.[124] The dominant trend towards a mechanical view of the universe was not, however, the only perspective which competed for the attention of individuals in society. The controversy over the Surrey Demoniac in the 1690s serves as a colourful case history which illustrates the avid interest that people had in demonic narratives at the turn of the century.[125] The ensuing debates surrounding the veracity of the possession and exorcism indicated that supernatural narratives were deeply entrenched in the psychological and social identification of individuals during the Enlightenment. Furthermore, a rapid exchange of charges and defences that canvassed the demoniac's authenticity revealed, at one level, that the idea of the supernatural was a powerful presence in the minds of people living in the period.

At a more complicated level, the exchanges, which compassed the controversy, indicated that people balked at the notion of a world with no traces of supernatural intervention.[126] The Surrey demoniac, moreover, was not an isolated case. Richard Baxter, the non-conformist pastor and theologian, collected narratives of individuals who detailed their alleged encounters with apparitions and witches. Through nearly three-hundred pages of text Baxter related stories which he believed would corroborate the existence of an invisible world. One example involved a pious woman who lived in London and was accosted in her home by the Devil during the day. "The Devil," reported Baxter, "stood before her in the shape of a Big, Black, Man, and pointed to the top of the Door, Tempting her there to hang herself."[127] Francis Hutchinson (1660-1739), a Whig prelate who emphasized the reasonableness of religion, cautiously published *A Historical Essay Concerning Witchcraft*, in which he questioned the reliability of popular testimony regarding the phenomena.[128] Fresh in Hutchinson's mind was the witch trials of the seventeenth century and his fear of recurring acts of persecution.[129] Later, the repeal of the Witchcraft Act passed in Parliament in 1736, but the idea of witchcraft as a viable explanation for acts of human malevolence and other disturbing occurrences continued to be accepted by some.

At a conceptual level, the continuance of beliefs in demoniac agency were enabled by the acceptance of the idea of the chain of being, first formulated in ancient philosophy, but widely accepted in an eighteenth-century form. Arthur Lovejoy observed that "the conception of the universe as a Chain of Being, and the principles which underlay this conception—plenitude, continuity, graduation—attained their widest diffusion and acceptance."[130] The Platonic concept, though not universally accepted, supported the idea of a hierarchal order which revealed the fabric of creation. From such a theory, it was not a huge breach to entertain the idea that life existed at different levels, natural and supernatural. As John Locke wrote in Book Three of his *Essay*:

> That there should be more Species of intelligent Creatures above us, than there are of sensible and material below us, is probable to me from hence; That in all

the visible corporeal World, we see not Chasms, or Gaps. All quite down from us, the descent is by easy steps, and a continued series of Things, that in each remove, differ very little from the other . . . And when we consider the infinite Power and Wisdom of the Maker, we have reason to think, that it is suitable to the magnificent Harmony of the Universe, and the great design and infinite Goodness of the Architect, that the Species of Creatures should also, by gentle degrees, ascend upward from us toward his infinite Perfection, as we see they gradually descend from us downwards.[131]

Locke's affirmation of "intelligent creatures above us" was fitting for those who believed that the invisible world was characterized by order and structure. William Whiston, author of *A New Theory of the Earth,* wrote a tract on demonic possession and exorcism one year after the repeal of the Witchcraft Act and insisted: "The belief of a real *Devil,* or *Satan,* the head of all the Demons, and Evil Angels; and of the reality of those Daemons, or Evil Angels themselves, under his dominion, and busy in perverting and ruining mankind, is one of the fundamental doctrines of Christianity."[132] Whiston's short essay gave evidence that demonology, especially as it was linked to the *unde malum* question, was not laid to rest in the eighteenth century.

A careful evaluation of sources reveals that ongoing debates about demonology was materializing in literary, philosophical, and theological circles. E. J. Clery notes in her book on supernatural literature that the radical nature of these discussions had profound results. "At this time," writes Clery, "the literary supernatural still had the power to disturb and, by the very force of the prohibitions against it, to voice otherwise unspeakable truths."[133] In fact, throughout the Enlightenment there emerged a steady stream of tracts, treatises, and published sermons about the legitimacy of supernatural phenomena—witches, demons, haunted houses, and apparitions—and the effect of these debates were carried on with vigor. A circumspect analysis of this aspect of religious rhetoric in this period, then, must resist the notion that the emergence of progress in the Enlightenment necessarily eclipsed belief in the rudiments of an invisible world. Additionally, the view of high and low cultures with a learned elite positioned above an unlearned and superstitious lower class also must be rejected.

It is true that there was a good deal of suspicion about particular claims to possession and unusual supernatural experiences. The notorious "Cock Lane Ghost" affair and the controversy surrounding the key characters of the incident in 1762 brought discredit and ridicule on those involved when the tale was found to be embarrassingly deceptive and lacking authenticity.[134] Despite a scepticism that louted claims to the supernatural as farcical and absurd, there remained a concerted defence for the belief in evil spirits and their malicious presence in the world. One of the key biblical stories at the centre of the debate was the healing of the Gadarene demoniac, which is found in all three synoptic gospels.[135] Rationalist interpreters of the Bible contended that the demoniac suffered from a mental distortion of one form or another. This was the interpretation advanced by Theophilus Lindsey (1723-1808), the Unitarian minister and theologian, who commented on the version found in Mark's gospel in a sermon preached in 1789. "According to the account," Lindsey argued, "we are to understand that he [the demoniac] was disordered in his mind. When it was said, that any one was possessed by many demons, it is to be understood that it was a case of deplorable insanity."[136] Thomas Chubb (1679-1747), a Deist, also gave similar expression to this New Testament pericope when he wrote in the debates on miracles in the first half of the eighteenth century.[137] However, others did not accept this sceptical commentary on the passage. In a letter to the *Gentleman's Magazine*, for example, one reader wanted to know how rationalist exegetes explained the act of Jesus sending madness into the swine who ran "for Shelter into a Lake, where instead of finding Refuge, they met an universal Ruin."[138] John Fell (1735-97), a Congregational minister, stated the orthodox view succinctly when he linked the denial of possession and exorcism portrayed in the biblical narrative to the refutation of the authenticity of the New Testament itself. Fell wrote:

> If we say, that these facts [concerning the demons and the swine] were not as recorded by the evangelists, we not only reject their competency as witnesses, but we also deny the truth of their history. To alter their terms in explaining these facts, and to introduce causes and agents different from those which they have mentioned, is in truth to tell the world, that the sacred penmen were in error, and that they ought not to have expressed themselves as they have done on this occasion.[139]

Fell's work, which came at the end of the eighteenth century, indicated that the issue of demonic possession was far from being an interesting topic for a few religious clerics but widely debated at the close of the century.[140] Nearly everyone who entered the debate commented on this passage in one way or another and the heated disputes that ensued were a sign that the belief in witches and demons was still very much alive.

"The Wesleyan Army": John Wesley, Demonic Possession, and The Sacramental Recovery Of Exorcism

At the beginning of the nineteenth century a Methodist broadsheet opened with the stanza:

> The WESLEYAN ARMY in one are combined,
> To war with the Devil, the foe of mankind:
> Jehovah their Captain commands from the skies,
> Death or victory their motto, and Heaven the prize.[141]

This document is revealing because it demonstrated that Wesley's idea of personified evil became embedded in the consciousness of the Methodists and survived after his death. As I previously have indicated, John Wesley's view of demonic agency was that of a transcendental will which intended to unsettle the harmony of God's created order. It is remarkable, in light of recent interest in the history of witchcraft and demonology theories, that Wesley has been ignored as a significant contributor in the philosophical and theological debates of the eighteenth century. Some, like Ian Bostridge, have too readily placed Wesley within a "fundamentalism" category which, at the end of the day, has been un-concerned with any close examination that would uncover the intricate dimensions of Wesley's life and thought. Bostridge writes: "John Wesley's commitment to witchcraft belief has to be seen in the context of his Tory upbringing and nonjuring affections, as well as his biblical fundamentalism."[142] Other Methodists, from the nineteenth century to present-day historians, like John Kent, have considered Wesley's idea of diabolical evil as crude and primitive for a man of his education.[143] Yet Wesley's attitude to the occult was more complicated than these judgments would allow. He was well aware of the debates which surrounded transcendental agency in the eighteenth century and even found himself at odds with some of his own Methodists; namely, Thomas Maxfield and George Bell, from whose ultra-supernaturalism he found it necessary to dissociate himself, privately and publicly. Certainly Wesley's association with such enthusiasts and their similiarities to marginal groups like the French Prophets became a serious point of contention. Especially problematical was their insistence on immediate inspiration. Nevertheless the connection between John Wesley and the belief in witches continued throughout his life and it is this aspect of Wesley's thought that I now turn to in greater detail.

Old Jeffrey: John Wesley's Fascination with Paranormal Phenomena

On 12 January 1717, while Wesley was at Charterhouse, Susanna Wesley wrote to Samuel Wesley, junior, then at Christ Church. Expressing fears that the rectory in Epworth was haunted by a poltergeist, she reported that in the previous month the maid had "heard at the door of the Dining room groans like a person in extremist at the point of death . . . This continued every night for a fortnight: sometimes it was in the garrack but most commonly in the nursery, or given Chambers."[144] For the next ten years the Wesley brothers—Samuel, John, and Charles—corresponded with their family in Epworth concerning the apparition, which in time they referred to as "Old Jeffrey."[145] The original letters are extinct but were transcribed by Charles Wesley in a notebook. First published by Joseph Priestley shortly after John Wesley's death they were printed again in 1801 by Adam Clarke under the title *Memoirs of the Wesley Family.*[146]

The collection is a fascinating source for understanding the Wesley family and their views of paranormal phenomena. The best known of the manifestations was the disruptive knockings of the poltergeist when prayers were being offered for King William III (1650-1702) at mealtime. Susanna Wesley wrote to Samuel junior and noted: "Only at the speaking of prayers for the King and Prince, when it usually begins; especially when my Father says 'Our most gracious Sovereign Lord etc.' This he is angry at, and intends to say Three instead of two for the Royal Family. We all heard this same noise at the same time, and as coming from the same place."[147] Other episodes occurred between 1717 and 1726; unleashing of secured door locks, trembling by the children while they were asleep, and physical assaults of family members by invisible forces—all played a role in Wesley family life at Epworth. One of the most spectacular incidents recounted in the correspondence was Anne Wesley's experience of levitation. In correspondence to John Wesley, she described the occasion:

> One night she [Anne Wesley] was sitting on the press-bed-end, playing at cards with some of my sisters: my sisters Molly, Hetty, Patty, and Kezzy, were in the room and Robin Brown. The Bed on which my Sister Nancy sat was lifted up with her on it. She leaped down and said "Surely Old Jeffrey will not run away with me." However they persuaded her to sit down again, which she had scarce done when it was lifted up again several times a considerable height: upon which she left her seat and would not be prevailed upon sit there any more.[148]

The correspondence documents are intriguing also because each member of the family initially manifested a spirit of scepticism about the poltergeist. However, as a result of their experiences and reflections, all came to believe that the rectory was inhabited by a spirit. Emily Wesley, in particular, related her erstwhile scepticism about the paranormal but found her encounter with the poltergeist "sufficient to convince anybody of the reality of the thing." As to its cause, she believed it was due to a disturbance at a nearby town coupled with the fact that her father had "preached warmly against consulting those that are called Cunning Men; which our people are much given to."[149]

At some point, however, the Old Jeffrey account was accepted by John Wesley as a valid and important supernatural manifestation. At the end of Charles Wesley's transcription of the family correspondence, there is a thirteen point summary of the decade long confrontations with Old Jeffrey written by his brother John.[150] Wesley's summary was significant not only because it signified the importance of the incident in the life of the Wesley family, but also because it disclosed Wesley's commitment to the empirical observation of supernatural phenomena. Even the sceptic biographer, Robert Southey (1774-1843), was constrained to admit: "An author who in this age relates such a story, and treats it as not utterly incredible and absurd, must expect to be ridiculed; but the testimony upon which it rests is far too strong to be set aside, because of the strangeness of the relation."[151]

Though the Old Jeffrey incident was a fascinating story in the history of the Wesley family, it should not be examined in isolation. There were scores of similar stories delineating the experiences of apparitions and strange occurrences in the Wesleyan corpus. On one occasion in 1723, for instance, John Wesley wrote home and disclosed how he discovered an empty house that, according to a countryman in Oxford, had been haunted. He expressed scepticism about the alleged story but vowed to return and test the countryman's claim.[152] An interesting commentary on the enduring appeal of supernatural narratives in Wesley's life is the fact that these stories were characteristic not only of the young Wesley but scattered throughout his journals, letter correspondence, *Arminian Magazine*, and uncatalogued manuscripts are hundreds of stories that explored the various dimensions of the supernatural in the lives of believers and non-believers alike. Frank Baker remarked about this feature of Wesley's life: "He remained eager to discover and describe to his friends examples of God's moving in mysterious ways."[153]

Malignos Spiritus in Corpore:
John Wesley's View Of Demonic Possession

All this indicates that John Wesley stood in a tradition of the Christian faith which understood humanity to be at odds with evil spirits; namely, what Owen Davies has articulated as "the old elite, theological conceptions of diabolism."[154] No apologies were made throughout his life for the belief in agents and forces acting in concert to destabilize God's created order.[155] Overlooking this facet of Wesley's life, modern scholarship has often concluded that Wesley's vision was anachronistic in an age dominated by mechanical science, industrial progress, and philosophical scepticism. This superficial reading of John Wesley's life and thought, however, does little justice to a figure of intellectual history and fails to recognize the nuances of a philosophical development that endeavoured to find a place for metaphysics against tremendous odds. It also slights the position of a leading religious figure that was highly complex and intelligent. Roy Porter, for one, offered a caricature of Wesley in this respect, picturing him as a quaint anomaly in his time.[156]

There was a huge number, however, for whom the sceptical mentality of mainstream Enlightenment thought was less than sufficient and John Wesley and his Methodist movement quickly tapped into a reservoir of supernatural beliefs in order to deepen their understanding of the Christian faith. There were many in the eighteenth-century who held to the idea of a cosmos whose structure allowed for many unusual and strange agents, seen and unseen, which allowed for both the existence of good and evil and the struggle between them to be made more intelligible. The message of John Wesley tapped into this sentiment and had a powerful congruity with a view of the world which was imagined in the framework of a battlefield between good and evil forces, unseen as well as visible. In such a picture, the dimensions of spirit and matter were configured in a symbiotic arrangement that enabled individuals to make sense out of their world and faith.

The commitment and conviction that Wesley brought to this aspect of religious rhetoric also eased the reception of his message among the popular audiences of Methodism. John Rule's frequently quoted statement about the marks of early Methodism certainly fit here too: "Methodism did not so much replace folk-beliefs as translate them into a religious idiom."[157]

At a different level, Wesley's ideas could very well be seen as countercultural and a collision with a particular strand of Enlightenment ideology that purported that human nature was merely a mechanism devoid of any spiritual or supernatural texture in its constitution. Despite the fact that there were some High Church bishops who embraced the notion of diabolical agency in the seventeenth and eighteenth centuries, large sectors of educated society, including many prominent figures in the Church of England hierarchy, maintained that the thought of demonic possession and the activity of exorcism should be avoided, mainly because they had been open to manipulation by enthusiasts and charlatans.[158] Both George Lavington of Exeter and William Warburton of Gloucester, blamed Wesley for preying on the fears of the plebeian class. Bishop Lavington, at the end of his anti-Methodist treatise, branded Wesley a man of "dubious character."[159] Bishop Warburton, a more serious opponent agreed, typifying Wesley as the paradigm of "modern Fanaticism."[160]

It was left to William Hogarth (1697-1764), however, to mock the Methodists portraying their gullibility and infatuation with a malicious aspect of the invisible world. In 1762, Hogarth produced his pictorial satire of Methodism—

first portrayed in "Enthusiasm Delineated" then later in a print entitled "Credulity, Superstition and Fanaticism."[161] In both, Methodism's obsession with an occult world was lampooned as superstitious and bizarre and an impassioned preacher, modelled after George Whitefield, was represented dangling effigies of demons and witches as a part of his pulpit technique. Also interesting was an orbed fixture with the inscription, "The New and Correct View of Hell."[162] A close inspection of Hogarth's engraving reveals that the globe was shaped in the form of a monster on whose face the topography of hell was divided by way of different facial expressions. The right eye marked the "molten lead lake" and the left the "bottomless pit" was separated by a river which was directed southward toward a nose entitled the "pitch and tar river." As one follows the stream southward, a horizontal marker across the globed face is entitled the "horrid zone" until the river passes into two tributaries which open into

Figure 2. William Hogarth, "Credulity, Superstition, and Fanaticism." Author's Copy.

"parts unknown," the "brimstone sea" and "eternal damnation gulf." On the right hand side in "Enthusiasm Delineated" is a disfigured mass labeled "Methodist Brain" which Hogarth replaced in "Credulity, Superstition, and Fanaticism" by a stack of books which consisted of Glanvill's *Sadducismus Triumphatus,* a celebrated treatise on witchcraft, and Wesley's *Sermons.* Above both brain and books in the engravings was a thermometer that measured the emotional intensity and intellectual level of the congregation. From despair and madness to heated love and hot lust to revelation and joy, Hogarth displayed the chasm that existed between the intelligentsia, on the one hand, and the devoted followers of Methodism, on the other.[163] The portraits and their imagery asserted unequivocally both Hogarth's view of the Methodists and what many considered a threat to a modern understanding of the world in the eighteenth century.

Figure 3. An Enlargement of the Globe in Hogarth's "Credulity, Superstition, and Fanaticism." Author's Copy.

Like Glanvill and Baxter, Wesley had been adamant that a belief in the supernatural consisted of a struggle between good and evil, which carried implications for the human soul. Furthermore, the validity of an invisible world was confirmed for Wesley by numerous spiritual case-histories evidenced in the *psychomachia* which raged in all believers. The struggle between good and evil spirits, angels and devils, an assortment of dreams, visions, and apparitions was often experienced in the life of believers who documented their accounts in written form along with various witnesses. At the end of his life, too, Wesley was more adamant than ever to outline his angelology and demonology. In 1783, Wesley included in the *Arminian Magazine* two sermons that he wrote on good and evil angels.[164] There Wesley profiled his belief in demonic activity against the background of the influential idea of the chain of being and maintained that a regiment of evil angels was positioned with diabolical tasks assigned to them.[165] This, Wesley concluded, was clearly based on the revelation of Scripture, where "we know that Satan and all his angels are continually warring against us, and watching over every child of man."[166] The purpose of the squadron of evil spirits was "hindering the work of God in the hearts of men."[167] The *modus operandi* of the demonic entourage, was much like the subtleness of the serpent in the Garden of Eden; it attacked Adam and Eve at their weakest point. Wesley explained:

> They are ever watching to see whose outward or inward circumstances, whose prosperity or adversity, whose health or sickness, whose friends or enemies, whose youth or age, whose knowledge or ignorance, whose business or idleness, whose joy or sorrow, may lay them open to temptation. And they are perpetually ready to make the utmost advantage of every circumstance. These skilful wrestlers espy the smallest slip we make, and avail themselves of it immediately; as they also are "about our bed, and about our path, and spy out all our ways." Indeed each of them "walketh about as a roaring lion, seeking whom he may devour," or whom he may "beguile through his subtlety, as the serpent beguiled Eve."[168]

Wesley also maintained that demonic assaults could come from external as well as internal temptations.[169] Jesus was tempted by the Devil with visible kingdoms, riches, and glory, which corroborated for Wesley, that "an astonishing measure of power is still left in the prince of darkness!"[170] Usually, however, evil spirits would begin their diabolical plots by infusing evil thoughts into the minds and hearts of men and women. Like Augustine of Hippo, Wesley believed that the Devil could penetrate the mind, will, and emotions through dreams.[171]

In 1781, Wesley buttressed this view and included in the *Arminian Magazine* the spiritual biography of Bathsheba Hall (1745-80) who described her life as tormented by diabolical dreams: "And the same have been again and again presented to me since I rose. My body is weak, my spirits faint, and I have many outward incumbrances. Satan well knows, this is his time to distress me."[172] Wesley admitted that it was not easy to differentiate between authentic demonic infiltration of the human senses and deceptions of the human imagination. One possible means of adjudication was the determination of thoughts that surfaced in the human mind which could not fit into a logical sequence of experienced events. Thoughts that spontaneously arose in the mind without any connection to antecedent thought patterns might be supernatural in origin. Wesley reasoned: "Those [thoughts] that are preternaturally suggested have frequently no relation to or connection (at least none that we are able to discern) with anything which preceeded. On the contrary they shoot in as it were across, and thereby show that they are of a different growth."[173] Satan, however, not only endeavoured to influence human thoughts but also tempted the human will with the intention of conjuring evil affections that are opposed to a righteous lifestyle. Asserting the reality of both the life of the Spirit and the demonic disfiguration of a holy life, Wesley maintained:

> He [the Devil] strives to instil unbelief, atheism, ill-will, bitterness, hatred, malice, envy—opposite to faith and love; fear, sorrow, anxiety, worldly care—opposite to peace and joy; impatience, ill nature, anger, resentment—opposite to long-suffering, gentleness, meekness; fraud, guile dissimulation—contrary to fidelity; love of the world, inordinate affection, foolish desires—opposite to the love of God.[174]

This passage, among others like it, indicated that—for Wesley—evil thoughts and deeds occurred with the assistance of a diabolical force, which was a "strong though secret power."[175] Moreover, an old theme which Wesley repeatedly addressed throughout his life and writings emerged; namely, should the modern mind continue to conceptualize supernatural agency in the same fashion as preceding generations had done? Previously I called attention to the cultural significance that Glanvill and others in the Royal Society considered an investigation of demons, witches, and apparitions within the perimeters of empirical science. Of course, sceptics were plenty, like D'Alembert and Diderot, who published an article on possession in their *Encylopaedia* which implied demonic possession was not a viable topic for modern scientific investigation but a hangover from a previous "fearful imagination."[176] Wesley was familiar with both sides of the debate and although sensitive to progressive discoveries of science he was resistant to abdicate a belief in either diabolical agency or demonic possession.

John Wesley substantiated his belief in the supernatural by including a psychological and theological ratiocination which he gathered from his observations of human nature and history.[177] Frequently he surveyed sundry accounts of experiences and recorded their peculiarities for the edifications of the Methodists. As a result, the journals showed both Wesley's meticulous observations for detail and his interest in supernatural and paranormal events. W. R. Ward in his introduction to the critical edition of the journals perceptively pointed out that, for Wesley, the issue of the causes of supernatural occurrences should be looked at within the tension of history and Christian realism. In Ward's estimation, "the conviction that the thought-world of the Bible, or thought-worlds to be found in the Bible, were obligatory for the awakened Christian of the eighteenth century, and urgently needed as a protest against what Wesley saw as the unrealistic, unscientific, unhistorical, premature dogmatism of the Enlightenment."[178] Certainly it was the case, in Wesley's evaluation, that the philosophical leaders of his era had determined that witchcraft and demonology were mythological constructions of an antecedent world view, which they considered unscientific and little help for either faith or reason. John Wesley, as the leader of the Methodist movement, however, contended that this was a transgression of the empirical principles on which modern science was founded. A case in point was found in his journal entry for 25 May 1768. Wesley related that there was a woman who had a tale of a strange account which he had transcribed for himself. He surmised that the woman's character eliminated fraud from her case and delusion was omitted by the circumstance itself, which Wesley did not directly reveal. He admitted that he did not understand all the facts of the incident but that did not prevent him from believing in the reality of the occurrence. "What pretence have I," asked Wesley, "then to deny well-attested facts because I cannot comprehend them?"[179] This was the mistake of the English and most Europeans, in Wesley's view. He linked his fundamental belief about witchcraft to a coherent view of Scripture which, Wesley believed, was substantiated by contemporary testimonies and asserted that a denial of witchcraft brought with it a high level of scepticism about the authenticity of the Bible itself:

> They well know (whether Christians know it or not) that the giving up witchcraft is in effect giving up the Bible. And they know, on the other hand, that if but one account of the intercourse of men with separate spirits be admitted, their whole castle in the air (deism, atheism, materialism) falls to the ground. I know no other reason therefore why we should suffer even this weapon to be wrestled out of our hands. Indeed, there are numerous arguments, besides, which abundantly confute their vain arguments, besides, which abundantly confute their vain imaginations. But we need not be hooted out of one; neither reason nor religion require this.[180]

Most commentaries on this statement have characterized Wesley's views as an anachronism of antiquity. However, I suggest that a closer look at the text will reveal a more nuanced argument. If one looks beyond this inflammatory statement in his journal, it will be noted that Wesley advanced his position by citing human testimony. Utilizing the principle of analogy, Wesley premised that because he had never seen a murderer did in no way mean that he doubted that the act of murder was being committed daily in English society. The reason for Wesley's belief in both the existence of natural and supernatural agents, i.e., murderers and witches, was because of the reliability of testimony. Then, for the next ten pages in the journal, he provided long and detailed testimonies of Elizabeth Hobson (1744-?) and her encounters with various apparitions.[181] Human testimonies, therefore, served an important function in Wesley's rhetoric of the invisible world.

On the surface, they evidenced occurrences that could not be contained within the boundaries of reason alone. The data of testimonies, especially in regard to human existence, was not a category which could be neatly compartmentalized. On a more substantial level, supernatural encounters that were witnessed by external sources had to be investigated and verified for their truth or error. In this regard, while it was the case that some professions could and should be discarded because of their fantastic nature it was nevertheless impossible to discount *a priori* all accounts of the supernatural. To do so, was to omit the epistemological component entailed in observation and the authentication of the empirical process itself. Instead, Wesley argued, the burden of proof fell squarely on those who denied the existence of the supernatural.

Up to this point, I have noted that Wesley based his belief in evil spirits on two fundamental criteria: the revelation of the Bible and human testimony. However, Wesley did not always rely on revelation or human testimony for his knowledge. Wesley's journals and letter correspondence contained ample evidence that he had direct encounters with individuals and groups that had come under the influence and possession of what he considered to be demonic spirits. The first occasion recorded in his journals occurred seven months after Wesley's own "heart warming" experience on Aldersgate street. On 5 December 1738, while preaching at St. Thomas he came into contact with a woman who, much like the Gadarene demoniac, was convulsing and screaming. Wesley described his feelings and actions: "I had a strong desire to speak to her. The moment I began she was still. The tears ran down her cheeks all the time I was telling her, 'Jesus of Nazareth is able and willing to deliver you.' O where is faith upon earth? Why are these poor wretches left under the open bondage of Satan? Jesus, Master! Give thou medicine to heal their sickness and deliver those who are now also vexed with unclean spirits!"[182] Within a year Wesley recorded two other cases of possession. On 25 October 1739, he was invited into a house at Bristol to care for a young woman who had taken ill the night before.[183] Upon entering her room, he saw a woman frantic and in convulsions on the floor. Following prayer, she became relaxed and they left her in peace for the night. On the following night, however, another situation arose and a similar summons came for Wesley. Initially he resisted the invitation but upon opening his Bible, *sorte biblicae*, his eyes fell upon the words of Matthew 25.25: "I was afraid, and went and hid thy talent in the earth." Admonished in his heart, Wesley went to see the girl, where he encountered the demonic presence again:

> She began screaming before I came into the room; then broke out into a horrid laughter, mixed with blasphemy, grievous to hear. One who from many circumstances apprehended a preternatural agent to be concerned in this asking, "How didst thou dare to enter into a Christian?" was answered, "She is not a Christian. She is mine." Q[uestion.] "Dost thou not tremble at the name of Jesus?" No words followed, but she shrunk back and trembled exceedingly. Q[uestion.] "Art thou not increasing thy own damnation?" It was faintly answered, "Ay, ay," which was followed by fresh cursing and blaspheming. My brother [Charles Wesley] coming in, she cried out, "Preacher! Field preacher! I don't love field preaching." This was repeated two hours altogether, with spitting and all the expressions of strong aversion.[184]

Narratives like the one cited in the above quotation were scattered throughout the journals. Sometimes Wesley recorded his own experiences in these affairs and at other times he related the accounts of others that seemed to him credible and worthy of consideration.

A closer examination of the possession narratives reveals that while they have particular nuances they also hold common characteristics that were emphasised for the benefit of Wesley's readers.

First, the condition of the possessed was always typified with hysteria which was characterized by a disruption of the personality. In either the case of the Devil who maintained control over the individual in possession; or, in the case of exorcism, the vocal demonstration of singing and prayers by Methodists votaries, there was produced an ambience which allowed the involuntary therapy on the subject to take centre stage. Throughout the possession narratives in Wesley's writings, there was an indiscriminate appearing and disappearing of personalities as malevolent forces emerged to make more subtle points of theological importance. Many times the individual's true personality became eclipsed and the identity of the demon emerged dominant over the mind and body of the possessed.[185] Closely aligned with the disappearance of human personality was the public display of diabolical agents in a drama of possession that often had socio-psychological implications.[186] Stephen Conner has argued that possession, as opposed to mystical experience, takes place in the public arena where it derives "its powers and meanings from the fact of being a visible event or series of events."[187] The idea of possession and hysteria posed particular problems that early Methodist preachers had to deal with in the activities of their open air preaching too. John Wesley, for example, never came to terms with the presence of convulsions in his preaching ministry.[188] He noticed, however, that when prayers were offered for those who were overwhelmed and manifested experiences of frenzy and fits, a peace and serenity would emerge in their bodies. John Wesley's transatlantic counterpart, Jonathan Edwards, also struggled with convulsions under his preaching ministry. Edwards had noted, like Wesley, that deliverance from convulsions should not be the measure of spiritual meaning and fulfilment because "the Scripture gives us no such rule."[189] For John Wesley, as with many of the Methodists in the eighteenth century, the presence of convulsions was an indication that the soul was disturbed by spiritual unrest and the possessed could be relieved by the act of emotional and spiritual deliverance.

Second, in Wesley's possession narratives, a vocalization of the demonic was disclosed. This meant either the acceptance of the existence of transcendental realities or a denial, *a priori*, of the existence of spiritual possession and therefore an assumption that such manifestations were acts of imposture. This was the circumstance that the Methodists confronted in the case of the Yatton demoniac in 1788. George Lukins, a forty-four year old tailor living in Somerset had been going from door to door, performing in Christmas plays when he was suddenly struck to the ground. When he recovered, he began to have uncontrollable fits, talking and singing in languages that others could not understand.[190] Often Lukins would sing sacred hymns but change the lyrics to praise Satan and his evil agents, offering a *Te Deum* to the Devil. When the demoniac spirit was addressed and asked why Lukins had been possessed, a voice protested: "That I may show my power among men."[191] This behaviour continued for eighteen years and news of the Yatton demoniac immediately made news in local papers, like the *Bristol Gazette* and *Bath Chronicle*.[192] Among those gathered in an attempt to exorcise the demon on Friday, 13 June, were John Broadbent (1751-94) and John Valton (1740-94), both Methodist preachers. There were others, however, who remained doubtful of Lukins's authenticity.[193] Did the Yatton demoniac, questioned the sceptics, actually possess a human being as a ventriloquist might, uttering curses and blasphemies or was George Lukins playing tricks and therefore merely a pretender? If the voice was not an instance of diabolical manipulation, how should it be explained with natural categories? Middleton had claimed that in ancient and modern societies there were "sort of Ventriloquists, who by a particular formation of their organs, managed by art and practice, could speak in such a manner, as to persuade the company, that the voice did not procede from them, but from some invisible being . . . by which means, weak and ignorant people have been terrified almost out of their senses, believing it to be the voice of a Spirit or Daemon."[194] John Wesley was aware that there were occurrences which were partially or completely fabricated. But the burden of proof, he believed, remained with the sceptics to disprove each paranormal occurrence as deceptive instead of categorically dismissing the phenomena out of hand. For Wesley's part, the existence of a demonic presence was one which had to be dealt with.

"I Charge Thee Not to Speak": John Wesley and the Sacramental Recovery of Exorcism

John Cennick (1718-55) one of Wesley's preachers who later left the Methodist connexion and became a Moravian, recounted several early Methodist encounters with evil spirits around the middle of the eighteenth century. At some point, he observed, the Methodist preachers discovered that it was better when the demonic spirits were prohibited from speaking and their voices silenced by those who professed faith. Furthermore, when the faithful commanded the evil spirits by the name of Jesus, divine power enabled believers to exercise control over the actions and words of the spirits. Cennick discussed an episode in which Wesley asked a demoniac, who appeared to have possessed a certain Betty Sommers of Kingswood, how they had taken control of her. After the demons responded with abuse to Wesley, Cennick observed:

> Experience proved that the more questions we asked them the stronger they grew and were more violent; so that I resolved neither to ask them anything nor suffer them to speak when they would say anything, and thus by a little and little it came to nothing in Kingswood. That was remarkable, if one said, I charge you in the name of Jesus Christ not to speak, they were always obedient; and so it was if one wanted them to give any answers.[195]

The above quotation demonstrated not only the belief in demonology in Bristol and Kingswood during the eighteenth century but also that John Wesley, along with other Methodists, were actively engaged in exorcism as a part of their mission and ministry.

The history of exorcism is an intricate and interesting story that space here does not allow a full description which it deserves.[196] However, by the eighteenth century, Church of England priests appeared to have abandoned the practice not only because there was controversy surrounding the act but also because Canon 72 prohibited a public exorcism without official sanction. The Canon expressly stated: "No minister or ministers shall, without the licence and direction of the bishop of the diocese first obtained and had under his hand and seal, appoint or keep any solemn fasts, either publicly or in any private houses, other than such as by law and or by public authority shall be appointed, nor shall be wittingly present at any of them, under pain of suspension for the first fault, of excommunication for the second, and of deposition from the ministry for the third."[197] With such laws in place coupled with the climate of the day it was easy to ignore the practice of exorcism.[198]

But, a cursory reading of John Wesley's journals and letter correspondence shows that he practiced and believed in the ministry of exorcism. In this he may have been influenced by his association with and reading of the nonjurors. In his sermon on *Evil Angels*, for example, Wesley mentioned that he had consulted an eminent physician about the relation of lunacy to demonic possession.[199] Albert Outler suggested that Wesley was speaking of Thomas Deacon (1697-1753), a physician in Manchester who performed exorcisms and healed the sick.[200] Wesley was not only influenced by Deacon but by many of the nonjurors. Several major figures among them actively sought to restore the minor sacrament of exorcism, as practiced in primitive Christianity, for the faith and practice of the church. Thomas Deacon, Joseph Bingham (1668-1723), and William Cave (1637-1713) all wrote about the office and practice of exorcism in the early church with approval.[201] Additionally, George Bull (1634-1710), Bishop of St. David's and much revered by High Churchmen, also added weight to the practice with his sermon on evil angels.[202] It is not difficult to imagine, then, that Wesley took some of these ideas to heart in his own theological development.[203] Furthermore, Wesley's inclusion of exorcism narratives in the published extracts of his journals amounted to an editorial marking of an ancient teaching that served both as an element for his practical theology which was fundamentally directed to the Methodists and a dimension of his rhetorical recovery of primitive Christianity that asserted the value of works of piety and mercy.[204]

The journals are a good place to end in the consideration of this aspect of Wesley and his ministry. Returning to one of the demonic narratives that I dealt with previously, the entry for 23 October 1739, offers insight into Wesley's idea of the meaning and significance of exorcism. In that occurrence, when the possessed woman began to pray to the Devil, Wesley abruptly interrupted her and declared: "We began [singing] Arm of the Lord, awake, awake."[205] This clarifies *inter alia* that for Wesley and the Methodists of the eighteenth century, singing was used as a technique in exorcism in addition to the singing of their faith. In this particular narrative, he discerned the malevolent character of the Devil's voice and prayed for the deliverance of the young girl, which after hours of prayer and singing was successful.[206] There were other exorcisms recorded too. Although Wesley's involvement in this act provided his enemies with an easy target for their attack it was a battle which Wesley had no intention of relinquishing, for he saw the healing of marred souls as part of his work in spreading scriptural holiness. Though he might be deceived at particular times, he believed that his life was unvarying: a liberation of those who had been possessed and oppressed by evil spirits in order that their lives might be under the influence of the Holy Spirit, the sanctifier of life.

Notes

1. Thomas Aquinas, *The De Mala of Thomas Aquinas*, ed., Brian Davies, trans. Richard Regan (Oxford: Oxford University Press, 2001), Q. xvi.

2. Wesley, "An Earnest Appeal to Men of Reason and Religion," *BEW* 11: 89-90.

3. Lactantius, "A Treatise on the Anger of God," xiii, in *ANF* 7: 271. See also *Glossarium Epicureum*; André J. Festugiere, *Epicurus and His Gods*, trans. C. W. Chilton (Oxford: Blackwell, 1955); and John M. Rist, *Epicurus: An Introduction*. (Cambridge: Cambridge University Press, 1972), 140-63.

4. Humphrey Ditton, *A Discourse Concerning the Resurrection of Jesus Christ. In Three Parts. Wherein I. The Consequences of the Doctrine are Stated Hypothetically. II. The Nature and Obligation of Moral Evidence, are Explain'd at large. III. The Proofs of the Fact of our Saviour's Resurrection are Propos'd, Examin'd, and fairly Demonstrated, to be Conclusive. Together with an Appendix concerning the Impossible Production of Thought, from Matter and Motion: The Nature of Human Souls, and of Brutes: The Animal Mundi, and the Hypothesis of the TO ΠAN as also, concerning Divine Providence, the Origin of Evil, and the Universe in General*, 2nd ed. (London: Printed by J. Darby, 1714), 501.

5. Throughout Wesley's works epicurean philosophy was used as a synonym for a type of Deism which conceptualized a deity separated from the activities of human existence. For example: "Let us even dare to own we believe there is a GOD: nay, and not a lazy, indolent Epicurean Deity, . . . who neither knows or cares what is done below." John Wesley, *Serious Thoughts Occasioned by the Late Earthquake at Lisbon*, 2nd ed. (Bristol: E. Farley, 1755), 25-26. Also, John Wesley, "The Spirit of Bondage and of Adoption" and "On Divine Providence," *BEW* 1: 251 and 2: 539-40.

6. John Wesley to Samuel Wesley, senior, 19 December 1729. *BEW* 25: 240-42. Wesley's *Diaries* from this time also indicate that he had "collected" part of Ditton's appendix on the origin of evil. See Frank Baker's comment in *BEW* 25: 240-241n2.

7. John Wesley to Samuel Wesley, senior, 11 December 1730. *BEW* 25: 258.

8. The letters to Samuel Wesley, senior from John Wesley about Humphrey Ditton and William King were published in the *Arminian Magazine* 3 (1780): 604-11.

9. John Wesley, "The End of Christ's Coming," *BEW* 2: 473. Albert Outler noted in his introductory comments on this sermon that Wesley preached on this passage no less than twenty-seven times from 1742 to 1789. See Albert Outler, "An Introductory Comment," *BEW* 2: 471.

10. See Michael J. Buckley, S. J., *The Origins of Modern Atheism* (New Haven: Yale University Press, 1987), 291-99.

11. Clyde A. Holbrooke, "Editor's Introduction to Jonathan Edwards's *The Great Christian Doctrine of Original Sin Defended; Evidences of it's Truth Produced, and Arguments to the Contrary Answered. Containing, in Particular, A Reply to the Objections and Arguings of Dr. JOHN TAYLOR, In his Book, Intitled, 'The Scripture-Doctrine of Original Sin proposed to, Free and candid Examination, &c,'*" in Clyde A. Holbrooke, ed., *Works of Jonathan Edwards* (New Haven: Yale University Press, 1970), 2: 1. Also, Clyde A. Holbrooke, "Original Sin in the Enlightenment," in John E. Cushman and Egil Grislis, eds., *The Heritage of Christian Thought: Essays in Honor of Robert Lowry Calhoun* (New York: Harper & Row, Publishers, 1965), 142-65.

12. Anthony Ashley Cooper, *Characteristics of Men, Manners, Opinions, Times*, ed., Lawrence E. Klein (1711; Cambridge: Cambridge University Press, 1999), 180.

13. For a view of scientific argumentation in the eighteenth century, see Alan G. Gross, Joseph E. Harmon, and Michael Reidy, *Communicating Science: The Scientific Article from the 17th Century to the Present* (Oxford: Oxford University Press, 2002), 68-116.

14. See Figure 1: "A Map of the Garden of Eden, before God Destroy'd it with the Flood." Also, R. Y., "Account of the Garden of EDEN by the Author of the Account of the Old World," *The Gentleman's Magazine* 8 (1738): 66-69.

15. For views of Hammond's Methodism and Moravianism see John Walsh, "The Cambridge Methodists," 249-83 and Colin Podmore, *The Moravian Church in England 1728-1760* (Oxford: Clarendon Press, 1998), 92, 127-28.

16. William Hammond, *Medulla Ecclesiae. The Doctrine of Original Sin, Justification by Faith, and The Holy Spirit, Fairly Stated and Clearly Demonstrated from the Homilies, Articles and Liturgies of the Church of England. Confirmed by Apostolic Texts of Scripture, with Proper Reflexiones, Inferences and Instructions Annexed to Each Head. Being the Substance of Several Discourses Preached in Cambridge* (London: Printed for J. Oswald, 1744), 22-23. "But as Serpents produce Serpents and all manner of venomous creatures bring forth creatures of the same kind, wild and venomous as themselves; so carnal, impure parents beget children as carnal and impure as themselves. As to the <u>modus</u> how this spiritual contagion is conveyed unto us, I do not pretend to determine it. That we are polluted from the womb is plain. The fact is too visible to be denied." John Bennet, *Mirror of the Soul: The Diary of an Early Methodist Preacher, John Bennet: 1714-1754*, ed., Simon R. Valentine (Peterborough: Methodist Publishing House, 2002), 17, who prefaced his vita with a theological discourse on the idea of the depravity of human beings and quoted Hammond almost verbatim.

17. Isaac Watts, *The Ruin and Recovery of MANKIND: Or An ATTEMPT to vindicate the SCRIPTURAL ACCOUNT of these great Events upon the plain Principles Of Reason. With an ANSWER to VARIOUS DIFFICULTIES, Relating to ORIGINAL SIN, The Universal DEPRAVATION of NATURE, And the Overspreading CURSE of DEATH; General OFFERS of GRACE to all Men, And the CERTAIN SALVATION of some; The CASE of the HEATHEN NATIONS, And the State of DYING INFANTS. Whereto Are subjoin'd, THREE SHORT ESSAYS, viz. The Proof of MAN'S Fall By his Misery; The Imputation of Sin and Righteousness; and The Guilt and Defilement of Sin. With a POSTSCRIPT.* 2nd ed. (London: Printed for James Brackstone, 1742), xvii.

18. Jeremy Gregory, "The Eighteenth Century Reformation: the Pastoral Task of Anglican Clergy after 1689," in Walsh, Haydon, and Taylor, eds., *The Church of England c. 1689—c. 1833: From Toleration to Tractarianism*, 70.

19. *Sermons or Homilies Appointed to be Read in Churches in the Time of Queen Elizabeth of Famous Memory* (London: Society for Promoting Christian Knowledge, 1839), 17. For a summary of attitudes to The Articles of Religion in eighteenth-century English religion, see John Walsh's "The Thirty Nine Articles and Anglican Identity in The Eighteenth Century," in Christiane d' Haussy, ed., *Quand Religions et Confessions se Regardent* (Paris: Didier-Erudition, 1998), 61-70.

20. *Sermons or Homilies*, 10.

21. Charles Wesley, *The Sermons of Charles Wesley: A Critical Edition with Introduction and Notes*, ed., Kenneth G. C. Newport (Oxford: Oxford University Press, 2002), 171. Kenneth Newport notes in his introductory comments that Charles Wesley's sermon register recorded him preaching this sermon on 21 January at Islington, 25 February at Bexley and 11 March at St. Catherine's.

22. John Wesley, "Original Sin," *BEW* 2: 176.

23. John Wesley, ed., *Arminian Magazine* 5 (1782): 27.

24. Locke, *Essay Concerning Human Understanding*, I.ii.15.

25. John Locke, "Is the Law of Nature Inscribed in the Minds of Men? No," in W. von Leyden, ed., *Essays on the Law of Nature and Associated Writings*, ed., (1663; Oxford: Clarendon Press, 2002), 139.

26. John Locke, *The Reasonableness of Christianity as Delivered in the Scriptures*, ed., John Higgins-Biddle (1695; Oxford: Clarendon Press, 1999), 5-11.

27. John Wesley, *The Doctrine of Original Sin: According to Scripture, Reason, and Experience* (Bristol: Felix Farley, 1757), 213.

28. Wesley, "Original Sin," *BEW* 2: 179.

29. Wesley, *Explanatory Notes*, 1: 16 (Genesis 3:6-8).

30. John Taylor, *The Scripture-Doctrine of Original Sin Proposed to Free and Candid Examination*, 2nd ed. (London: Printed and Sold by M. Fenner, 1741).

31. See, Geoffrey T. Eddy's, "Formica Contra Leonem: An Eighteenth Century Conflict Reassessed," *Methodist History* 38 (2000): 71-81; "Sartor Resartus: or Taylor New-Tailor'd," *Epworth Review* 26 (1999): 88-98; "There Goes the Arch-Heretic: The Revd Dr John Taylor of Norwich and Warrington Academy," *Faith and Freedom* 52 (1999): 39-50; and *Dr Taylor of Norwich: Wesley's Arch-heretic* (Peterborough: Epworth Press, 2003).

32. "I find no more than five places in all the Bible where the Consequences of the first Sin are *certainly* spoke of." Taylor, *The Scripture-Doctrine of Original Sin*, 5. The five citations that Taylor marked out for consideration were Genesis 2. 7; 3.7-24; Romans 5.12-20; I Corinthians 15. 21-22; and I Timothy 2.14.

33. Taylor, *The Scripture-Doctrine of Original Sin*, 93.

34. Taylor, *The Scripture Doctrine of Original Sin*, 252-53.

35. Watts, *The Ruin and Recovery of Mankind*; Jonathan Edwards, *The Great Christian Doctrine of Original Sin Defended; Evidences of it's Truth Produced, and Arguments to the Contrary Answered. Containing, in Particular, A Reply to the Objections and Arguings of Dr. JOHN TAYLOR, In his Book, Intitled, "'The Scripture-Doctrine of Original Sin proposed to, Free and candid Examination, &c,' (1757),"* in Clyde Holbrooke, ed., *The Works of Jonathan Edwards*, 3: 103-444; David Jennings, *A Vindication of the Scripture-Doctrine of Original Sin, From Mr TAYLOR's free And candid Examination of it* (London: John Oswald, 1740).

36. Clyde Holbrook, "Editor's Introduction," in Holbrook, *Works of Jonathan Edwards*, 3: 12. The work of Samuel Webster, *A Winter Evening's Conversation upon the Doctrine of Original Sin . . . Wherein the Notion of Our Having Sinned in Adam and Being on That Account Only Liable to Eternal Damnation, Is Proved To Be Unscriptural, Emotional, and of Dangerous Tendency* (Boston: Printed and Sold by Green and Russell, 1757) was first published anonymously. See Peter Clark's defence, *Scripture-Doctrine of Original Sin Stated and Defended. A Summer Morning's Conversation between a Minister and a Neighbor, a Reply to a Winter Evening's Conversation* (Boston: Printed by S. Kneeland, 1758). There were many exchanges in the debate which also included Charles Chauncy's *The Opinion of One Who Has Perused the Summer Morning's Conversation* (Boston: Printed by Green and Russell, 1758) and Joseph Bellamy's *A Letter to the Reverend Author of the Winter-Evening's Conversation on Original Sin* (Boston: Printed by S. Kneeland, 1758).

37. Wesley, *The Doctrine of Original Sin*.

38. Wesley, *The Doctrine of Original Sin*, iv-v. Compare Edwards attack on Taylor in 1757: "According to my observation, no one book has done so much towards rooting out of these western parts of New England, the principles and scheme of religion maintained by our pious and excellent forefathers, the divines and Christians who first settled this country, and alienating the minds of many from what I think are evidently some of the main doctrines of the gospel, as that which Dr. Taylor has published against the doctrine of original sin." Edwards, *The Great Christian Doctrine of Original Sin Defended*, 102.

39. Wesley, *The Doctrine of Original Sin*, v.

40. Taylor, *The Scripture-Doctrine of Original Sin*, 252-53.

41. Taylor, *The Scripture-Doctrine of Original Sin*, 253.

42. "*Shame*—Sin, which causes shame, for that brought shame first into the world." Wesley, *Explanatory Notes*, 3: 2135 (Jeremiah 3.24).

43. Wesley, "Original Sin," *BEW* 2: 177. "*And being without God*—Wholly ignorant of the true, and so in effect atheists. Such in truth are, more or less, all men in all ages, till they know God, by the teaching of his own Spirit; *in the world*—The wide, vain world, wherein ye wandered up and down, unholy and unhappy." Wesley, *Explanatory Notes*, 4: 493 (Eph. 2: 12).

44. John Wesley to Susanna Wesley, 24 January 1727. *BEW* 25: 208n1.

45. John Wesley, "The Image of God," *BEW* 4: 293-94.

46. Bryant, *John Wesley's Doctrine of Sin*, 151.

47. Wesley, *The Doctrine of Original Sin*, 60. "What a glorious work of God was at Cambuslang and Kilsyth from 1740 to 1744! But the war that followed tore it all up by the roots and left scarce any trace of it behind; insomuch that when I diligently inquired a few years after, I could not find one that retained the life of God!" John Wesley to Thomas Rankin, 19 May 1775. *LJW* 6: 150-51. For treatments of Wesley and political ethics, David Hempton's, *Methodism and Politics in British Society 1750-1850* (Stanford: Stanford University Press, 1984); *Religion and Political Culture in Britain and Ireland: From the Glorious Revolution to the Decline of Empire* (Cambridge: Cambridge University Press, 1996), 25-48; and Theodore Weber, *Politics in the Order of Salvation* (Nashville: Kingswood Books, 2001).

48. Peter Harrison, "Original Sin and the Problem of Knowledge in Early Modern Europe," *Journal of the History of Ideas* 63 (2002): 239-59.

49. David Spadafora, *The Idea of Progress in Eighteenth-Century Britain* (New Haven: Yale University Press, 1990).

50. Taylor, *The Scripture-Doctrine of Original Sin*, 231-32.

51. Wesley, *The Doctrine of Original Sin*, 84-85.

52. Wesley, *The Doctrine of Original Sin*, 136.

53. John Wesley, "The Reward of Righteousness," *BEW* 2: 403.

54. Wesley, *The Doctrine of Original Sin*, 271.

55. Nicholas Malebranche, *Father Malebranche's Treatise Concerning The Search After Truth. The Whole Work Compleate. To Which is Added The Author's Treatise of Nature and Grace. Being a Consequence of the Principles Contain'd in the Search: Together with His Answer to the Animadverions Upon the First Volume: His Defense Against the Acussations of Mr. De La Ville, &c. Relating to the Same Subject*, trans. Richard Sault (London: John Dunton & Steve Manship, 1694), 55-63.

56. Malebranche, *The Search After Truth*, 61.

57. John Wesley to Miss. L," nd. *WJW* 12: 260-62, and John Wesley to Miss. Bishop," 18 August 1784. *WJW* 13: 38-39. Wesley's indirect defence of Malebranche regarded the Count de Buffon's attack which may be found in John Wesley's "Remarks on The Count De Buffon's 'Natural History,'" *WJW* 13: 448-49. Wesley also recommended Malebranche in his "An Address to the Clergy," *WJW* 10: 492, and was also listed as required reading for students in the fourth year at Kingswood in "A Short Account of the School in Kingswood," *WJW* 13: 298.

58. See Albert Outler's note in John Wesley, "The Witness of Our Own Spirit," *BEW* 1: 301n8.

59. Ephraim Chambers, *CYCLOPAEDIA: OR, an UNIVERSAL DICTIONARY of ARTS AND SCIENCES; Containing An Explication of the terms, and an account of the things signified Thereby, in the SEVERAL ARTS, BOTH LIBERAL AND MECHANICAL; And the SEVERAL SCIENCES, HUMAN AND DIVINE: The Figures, Kinds, Properties, Productions, Preparations, and Uses of Things Natural and Artificial: The Rise, Progress, and State of Things ECCLESIASTICAL, CIVIL, MILITARY, AND COMMERCIAL: With the Several Systems, Sects, Opinions, &c. among PHILOSOPHERS, DIVINES, MATHEMATICIANS, PHYSICIANS, ANTIQUARIES, CRITICS, &c. The whole intended*

as a Course of antient and modern Learning. Extracted from the best Authors, Dictionaries, Journals, Memoirs, Transactions, Ephemerides, &c. in several Languages, 2 vols., 2nd ed. (London: Printed for D. Midwinter, 1738), "Original Sin." See Chamber's reference to "Concupiscence" where he cited Malebranche again in explicating the theological concept.

60. Wesley, *The Doctrine of Original Sin*, 185.

61. John Wesley, *The Doctrine of Original Sin. Extracted From a Late Author* (London: J. Paramore, 1784), 6. See Thomas Boston, *Human Nature in its Fourfold State of Primitive Integrity Subsisting in The PARENTS of Mankind in Paradise, ENTIRE DEPRAVATION Subsisting in the Unregenerate, BEGUN RECOVERY Subsisting in the Regenerate, and CONSUMMATE HAPPINESS or MISERY Subsisting in All Mankind in the Future State in SEVERAL PRACTICAL DISCOURSES*, 4th ed. (Edinburgh: R. Drummond and Company, 1744), 27.

62. "The Word *Sin* having so many Significations, you should have begun by determining even in your short Proposals, if *that* Original *Sin* is an original Crime, or only an original Fault, or Defect, Imperfection, or Falsity, or Error, or Lie, or Illusion, of Superstition, or Idolatry, or Ignorance, or Infidelity, or Unfaithfulness. Thus you are a bad Teacher of a Doctrine as bad, as the Sin it's Substance of whatever of all these kinds, this *Sin* may be." John Baptist Malaiss de Sulamar The Arch Teacher, *A Short Examen of Mr. John Wesley's System, as it Appears in his Publick Proposals Concerning THE DOCTRINE of Original Sin; or The Doctrine of Original Sin Examined at the Living Light of The Doctrine of Truth, In a Letter Publickly Directed to Mr. John Wesley, by John-Baptist, The Arch-Teacher* (London: J. Marshall, 1757), 4-5, an anonymous anti-Wesleyan pamphlet under the pseudonymn, criticized both doctrine and teacher when he wrote about Wesley.

63. T. D. Kendrick, *The Lisbon Earthquake* (London: Methuen, 1956), 34. For recent evaluations of the Lisbon earthquake, Regina Ammicht-Quinn, *Von Lissabon bis Auschwitz: Zum Paradigmawechsel in der Theodizeefrage* (Freiburg im Breisgau: Herder, 1992), 217-21; Wolfgang Breidert, ed., *Die Erschütterung der vollkommenen Welt: Die Wirkung des Erdlebens von Lissabon im Spiegel europäischer Zeitgenossen* (Darmstadt: Wissenschaftliche Buchgesellschaft, 1994); Horst Günther, *Das Erdbeben von Lissabon und die Erschütterung des Aufgeklärten* (Frankfurt am Main: Fischer Taschenbuch Verlag, 2005); Gerhard Lauer and Thorsten Unger, eds., *Das Erdbeben von Lissabon und der Katastrophendiskurs im 18. Jahrhundert* (Göttingen: Wallstein Verlag, 2008); Susan Nieman, "What's The Problem with Evil?" in Maria Pía Lara, ed., *Rethinking Evil: Contemporary Perspectives* (Berkeley: University of California Press, 2001), 29-31; Susan Nieman, *Evil in Modern Thought: An Alternative History of Philosophy* (Princeton: Princeton University Press, 2002), 240-50; and Claudia Sanides-Kohlrausch, "The Lisbon Earthquake, 1755: A Discourse about the 'nature' of nature," in William Drees, ed., *Is Nature Ever Evil? Religion, Science and Value* (London: Routledge Taylor & Francis Group, 2003), 106-19.

64. 8 February 1750. *BEW* 20: 320.

65. Tyerman, *The Life and Times of Rev. John Wesley*, 2: 71-72.

66. John Wesley to Grace Bennett, nd [1750]. *BEW* 26: 408.

67. Horace Walpole, *The Letters of Horace Walpole 4th Earl of Orford*, ed., Peter Cunningham, 9 vols. (Edinburgh: John Grant, 1906), 2: 200-06.

68. Daniel Defoe, *The Storm: Or, A Collection of the Most Remarkable Casualties and Disasters which Happen'd in the Late Dreadful Tempest, Both by Sea and Land* (London: Printed for G. Sawbridge, 1704), np.

69. Sampson Letsome was an obscure indexer who in 1753 published his compilation of all known sermons since the Restoration, over 13,000 entries along with listing scrip-

ture text, topic of sermon, and homiletical occasion. Thirty years later John Cooke updated Letsome's edition and included 24,000 entries in two volumes under the title *The Preacher's Assistant, (after the Manner of Mr. Letsome) containing a Series of Texts of Sermons and Discourses Published Either Singly, or in Volumes, By Divines of the Church of England, and by the Dissenting Clergy, since the Reformation to the Present Time, Specifying Also the Several Authors Alphabetically Arranged Under Text—With Size, Date, Occasion or Subject-Matter of Each Sermon or Discourse*, 2 vols. (Oxford: Printed for John Cooke at the Clarendon Press, 1783). A copy of Sampson Letsome's 1753 edition containing various *marginalia* additions and mss. notes is held by the Bodleian Library in the Gough collection. See also Francoise Deconinck-Brossard, "Eighteenth-Century Sermons and the Age," in W. M. Jacob and Nigel Yates, eds., *Crown and Mitre: Religion and Society in Northern Europe Since the Reformation* (Maidstone: Kent County Council, Arts, & Library, 1993), 105-21.

70. Nathaniel Dodge, *God's Voice in the Earthquake, or, a Serious Admonition to a Sinful World. A Sermon Preached in the Parish Church of Sheffield, on Sunday December 7, 1755* (York: Printed by Caesar Ward for the Author, 1756).

71. Thomas Sherlock, *A Letter from the Lord Bishop of London, to the Clergy and People of London and Westminster, on Occasion of the Late Earthquakes* (London: Printed for John Whiston, 1750).

72. Sherlock, *A Letter from the Bishop of London*, 3.

73. Representative of Sherlock's opponents were the Quaker, Joseph Besse, *Modest Remarks upon the Bishop of London's Letter Concerning the Late Earthquakes By One of the People Called Quakers* (London: Printed for T. Howard, 1750) and Richard Glover's anonymous pamphlet entitled *A Serious Expostulation with the Right Reverend the Lord Bishop of London on his Letter to the Clergy and People of London and Westminster* (London: np, 1750). Representative of those who supported Sherlock's view were Samuel Hull, *The Fluctuating Condition of Human Life, and the Absolute Necessity of a Preparation for the Eternal World, Consider'd, in a Sermon Occasioned by the Late Shocks of Earthquake, Preached at Lorriners Hall, March 11, 1750: Humbly Recommended to the Serious Perusal of the Inhabitants of London and Westminster* (London: Printed for J. Fuller, 1750) and William Stukeley, *The Philosophy of Earthquakes, Natural and Religious. Or An Inquiry into their Cause, and their Purpose* (London: Printed for C. Corbet, 1750).

74. Schechner, *Comets, Popular Culture, and the Birth of Modern Cosmology*, 111.

75. Thomas Burnet, *The Sacred Theory of the Earth: Containing an Account of the Original of the Earth, and of all the General Changes which it hath Already Undergone, or is to Undergo, till the Consummation of all Things with a Review of the Theory, and of its Proofs; especially in Reference to Scripture and The Author's Defence of the Work, from the Exceptions of Mr. Warren & An Ode to the Author Mr. Addison*, 2 vols., 4th ed. (London: Printed for John Hooke, 1719).

76. John Keill, *An Examination of Dr. Burnet's Theory of the Earth. Together with some Remarks on Mr. Whiston's New Theory of the Earth* (Oxford: Printed at the Theatre, 1698).

77. William Whiston, *A New Theory of the Earth, From its Original, to the Consummation of all Things. Wherein The Creation of the World in Six Days, The Universal Deluge, and the General Conflagration, as laid down in the Holy Scriptures, are shewn to be perfectly agreeable to Reason and Philosophy. With a large Introductory Discourse Concerning the Genuine Nature, Stile, and Exent of the Mosaick History of the Creation*, 5th ed. (London: Printed for John Whiston, 1737).

78. John Woodward, *An Essay Toward A Natural History of the Earth: and Terrestrial Bodies, Especially Minerals: As Also of the Sea, Rivers, and Springs. With an Ac-*

count of the Universal Deluge: And of the Effects that it had upon the Earth (London: Printed for Richard Wilkin, 1695).

79. Wesley, *Survey of the Wisdom of God in Creation*, 3: 328-40, where he provides a survey of modern astronomy. See also, John Wesley to the Editor of the *London Magazine*, 1 January 1765. *LJW* 4: 281-87.

80. John Wesley, *Serious Thoughts Occasioned by the Late Earthquake at Lisbon*, 2nd ed. (Bristol: E. Farley, 1755); John Wesley "The Great Assize," *BEW* 1: 355-75. See my chapter, "The Lisbon Earthquake: John and Charles Wesley Reconsidered," in Theodore E. D. Braun and John B. Radner, eds., *The Lisbon Earthquake of 1755: Representations and Reaction* (Oxford: Voltaire Foundation, 2005), 116-26.

81. Wesley, "The Great Assize," *BEW* 1: 357-58.

82. "Now, that God is himself the author, and sin the *moral* cause, of earthquakes, (whatever the natural cause may be) cannot be denied by any who believe the scriptures; for these are they which testify of him, that 'it is God who removeth the mountains, and overturneth them' in his anger; 'who shaketh the earth out of her place, and the pillars thereof tremble' (Job 9: 5)." Kenneth Newport, ed., *The Sermons of Charles Wesley*, 227.

83 Wesley, *Serious Thoughts*, 4-5. George Whitefield had stopped at Lisbon in 1739 on his way to America and recorded his anti-Catholic sentiments in regard to the Inquisition as well. See George Whitefield, *Whitefield at Lisbon. Being a Detailed Account of the Blasphemy and Idolatry of Popery, as Witnessed By the Late Servant of God, George Whitefield, at the City of Lisbon, During His Stay There. Printed Verbatim From His Account Sent to a Friend. Also, A Narrative of the Commencement and Continuation Of the Dreadful Earthquake that Totally Destroyed The Above City, with Sixty Thousand Inhabitants, A Few Months After Mr. Whitefield's Visit, on All-Saints Day, Being A Great Festival, and At a Time of High Mass Being Performed at All the Churches. Printed from an Account communicated by an English Merchant, residing at that time in Lisbon. With Mr. Whitefield's Remarks Thereon* (London: R. Groombridge & Sons, 1851), 13. For miracles occurring during and after the Lisbon Earthquake, Kendrick, *The Lisbon Earthquake*, 73-79.

84. Thomas Herring, *Letters from The Late Most Reverend Dr. Thomas Herring, Lord Archbishop of Canterbury, to William Duncombe, Esq., Deceased, from the Year 1728 to 1757. With Notes and an Appendix* (London: Printed for J. Johnson, 1777), 173-74.

85. Clark, "Providence, Predestination, and Progress," 559-89.

86. Wesley, *The Doctrine of Original Sin*, 96-97.

87. Wesley, *The Doctrine of Original Sin*, 99.

88. Charles Goodwin, "The Terrors of the Thunderstorm: Medieval Popular Cosmology and Methodist Revivalism," *Methodist History* 39 (2001): 101.

89. Wesley, *Serious Thoughts*, 21.

90. *DEB*, "Hopper, Christopher."

91. John Wesley to the Editor of the London Magazine, 1 January 1765. *LJW* 4: 284. "When a land is visited with famine or plague or earthquake, the people commonly see and acknowledge the hand of God." John Wesley to Thomas Rankin, 19 May 1775. *LJW* 6: 150-51.

92. "Moreover, the Lisbon earthquake and similar natural disasters cast doubt on the regularity and justice of God's general plan for the universe. The 'laws of nature' did not appear to embody an ordered and beneficent scheme of creation, but instead consisted of random physical forces established but not controlled by God." Nicholas Hudson, *Samuel Johnson and Eighteenth-Century Thought* (Oxford: Clarendon Press, 1988), 106.

93. Robin Briggs, *Witches & Neighbours: The Social and Cultural Context of European Witchcraft*, 2nd ed. (Oxford: Blackwell Publishers, 2002), 1.

94. "Christian theodicies have existed and will exist, but no theodicy that does not take the Devil fully into consideration is likely to be persuasive." Jeffrey Russell, *The Devil: Perceptions of Evil from Antiquity to Primitive Christianity* (Ithaca, NY: Cornell University Press, 1977), 228. Other volumes in Russell's history of the Devil are *Satan: The Early Christian Tradition* (Ithaca, NY: Cornell University Press, 1981), *Lucifer: The Devil in the Middle Ages* (Ithaca, NY: Cornell University Press, 1985), and *Mephistopheles: The Devil in the Modern World* (Ithaca, NY: Cornell University Press, 1990).

95. Recent approaches to the problem of evil that deal with evil in its ancient and modern context include Marilyn Adams, *Horrendous Evils and the Goodness of God* (Ithaca, NY: Cornell University Press, 1999); Marilyn Adams, *Christ and Horrors: The Coherence of Christology* (Cambridge: Cambridge University Press, 2006); Claudia Card, *The Atrocity Paradigm: A Theory of Evil* (New York: Oxford University Press, 2002); Drees, ed., *Is Nature Ever Evil? Religion, Science and Value*; Mary Midgley, *Wickedness: A Philosophical Essay* (1984; repr., London: Routledge Classics, 2001); Neiman, *Evil in Modern Thought*; and Maria Pia Lara, ed., *Rethinking Evil.*

96. Stuart Clark, *Thinking with Demons: The Idea of Witchcraft in Early Modern Europe* (Oxford: Oxford University Press, 1997), 10. On this point see also the essays in Stuart Clark, ed., *Languages of Witchcraft: Narrative, Ideology and Meaning in Early Modern Culture* (Houndmills and New York: Macmillian Press Ltd., and St. Martin's Press, 2001), Carlo Ginzburg, *The Night Battles: Witchcraft and Agrarian Cults in the Sixteenth and Seventeenth Centuries*, trans. John and Anne Tedeschi (Baltimore, MD: The John Hopkins University Press, 1983), and Armando Maggi, *Satan's Rhetoric: A Study of Renaissance Demonology* (Chicago: University of Chicago Press, 2001).

97. "They [rhetorics of disorder] were entailed by a metaphysical system with its own criteria of what was real." Stuart Clark, *Thinking with Demons*, 78. Also, "Love, for the witch, is a consuming passion, never love for one's neighbour. When she works for someone else, it is for some perverted purpose or for financial gain." Julio Baroja, *The World of the Witches*, trans. Nigel Glendinning (1964; repr., London: Phoenix Press, 2001), 24-34, and esp. 31 is instructive.

98. Clark, *Thinking With Demons*, 130-31.

99. Stuart Clark, "Inversion, Misrule and the Meaning of Witchcraft," *Past & Present* 87 (1980): 118-19.

100. See Philip C. Almond, ed., *Demonic Possession and Exorcism in Early Modern England: Contemporary Texts and their Cultural Contexts* (Cambridge: Cambridge University Press, 2004) and Nathan Johnston, *The Devil and Demonism in Early Modern England* (Cambridge: Cambridge University Press, 2006).

101. Keith Thomas, *Religion and The Decline of Magic: Studies in Popular Beliefs in Sixteenth and Seventeenth Century England* (1971; repr., London: Weidenfeld & Nicolson, 1997), 449.

102. There is some debate as to how influential the *Malleus Maleficarum* actually was in the modern world. On the one hand, James Sharpe, *Instruments of Darkness: Witchcraft in Early Modern England* (Philadelphia, PA: University of Pennsylvania Press, 1997), 21, labels it as one of the "key tracts in the witch-hunting canon." Edward Peters, "The Medieval Church and State on Superstition, Magic and Witchcraft: From Augustine to the Sixteenth Century," in Bengt Ankarloo and Stuart Clark, eds., *Witchcraft and Magic in Europe: The Middle Ages* (London: The Athlone Press, 2002), 239, agrees classifying it as "the most important of all demonological treatises." See also Heiko Oberman, *Masters of the Reformaiton: The Emergence of a New Intellectual Climate in Europe*, trans. Dennis Martin (Cambridge: Cambridge University Press, 1981), 167. On the other hand, Clark, *Thinking With Demons*, 81, denies it paradigm status for "archetypal demonology." See also Stuart Clark, "Witchcraft and Magic in Early Modern

Culture" in Bengt Ankarloo and Stuart Clark, eds., *Witchcraft and Magic in Europe: The Period of the Witch Trials* (London: The Athlone Press, 2002), 97-169, esp. 121 and Erik Midelfort, *Witch Hunting in Soutwestern Germany 1562-1684: The Social and Intellectual Foundations* (Stanford: Stanford University Press, 1972), 22: "The *Malleus Maleficarum* failed to become generally accepted doctrine, and its influence and authority have vastly been exaggerated by most scholars."

103. Jacobus Sprenger and Heinrich Kramer, *Malleus Maleficarum*, 2.1.a. For more about demonology and sexuality consult Lyndal Roper, *Oedipus & The Devil: Witchcraft, Sexuality and Religion in Early Modern Europe* (1994; repr., London: Routledge, 2003); Lyndal Roper, *Witch Craze: Terror and Fantasy in Baroque Germany* (New Haven: Yale University Press, 2004), 82-103 and Walter Stephens, *Demon Lovers: Witchcraft, Sex, and the Crisis of Belief* (Chicago: University of Chicago Press, 2002).

104. Sprenger and Kramer, *Malleus Maleficarum*, 1. 6.

105. See Kathryn A. Edwards, ed., *Werewolves, Witches, and Wandering Spirits: Traditional Belief & Folklore in Early Modern Europe* (Kirksville, MO: Truman State University Press, 2002); Alan Macfarlane, *Witchcraft in Tudor and Stuart England: A Regional and Comparative Study*, 2nd ed. (London: Routledge, 1999), 23-65, 147-207; Marion Gibson, *Reading Witchcraft: Stories of English Witches* (London: Routledge, 1999), 50-77; Marion Gibson, *Early Modern Witches: Witchcraft Cases in Contemporary Writing* (London: Routledge, 2000).

106. *I. JAC. I. C. 12.*

107. "Witchcraft is itself a reification, an imposed category whose boundaries are anything but clear." Robin Briggs, "'Many Reasons Why': Witchcraft and the Problem of Multiple Explanation," in Jonathan Barry, Marianne Hester, and Gareth Roberts, eds., *Witchcraft in Early Modern Europe: Studies in Culture and Belief* (Cambridge: Cambridge University Press, 1996), 53.

108. Bostridge, *Witchcraft and its Transformations*, 38-52, 85-154.

109. "The notion that the universe was subject to immutable natural laws killed the concept of miracles, weakened the belief in the physical efficacy of prayer, and diminished faith in the possibility of direct divine inspiration." Thomas, *Religion and the Decline of Magic*, 643.

110. Johann Weyer, *Witches, Devils, and Doctors in the Renaissance: Johann Weyer, De Praestigiis Daemonum* (1563; Binghampton: Medieval & Renaissance Texts & Studies, 1991); Reginald Scott, *The Discouerie of witchcraft, Wherein the lewde dealing of witches and witchmongers is notablie detected, the knauerie of coniurors, the impietie of inchantors, the follie of soothsayers, the impudent falsehood of cousenors, the infidelitie of atheists, the pestilent practises of Pythonists, the curiositie of figurecasters, the vanitie of dreamers, the geggerlie art of Alcumysterie, The abhomination of idolatrie, the horrible art of poisoning, the virtue and power of naturall magike, and all the conueiances of Legierdemaine and iuggling are deciphered: and many other things opened, which haue long lien hidden, howbeit verie necessarie to be knowne. Heerevnto is added a not be doubted of; who instead of learning and wtretatise upon the nature and substance of spirits and diuels, &c* (1584; London: Elliott Stock, 1886). The influence of Weyer and Scott can be seen in that King James VI and I in his *Daemonologie in the Form of a Dialogue Divided into Three Books* (Edinburgh: Robert Waldegrave, 1597) mentioned Weyer and Scott as the reason for his apologetical defense of belief in demons.

111. Scott, *Discoverie of Witchcraft*, 1.

112. Balthasar Bekker, *De Betoverde Weereld, Zynde een Grondig Ondersoek Van't Gemeen Gevoelen Aangaande de Geesten, DerselverAart en Vermogen, Bewind en Dedryf: als Ook't Genede Menschen Door Derselver Kraght Gemeenschap Doen* (Deventer: Heronauta, 1691). See also, Israel, *Radical Enlightenment*, 377-405.

113. Balthasar Bekker, *The World turn'd upside down: or , a Plain Detection of Errors, in the Common Or Vulgar Belief, Relating to Spirits, Spectres or Ghosts, Daemons, Witches &c. In a Due and Serious Examination of their Nature, Power, Administration, and Operation. In What Forms or Shape Incorporeal Spirits Appear to Men, by what Means, and of what Elements they take to Themselves, and form Appearances of Bodies, visible to mortal Eyes; why They appear, and what Frights and Force of Imagination often delude us into The Apprehensions of supposed Phantasms, through the Intimidation of the Mind, &c. ALSO What evil Tongues have Power to produce of Hurt to Mankind, or Irational Creatures; and the Effects Men and Women are able to Produce by their Communication with Good or Evil Spirits, &c.* (London: Printed for Elizabeth Harris, 1700), 3.

114. On the old view, see W. E. H. Lecky, *History of the Rise and Influence of the Spirit of Rationalism in Europe*, 2 vols., 2nd ed. (London: Longmans, Green, and Company, 1904), 1: 1-205; Thomas, *Religion and the Decline of Magic*, 452; and Bostridge, *Witchcraft and its Transformations*. On the new, see Owen Davies, *Witchcraft, Magic, and Culture 1736-1951* (Manchester: Manchester University Press, 1999) and H. C. Erik Midelfort, *Exorcism and Enlightenment: Johann Joseph Gassner and the Demons of Eighteenth-Century Germany* (New Haven: Yale University Press, 2005).

115. Bostridge, *Witchcraft and its Transformations*, 233, who in the end classifies his work as "a history of the disavowal of witchcraft theory." Nevertheless, Bostridge cannot escape the historical fact that well into the eighteenth century people in England, Germany and France continued to be attracted to the ideas of the supernatural, witchcraft theory, and exorcism. See Sarah Ferber, *Demonic Possession and Exorcism in Early Modern France* (London: Routledge Taylor & Francis Group, 2004); Roper, *Witch Craze*; and Chadwick Hansen, *Witchcraft at Salem* (New York: George Braziller, 1969).

116. A fascinating study in this regard is Ronald Hutton's *The Triumph of the Moon: A History of Modern Pagan Witchcraft* (Oxford: Oxford University Press, 1999).

117. Keith Hutchison, "What Happened to Occult Qualities in the Scientific Revolution?" *Isis* 73 (1982): 233-53 and Ron Millen, "The Manifestation of Occult Qualities in the Scientific Revolution," in M. J. Osler and P. L. Farber, eds. *Religion, Science, and Worldview: Essays in Honour of Richard Westfall* (Cambridge: Cambridge University Press, 1985), 185-216.

118. Glanvill, *Saducimus Triumphatus*. Bostridge, *Witchcraft and Its Transformations*, 73-77.

119. Glanvill, *Saducimus Triumphatus*, 1: 86-87.

120. Joseph Glanvill, *Scepsis Scientifica: or, Confest Ignorance, the Way to Science; in an Essay of the Vanity of Dogmatizing, and Confident Opinion* (London: Printed for Henry Eversden, 1665).

121. Moody Prior, "Joseph Glanvill, Witchcraft, and Seventeenth-Century Science," *Modern Philology* 30 (1933): 184. See also Burns, *An Age of Wonders*, 68-80.

122. Davies, *Witchcraft, Magic and Culture 1736-1951*, 8.

123. Thomas Hankins, *Science and the Enlightenment* (Cambridge: Cambridge University Press, 1985), 1-16. See also the essays in William Clark, Jan Golinski, and Simon Schaffer, eds., *The Sciences in Enlightened Europe* (Chicago: University of Chicago Press, 1999).

124. Jonathan Swift, *The Story of the St. Alb-ns Ghost, or the Apparition of Mother Haggy* (London: np, 1712), 3. See, Malcolm Gaskill, *Crime and Mentalities in Early Modern England* (Cambridge: Cambridge University Press, 2000), 87.

125. Thomas Jolley, *The Surey Demoniack: or, an Account of Satan's Strange and Dreadful Actings in and about the Body of Richard Dugdale of Surey, near Whalley in Lancashire: And how he was Dispossest By Gods Blessing on the Fastings and Prayers*

of Divers Ministers and People. The Matter of Fact Attested by the Oaths of Several Credible Persons, Before Some of His Majesties Justices of the Peace in the Said County. (London: Printed for Jonathan Robinson, 1697); Thomas Jolley, *A Vindication of the Surey Demoniack as no Imposter: or, A REPLY to a certain PAMPHLET published by Mr. Zach Taylor, called The Surey Imposter. With a further clearing and confirming of the Truth as to Richard Dugdale's Case and Cure* (London: Printed for Nevill Simmons, 1698).

126. See Michael Snape, "'The Surey Imposter': Demonic Possession and Religious Conflict in Seventeenth-Century Lancashire," *Transactions of the Lancashire and Cheshire Antiquarian Society*, 90 (1994): 93-114.

127. Baxter, *The Certainty of the World of Spirits*, 38.

128. Francis Hutchinson, *A Historical Essay Concerning Witchcraft. With Observations Upon Matters of Fact; Tending to Clear the Texts of the Sacred Scriptures, and Confute the Vulgar Errors About That Point. And Also Two Sermons: One in Proof of the Christian Religion; The Other Concerning the Good and Evil Angels* (London: Printed for R. Knaplock and D. Midwinter, 1718).

129. "Our present Freedom from these Evils are no Security, that such a Time may not turn up in one Revolution or another." Hutchinson, *A Historical Essay Concerning Witchcraft*, 182: See Bostridge, *Witchcraft and its Transformations*, 143-54.

130. Arthur Lovejoy, *The Chain of Being: A Study of the History of An Idea* (1936; repr., Cambridge, MA: Harvard University Press, 1964), 183. For a contemporary treatment of this theme, see Donald R. Kelley, *The Descent of Ideas: The History of Intellectual History* (Aldershot: Ashgate Publishing Ltd., 2002).

131. Locke, *Essay Concerning Human Understanding*, 3.6.12.

132. Whiston, *An Account of the Daemoniacks*, 49.

133. E. J. Clery, *The Rise of Supernatural Fiction 1762-1800* (1995; repr. Cambridge: Cambridge University Press, 1996), 9.

134. Oliver Goldsmith, *The Mystery Revealed; Containing a Series of Transactions and Authentic Testimonials, Respecting the Supposed Cock-Lane Ghost; Which have hitherto been Concealed from the Public* (London: Printed for W. Bristow, 1762). James Boswell, *The Life of Samuel Johnson* (1793; repr., London: Everyman's Library, 1992), 256. See, Douglas Grant, *The Cock Lane Ghost* (London: Macmillan, 1965); Paul Chambers, *The Cock Lane Ghost: Murder, Sex & Haunting in Dr Johnson's London* (Phoenix Mill: Sutton Publishing Ltd., 2006); and Clery, *The Rise of Supernatural Fiction*, 13-32. See also, Sasha Handley's, *Ghost Narratives in Modern British Culture* (Ph. D. thesis, University of Birmingham, 2004), 218-69 and *Visions of an Unseen World: Ghosts Beliefs and Ghost Stories in Eighteenth-Century England* (London: Pickering & Chatto, 2007), 141-53.

135. Matthew 8. 28-34; Mark 5. 1-20; Luke 8. 26-39.

136. Theophilus Lindsey, *Sermons, with Appropriate Prayers Annexed.* 2 vols. (London: Joseph Johnson & Co., 1810), 1: 487.

137. Thomas Chubb, *A Discourse on Miracles Considered as Evidence to Prove the Divine Original of Revelation wherein is Shewn, what Kind and Degree of Evidence arises from them, and in which the Various Reasons on Those Questions that Relate to the Subject are Fairly Represented* (London: Printed for T. Cox, 1741).

138. Anonymous, *Gentleman's Magazine* 8 (1738): 70.

139. John Fell, *Daemonics. An Enquiry into the Heathen and the Scripture Doctrine of Daemons. In Which the Hypothesis of the Rev. Mr. Farmer, and Others on this Subject, are Particularly Considered* (London: Printed for Charles Dilly, 1779), 233. See also, Hugh Farmer, *An Essay on Daemonics in the New Testament* (London: Printed for G. Robinson, 1775). Also in the debate over the Gadarene demoniac was Nathaniel Lard-

ner, *The Case of Demoniacs Mentioned in the New Testament: Four Discourses upon Mark v. 19. With an Appendix for Farther Illustrating the Subje*ct (London: Printed for C. Henderson, 1758); William Worthington, *An Farther Enquiry into the Case of the Gospel Demoniacks. Occasioned by Mr. Farmer's Letters on the Subject* (London: Printed for J. F. and C. Rivington, T. Payne and Son, B. White, and H. Payne, 1779), and Bishop William Warburton, "Sermon x: The Fall of Satan" in *The Works of William Warburton*, 6 vols. (London: Printed by John Nichols, 1788), 5: 415-35.

140. Philip Doddridge in his commentary on the passage listed, in addition to Fell's work, nine other works of recommended reading on the topic. See Philip Dodderidge, The *Works of the Rev. Philip Doddridge*. Eds., Job Orton and Edward Williams, 10 vols. (Leeds: np, 1802-05), 5: 360-63. "Thus well over a hundred years after the Witchcraft Act of 1736 people still continued to expect official succour against the malicious power of the witch." Davies, *Witchcraft, Magic, and Culture*, 80.

141. *The Wesleyan Army At War With The Devil*. Bodleian Library, Ballads Catalogue: Harding B 20 (186).

142. Bostridge, *Witchcrafts and its Transformations*, 158. The problem with Bostridge using the term "fundamentalism" to describe Wesley is that the appellation is a twentieth-century term that has taken on pejorative connations in the twenty-first century. Additionally, Bostridge seems to be unaware of the ways that John Wesley does not fit into either the twentieth or twenty-first century characterizations of biblical fundamentalism.

143. Kent, *Wesley and the Wesleyans*, 187-207.

144. Susanna Wesley to Samuel Wesley, junior, 12 January 1717. MARC, DDCW 8/15, 8. For a discussion of Ghosts in eighteenth-century Methodism, see Sasha Handley, "Reclaiming Ghosts in 1690s England." In Kate Cooper and Jeremy Gregory, eds., *Signs, Wonders, Miracles: Representations of Divine Power in the Life of the Church* (Woodbridge: Boydell Press, 2005), 345-55.

145. The original letters are extinct but were transcribed by Charles Wesley in a notebook and are now held in MARC, DDCW 8/15, 8-43.

146. Joseph Priestley, *Original Letters of Rev'd John Wesley and His Friends, Illustrative of His Early History, with Other Curious Papers Communicated by The Late Rev. S. Badcock. To Which is Prefixed, an Address to the Methodists* (Birmingham: Printed for Thomas Pearson, 1791), 117-48; Adam Clarke, *Memoirs of the Wesley Family; Collected Principally from Original Documents* (London: Printed by J. & T. Clarke, 1823), 161-200. John Wesley also included sections about the Epworth poltergeist in the Arminian Magazine 7(1784): 548-50, 606-08, 654-56. According to Adam Clarke, *Memoirs of the Wesley Family*, 195, most biographers of John Wesley were unaware of the fact that after 1726, Old Jeffrey "continued to molest some branches of the family for *many years* after." Emily Wesley was credited with naming the spirit "Old Jeffrey" and in 1750 was still writing letters to her brother John concerning the supernatural disturbances. See Mrs. Emilia Harper to John Wesley, 16 Febuary, 1750. *BEW* 26: 449.

147. Susanna Wesley, junior, to Samuel Wesley, junior, 24 January 1717. MARC, DDCW 8/15, 15-16. For other apparitions concerning King William III see the anonymous tract entitled *A True and Impartial Relation of a Wonderful Apparition that Happen'd in the Royal Camp in Flanders, The Beginning of this Instant September 1692. Concerning King William. In a Letter to a Gentleman in London, from his Friend, a Captain in the King's Camp* (London: Printed for Randall Taylor, 1692).

148. Anne Wesley to John Wesley, 10 September 1726. MARC, DDCW 8/15, 37

149. Emily Wesley to Samuel Wesley, Junior, nd [1717]. MARC, DDCW 8/15, 17.

150. See Appendix 1: "John Wesley's Summing Up the Matter of Old Jeffrey, 1726."

151. Robert Southey, The *Life of Wesley and the Rise and Progress of Methodism*, 2 vols. (London: Oxford University Press, 1925), 1:19.

152. "I designed to go thither the first opportunity, and see if it be true; which I shall hardly believe till I am an eye-or ear-witness of it." John Wesley to Susanna Wesley, 18 December 1724. *BEW* 25: 156.

153. Frank Baker, "Introduction: Wesley as Seen in his Letters," in *BEW* 25: 5.

154. Owen Davies, "Methodism, the Clergy, and the Popular Belief in Witchcraft and Magic," *History* 82 (1997): 264.

155. See my article, "'Those Distracting Terrors of the Enemy': John Wesley's Rhetoric of Evil," *Bulletin of the John Rylands University Library of Manchester* 85 (2003): 373-85.

156. Porter, *Enlightenment: Britain and the Creation of the Modern World*, 128.

157. John Rule, "Methodism, Popular Beliefs and Village Culture in Cornwall, 1800-50," in Robert Storch, ed., *Popular Culture and Custom in Nineteenth-Century England* (London: Croom Helm, 1982), 63.

158. M. J. Naylor, *The Inanity and Mischief of Vulgar Supersitions. Four Sermons Preached at All-Saint's Church, Huntingdon, On the 25th Day of March, in the Years 1792, 1793, 1794, 1795* (Cambridge: Printed for B. Flower, 1795), preached four sermons against fanaticism, which he meant Methodism, at the end of the eighteenth century. See also, Arthur Bedford, *The Doctrine of Assurance: OR, The Case of a Weak and Doubting Conscience. A Sermon Preached at St. Lawrence Jewry, in the City of London on Sunday, August 13, 1738 with an Appendix, answering the Objections From the Texts of Scripture* (London: Charles Ackers, 1738).

159. Lavington, *The Enthusiasm of Methodists and Papists Compar'd*, 1: 333.

160. William Warburton, *The Doctrine of Grace: or, The Office and Operations of the Holy Spirit Vindicated From The Insults of Infidelity, and The Abuses of Fanaticism: with Some Thoughts (humbly offered to the consideration of the Established Clergy) Regarding The Right Method Defending Religion Against The Attacks of Either Party. In Three Books*, 3rd ed. (London: Printed for A. Millar & T. and R. Ronson, 1763), 87.

161. See Figure 2. William Hogarth, "Credulity, Superstition, and Fanaticism."

162. See Figure 3. An Enlargement of the Globe in Hogarth's "Credulity, Superstition, and Fanaticism."

163. Castle, *The Female Thermometer*, 28-29.

164. John Wesley, "Of Good Angels" and "Of Evil Angels," *BEW*, 3: 3-15 and 16-29 respectively. See also, *Arminian Magazine* 6 (1783): 12-13. Wesley's early sermon "Guardian Angels," *BEW*, 4: 225-35, addressed the topic as well.

165. See Barry Bryant, "John Wesley on the Origins of Evil," *Wesleyan Theological Journal* 29 (1994): 120-24.

166. Wesley, "Of Evil Angels," *BEW* 3: 20.

167. Wesley, "Of Evil Angels," *BEW* 3: 23.

168. Wesley, "Of Evil Angels," *BEW* 3: 21-22.

169. Wesley, ed., "An Account of Mr. J. V. [John Valton]," *Arminian Magazine* 6 (1782): 517.

170. Wesley, "Of Evil Angels," *BEW* 3: 21. Compare, Lindsey, *Sermons*, 2: 100-01, who interpreted the temptations story as a vision of Jesus.

171. "They [demons] persuade them [men], however, in marvellous and unseen ways, entering by means of that subtlety of their own bodies into the bodies of men who are unaware, and through certain imaginary visions mingling themselves with men's thoughts, whether they are awake or asleep." Augustine, "The Divination of Demons," in Ruth Wenworth Brown, trans. and Roy Deferrari, ed., *The Fathers of the Church: A New Translation*, 110 vols. (New York: Fathers of the Church, 1955), 27: 430. Also, Bishop

George Bull, *Some Important Points of Primitive Christianity Maintained and Defended; in Several Sermons and Other Discourses* (London: Printed by W. B., 1713), 2: 456, who claimed that demons had possessed people with *"tenatio horrenda, the Temptation of blasphemous Thoughts,* abhorr'd by the Person who is continually molested with them."

172. Wesley, ed., *Arminian Magazine* 4 (1781): 257-58.

173. Wesley, "Of Evil Angels," *BEW* 3: 23.

174. Wesley, "Of Evil Angels," *BEW* 3: 24.

175. Wesley, "Of Evil Angels," *BEW* 3: 24.

176. Jean Le Rond D'Alembert and Denis Diderot, *Encyclopédie*, 13: 162. See Roy Porter, "Witchcraft and Magic in Enlightenment, Romantic and Liberal Thought," in Ankarloo and Clark, eds., *Witchcraft and Magic in Europe: The Eighteenth and Nineteenth Centuries*, 224.

177. Bruce Edward Rose, *The Influence of Genre in John Wesley's Journal* (Ph.D. thesis, University of North Carolina at Chapel Hill, 1999).

178. W. R. Ward, "Introduction," *BEW* 18: 49-50. "He [John Wesley] evidently saw these as in part an answer to contemporary skepticism and deism—hence one reason for belief in witchcraft." Rack, "Doctors, Demons and Early Methodist Healing," 145.

179. 27 May 1768. *BEW* 22: 135.

180. 27 May 1768. *BEW* 22: 135.

181. 27 May 1768. *BEW* 22: 135-45. A decade later John Wesley and Samuel Johnson discussed the affair but Johnson remained sceptical. See James Boswell, *The Life of Samuel Johnson* (1791; repr., London: Everyman's Library, 1992), 837. "I know those who fashionably deny the existence of spirits are hugely disgusted at accounts of this kind. I know that they incessantly labour to spread this disgust among those that are of a better mind; because if one of these accounts be admitted, their whole system falls to the ground . . . Indeed I never myself saw the appearance of an unbodied spirit; and I never saw the commission of a murder. Yet, upon the testimony of unexceptionable witnesses, I can firmly believe both one and the other." John Wesley, "An Answer to a Report," *JWJW*, 11: 503, where Wesley discounted on 12 September 1782 a Quaker who questioned the authenticity of Hobson's account. In his rebuttal Wesley again affirmed the power of testimony.

182. 5 December 1738." *BEW* 19: 23. Contrary to Mack, *Heart Religion in the British Enlightenment*, 266-67 and Wesley's own disavowal to Warburton, these stories read like exorcism narratives. Mack incorrectly sites Wesley letter to Warburton. It is found in *LJW* 4: 435, not 6: 435.

183. 25 October 1739 (London Diaries 2). *BEW* 19: 413.

184. 25 October 1739. *BEW* 19: 110-11.

185. Baroja, *The World of the Witches*, 131-32, has noted this disappearance of personality as one of the fundamental characteristics of possession.

186. For an interesting discussion of the Devil and demoniac in English drama during the medieval and renaissance periods of intellectual history see John D. Cox, *The Devil and the Sacred in English Drama, 1350-1642* (Cambridge: Cambridge University Press, 2000).

187. Stephen Conner, *Dumbstruck: A Cultural History of Ventriloquism* (Oxford: Oxford University Press, 2000), 111.

188. Frederick Dreyer, "Faith and Experience in the Thought of John Wesley," *The American Historical Review* 88 (1983): 15. See also Bernard Holland, "'A Species of Madness': The Effect of John Wesley's Preaching," *Proceedings of the Wesley Historical Society* 39 (1973): 77-85.

189. Edwards, *The Distinguishing Marks of the Work of the Spirit*, 91. Edwards, *Some Thoughts Concerning the Present Revival in New England*, 18.

190. John Wesley published the story of the Yatton Demoniac in the *Arminian Magazine* in five segments. See *Ariminan Magazine* 12 (1789): 155-59, 205-10, 264-69, 324-27, and 373-75.

191. Joseph Easterbrook, *An Appeal to the Public Respecting George Lukins (Called the Yatton Demoniac,) Containing an Account of His Affliction and Deliverance; Together with A Variety of Circumstances which Tend to Exculpate him from the Charge of Imposture* (Bristol: Printed for T. Mills, 1788), 16.

192. I have been unable to locate a copy of the *Bristol Gazette* for the year 1788 but the article was reprinted in the *Bath Chronicle* 27 (July 17, 1788): 2.

193. Samuel Norman, *Authentic Anecdotes of George Lukins, The Yatton Demoniac; with a View of the Controversy, and a Full Refutation of the Imposture* (Bristol: Printed by G. Routh, 1788). See also the anonymous article that criticized both Lukins for being an imposter and Wesley for supporting his fraud, in *European Magazine*, 15 (1789): 42.

194. Middleton, *A Free Inquiry*, 92.

195. John Cennick, "An Account of the Most Remarkable Occurrences in the Awakenings at Bristol and Kingswood till the Brethern's Labours Began There in 1746: Written by John Cennick in April, 1750, for the Archives of Bristol and Kingswood," *Proceedings of the Wesley Historical Society* 6 (1907): 110.

196. See Nischan Bodo, "The Exorcism Controversy and Baptism in the Late Reformation," in Nichan Bodo, ed., *Lutherans and Calvinists in the Age of Confessionalism* (Aldershot: Ashgate, 1999), 31-51; Franz Dölger, *Der Exorzimus im Altchristlichen Taufritual* (Paderborn: n. p., 1909); E. E. Evans-Pritchard, *Witchcraft, Oracles, and Magic among the Azande* (1937; Oxford: Clarendon Press, 1976); Horst Figge, "Exorzismus," *Religion in Geschichte und Gegenwart* 2: 790-95; Balthasar Fischer, "Baptismal Exorcism in the Catholic Baptismal Rites after Vatican II," *Studia Liturgica* 10 (1974): 48-55; Felicitas Goodman, *How About Demons?* (Bloomington, IN: Indiana University Press, 1988); Elizabeth Leeper, "From Alexander to Rome: The Valentinian Connection to the Incorporation of Exorcism as a Prebaptismal Rite," *Vigiliae Christianae* 44 (1990): 6-24; Elizabeth Leeper, "The Role of Exorcism in Early Christianity," *Studia Patristica* 26 (1993): 59-62; and D. P. Walker, *Unclean Spirits: Possession and Exorcism in France and England in the Late Sixteenth and Early Seventeenth Centuries* (London: Scholar Press, 1981).

197. Gerald Bray, ed., *The Anglican Canons 1529-1947* (Woodbridge: Boydell Press, 1998), 363-64. See also, E. Caparros, M. Thériault, J. Thorn, eds., *Code of Canon Law Annotated* (Montreal: Wilson and LaFleur, 1993), 736, for the regulations of the Roman Catholic rite of Exorcism.

198. It was also the case that this Canon Law had become relaxed at this time. See, William Lyndwood, *Constitutiones Provinciales*, L, 3.24.2.

199. Wesley, "Of Evil Angels," *BEW* 3: 26.

200. Wesley, "Of Evil Angels," *BEW* 3: 23, n. 54. See also, Henry D. Rack, "Between Church and Sect: The Origins of Methodism in Manchester," *Bulletin of the John Rylands University Library of Manchester* 80 (1998): 68; Rack, *Reasonable Enthusiast*, 90-93.

201. Joseph Bingham, *Origines Ecclesiasticae: Or, The Antiquities of the Christian Church. In Twenty Book in The Works of the Learned Joseph Bingham, M. A. Later Rector of Havant, and Sometime Fellow of University-College in Oxford*, 2nd ed., 2 vols. (London: Printed for Robert Knaplock, 1726), 1: 112-14; William Cave, *Primitive Christianity: Or, The Religion of the Ancient Christians in the First Ages Of the Gospel. In Three Parts*, 3 vols. (London: Printed for Richard Chiswell, 1673), 1: 63-64. Thomas Deacon, *A Full, True, and Comprehensive View of Christianity: Containing a Short Historical Account of Religion from the Creation of the World to the Fourth Century After*

our Lord Jesus Christ. As also the Complete Duty of a Christian in Relation to Faith, Practice, Worship, and Rituals, set forth Sincerely, without Regard to any Modern Church, Sect, or Party, as it is taught in the Holy Scriptures, was delivered by the Apostles, and received by the Universal Church of Christ during the Four First Centuries. The Whole Succinctly and Fully Laid Down in Two Catechisms, A Shorter and a Longer, each Divided Into Two Parts; Whereof the one Comprehends the Sacred History, the other The Christian Doctrine. The Shorter Catechism being suited to the meanest Capacity, and calculated for the Use of Children; And the Longer for that of The More Knowing Christian to which is Prefixed A Discourse upon the Design of these Catechisms, and upon the Best Method of Instructing Youth In them* (London: Printed for S. Newton, 1747), 70.

202. George Bull, *Some Important Points of Primitive Christianity* (London: np, 1713), 2: 435-77.

203. This reading finds support also in Eamon Duffy's remark that Wesley was the sea in which the non-juror river finally rested. See, Eamon Duffy, "Primitive Christianity Revived: Religious Renewal in Augustan England," in Derek Baker, ed., *Renaissance and Renewal in Church History* (Oxford: Basil Blackwell, 1977), 299-300. See Robert Cornwall, *Visible and Apostolic: The Constitution of the Church in High Church Anglican and non-Juror* [sic] *Thought* (Newark: University of Delaware Press, 1993); idem., "The Search for the Primitive Church: The Use of the Early Church Fathers in High Anglican Church Tradition 1680-1745," *Anglican and Episcopal History* 59 (1990): 303-29.

204. For an argument that works of piety and mercy should never be bifurcated in Wesley's thinking, see Joerg Rieger's "Between God and the Poor: Rethinking the Means of Grace in the Wesleyan Tradition," in Richard P. Heitzenrater, ed. *The Poor and the People Called Methodists 1729-1999* (Nashville: Kingswood Books, 2002), 83-99.

205. 23 October 1739. *BEW* 19: 109. The hymn comes from *Hymns and Sacred Poems* (London: Printed for William Strahan, 1739), 222.

206. Another method used by the Methodists was prayer and fasting. See, for example, John Wesley, ed., "An Extract from the Journal of Mr. G. C.," *Arminian Magazine* 6 (1783): 352.

Chapter 4

Seeing Salvation: Dreams, Visions, and Perfection in the Thought of John Wesley

> If bodies have a language by which they can convey their thoughts to each other, though sometimes at a distance, have spirit no language, think you, by which they can converse with our spirits and, by impressions on the mind, speak to us as easily as before they did by the tongue?[1]

> I found a lovely congregation at Stockport, much alive to God. So was that at Oldham the next day, which was not perceptibly lessened, though it blew a storm and poured down with rain. Here a young woman of unblameable character (otherwise I should not have given her any credit) gave me a remarkable account. She said, "I had totally lost the sight of my right eye, when I dreamed one night that our Saviour appeared to me, that I fell at his feet, and he laid his hand upon my right eye. Immediately I waked and, from that moment, have seen as well with that eye as with the other."[2]

Mary Bosanquet (1744-1812), a female Methodist leader in Madeley, wrote in her autobiography of a dream that guided her in a unique manner.[3] In her dream an unidentified man came and offered her a tithe offering.[4] After refusing the monetary gift, Bosanquet informed her family that she felt compelled to travel to a place "that she knew not where, nor even to what country."[5] Walking on a few steps Bosanquet was transferred in her dream to a church where she was commanded to enter. Upon setting foot into the church, she encountered a woman who announced that this was the place where God intended her to reside. After some discussion, she entered into another room to reflect on her circumstance, when a coach driver came to the house inquiring if she needed assistance in travelling to a destination. Bosanquet related the incident which she interpreted in providential terms:

> Seeing a coach ready to be hired, I beckoned to it. The man opened the door. As I was stepping in, he said, "Where will you be carried to?" I strove to say, "Cross-hall in Yorkshire," but could not. Then I strove to name various habitations I had formerly lived in, but could remember the name of none. As he still persevered in his question, God had taken the remembrance of every other out of my heart.[6]

Dreams, Visions, and the Condition of the Soul

Dreams and visions have a long and complicated history in western and eastern cultures. What can be acknowledged is that, at least from early antiquity, men and women have been fascinated with the experience of dreams and their significance has been debated and chronicled throughout civilization.[7] Many in the ancient period wrote about dreams but it was Artemidorus (2nd century A.D.) who first catalogued dreams in the ancient world.[8] The early church, however, showed caution when it considered dreams and their place in the early Christian world. Justin the Apologist (100-65), for example, inveighed against those who gave credence to "dream-senders."[9] Tertullian (160-225), too, in his *A Treatise on the Soul*, voiced concern about the validity of dreams. "We declare, then," wrote Tertullian, "that dreams are inflicted on us mainly by demons, although they sometimes turn out true and favourable to us."[10] W. H. C. Frend, the historian of early Christianity, maintained that the early church's thoughts about dreams were linked to their ideas about the demonic invasion of human consciousness.[11] As a result, during early Christianity there was a suspicion of dreams and the dominant trend of the era was to view them with caution.

It fell to the medieval mind, however, for a more positive assessment of visionary experiences.[12] Mainly because of the influential Macrobius (395-423) and his commentary on a passage in Cicero's (106-43) *De Republica*, a renewed interest in dreams emerged during the twelfth century.[13] Whereas classical culture had conceptualized dreams within natural categories and the early Christian community had portrayed their perils, the medieval world presented a major heuristic shift in dream theory and asserted that dreams might be analyzed both for their immanent and transcendental qualities. Steven Kruger has demonstrated that the merging of these aspects in medieval dream theory occurred, for the most part, because dreams were codified within a psychosomatic framework in the medical discourses of the era. In such a view, Kruger writes "the most important consequence of the new somatic treatment of dreaming is in the ways it enables a bringing together of different kinds of dream—internally and externally motivated, celestial and mundane, angelic, demonic, and human—on the common ground of one unitary dream process involving certain universal psychosomatic elements."[14] In the medieval mind, crisscrossing of categories validated these dual elements of human experience and implied a dialogic character for dreams.

From the Renaissance to the Enlightenment, conflict persisted over the place of dreams in the human imagination. There continued, however, to be an impressive body of literature that opted for a view of visionary experiences which went beyond the notion of psychobiology, which at one level, indicated that dreams served an important role in hammering out the concept of the mind among a variety of social and religious figures in the seventeenth and eighteenth centuries.

More germane for the issues that I will raise in this chapter, the discussions and debates about visionary experiences caused numerous questions to emerge about human nature and at what level, if any, that the human psyche intersected with transcendental categories. René Descartes (1596-1650), the French philosopher and mathematician, for example, wrote and recorded his own reflections on dreams and noted their revelatory character when he claimed a non-human agency for their origin.[15] John Bunyan (1628-88), a dissenting preacher and writer, wrote his famous *Pilgrim's Progress in the Similitude of a Dream*, from his prison cell in Bedford and, as his subtitle indicated, set the journey of his hero within the context of a dream.[16] Notwithstanding, John Locke had noted in his *Essay* that dreams were "little conformable to the Perfection of and Order of a rational Being."[17] Francois-Marie Arouet, more commonly known as Voltaire (1694-1778), followed suit in his *Philosophical Dictionary* when he glibly remarked: "Dreams have always been a great object of superstition: nothing was more natural."[18] All of which attests that individuals in this period of intellectual history had various but specific concerns about the nature and role of dreams. Furthermore, the articulation of visionary experiences played a decisive role in fleshing out a determinate self-understanding for individuals living in a world that was constantly changing and challenging preconceived ideas about human existence. For example, Thomas Tyron (1634-1703), a physician, wrote a treatise on dreams and maintained,

> it is from the Soul or Spirit in man, which is the Image of the divine Eternal Spirit, and never standeth still, Sleepeth or Slumbereth, when *Dreams* and all Nocturnal Visions do arise and proceed; for whilst the Senses and Powers and Faculties of the outward Nature do sleep, rest or cease from their Functions, the Soul and Spirit ceaseth not from its operation, but goeth on forming, figuring and Representing of things as real, and substantial.[19]

A more detailed argument came from the Scottish philosopher, Andrew Baxter (1686-1750), who registered his anti-Lockean analysis of dreams. Issued in three editions in 1740, 1745, and 1765, *An Enquiry into the Nature of the Human Soul; Wherein The Immateriality of the Soul is Evinced from the Principles of Reason and Philosophy*, Baxter contended that matter was inert and any modification or change in its structure or motion must be caused by an immaterial force.[20] It was both reasonable and a point of comfort to assert that an immaterial force which acted on the sensations of the mind in dreams also gave credence to their supernatural origin. Baxter surmised that a world inhabited by spirits was preferable to one that was empty and barren. He argued: "How delightful is it to think that there is a *world* of spirits; that we are surrounded with intelligent living Beings, rather than in a *lonely, unconscious Universe, a wilderness of matter!* It is a *pledge* give us of *immortality itself,* and that we shall not be extinguished all at once, nor cut off from existence . . . This appearance is offered to us as a *counter-part* to dead matter."[21]

In North America, previous to the colonies declaring their independence from England, dreams played a significant part in developing a social rhetoric that was far from being eclipsed from religious and political discourse.[22] Throughout the period, dreams fostered a sense of value and self-worth for the dreamer. Mechal Sobel, in her *Teach Me Dreams: The Search for Self in the Revolutionary Era,* has documented over two hundred cases where dreams and visions became a primary catalyst in the formulation of a self-identity that was marked by conversion, fulfilment, and destiny. Sobel explains: "Unlike those who continued to regard themselves as observers of their own lives, the dramatic narrators and the self-fashioners did not simply see their dreams as foretelling the future; they came to believe that they had to find ways to achieve goals posited in dreams in order to change themselves and their lives."[23] Pioneers like Freeborn and Catherine Garrettson (1752-1827 and 1752-1849), Chloe Russell (18th and 19th centuries), and John Woolman (1720-72), all saw their social and spiritual experiences punctuated by dreams.[24]

Furthermore, dreams maintained a sense of authenticity when people in the modern era determined that particular apparitional encounters could not be explained solely within the boundaries of rational discourse. John Wigger has recently summarized the influence of visionary experiences in the context of the American camp meetings. "The enthusiasm of the camp meetings is well known," writes Wigger, "but what is less frequently acknowledged is that a great many early Methodists believed in the efficacy of prophetic dreams, visions, and supernatural impressions and were not afraid to base day-to-day decisions on such phenomena."[25] On both sides of the Atlantic, dreams gained a tone of public authority when they were published in court trials, newspapers, and diaries which gave evidence of their spiritual and social importance in society.[26] The function of dreams and visions became an indicator that signalled a level of influence on individual and collective behaviour that had to be sorted out among people living in the world.[27]

The Dream of Salvation: Moving from the Visible to the Invisible and Back Again

One of the first recorded portents found in John Wesley's journals was the tragic suicide of an undergraduate known to him while he was a tutor at Lincoln College. Around eleven o'clock Wesley found himself suddenly disturbed in his sleep during the night. The next morning he learned of the terrible incident which transpired in the Porter's Lodge at Lincoln College, Oxford, which he interpreted clairvoyantly:

> About that time (as I found in the morning) one who had been designed to be my pupil, but was not, came into the porter's lodge (where several persons sitting)

with a pistol in his hand. He then attempted twice or thrice to shoot himself, but it would not go off. Upon his laying it down, one took it up and blew out the priming. He was very angry, went and got fresh prime, came in again, sat down, beat the flint with his key; and about twelve, pulling off his hat and wig, said he would die like a gentleman, and shot himself through the head.[28]

For Wesley, this incident illustrated, not only the tragic nature of a terrible decision by a student but also the urgency of the human condition, which might be revealed at various levels of human consciousness. Of an equally serious nature, Wesley recorded in his journal of a woman who had a premonition in a dream of drowning at Haxey Carr.[29] After being ridiculed by her friends she reluctantly set off on horseback to market only to fall off into drains where she drowned.[30]

Throughout the eighteenth century important theological issues surfaced in the dreams and lives of individuals. As was the case in other issues, there was not always a fine line of distinction between the conceptual articulation of an issue and the lived out experience of those who were encountering the reality of the matter. This was particularly the case in relation to the issue of salvation as individuals would often have dreams and visions that they interpreted in ways that provided theological verification and direction for their lives.[31] In the following discussion, I will show how Methodists in the eighteenth century joined theological articulation and unconscious experiences in their understandings of divine presence. Additionally, I will demonstrate that for Wesley this union became problematic and caused continual internal and external accusations that the leader of the Methodists was not only lacking in discernment but also selective in the experiences he censored as opposed to the ones he found authentic.

The ideas of psychological and spiritual well-being preoccupied many of the writings and dreams of individuals during the Enlightenment. Particularly, the topic of happiness and holiness attracted the attention of numerous writers such as the Latitudinarians, for example, with their emphasis on moral duty and the assertion that happiness was the purpose and end of human beings. John Tillotson (1630-94), Archbishop of Canterbury from 1691 to 1694, proclaimed in his sermon "On the Happiness of a Heavenly Conversation": "Holiness is not only a condition but a necessary qualification for the happiness of the next life."[32] It was John Wesley's view that the experiences of justification and sanctification were antecedent to the notions of authentic holiness and happiness. The focus of the religious person (*homo religiosus*), Wesley maintained in a sermon at the end of his life, was aimed solely on God. The temperaments of many, however, were callow and insensitive to God's presence and what scriptural Christianity asserted concerning its nature and essence. "How totally ignorant are they of God," he wrote, "and of the things of God! How unacquainted both with the invisible and the eternal world!"[33] Because the unregenerate had not pursued God there was no peace or rest, which Wesley deemed the primary indicators of happiness. Quoting Augustine's *Confessions*, Wesley stressed: "The hungry soul, like the busy bee, wanders from flower to flower; but it goes off from each with an abortive hope and a deluded expectation. Every creature cries . . . 'Happiness is not in *me*'. The height and the depth proclaim to an attentive ear, 'The

Creator hath not implanted in me a capacity of giving happiness; therefore with all thy skill and pains thou canst not extract it from me.'"[34] It was the unhappy state of the soul that provided Wesley and his Methodist followers with an evangelical agenda during the eighteenth century. "We learn hence," wrote Wesley in another sermon, "that none but a Christian is happy; none but a real, inward Christian."[35]

In Wesley's view, both human unrest which was caused by an unregenerate self and the quest for lasting happiness were often revealed in visionary experiences. Therefore, as in awakened consciousness, one could encounter the grace of God and throughout the published extracts of his journal, Wesley included several dream narratives which addressed the topics of spiritual and emotional disturbances. His journal entry for 3 March 1748, for instance, he related the story of a Mrs. Holloway who scoffed at her husband's rejuvenated faith. Previously she had experienced a belief in God, when she had been struck to the ground by a bolt of lightning, but later had fallen back into discouragement and cynicism. John Wesley contended, however, that God would not let her be; divine beings appeared to her in dreams with an apocalyptic message:

> Yet God called her again, in dreams and visions of the night. She thought she was standing in the open air, when one appeared in the clouds, exceeding glorious, above the brightness of the sun. She soon after saw a second, and then a third. One had a kind of spear in his hand; the second, a besom, wherewith he was going to sweep the earth; the third, an hour-glass, as thou the time was short. This so deeply affected her that she began from that time to seek God with her whole heart.[36]

This visionary experience, like so many in Wesley's writings, showed that the Methodists believed in the revelatory character of dreams and visions and demonstrated not only the depraved condition of the soul but, more importantly, asserted that the consciousness of the sinner was capable of perceiving transcendental realities.

Reading Dreams in Wesley's *Arminian Magazine*

One of the principal avenues that Wesley used in pressing his point of view about the power of the supernatural was *The Arminian Magazine, Consisting Chiefly of Extracts and Original Treatises on Universal Redemption*. Scattered throughout this periodical were various narratives and testimonies by those who had experienced miraculous and supernatural events.[37] Often, it must be remembered, Wesley saw dreams and visions as miraculous occurrences in the lives of believers and sceptics alike and treated them as miraculous events with no apparent level of distinction.[38] Modelled after Augustus Toplady's (1740-78) *The Gospel Magazine, or, Treasury of Divine Knowledge: Designed to Promote Experimental Religion*, the first issue of the *Arminian Magazine* appeared in 1778 with monthly instalments released throughout Wesley's lifetime and, after his death in 1791, well into the twentieth century.

An examination of his diaries for this period shows that Wesley was active as an energetic editor, assimilating materials for inclusion into the publication.[39]

For fourteen years he edited and wrote for the magazine which contained abbreviated editions of theological works, sermons, letters, poetry, biographical narratives, autobiographies, and portraits of leading lights in the Methodist movement. In 1789, a version of the magazine was initiated in North America under the editorial supervision of Thomas Coke (1747-1814) and Francis Asbury (1745-1816) but was discontinued after only one year. After Wesley's death in 1791, the editorial supervision in England was assumed by George Story (1745-1800), the Yorkshire Methodist preacher. In 1798, with the assistance of Joseph Benson (1748-1821), the name changed to *The Methodist Magazine* whereby it was circulated until Benson's death in 1821. Then for over a century, the Methodist periodical was known under the title of the *Wesleyan Methodist Magazine* until 1932 when it returned to its former title of *The Methodist Magazine*.[40] Arguably then, the *Arminian Magazine*, became one of the longest running religious periodicals in modern publishing history.

Certainly Wesley was both pleased and surprised by the magazine's success. At the beginning of its seventh year, in 1784, he wrote in the preface: "*I could not very easily have believed, had one told it me long ago, that this Work would have grown under my hands, so as to extend to the beginning of the seventh Year!*"[41] However, increasing subscriptions underscored its importance and influence throughout the plebeian population of eighteenth-century England. At the time of Wesley's death, there were over 13,000 copies for sale at the Book Room in London, twice the circulation of the popular middle-class *Gentleman's Magazine*. A brief examination of Wesley's book inventory held at the John Rylands Library in Manchester suggests its remarkable growth: "The number of *Arminian Magazine* printed at the press of Mr. Wesley's Decree were 7,000 they continued to increase to the number of 24,000 & have succeeded to the . . . Number 13,500 . . . constantly been on sale at the Book Room from 1749 to his Death when the Stock on Hand was 7,300—the sale being constantly large."[42] The success of the magazine pleased Wesley, who insisted that the Methodist people should always be a reading people and the materials they digested ought to inculcate a life of piety.[43] In November 1790, the aged leader of the Methodist movement answered George Holder in correspondence: "It cannot be that the people should grow in grace unless they give themselves to reading. A reading people will always be a knowing people . . . Press this upon them with all your might; and you will soon see the fruit of your labours."[44] Reinhard Wittmann maintains that the act of reading provided the marginalized masses with a particular intellectual and social space in the modern world. "Reading," writes Wittman, "acquired an emancipatory function, and became a productive social force: it explained one's moral and intellectual horizon."[45] The Methodists, like others in the eighteenth century, became increasingly aware of the political and social implications of reading and its effect on their image and self-identification. In this respect, the dream narratives played an important part in the *Arminian Magazine*.

First, and most importantly, Wesley believed the narratives in his periodical gave evidence of the reality of an invisible world; empirical corroboration of the existence of a supernatural world which could be substantiated repeatedly throughout human history. Second, the fact that Wesley continually collected such stories for the *Arminian Magazine* demonstrates that his interest in the supernatural aspects of human experience was more than a passing fad of his youthful days but a sustained interest throughout his life; indeed, a legacy of his mission and ministry. The narratives that Wesley included for publication buttressed, in his mind at least, how the spiritual struggle of flesh and Spirit, God and the Devil, were fought out in the deeper recesses of the human consciousness.

Amidst the many narratives of dreams and visions found in Wesley's periodical were those that depicted the reality of sin and its corruptive effect on human nature. Christopher Hopper, for example, recorded how he would take pleasure in killing dogs, cats, birds, and insects; dissecting them into small pieces. After an afternoon when Hooper and his friends stoned a marsh full of frogs he experienced retribution in a dream, in which he was attacked until he was "in great terror, and found exquisite pain until I awoke, sweating, and trembling, and half dead with fear."[46] Other dreams had a theological focus and illustrated the plight of the soul separated from the presence of Christ. A Mr. Roe's sight of eternity and of the judgment to come was revealed to him in a dream:

> Conscience however, often did its part, in frequently urging me to repent, particularly in dreams. Once I thought the day of judgment was come. My sins were all brought in dreadful array before me! And I remained in a miserable suspence, whether heaven or hell was to be my portion for ever! This made some impression on me for a season; but though God followed me with conviction I was not willing to obey.[47]

Dreams could also be construed as diabolical attacks on the soul and symptomatic of a time of trial. John Valton wrote a letter to John Wesley which was later included in the *Arminian Magazine* describing a night where Valton, much like a panic-attack, "was sadly harassed with dreaming of a lion pursuing me up and down. The next day, the lion roared upon me indeed! It was a day of sore temptation . . . O how I was torne and tempted! . . . I was much harassed concerning visiting the sick, that I had no knowledge of, nor knew how to get admittance to. I believe Satan drove me into extremes in order to weary me out."[48] For many of the Methodists in the eighteenth century, then, dreams revealed a gulf that existed between the unregenerate self and true happiness.

Another type of visionary experience characterized in eighteenth-century Methodism portrayed the salvation of the sinner and directly linked the redemption of humanity to the atonement of Christ portrayed in the crucifixion of Christ at Calvary. Many times these dreams were played out on the believer's death bed, as was the case with a Mr. Pigot: "Last Monday our dear friend Mr. *Pigot*, made a very happy change. A little before his departure (having prayed with him) I asked, How he felt himself? He answered, . . . 'I am viewing him on the cross, dying in my stead.'"[49] Often the image of the suffering Christ was impressed onto the consciousness of votaries in ways which altered their self-understanding.[50] In 1755, John Cennick preached a sermon entitled *The Beatific Vision; or, Beholding Jesus Crucified,* and highlighted the importance of the cross for believers. In the presence of an evil world, noted Cennick: "Our eyes shall be fastened on him, we will look to him in all times of need; we will praise and pray, looking to him crucified, till we behold the Lamb of God face to face in heaven, where I pray him to hasten our appearing, for his blood's sake! Amen."[51]

One of the most dramatic narratives that came to Wesley's attention, was through the bigamous but later reformed housekeeper, Sarah Ryan (1724-68).[52] Though her character was questionable, her visions were inserted at the beginning of the *Arminian Magazine* as a model of divine grace and love.[53] After a period of spiritual unrest and soul searching, which lasted for seven years, Ryan went to live with a Jewish family. One night she dreamed about Wesley preaching in a society room and was admonished by an angel in a dream to leave the residence of her Jewish hosts. Thereafter, in April of 1754, Ryan went to the Spitalfields church where she found Wesley preaching on the parable of the sower and presiding at Eucharist. At the altar, Ryan became faint, and when Wesley offered her the host she was unable to receive it. Later in the service he returned a second time and offered the sacrament again to Ryan and heard him to speak: "When he spoke those words, 'the Blood of the Lord Jesus Christ,' they pierced my heart, and filled my soul with love to him. Immediately I said, 'This is the Faith by which the martyrs went to the flames.'"[54] Three weeks later, however, in a society meeting where her sister too yearned for forgiveness of sin, Ryan prayed for her sibling, and then, in her narrative, recorded a fantastic event:

> I felt the burden of her soul laid upon mine in an inexpressible manner: and while I was exhorting her to believe, the power of God overwhelmed my soul, so that I fell back in my chair, and my eye-sight was taken from me: but in the same moment the Lord Jesus appeared to my inward sight, and I cried out three times, "O the beauty of the lovely Jesus, Behold him in his vesture dipt in blood!" A little after my leader asked me, "Do you now believe?" I faintly answered "Yes."[55]

Dreams were sometimes positioned in a Trinitarian context too. Henry Rack argues that Trinitarian dreams were unique to Methodists in the eighteenth century.[56] Rack contends that visionary experiences of the Trinity were often linked with the pursuit of spiritual perfection and can be read at one level as expressions of the religious imagination, where "there is no conscious interruption (i.e. no sense of known sin)."[57] In a letter to Hester Ann Roe (1756-94) on 11 February 1777, Wesley recounted how he had come across a written account of a vision experienced by Charles Perronet (1723-76), the son of Vincent Perronet (1693-1785). Charles had claimed shortly after uniting with the Methodists to have had a vision of the Trinity where he, "beheld the distinct persons of the Godhead, and worshipped one undivided Jehovah and each Person separately."[58] After many years, when Perronet had affirmed that he had enjoyed communion with the Trinity, he asserted that his experiences were indescribable and concluded his comments with the declaration: "I was overwhelmed with it; body and soul were penetrated through with rays of Deity."[59]

Some of the most dramatic experiences of the Trinity, moreover, published in the *Arminian Magazine* came from the accounts of female Methodists.[60] An interesting narrative that Wesley included at the beginning of his *Arminian*

Magazine came from the *Diaries* of Bathsheba Hall (1745-80), which occurred during the middle of the eighteenth century.[61] They convey a charismatic awareness of the spiritual life enfolded by the Trinity-in-Unity theme. In one early morning meditation Hall confessed: "I feel this morning the holy presence of the blessed Three in One."[62] And in another, she recorded: "Within these few days, Satan has stirred up all his forces against me . . . I was enabled patiently to endure, and see in him that is invisible. I have felt to-day what no language can express: the triune God dwelling in my heart."[63] Another instance was a death bed experience of a Sarah Brough and her husband Barnabas. It read in the October issue for 1780:

> I beheld the great Three-One . . . For I travelled with her in my very heart and arms through the valley of the shadow of death. I never was, before so far out of the body: I went with her to the very threshold of heaven; as when she expired, she with her arms round me seemed to draw me after her. So my soul conducted her to the very presence of the angels, and then fell back again to its poor habitation. Oh how did I long, to keep my hold, and return back no more![64]

In her study of Quaker women in Seventeenth-century England, Phyllis Mack has suggested that women in the modern world were seen to have capabilities that embraced and internalized supernatural qualities.[65] The feminization of the supernatural continued into the eighteenth century. Mack writes: "Since women's bodies were believed to be more moist and porous than men's, women were thought to have a particular susceptibility to outside influences, including invasion by spiritual forces."[66] Though male experiences of dreams and visions were included in Wesley's *Arminian Magazine*, there was indication that he accepted the eighteenth-century idea that the feminine was especially receptive to supernatural occurrences, an issue that Wesley took advantage of for his agenda in a variety of ways. [67]

These examples, though a small sample of accounts included under Wesley's editorship, were important for their information about Methodist practices. What is more important for the thesis of this study is the influence that dreams and visions carried with fledging religious groups in eighteenth-century society. The narratives of Ryan, Perronet, and Hall confirmed that visionary experiences were an active ingredient in the development of the Methodists and their religious consciousness. By the citation of dreams and visionary experiences in the pages of Wesley's influential periodical, he clearly intended them to be viewed as models for apprehension of the supernatural, making the invisible world visible for his readers, who should be instructed and inspired by the knowledge of such phenomena. Though not normative, they were of great significance. At the very least, as Rack observes, such narratives became "a constant challenge to the rationalising and desupernaturalising tendencies of the century."[68] At another level, though, the publication of these narratives was a bold assertion to the Methodists, and those who would listen to their message, that encounters such as those catalogued in the *Arminian Magazine* should not be tucked away into obscurity but openly professed and utilized as testimony to the existence of an invisible world. "There was nothing particularly unusual in this," writes Rack, "for a Methodist."[69]

Dreaming Too Much: Opposition to Wesley's Visions

Not everyone shared John Wesley's excitement about visionary experiences. Thomas Church (1698-1777), Vicar of Battersea and Prebendary of St. Paul's, attacked the fourth extract of Wesley's journal in 1744 and lampooned the Methodist leader as a man whose "own dreams must be regarded as oracles."[70] John Wesley, for his part, responded that any notion about dreams and visions should be tested, like all theological claims, against the "oracles of God."[71]

It was from his older brother Samuel that John Wesley faced one of the most interesting challenges on this issue.[72] From 30 October 1738 to 27 October 1739, Samuel Wesley, junior, and John Wesley rigorously exchanged views about the importance and function of visionary experiences. The debate was ignited by a report that Samuel received from Mrs. John Hutton, the wife of the Moravian bookseller. A few days after John Wesley had attended his famous Aldersgate society meeting in London he was in the Hutton home. They were outraged because Wesley had declared that he had not been a Christian before his experience on 24 May 1738. In a letter to John Wesley's older brother, Mrs. Hutton outlined her ire and bolstered her case by mentioning the suppositious dream of one of Wesley's company:

> A woman had besides a previous dream, a ball of fire fell upon her, and burst, and fired her soul. Another young man when he was in St. Duncan's church, just as he was going to receive the sacrament, had God the Father come to him, but did not stay with him, but God the Son did stay, who came with him holding his cross in his hands.[73]

The response from Samuel was immediate both to the Hutton's and his younger brother John.[74] Despite John Wesley's disparagement of the woman's "ball of fire" dream, the discussion that ensued between Samuel and John was sharp. Samuel considered dreams too subjective and prone to error. Thus, dreams not only negated the necessity of the Bible as objective truth but also served as inadequate gauges of divine presence in the human psyche. As long as there were those who played up the importance and significance of dreams, Samuel advised John, "then I will use my utmost strength that God shall give me to expose these bad branches of a bad root, and thus—Such doctrine as encourages and abets spiritual fireballs, apparitions of the Father, etc., etc., is delusive and dangerous."[75]

John Wesley, for his part, readily admitted that there were cases in which individuals tended to hallucinate and display fits of fantasy. Nevertheless, he refused to disallow dreams a place in the spiritual experiences of believers and instead asserted that there were cross-over dimensions between dreams and awakened consciousness.[76] Scripture plainly gave credence to the existence and influence of dreams and visions in the life of the faithful. Furthermore, Wesley reasoned, throughout post-apostolic Christianity, there were individuals who ascribed to the efficacious nature of visionary experiences in their lives. In a letter to Samuel on 4 April 1739, John wrote:

My dear brother, the whole question turns chiefly, if not wholly, on matter of fact. You deny that God does now work these effects, at least that he works them in such a manner. I affirm both, because I have heard those facts with my ears, and seen them with my eyes. I have seen (as far as it can be seen) very many persons changed in a moment from the spirit of horror, fear, and despair, to the spirit of joy, peace; and from sinful desires, till then reigning over them, to a pure desire of doing the will of God . . . This I know: several persons in whom this great change from the power of Satan unto God was wrought either in sleep, or during a strong representation to the eye of their minds of Christ either on the cross or in glory. This is the fact. Let any judge as they please[77]

An important element of Wesley's understanding of dreams was revealed in his words "matter of fact" in the above quotation. For visionary experiences, as with other supernatural occurrences, Wesley considered the empirical nature of human experience crucial in determining the authenticity of the event itself. The radical change of behaviour which necessarily required a *raison d'être* was viewed by Wesley to be an important item in the examination of the supernatural. Like anyone trained in empirical methods, Wesley was always on the lookout for a link between cause and effect. In this case, it was the demonstration of the reality of Christ which had effected a change in an individual's thoughts and actions that he considered indisputable and ample proof that the experience was a valid one.

As one might imagine, the exchange between the brothers became vitriolic at times. For example, when John Wesley self righteously parodied his brother and charged him with discounting the Articles of the Church of England, the correspondence became inflamed with sarcasm and Samuel's orthodoxy became a point of insult. John Wesley wrote on 3 February 1739: "I fear you *dissent* from the fundamental Articles of the Church of England . . . I doubt you do not hold justification by faith alone . . . O may the God of love, if my sister or you are otherwise minded, reveal even this unto you."[78] Samuel turned the screw tighter in his follow-up letter of 26 March 1739, and claimed that Charles sided with him in the debate.[79] Samuel received another letter in which John Wesley expressed disbelief that his older brother could not acknowledge the power of God at work in the lives of men and women who were being converted throughout England. Then he concluded his letter boldly: "What would you think of our new faith (as you term it) if God should send two or three that believe in his name (I lightly touch upon it, because the thing is not yet clear to me) and the prayer of faith should save the sick, and your health be restored from that hour?"[80] Less than two weeks after the letter was postmarked Samuel died without having read or responded to John's inquiry.[81]

Whatever opposition Wesley faced in his lifetime, even among his own family, visionary experiences became a defining characteristic of Methodists during the eighteenth century. Throughout the period Methodists were known as a people who dreamed and associated dreaming with a supernatural presence in their lives. Moreover, the experiences of dreams that portrayed supernatural and providential events in great detail were considered reliable data on which important decisions were made during moments of awakened consciousness.

A more cautious approach among the Evangelical parish clergy of the eighteenth and nineteenth centuries was represented, however, by the Eclectic Society of London, a group originally founded in 1783 and composed primarily of Evangelical Anglican clergymen and one or two Nonconformist ministers. By and large they accepted the authenticity of dreams but correspondingly warned, "we must not lean too much towards the superstitious side. Mr. Wesley's people do this. Dreams can afford no implicit ground of comfort and guidance."[82] Despite this monitory advice, there were many devout figures in the Evangelical Revival who agreed with the Methodists and maintained that visionary experiences, including dreams, played an important role in the development of religious consciousness. Cornelius Cayley (1729-80), an itinerant evangelical preacher whose autobiography went through three editions in the eighteenth century and was reprinted in several editions in the nineteenth century unabashedly asserted his belief in visionary experiences. "I think they greatly err," wrote Cayley, "who say, that God doth not in a particular manner, sometimes visit his Children now, by dreams and visions, for their spiritual Edification, in Divine Things."[83] Still, the charge of superstition associated with dreams was one that taxed Wesley throughout his lifetime. The criticisms he faced, however, never overshadowed the appeal that he found among the plebeian classes. Various claims of those who claimed to have experienced the supernatural eased the path of his rhetoric as he continued to utilize the testimony of devout and pious individuals and accumulated one by one a vast amount of evidence to support his argument for the belief in the reality of an invisible world. The concentration of people who found the Church of England waning and the promise of Methodism encouraging were particularly in the North and in the West, in Cornwall and Wales.[84] John Rule, writing on Methodism in Cornwall notes: "The miners of Cornwall formed an occupational community to which Methodism came early and prospered greatly. By the early nineteenth century west Cornwall had become one of the movement's greatest strongholds."[85] This was sustainable, in part, because of a thread of religious sentiment that moved throughout the social and intellectual fabric of society in the eighteenth and nineteenth centuries in which dreams continued to hold a viable place for individuals as they attempted to make a connection between a visible realm of existence that was temporal with an invisible dimensionality that offered spiritual sense for the reason and ritual of their lives.[86] John Wesley, then, at this point, was tuned into a climate that refused to be jettisoned from a religious consciousness that was present in the modern world. As such, he was able to touch a strata of the human psyche that gave it a reference point in both its natural and supernatural dimensions.

Envisioning Salvation:
Justification and Sanctification Realized

Thusfar, I have argued that John Wesley's endorsement of visionary experiences was a significant statement that shored up support for his commitment to the idea of the supernatural in the daily life of individuals living in the modern world. What must be addressed in some detail now is how Wesley's confidence in particular dreams and visions gave him evidence for the integrity of key theological affirmations of the Christian faith. For Wesley, the whole Christian message of redemption rested on the doctrines of justification and sanctification.[87] Ample commentary has been made on the importance of these doctrines which secured Wesley a place in Reformation theology and positioned him as a force to be reckoned with in the Evangelical Revival of the eighteenth century.[88]

What has been left largely untouched in eighteenth-century studies, however, is an examination of Wesley's view of salvation as a supernatural event. Briefly stated, the Wesleyan corpus unequivocally demonstrated that John Wesley viewed salvation first and foremost a supernatural event with empirical consequences. Moreover, Methodists in the eighteenth century believed they could experience redemption in the context of either dreams or awakened consciousness. Scattered throughout Methodist biographies, diaries, and letters were accounts of dreams that displayed providential epiphanies of God's power that culminated in experiences of justifying and sanctifying grace. Mary Bosanquet recorded multiple supernatural encounters in her autobiography and multifarious letter correspondence portrayed her life filled with dreams, visions, and apparitional manifestations. Characteristic of these accounts was one where Jesus appeared to her, as she stood in a room of people who she qualified as having no faith in God. She recorded her dream:

> The awful majesty of his presence had such an effect on me as I cannot express. It seemed to me I sunk down before him as if I were sweetly melting into nothing. I saw no shining brightness or anything dazzling to the eye. He appeared only as a man clothed in white . . . It was the glory of holiness which so overcame me! There seemed but about a yard distance between my Saviour and me when he spoke with a voice, clear and distinct, these words, "I will send thee to a people that are not a people, and I will go with thee. Bring them unto me, for I will lay my hand upon them and heal them. Fear not, only believe!"[89]

An interesting facet of Bosanquet's account was the empirical qualities of her expeience. Not only did she notice the color of Christ's garments, but the approximate distance which he stood from her, and, of course, the words of Christ's message. The implicit conclusion found in her account, as with other Methodists in the eighteenth century, was the connection which existed between the natural and supernatural and its availability to the spiritual senses of the person of faith. John Wesley's sermons, too, displayed a soteriological emphasis that merged the natural and supernatural. For example, in his homily on John 3.7 Wesley stressed: "If any doctrines within the whole compass of Christianity may be properly termed fundamental they are doubtless these two—the doctrine of justification, and that of the new birth: the former relating to that great work which God does *for us*, in forgiving our sins; the latter to the great work God does *in us*, in renewing our fallen nature."[90] There was, then, in the Methodist experience of visionary experiences both a subjective and objective feature of their understanding of agency and its role in forming their self-identification had dimensions that affected both their heart and behavior.

A clue to understanding this dual aspect of Wesley's understanding of dreams and how it impinged on his soteriological concerns emerges within the context of an apologetic portrayal of the invisible world that he outlined in an often overlooked sermon that was composed at the end of his life. In 1789, his "Human Life A Dream," was a homily that posited dreams in human nature and developed a trajectory of the human self where a type of dream analysis was incorporated.[91] First, in logical order, Wesley addressed the origins of dreams and hinted at his knowledge of dream theory, when he wrote:

> There can be no doubt but some of them arise from the present constitution of the body, while others of them are probably occasioned by the passions of the mind. Again, we are clearly informed in Scripture that some are caused by the operation of good angels (if we may dare to suppose that there are any such now, or at least that they have anything to do in the world!).[92]

Though human experience may be accentuated by dreams, they also functioned as a conduits to altered levels of consciousness that the biblical writers called eternity. The transfer from a finite point of perception where knowledge is subject to hypothesis, tests, and conjecture to an echelon of awareness that is multidimensional was equated to sleeping and awakened concentration: "See, all is *real* here! All is permanent, all eternal! Far more stable than the foundations of the earth; yea, than the pillars of that lower heaven. Now that your eyes are open, see how inexpressibly different are all the things that are now round about you! What a difference do you perceive in yourself!"[93] Additionally, for Wesley, the association of two worlds, i.e., visible and invisible, was a hallmark of wisdom. Those sensible of this association exhibited an awareness of the human condition and the importance of religious discourse. Wesley admonished:

> How advisable by every possible means to connect the ideas of time and eternity! So to associate them together that the thought of one may never recur to your mind without the thought of the other! It is our highest wisdom to associate the ideas of the visible and invisible world, to connect temporal and spiritual, mortal and immortal being . . . . What an admirable foundation for thus associating the ideas of time and eternity, of the visible and invisible world, is in the very nature of religion! For what is religion? (I mean scriptural religion; for all other is the vainest of all dreams) . . . It is Immanuel, God with us! God in man! Heaven connected with earth! The unspeakable union of mortal with immortal.[94]

A fundamental issue in John Wesley's theology, as the above quotation illustrates, was the integrity of belief in a supernatural realm of existence that was empirically contextualized by human experience. In this way, he moved easily between theoretical and practical concepts in his rhetorical defence of historical Christianity. On the one hand, Wesley's theoretical juxtaposition of the visible and invisible provided a matrix whereby an association of ideas from transcendental and immanent categories enabled, at least to his own satisfaction, a coherent portrait of reality. On the other hand, Wesley's practical emphasis on the incarnation showed that salvation primarily functioned within human history as a realization of universal qualities with particular implications. For Wesley, the supernatural was revealed in the natural and could not be sidelined without intellectual repercussions.

With this in mind, Wesley's call to conversion, "Do you desire to flee the wrath to come?" was not only an evangelical affirmation of faith but a rhetorical device which was utilized to drive home the importance of key theological concepts for his listeners. Notes Jean-Pierre van Noppen, the success of Methodist discourse in the eighteenth century rested, in part, on John Wesley's ability to highlight this divine-human intersection, and target an audience that was receptive to his message.[95] In December 1738, when Wesley drew up his *General Rules of the Band Societies*, Methodists were beginning to attract individuals who desired to meet in small groups. Many were interested in the Methodist concept of salvation but, as Rupert Davies noted, "did not necessarily understand the full implications of belonging to the societies."[96] On several occasions, Wesley excluded individuals from society who were not living up to the standards of membership.[97] Later, in 1743, Wesley published the General Rules under the title, *The Nature, Design, and General Rules, of the United Societies, in London, Bristol, King's-wood, and Newcastle upon Tyne*, which went through thirty-nine editions during his lifetime.[98] In that document, Wesley stated the primary condition for admittance into the Methodist societies: "There is one only condition previously required in those who desire admission into these societies, 'a desire to flee from the wrath to come, to be saved from their sins.'"[99]

This concern, "a desire to flee from the wrath to come," was lived out throughout John Wesley's life and became a fundamental dictum among Methodists in the eighteenth century. The sense of urgency marked by Wesley and his preachers illustrated an understanding of the finite and infinite nature of the human psyche, which entailed a conceptualization of the soul that consistently appeared throughout Wesley's journals, sermons, theological tracts, and miscellaneous manuscript documents. A manuscript dated 19 February 1756, and titled *Two Remarkable Stories, 1756, 1758* is a case in point.[100] It is in Wesley's handwriting but, as far as scholarship has been able to determine, Wesley never published or edited it. It is unlikely that the document was from Wesley's own personal experience but it is also uncertain where it originated. Throughout his life, Wesley collected and solicited various narratives, journals, and autobiographical accounts from people inside and outside the Methodist fold. This particular document illustrates both Wesley's concern for the supernatural in general and salvation in particular. According to the account, an apparition pleaded with the inhabitant of a house to take dictation for a letter to the specter's living nephew. Apparently, the apparition had knowledge of the future as he knew that his unbelieving nephew would die the following month. The letter described "the torments of Hell in such words as I had never heard in my life, enough to make one's blood run cold."[101] Like the biblical parable which it emulated (Luke 16.19-31), the apparition in the story communicated a message that both transcended and affected human existence. In a sermon on this theme, written in 1788 while on a visit to Birmingham, Wesley maintained: "It is not impossible that other unhappy spirits may wish well to the relations they have left behind them. But this is the accepted time, for them as well as for us."[102] The crux of the issue for Wesley, however, was the necessity of repentance and the belief in the importance of responding to divine grace which implied a fixed condition of the soul in eternity.

This evidence illustrates, repentance for Wesley was a pivotal turning point in the *ordo salutis*.[103] In his sermon, *The Scriptural Way of Salvation*, he had outlined the Christian idea of repentance and its necessity for a proper understanding of salvation. For Wesley, the idea of self-reliance and its weakness for Christian theology was highlighted throughout history by the notion of repentance. Authentic repentance, he posed, conveyed a scheme that was more in line with human experience, for it constituted "a conviction of our helplessness, of our utter inability to think one good thought, or to form one good desire; and much more to speak one word aright, or to perform one good action but through his free, almighty grace, first preventing us, and then accompanying us every moment."[104] However, the realization of repentance was not merely an awareness of the fragility of human life but an awakening to the sinful quality of human existence.[105] It was the emphasis on the sinful nature of humanity that not only set Methodism at odds with the hierarchy of the Church of England but also provided visible unrest among those who came out to hear the Methodists preaching in the open fields.

As I indicated in the previous analysis of Ryan and Hall, many of the Methodists in the eighteenth century had vivid dreams where grace was experienced under the preaching of men like Whitefield and Wesley. A corollary of dreams was the experiences of convulsions and trances that Methodists and others experienced in the eighteenth century and which may be considered within the category of visions in a broad sense of the word. These encounters demonstrated that Methodists understood convulsions, and in a broader way visions, as channels or passage ways for dissociative altered states of consciousness with other-worldly phenomena.[106] As with dreams and visions, these episodes exposed the Methodists to further ridicule by their opponents. It also allowed Wesley and his followers to flesh out the meaning of these incidents for their self-understanding and referenced them as encounters with transcendental realities. David Hempton makes a point worth considering: "Religious insiders and outsiders heard noise differently, the phrase 'all nonsense and noise' was a favorite of critics of Methodists revival meetings, but for those enraptured attendees at love feasts or camp meetings there was nothing nonsensical about the noise."[107] To draw upon Taves's language, the dissociative experience of the Methodists affirmed a relationship with the one who had altered ordinary consciousness. Taves writes: "I would argue that direct, perceivable religious experiences entail some degree of dissociation, that is, some degree of displacement of ordinary, waking consciousness such that 'I' enter into relationship with that which I either experience of believe is 'not me.'"[108]

If there was a theatre for these altered forms of divine communication, it was certainly the field-preaching in England and later the camp meetings in North America and Methodists were well known in both for the promotion of their evangelical causes. George Whitefield had preceded John Wesley in the use of this strategy with remarkable success and in May of 1739 Whitefield recorded in his journal: "After God had enabled me to preach to about twenty thousand for above an hour at Kennington, He inclined the hearers' hearts to contribute most cheerfully and liberally towards the Orphan House."[109] The attraction of large crowds for preachers like Wesley, Whitefield, and Cennick, were meet with uncontrollable fits and convulsions with common regularity in the eighteenth century.[110] Leigh Eric Schmidt aptly describes the milieu of the crowds who had come to hear these preachers and others like them. "The distance between this world and the next narrowed in the ears of the devout. Heaven was so close that on a good day they could hear it."[111] Of course, there were detractors. *The Gentleman's Magazine* ran one of its many anti-Methodist articles in September 1744, where field-preaching was openly disparaged:

> It being too well known that there are several (as we are advised illegal Field and other Meetings of Persons), styl'd *Methodists*, whose Preachers pretend to expound the holy Scriptures by Virtue of Inspiration by which Means they collect together great Numbers of disorderly Persons, very much endangering the Peace of our Sovereign Lord the King; which Proceedings, unless timely suppressed, may endanger the Peace of the Kingdom in general; and at all Adventures the pretended Preachers, or Teachers, at their irregular Meetings, by their *enthusiastic* Doctrines, do very much confound and disorder the Minds of great Numbers of his Majesty's good subjects.[112]

Nonetheless, one historian of the Evangelical Revival describes the mentality of the itinerant evangelists as one that believed he or she was participating in a diffusion of spiritual power. "What distinguished eighteenth-century revivalists from other evangelicals," Frank Lambert contends, "was their belief that God periodically pours out his grace in an extraordinary way to redeem a sinful people, and that they were participating in one of those unusual outpourings."[113]

For Wesley's part, the deluge of people who came out to hear him preach and ended up convulsing in the open fields was a matter that he continually struggled with but could not deny. As a high church Tory, he was not comfortable with fits of passion and repeatedly asserted that he had not encouraged or manipulated his audiences to mimic such experiences. Other leaders in the Revival disagreed. John Cennick, George Whitefield, and Charles Wesley all suggested that John Wesley might have contributed to the cries, swoonings, perturbations of mind, and bodily convulsions of those who heard him preach.[114] More contemporaneously, William Sargent in his *Battle for the Mind* claimed that Wesley participated in a type of religious brain-washing with the aid of particular homiletic methods.[115] As a master of logic and rhetoric, exercises that Wesley took pride in from his Oxford days, he was familiar with techniques of persuasion that would enable him to influence the plebeian populations he addressed in his preaching.[116] However the case may be, the influences of and reactions to Wesley's preaching were dynamic.[117] On one occasion, John Nelson (1707-74), a travelling stonemason who found the first Methodist society in Birstall in 1741, recorded that Wesley threw back his hair while preaching a sermon and Nelson felt his "heart beat like the pendulum of a clock."[118] Richard Heitzenrater's evaluation of Wesley's preaching is instructive at this juncture. Heitzenrater notes: "If Wesley's stature as a theologian has been underestimated, his reputation as a preacher has probably been overestimated. Wesley's primary skill was not in the techniques of preaching; he certainly did not have the homi-letical flair of a Whitefield."[119] Nevertheless, the fanatical display of emotion during his preaching tours and subsequent charges of enthusiasm were continual issues in the polemical attacks on Wesley and the Methodists.[120]

The heart of the problem was Wesley's insistence that sin had a detrimental effect on human nature. The conviction of sin, Wesley maintained, was a neces-sary component in the understanding and formulation of the *ordo salutis*. Throughout his writings and reflections on the Revival, Wesley adamantly con-tended that those enraptured in the open fields had *seen* in their fits and trances the great chasm which existed between human sinfulness and the holiness of God.[121] The emotional energy that was present in these meetings was intense; loud cries of agony, coupled with psychic trances, until physical fatigue caused individuals to collapse under exhaustion. Wesley recorded similar cases in the published extracts of his journal: "Several said they were afraid of the devil, and this was all they knew. But a few gave a more intelligible account of the pierc-ing sense they then had of their sins, both inward and outward, which were set in array against them round about; of the dread they were in of the wrath of God and the punishment they had deserved, into which they seemed to be just falling, without any way to escape."[122]

One of the most dramatic and sustained occurrences was during the meetings held at Everton in Huntingdonshire. Not specifically a Methodist revival, never-theless Wesley included accounts of it in his journal and *Short History of the People Called Methodists*.[123] The noteworthy account provided by Wesley in-cluded men, women, and children who were "in violent contortions of body and weeping aloud—I think incessantly during the whole service."[124] Wesley further highlighted the agonies of the congregation:

> And while poor sinners felt the sentence of death in their souls, what sound of distress did I hear! The greatest number of them who cried or fell were men, but some women, and several children, felt the power of the same almighty Spirit and seemed to be sinking into hell. This occasioned a mixture of various sounds, some shrieking, some roaring aloud. The most general was a loud breathing, like that of people half strangled and grasping for life. And indeed almost all the cries were like those of human creatures, dying in bitter anguish.[125]

Additionally, Wesley observed that there were young boys who experienced convulsions with agitations accompanied by a physical strength that paralleled a grown adult. And, in one particular case, a young girl about the age of twelve, came out of a trance and declared: "Oh what can Jesus do for lost sinners! He has forgiven all my sins! I am in heaven! I am in heaven! Oh, how he loves *me*! And how I love him!"[126] Some cried out for spiritual liberty and were released in an instant while others only after extended periods of prayer.

There are several considerations that surface in an analysis of these experi-ences of ecstasy. First, a study of these experiences reveals that they were, to some extent, psychologically conditioned by the emotional ambience of the Re-vival. As we have noted, this fuelled criticism which was levelled at Wesley from both inside and outside the movement, and at times put him in a defensive posture. John Hampson, junior (1760-1817?), Wesley's first biographer, was

offended by the plethora of emotional outbursts and labelled them "highly ridic-
ulous," then concluded: "If the Almighty has any work to accomplish in the
world, he can surely conduct it without such auxiliaries."[127] E. P. Thompson
inveighed against the Methodists with his "chiliasm of despair" accusation.[128]
Like William Lecky before him, Thompson saw Methodism chiefly, as "religious terrorism;" an anti-life movement which in Thompson's words was a
"chiliasm of the defeated and the hopeless."[129] Furthermore, Thompson argued,
Methodism provided the lower class with a "ritualized form of psychic mastur-
bation."[130] John Wesley conceded that a fine line must be utilized in adjudicat-
ing such phenomena. As in other issues which touched upon religious themes,
here too he embraced a *via media* which held extreme judgments from both fanatical and sceptical positions in a healthy balance.

Looking back on these early religious expressions Wesley noted In his journal entry for 25 November 1759: "The danger *was* to regard *extraordinary* circumstances too much, such as outcries, convulsions, visions, trances, as if these
were *essential* to the inward work, so that it *could not* go on without them. Perhaps the danger *is* to regard them too little, to condemn them altogether, to imagine they had nothing of God in them and were an hindrance to his work."[131]
While Wesley defended the authenticity of a vast assortment of supernatural
experiences, he also conceded that there were occasions when individuals mimicked ecstatic encounters. In some cases, he admitted, there was "a mixture of
dissimulation . . . persons pretended to see or feel what they did not and imitated
the cries or convulsive motions of those who were really overpowered by the
Spirit of God."[132] Nevertheless, genuine experiences, could only be denied at the
cost of becoming "irrational and unchristian."[133]

Second, social historians have misunderstood John Wesley precisely at this
point, without a due consideration of the internal logic of the Evangelical Revival and Wesley's own theological development. This easier path has led to a simplistic caricature of Wesley and an inaccurate and fallacious description of the
movement he sustained. A resistance of surface readings of the Wesleyan corpus
will reveal that Wesley and the Evangelical Revival, with which he was integral-
ly involved, maintained an internal consistency throughout its development
throughout the eighteenth century.[134] David Hempton, for one, cogently argues:
"Although there is some evidence to link revivalism to economic dislocation and
political repression, there is a general acknowledgement that religious revivals
had internal social and psychological dynamics regardless of external circumstances."[135] Additionally, Jonathan Clark's assertion that Methodism inherited a
political theology that was already present in the Church of England gives
weight, at one level, to a logic that was consistent and available in the broader
spectrum of popular culture during the period.[136] The Methodists highlighted in
their preaching the fragmentation of the human soul and the detrimental implications of sin for society. Wesley's message of repentance and championing of the
doctrine of justification by faith appealed to the human experience of many individuals and tapped into a historical continuum that votaries considered a necessary component for their living out the Christian faith, though they might have
disagreed with him about the meaning of certain displays of religious exurbance.

Third, and counter to many charismatic elements in contemporary religious discourse, the ecstatic experiences of these Methodists of the eighteenth century were not viewed primarily as divine intrusions of the Spirit but outbursts of demonic oppression.[137] John Wesley candidly admitted that he could not dismiss the thought that some of the bodily contortions and bizarre outcries in the convulsionaries was due to a demonic presence.[138] In his *A Farther Appeal to Men of Reason and Religion*, for example, Wesley responded to Bishop Warburton's attack on the Methodists by quoting a letter he had received from Ralph Erskine (1685-1752), the Scottish evangelist. The full version of the letter was entered into his journal for 30 June 1739, which a part reads: "what influence sudden and sharp awakenings may have upon the body I pretend not to explain. But I make no question Satan, so far as he gets power, may exert himself on such occasions, partly to hinder the good work in the persons who are thus touched with the sharp arrows of conviction, and partly to disparage the work of God, as if it tended to lead people to distraction."[139] Jane March (1743-1816), a female Methodist wrote to Mary Bonsanquet and related that some had experienced what she characterized as "the malice of Satan."[140] The realization of sin was intense for eighteenth-century Methodists, and individuals longed for a peace that could only be relieved by God's grace and love.

Justification by Faith Alone: God's Radical Answer to Humanity's Radical Problem

In 1735, when John Wesley set sail for America, he was disturbed and perplexed about many things. The voyage journals and diaries in this episode of his life revealed a man concerned about the mortality of life and the uncertainty which impinged on his own existence.[141] Sea journeys were not an easy or pleasant adventure in the eighteenth century and those aboard the *Simmonds* faced various tumultuous storms in the five month trip across the Atlantic ocean.[142] One particular crisis arose on 17 January 1736, just three weeks before the travellers set foot on American soil. The waters and violent winds burst throughout the boat and Wesley's journal recorded his fear: "I laid me down in the great cabin, very uncertain whether I should wake alive, and much ashamed at my unwillingness to die. O how pure in heart must he be who would rejoice to appear before God at a moment's warning."[143] In the midst of the turbulent storms, Wesley noted that the Moravians who were on board seemed unconcerned for their lives but "looked up, and without intermission sang on."[144] Wesley's own fear of death caused him to ponder eternity and the condition of his soul. Why was he not rejoicing in the midst of danger but only concerned about the preservation of his own mortal life? These were questions that disturbed the young Wesley and caused him anxiety.

It was through his association with the pietists, August Gottlieb Spangenberg (1704-92) and Peter Böhler (1712-75), however, that John Wesley's sights became more focused on experiential views of salvation and the importance of the Reformation doctrine, justification by faith alone. Spangenberg had returned from Savannah with General James Oglethorpe (1696-1785), MP of Haslemere and chairman of the parliamentary commission on debtors prison, when the former had met the Oxford don turned missionary in early February 1736. Wesley's journal entry of this event, suggested he was impressed with Spangenberg, and determined that his character and demeanour were above reproach. Moreover, soon after the two met, Wesley displayed his confidence in Spangenberg when he asked the Moravian for an evaluation of his character and conduct. Straightway Spangenberg probed Wesley about his personal knowledge of Jesus Christ, to which Wesley weakly replied: "I know he is the Saviour of the world." [145] The reaction was not sufficient and Spangenberg quickly steered Wesley to the notion that it was an internal knowledge of Jesus Christ that would bring about a lasting and true consolation for his life.

After nineteen months of failed ministry in Georgia John Wesley returned to England on the run from William Williamson and his newfound wife Sophey Hopkey. [146] Wesley had developed a close relationship with Hopkey and had privately considered marriage to her. However, as with most of his romantic ties to members of the opposite sex, Wesley pondered the possibilities of matrimony too long. Presumably tired of waiting on Wesley to make a commitment, Hopkey developed a relationship with Williamson, and soon thereafter the two married. Wesley was both heartsick and outraged, and refused communion to them the following Sunday. Williamson equally outraged filed suit against Wesley which required him to give an account of his actions in court. [147] Wesley's time in the American colonies had been, evangelically speaking, dismal and he met with little success, especially among the Indians in Georgia. [148] Tomochichi, chief of the Yamacraw tribe, had expressed a desire to hear Wesley and the other English missionaries who had been sent under the auspices of the Society for the Propagation of the Gospel. For the most part the curiosity of the Indians was superficial and Wesley's countless attempts to preach and teach the gospel to them were met with minimal results. In an extended summary of the Georgia province Wesley wrote concerning the Indians: "They [the Creek Indians] know not what friendship or gratitude means. They show no inclination to learn anything, but least of all Christianity, being full as opinionated of their own parts and wisdom as either modern Chinese or ancient Roman."[149] Despite Wesley's failure among the Indians, his time with the Moravians had captivated his mind and heart. His observations of the Moravians in the midst of physical perils had peaked an interest that simultaneously caused him to have fear about the salvation of his own life.

On his return to England, Wesley continued his evangelical exercises with his fellow travellers but was still fearful for his own life. [150] Wesley reasoned: "Whoever is uneasy on any account (bodily pain alone excepted) carries in himself his own conviction that he is so far an unbeliever. Is he uneasy at the apprehension of death? Then he believeth not that 'to die is gain.'"[151] When Wesley caught sight of English soil, he turned on himself and admitted his failure as a missionary and a Christian. Wesley's acerbic tone showed not only his inability to live up to his personal ideals about holiness but also made plain his misgivings about the nature of faith and the purpose of Christianity in the world:

It is now two years and almost four months since I left my native country in order to teach the Georgian Indians the nature of Christianity. But what have I learned myself in the meantime? Why (what I least of all suspected), that I who went to America to convert others, was never myself converted to God. "I am not mad," though I thus speak, but "I must speak the words of truth and soberness," if haply some of those who still dream may awake, and see that as I am, so are they.[152]

Within seven days of his return to England, Wesley came to the acquaintance of the German Moravian, Peter Böhler, and the two developed an amicable relationship that offered one another mutual support and admiration. Böhler had come with a group of German Moravians from their homeland and had their sights set on Georgia where they intended to minister to blacks in the region. Wesley found them lodging, and determined to engage them in conversation while he had their company. John Wesley's discussions with Peter Böhler, much like the one he had with Spangenberg, was influential for his life. Skevington Wood's suggestion, though hagiographically shadowed, carried merit. "Böhler played," wrote Wood, "Bilney to Wesley's Latimer."[153]

While Spangenberg had opened Wesley's mind to the experiential dimensions of salvation, it was Böhler who impressed upon Wesley the critical importance of faith itself. Peter Böhler had studied theology at Jena where he came into contact with small Moravian societies, primarily led by August Spangenberg, and Nicholas Ludwig Graf von Zinzendorf (1700-60). Under Zinzendorf's tutelage, Böhler was converted and ordained to the Moravian ministry. He became one of the leaders of the Moravian movement in the eighteenth century and Clifford Towlson remarked about him: "Böhler is probably the most attractive figure in this period of the history of the Brethren."[154] At the centre of Böhler's dialogues with Wesley was the nature of faith and its role in the Christian life. For Wesley, as previously indicated, the fear of death led him to the conclusion that his faith was deficient and weak. After he returned to England, Wesley lapsed into former methods for working out his salvation, renewing with himself a written contract that demanded renunciation of worldly passions and engagement in holy living.[155] The fundamental conundrum for Wesley was a lack of assurance.[156] While an undergraduate at Oxford he had entertained the idea that faith was grounded in assent, which he viewed within rational categories.[157] Susanna Wesley responded to her son in letter correspondence with determination. "You are quite mistaken," wrote Susanna to her son, "in your notion of faith. All faith is an assent, but all assent is not faith . . . The true measure of faith is the authority of the revealer, the weight of which always holds proportion with our conviction of his ability and integrity. Divine faith is an assent to whatever God has revealed to us, because he has revealed it."[158]

At this stage in Wesley's life, the chasm between an orthodox, but barren, representation of Christian doctrine and a practical and living faith plagued him. Peter Böhler, however, thought that Wesley was fundamentally confused in his thinking about faith, and possibly had no faith at all. On one occasion, Böhler frankly told Wesley, "my brother, my brother, that philosophy of yours must be purged away."[159] John Wesley was reluctant but a fortnight later, on 4 March 1738, engaged Böhler in another conversation at Oxford. If he had not faith—

and faith alone—for his assurance of salvation, then how could he logically proclaim the much cherished reformation teaching? Böhler's instruction transgressed both Wesley's egoism and logic; instead, the focus was squarely placed on the saving efficacy of faith itself. "Preach faith *till* you have it, and then, *because* you have it, you *will* preach faith."[160] This famous exchange revealed that, for Wesley at least, there was a desire for salvation. Robert Moore in his study of Wesley has noted the "religious egoism" of Wesley caused him intense anxiety and outlined a fundamental difference between the high churchman and the Moravian minister: "For the Moravian the power of God's word of grace had an objective reality and efficacious power that did not depend on the subjective condition of the preacher no matter how petty and self-centered that subjective condition might be. Wesley experienced a great deal of personal conflict over the idea that God might use him without his own spiritual house being in order."[161] At the core of Wesley's confusion was his inability to discover spiritual peace for his own soul after he believed he had sinned away his baptism, or what he termed, "the washing of the Holy Ghost."[162] Consequently, he began at the young age of ten to seek for his salvation through external measures. The teaching he received, Wesley remembered, "carefully taught that I could only be saved *by universal obedience, by keeping all the commandments of God,* in the meaning of which I was diligently instructed."[163] Inculcating young boys and girls in the role and intendment of deeds of obedience along with a fretfulness about their negligence were not uncommon in the ecclesiastical and social climate of eighteenth-century England. Donald Spaeth documents the anxiety concerning salvation in the following way: "Villagers were anxious about their salvation because they believed that they could jeopardise it by their own actions."[164] John Wesley preached the message of faith, notwithstanding with mixtures of both reception and rejection in these early and confused days, and found that his life needed more focus and determination which also fit into an acceptable social pattern during the Enlightenment.

Later, John Wesley's thinking was filtered in a way that was important for his own faith development and decisive for shaping an evangelical ethos throughout Wesleyan and Methodist history.[165] On 24 May 1738, he reluctantly went with a friend to a society meeting on Aldersgate street in London.[166] It was there that Wesley heard the reading of Luther's preface to the book of Romans and consequently made the observation about the topography of his heart: "I felt my heart strangely warmed. I felt I did trust in Christ, Christ alone for salvation, and an assurance was given me that he had taken away *my* sins, even *mine*, and saved *me* from the law of sin and death."[167] The rehearsal of the story in his journal became a model for early Methodist conversions and highlighted the *ordo salutis*; some even emphasized the personal pronoun, as Wesley had done in his journal account. This literary technique became a signal confirmation of both the restless soul which was awakened to spiritual life by an encounter with God's grace and underscored the significance of experienced religion in the modern world.

The significance of John Wesley's Aldersgate experience has been a topic of considerable debate. What was the nature of the experience which became so influential in Methodist circles?[168] According to older views of Wesley's "heart warming experience," he first encountered justifying grace on that evening in 1738. References to his own spiritual unrest on the way to and from Georgia are cited in support of this view.

However, another view indicates that what occurred at the Moravian society meeting is more realistically understood as a renewal of Wesley's understanding of holiness and a commitment in his own life which fundamentally shaped his mission and ministry. There is a sufficient amount of evidence that gives weight to the idea that Wesley struggled with his own understanding of faith before and after this experience. The clearest indicator was Wesley's editing of the voyage journals for publication. When he wrote about the matter, Wesley qualified the experience in both the 1774 and 1775 editions of the journal with footnotes that suggested he had changed his mind on his initial view of the experience.[169]

But what was Wesley's rationale in his self-evaluation of this episode? On the one hand, he combated the quietist and antinomian tendencies of the Moravians and came to believe that they had misunderstood faith alone (*sola fide*). Writing in the midst of heated debates, Wesley barbed those at the Fetter Lane Society who had excluded the means of grace in their affirmation of faith. To such individuals Wesley acidly remarked in the summer of 1740: "But as I find you more and more confirmed in the error of your ways, nothing now remains but that I should give you up to God."[170] On the other hand, Wesley never returned to a minimalist view of faith which submitted the Reformation dogma of justification by faith to a category that relegated acts of piety and mercy to a marginal status for Christian theology.

Under Peter Böhler's tutelage, John Wesley had embraced the notion that faith was not merely a personal confidence in God (*fiducia*) but a vital element of divine life that permeated human consciousness and which conversion was a signal indicator. This was a tenet that Wesley embraced, formulated, and appropriated throughout his life. It is clear from an examination of a variety of published sermons that Wesley conceptualized faith in terms of both "confidence" and "conviction," which explained why he repeatedly used the terms interchangeably. His much repeated definition of faith was supported by his favourite scriptural passage on this topic, Hebrews 11.1, from which he gleaned fundamental insight. "Faith is," wrote Wesley in his last mediation on the topic in 1791, "in one sense of the word, a divine conviction of God and of the things of God; in another (nearly related to, yet not altogether the same) it is a divine conviction of the invisible and eternal world."[171] Earlier, in his *Explanatory Notes*, Wesley had linked the faith in Hebrews 11.1 to the theological doctrine of justification. There Wesley commented: "And yet they may all be considered as evidences of the power of justifying faith in Christ, and of its extensive exercise, in a course of steady obedience, amid difficulties and dangers of every kind."[172] It was faith that enabled the spiritual senses of the believer to apprehend both the presence of God in the course of life and the contours of a world that was invisible to the physical eye.[173] It was also, in this respect, that Wesley's commitment to the idea of *sola fide* marked him as *homo perturbatus* and led to a radical separation between the ecclesiastical hierarchy of the Church of England and his

Methodist movement which sought to reform both church and nation. Stephen Gunter has succinctly remarked on the radical nature of John and Charles Wesley and their proclamation of the doctrine of justification. "John Wesley," writes Gunter, "was full of 'holy boldness' when he moved from the quadrangles of the colleges to the pulpits of the cathedrals, and no less daring was his brother Charles. With regard to this issue of salvation by faith, the Wesleys assaulted the citadel with a united front."[174]

The assault that the Wesley brothers received became divisive not solely because it transgressed the consensus of the church's leadership but it attacked the philosophical presuppositions of sceptical religion. The Deists, for instance, saw no need of a supernatural element for religion and repeatedly made their point with zeal. Anthony Ashley Cooper (1671-1713), the third Earl of Shaftsbury, for example, wrote an essay entitled "The Moralists, a Philosophical Rhapsody, Being a Recital of Certain Conversations on Natural and Moral Subjects" published with other essays under the title of *Characteristics of Men, Manners, Opinions, and Times*, where he besmirched supernatural beliefs as counterproductive to true religious discourse. Shaftsbury contended:

> For, while you are labouring to unhinge nature, while you are searching heaven and earth for prodigies and studying how to "miraculize" everything, you bring confusion in the world, you break its uniformity and destroy that admirable simplicity of order from whence the one infinite and perfect principle is known. Perpetual strifes, convulsions, violences, breach of laws, variation and unsteadiness of order show either no control or several uncontrolled and unsubordinate powers in nature. We have before our eyes either the chaos and atoms of the atheists or the magic and daemons of the polytheists.[175]

Matthew Tindal (1657-1733), twenty years later in his celebrated *Christianity as Old as the Creation: or, the Gospel, A Republication of the Religion of Nature*, maintained that, at the conclusion of the matter, the belief in supernatural religion begged the question. Rational religion, for Tindal, rested on logical argument and deductive reason which was the foundation of all true religious discourse. Therefore, to weaken the force of demonstration, Tindal argued, "is to strike at all Religion, and even the Being of God; and not to give Probability its due Weight, is to strike at the Authority of that Revelation you contend for; because, that God reveal'd his Will by *Visions, Dreams, Trances*, or any other Way besides the Light of Nature, can only come under the Head of Probability."[176] In Wesley's view, Tindal's assessment was off the mark. Conceptions that bracketed the supernatural from human experience committed the double error of falling victim to a philosophical prejudice which excluded transcendental events from the world *a priori* and thereby maligned the category of experience itself.

Soon after his Aldersgate experience in 1738, Wesley read various works on the history of justification and observed that the crowds which heard his preaching responded in ways that could not be reconciled with traditional religious expression. His diaries recorded that he was reading and making notes on Luther in February 1739, which was the latter's preface that had so impressed Wesley a few months before.[177] Also, in 1739 Wesley, extracted and published an edition of Robert Barnes's (1495-1540) *Treatise on Justification by Faith Only, According to the Doctrine of the Eleventh Article of the Church of England* and *The Doctrine of Salvation, Faith, and Good Works: Extracted from the Homilies of the Church of England.*[178]

However, foremost in importance, was John Wesley's sermon, "Justification by Faith."[179] The first record of Wesley preaching on this topic was four days after his Aldersgate experience. On 28 May 1738, Wesley contended he had been the victim of attacks being labelled "as a enthusiast, a seducer, and a setter-forth of new doctrines."[180] Later in the evening, Wesley went to chapel in Long-Acre where he preached on justifying faith and was received poorly there, as he had been in the morning at St. George's in Bloomsbury. Wesley thus concluded: "The last time I am to preach at either."[181] Wesley preached from Romans 4.5, at least eight times before 8 June 1742, when he stood atop his father's tombstone in Epworth.[182] His published sermon in 1746 noted that the divine plan for humanity was "'an image of his [God's] own eternity' an incorruptible picture of the God of glory."[183] However, when Adam sinned there emerged a vast chasm separating God from him, and by generational transmission of his sin, to the whole human race. The corrupted status (*status corruptionis*) of the soul, for Wesley, became a characteristic mark of depravity in general and a sign that humanity needed an external agency in order to induce repair.[184] Furthermore, the soul required justification, which Wesley defined as "forgiveness of sins," for its correction.[185] In this way the idea of salvation was both individually and socially determined. He developed this idea emphatically and pronounced, "for it is not a saint but a sinner that is forgiven, and under the notion of a sinner. God justifieth not the godly, but the ungodly; not those that are holy already, but the unholy. Upon what condition he doth this . . . cannot be holiness. To assert this is to say that the Lamb of God takes away only those sins which were taken away before."[186] The gospel was not designed for human assistance in the fulfilment of moral duties, as the Latitudinarians and others had suggested, but to magnify the futility of human righteousness altogether and provide a solution for the human condition. For Wesley, it was only faith in the God who performed the act of love incarnated in Jesus Christ which produced justification and demonstrated in the life of the believer both the universal and particular dimensions of salvation simultaneously. "Justifying faith implies," averred Wesley, "not only a divine evidence or conviction that 'God was in Christ, reconciling the world unto himself' but a sure trust and confidence that Christ died for *my* sins, that he loved *me*, and gave himself for *me*."[187] Faith, then, was the only sufficient condition for justification and that which, Wesley believed, overwhelmed the crowds in the midst of his preaching.

The journals of John Wesley, like many of the spiritual narratives of evangelicals in the eighteenth century, are highlighted with fantastic stories which contain passion and fervour. One such incident, which Wesley fondly recounted was that of John Haydon, a common weaver in Newgate, who had been offended at Wesley's preaching of justification by faith. In the context of his preaching tour in Newgate, Wesley had encountered Haydon, an individual whom Wesley described in his journal as a "man of a regular life and conversation, one that constantly attended the public prayers and sacrament, and was zealous for the Church and against Dissenters of every denomination."[188] Haydon had taken offence at the wild and frantic experiences that occurred under Wesley's field preaching and sought to convince people that convulsions and trances were examples of demonic influence.[189] However, Haydon sat down after an evening meal, and as was his custom, finished reading a sermon. On this occasion, after reading Wesley's sermon on justification by faith, the defiant Haydon was struck to the ground and exhibited characteristics for which he had previously expressed criticism and disdain.[190] The account published in Wesley's journal described Haydon's agitated state: "In reading the last page he changed colour, fell off his chair, and began screaming terribly and beating himself against the ground."[191] Wesley's summary of the incident exhibited both the disorder of Haydon's convulsion and the transformation of his attitude to Wesley himself. When Wesley entered Haydon's home he encountered his opponent, being held on the floor by several men, and Wesley observed that Haydon "immediately fixed his eyes upon *me* and, stretching out his hand cried, 'Ay, this is he, who I said was a deceiver of the people. But God has overtaken me.'"[192] Not only did Wesley see this event as a dramatic occurrence of divine power impinging on a human life but also a lucid depiction of the supernatural dimension of religious experience. In this regard, it should be remembered, Wesley often defined faith as a "supernatural persuasion."[193] With the case of Haydon, as with others throughout the Evangelical Revival, an overwhelming presence was tempered by justifying grace that produced peace of soul and a recreation of a self, which could be seen in light of what Robert Cushman described as a "cognition . . . whose verity becomes self-evident in virtue of the work of the Holy Spirit in the transformation of the mind and its conformation of the Holy."[194]

Many other examples contained in Wesley's works offered vivid displays of emotion and featured visionary experiences which transcended the boundaries of natural consciousness and a rational interpretation of religion.[195] However, the association of the doctrine of justification by faith with dreams and visions became a matter of concern for the Methodists and led an early conference at Bristol on 1-2 August 1745, to examine the link between dreams and the experience of justifying grace. "Do we not discourage," question 2.16 asked, "Visions and Dreams too much? As if we condemned them *toto genere*." Wesley's response made known both his belief in the divine-human quality of dreams and his perception that they had in the place of salvation: "We do not intend to do that. We learn from Acts 2.19 &c to expect something of this kind in the last Days. And we cannot deny that saving Faith is often given in Dreams and Visions in the Night, which Faith we account neither better nor worse, than if it comes by any other means."[196] The experiences of converts in the Evangelical Revival seemed to support the idea that the work of the Spirit could come through the medium of dreams.

John Bennet (1714-59), who began as a Methodist minister in 1743 and then separated from Wesley's connexion in 1752, experienced justifying grace by way of a visionary trance that was not unlike other Methodists of his day. In Bennet's vision, Jesus approached a tree and upon climbing it turned around, and Bennet noticed Christ's hands and feet "which seem'd to be newly pierced. Having extended his arms very wide, he looked up with his eyes towards heaven & gave up the ghost."[197] All this, Bennet professed, happened while "[I] lay up-on my Face on the Bed and was as broad awake during the whole time, as ever I was in any part of life."[198] Upon returning to awakened consciousness, Bennet left his room where he related his experience to a group that had gathered down-stairs in the house where he resided but the effects of the vision lingered in Bennet's mind. "From that very moment," he related, "I found a disinclination and abhorrence of all sin, and was sensible of that horrible ingratitude I had all my life shown to the God of my life, and to that blessed Redeemer who had been in so an affecting manner set forth as <u>crucified</u> before me."[199] About four o'clock the next morning he awoke and "sang hymns as the Spirit gave me utterance and my heart rejoiced in GOD <u>my Saviour</u>. The room was so light that for some moments I could have seen to have written, but afterwards went dark."[200] There are three instructive features in Bennet's vision that are revealing.

First, there was the symbolism of agrarian elements. The presence of trees played an interesting and significant place in Methodist visionary experiences. Often trees pointed to the redemptive power of the crucifixion of Jesus. Trees could also signal the "tree of life," an image taken from the creation account of Genesis 1-2. A anonymous print by that title was issued around the 1780s and showcased John Wesley and George Whitefield preaching their evangelical messages in the open air. In America, it was printed for John Haggerty (1744-1823) in 1791, an American Methodist preacher in Baltimore. In that edition several changes were made including the positioning of Wesley and Whitefield, some of the smug sinners below, and the demon in the bottomless pit. However, the general message of the print was maintained. Again, in the Victorian nine-teenth century another print was issued in 1845 but significantly updated to reflect the fashions and styles of the day. In the background, the tree of life which looms large over Methodist preachers inquire passers-by if they are ready to flee the wrath to come? Demons are also represented at a strategic point in the portrait luring people into a bottomless pit that is characterized by eternal flames.[201] The distinction is obvious between the vitality that is an offspring from the tree and the presence of hell-fire that is destroying the created world. At times the tree of life and the cross of Christ are equated with one another in Methodist narratives. Thus, Jane March wrote in correspondence to Mary Fletcher on 10 November 1812:

> I dreamed I was in Pursuit of the Tree of Life—& went a long travel all up & round the Gallery from the right side to the left, & down again to the Door I en-ter'd in—I then turn'd into an Alley which went into Austin friars—and came in-to a gravel'd Garden—where the *Tree* of *Life was railed in*—the path which was a *direct short cross path*—the sun shone with transparent Brightness.[202]

Figure 4. John Haggerty's "The Tree of Life." (1780s).
Methodist Archives. University of Manchester

Figure 5. John Haggerty's "The Tree of Life." 1791.

Figure 6. E. B. & E. C. Kellog, "The Tree of Life." (1846).

Second, many of the dream narratives of Methodists in the eighteenth century addressed the idea of whether salvation was progressive or instantaneous. From his early days with the Moravians, John Wesley had struggled with the idea of instantaneous salvation because he felt it negated the idea of righteousness and the importance of works. It was Böhler who instructed Wesley, suggesting that the person with doubt had no saving faith. The issue was never completely settled in Wesley's mind, however.[203] For Wesley, the concern about works never eclipsed, as it had for the Moravians, the need of the means of grace and many of the Methodist visions and dreams of salvation occurred while they were actively practicing the statutory and prudential means of grace.

Third, and what became a sticky issue for the Arminian Methodists, was the matter of God's sovereignty and the question of predestination. John Wesley never addressed the problem of election and its implied presence in the dreams of Methodists in either his publications or letter correspondence. Nevertheless, in many of the visionary experiences of Methodists during this era a forecast about future events in the life of the dreamer surfaced and salvation was realized in the consciousness of the subject by delineating the physiological development of the believer to sin, conviction, conversion, and holiness.

This problem, though, was one that John Wesley faced on other levels when he combated, for instance, Calvinism in the 1770s.[204] In his essay, *Predestination Calmly Considered*, Wesley expressed his belief in free-will as a supernatural restoration of human nature. "Natural free-will, in the present state of mankind, I do not understand," Wesley confessed, "I only assert, that there is a measure of free will supernaturally restored to every man, together with that supernatural light which "enlightens every man that cometh into the world.'"[205] Sin, however, as was previously mentioned, all but obliterated the *imagio dei* in the soul of man.[206] The Sovereignty of God, in Wesley's estimation, however, allowed for a divine work in the life of the soul that enabled human beings to respond, either positively or negatively.[207]

In response to the Calvinist viewpoint that works must be contextualized within the dogma of imputed righteousness, Wesley found no fundamental disagreement: "We affirm, that God alone does the whole work, without man's working at all; in one sense, we allow this also."[208] It was this conviction, moreover, that would lead to one undeniable conclusion for Wesley. In an undated sermon he proclaimed: "For if we are thoroughly sensible that we have nothing which we have not received, how can we glory as if we had not received it . . . If it is God that not only infuses every good desire, but that accompanies and follows it, else it vanishes away—then it evidently follows that "he who glorieth must glory in the Lord.'"[209]

The operative concept for Wesley was what Randy Maddox has termed, "the co-operant character of Salvation."[210] Throughout his life and writings, Wesley maintained a belief in the connection between divine and human agency and concomitantly that the works of God and the responses of individuals operated in tandem. Dreaming, in the Methodist narratives of the eighteenth century, then, was not an exercise in psychological illusion but a limpid argument that showed God was at work in the soul; a presence whose goal was the transfor-

mation of consciousness into a wider and more impressive level of spiritual existence. As such, it was also an indication that justification was, for Wesley who
stood in the Reformation lineage, *articulus stantis et cadentis ecclesiae* (the article on which the church stands or falls).[211]

Sanctification: God's Spirit at Work in Creation

When R. Newton Flew published his book entitled *The Idea of Perfection in
Christian Theology: A Historical Study of The Christian Ideal for the Present
Life* in 1934, he made a significant point for his readers: "There are three useful
historical sketches of the doctrine of perfection all by Wesleyan writers."[212]
Throughout the history of modern Christianity scholars have tended to under-
score the idea that the Methodist movement provided a formidable thrust to the
importance of the doctrine of the Holy Spirit and the appeal to view life within a
pattern of spiritual principles that considered holiness to be a crucial axiom of
Christian existence.[213] From its inception, the prism of holiness was one through
which John Wesley's view of religious experience was refracted. In the *Large
Minutes*, a document that intended to establish standards of conformity during
the Perfectionist disputes of the 1760s, Wesley described the central purpose of
the rise of Methodism:

> Q. What may we Reasonably believe to be God's Design in Raising up the
> Preachers Called Methodists?
>
> A. Not to form any new sect, but to reform the Church, and to spread Scriptural
> Holiness over the Land.[214]

The history of modern Christianity, especially in England and North America, indicates that Methodism emphatically embraced this idea. Methodist converts were made on both British and American soils during the eighteenth and
nineteenth centuries with incredible rapidity.[215] In Britain, on the one hand,
Methodists made their greatest increases in places where traditional religious
approaches were struggling. The historian, David Hempton, recounts: "Methodism . . . made its fastest gains in areas least amenable to paternalistic influence,
including freehold parishes, industrial villages, mining communities, marketing
towns, canal- and sea-ports and other centres of migratory populations."[216] By
the end of the eighteenth century, the renewal movement which had begun with
a small group of undergraduates and fellows at Oxford University had grown
into an impressive social and religious presence in the modern world. When
John Wesley died in early 1791 there were 75 circuits in England and Wales
alone. Additionally, some 70,000 British citizens understood themselves as
"Methodists," and nearly three-hundred active preachers itinerated in Wesley's
connexion.[217] At the core of Wesley's message, moreover, was perfection and
what it meant to live within an taxonomy of sanctification. However, as James
Logan observed, by the time the Methodist *Discipline* had been published in
1797 the answer to the question of the *Large Minutes* had radically changed.[218]

The goal and destiny of Methodist preachers, stated in the *Discipline* of 1797
was "above all to reform the nation, *by* spreading scriptural holiness over the

land."[219] John Wesley and his band of preachers travelled tirelessly in an attempt to fulfil this mission. Over the span of the eighteenth century Wesley himself travelled and preached his message of justification and sanctification with zeal and urgency.[220] The preachers, furthermore, found a common ground for the pursuit of spiritual perfection in the dreams, visions, and trances of their open-field congregants so that by the nineteenth century George Eliot's *Adam Bede* portrayed her Methodist characters Seth and Dinah with a staunch commitment to the supernatural. Eliot narrated: "They believed in present miracles, in instantaneous conversions, in revelations by dreams and visions."[221]

It was left to John Wesley, however, who in his organized and meticulous preaching tours, observed and articulated a rationale for the various religious experiences of the Methodists.[222] His defence of their significance and role in the larger picture of salvation was woven in and out of his writings, being duly noted in letters, sermons, theological documents, and through his editorial supervision of the *Arminian Magazine*. Wesley was forced by the volume of incidents to consider the multi-dimensional character of salvation and how religious encounters could be both understood and framed for the benefit of the societies. At the heart of Wesley's sermons, for example, was his concept of perfection and its necessary component in the religious life of the believer. Also, the dreams of Methodists signaled a type of symbiotic lattice in which both enlightenment and enthusiasm were held in what Hempton has termed "dialectical friction."[223] In North America, on the other hand, the pervasive embrace of Methodism was nothing short of extraordinary. The focus of Methodists and their emphasis on spiritual conversion in the camp meetings resolutely included the souls of men, women, and children. Richard Carwardine, in his essay "Methodist Ministers and the Second Party System," touches on the impressive nature of transatlantic Methodism in nineteenth-century America: "Numbering only 73,000 members in 1800, the Methodist Episcopal Church [MEC] grew at a rate that terrified other religious bodies, reached a membership of a quarter of a million by 1820, doubled its members in the following decade, penetrated into every quarter of the country, including traditionally hostile New England, and became the largest denomination in America."[224] But the impressive nature of American Methodism was not only in the numeric additions of converts but in the breadth of the populace it appealed to.

Contrary to its British counterpart, which mainly secured an audience among the plebeian populations, American Methodism reached out and incorporated a vast spectrum of social classes.[225] At one level, the success of the Methodist church in America was due to a tremendous company of preachers that portrayed the gospel with passion and flair.[226] Peter Cartwright (1785-1872), for example, in his *Autobiography* related how he entered into a debate on a riverboat with a Lieutenant Baker who was defending rational religion against "the religion of the bastard."[227] Cartwright responded with equal passion but it was when he criticized Thomas Paine (1737-1809), the free-thinking Deist, that the encounter moved from verbal debate to physical violence. Cartwright remembered:

> My opponent flew into a violent passion, and swore profanely, that God Almighty never made a man purer and more honourable man than Tom Paine. As he belched forth these horrid oaths, I took him by the chin with my hand, and moved his jaw together, and made his teeth rattle together at a mighty rate. He rose to his feet, so did I. He drew his fist, and swore he would smite me to the floor.[228]

Francis Asbury also reflected in his journal when he travelled across Virginia in the autumn of 1780: "The people are kind, and appear loving; but there is a great falling away; the devil has not been idle, and opposers have preached to them water, more than holiness; and have thus brought confusion among the Methodists."[229] The issue at stake for these Methodist preachers of the American frontier was both the place of perfection in their theological agenda; but, what is more important, the establishment of the life of holiness for future generations.

Christian Perfection:
Promise, Problem, and Perseverance

Howard Watkin-Jones's survey of the doctrine of the Holy Spirit in modern ecclesiastical history assessed John Wesley's primary significance in light of his pneumatology. In *The Holy Spirit from Arminius to Wesley*, Watkin-Jones observed that "Wesley's principal contribution to this subject is found throughout his emphatic teaching on the work of the Spirit, which rests altogether upon an assumption of His Deity."[230]

In John Wesley's estimation, the proper understanding of the Spirit had been eschewed by divines who were afraid that radical enthusiasts had formulated ideas which complicated spiritual presence altogether. Wesley's meeting with Joseph Butler (1692-1752), fellow of Oriel College, Oxford, and Bishop of Bristol in 1738 and later of Durham in 1750, exhibited a sharp discrimination that existed between John Wesley's Methodism and the hierarchy in the Church of England during the Enlightenment. After various disturbances associated with Wesley's preaching in the open fields, Butler declared to Wesley in August of 1739, "Sir, the pretending to extraordinary revelations and gifts of the Holy Ghost is a horrid thing, a very horrid thing."[231] In contradistinction to Butler's opposition, Wesley maintained that the manifestations should be conceptualized within an egalitarian framework whereby revelation was equally available to every Christian—man, woman, and child. "I pretend," answered Wesley to Butler, "to no extraordinary revelations or gifts of the Holy Ghost—none but what every Christian may receive, and ought to expect and pray for."[232] Additionally, Wesley was equally concerned about the isolation of holiness from scripture, tradition, and reason. From the very outset, he was constrained to rebut accusations of enthusiasm against the Methodist movement that, on the one hand, was transparently open to the idea of spiritual inspiration and, on the other hand, had to recoil and maintain its distance from fringe groups, like the French Prophets, which embraced the idea of immediate inspiration.[233] At the root of enthusiasm, in Wesley's mind, was a self-deception that was fuelled by an inaccurate view of spiritual presence, as one of his sermons warned.

Every the logician, Wesley set his case in propositional form: "Suppose his premises true, and his conclusions would necessarily follow. But here lies his mistake: his premises are false. He imagines himself to be what he is not. And therefore, setting out wrong, the farther he goes the more he wanders out of the way."[234] He then, concluded:

> Every enthusiast then is properly a madman. Yet his not an ordinary, but a religious madness. By religious I do not mean that it is any part of religion. Quite the reverse: religion is the spirit of a sound mind, and consequently stands in direct opposition to madness of every kind . . . And so the enthusiast is generally talking of religion, of God or of the things of God; but talking in such a manner that every reasonable Christian may discern the disorder of his mind. Enthusiasm in general may then be described in some such manner as this: a religious madness arising from some falsely imagined influence or inspiration of God; at least from imputing something to God which ought not to be imputed to him, or expecting something from God which ought not to be expected from him.[235]

In John Wesley's estimation, the activity of the Holy Spirit was principally located in the human soul where holiness could be observed both in particular and universal categories. In a homily on the Trinity, a subject to which Wesley gave no extended theological treatment during his lifetime, he asserted that the presence of the Spirit in the life of the believer was crucial to a proper Christian identity.[236] "But I know not how anyone can be a Christian believer till God the Holy Ghost witnesses that God the Father has accepted him through the merits of God the Son—and having this witness he honours the Son and the blessed Spirit 'even as he honours the Father.'"[237] A quarter of a century earlier, while preaching in Ireland, Wesley had composed a short letter to a Roman Catholic. The letter was written in a conciliatory tone and accentuated a bridge of reconciliation between the Catholic faith of the priest and Wesley's own Protestant understanding of Christianity. In his outline of the Protestant faith, Wesley affirmed:

> I believe in the infinite and eternal Spirit of God, equal with the Father and the Son, to be not only perfectly holy in himself, but the immediate cause of holiness in us; enlightening our understandings, rectifying our wills and affections, renewing our natures, uniting our persons to Christ, assuring us of the adoption of sons, leading us in our actions; purifying and sanctifying our souls and bodies, to a full and eternal enjoyment of God.[238]

The letter that Wesley composed showed that he was fundamentally orthodox in his theological understanding of the Holy Spirit; indeed, the gist of his comments were lifted from John Pearson's (1613-86) *An Exposition of the Creed*, which was widely revered as an authoritative exposition of the doctrine in the seventeenth and eighteenth centuries.[239] What set Wesley in the crossfire with his contemporaries was not only his understanding of the work of the Spirit in the soul but his view of the radical dimension of that work. When, in 1732, at the age of twenty-nine, John Wesley sat down to read William Law's essay on Christian perfection, it was a seminal moment in his theological development with practical issues that would stay with him throughout his life.[240] It should not be forgotten that during his days as an undergraduate at Christ Church and later as a fellow at Lincoln College, Wesley had also been favourably impressed by the writings of Thomas à Kempis (1380-1471) and Jeremy Taylor (1613-67). In these three works, especially Taylor's *Rule and Exercise of Holy Living,* Wesley was struck with the idea of circumspectly monitoring his daily activities.[241] He began with an "exact diary" which, in addition to recording his activities for the day, also divided his time into hourly segments. Later Wesley used his diaries as primary source material for the journals and published extracts from the journals for the wider public.[242] These early influences on the young Wesley occurred prior to his missionary trip to America, where by his own admission he endeavoured to "save his own soul."[243] The management of his life, then, was crucial to the pursuit of holiness and became his principal focus from the start.

Contrary to the view that compartmentalized the history of salvation into separate elements, Wesley conceptualized salvation as an event of religious experience where one encountered God's grace in one continuum which influenced and characterized all of human life. Throughout his life, however, Wesley's emphasis fell on salvation as the restoration of the *imago Dei* where the doctrine of Justification opened a window to a larger landscape. Kenneth Collins maintains:

> This larger process of sanctification, of which regeneration is ever an important part, entails the implanting of the love of God, in all its richness and power, in the human heart, and therefore involves the inculcation of holy tempers such as faithfulness, humility, meekness, and patience, which will displace such ungodly tempers as atheism, pride, self-will, and love of the world. This process of cleansing, of purifying human hearts so that the divine glory shines through, is nothing less than the very substance of salvation.[244]

At the beginning of 1740, Bishop Edmund Gibson had requested the presence of Wesley at an unofficial meeting at Whitehall. The ecstatic disturbances which emerged from the field preaching of Wesley and Whitefield along with the growing numbers who displayed rapturous experiences in the society meetings had dramatically increased and many faithful adherents in the Church of England were distraught at the widening influence and success of the Methodists. When Wesley responded to Gibson, he not only asserted his personal belief in the biblical teaching of perfection but outlined for the Bishop what the Methodists understood holiness to signify. Accordingly, after Wesley's explanation to Gibson, he was allowed to continue preaching and publishing on the topic.

What ensued from the encounter between the two men was a sermon which John Wesley published in 1741 and sold for six pence. The homily was divided into two parts: What perfection is *not* and what it *is*. He began negatively, with a categorical denial that spiritual perfection was linked to the idea of "perfectionism" where all human acts are free from ignorance, mistakes, weaknesses, or temptations.[245] Instead, Wesley equated perfection to holiness. "Indeed," he stipulated, "it is only another term for holiness. They are two names for the same thing. Thus, everyone that is perfect is holy, and everyone that is holy is, in the Scripture sense, perfect."[246] Inferentially, then, a quest for perfection logically leads to a definition of holiness. Throughout John Wesley's writings and Charles

Wesley's poetry too, holiness, sanctification, and perfection were all used interchangeably so that, the idea properly understood, bowed to the curious idea that the sanctified were "made free from outward sin."[247] However, a claim to external perfection necessarily involved a consideration of freedom from evil inclinations; namely impure thoughts and tempers. In other words, the lasting change that was required included a new orientation that endeavoured to mirror the purity of the love of Christ which was incarnated in Jesus of Nazareth. For Wesley, this possibility emerged for the Christian community not at the Crucifixion or Resurrection but at Pentecost. Utilizing John 7.38 and the image of "living water," Wesley contended that sanctification did not mean that miraculous powers were provided for an elite few, but that at Pentecost humanity was "made more than conquerors over sin by the Holy Spirit."[248] Certainly inbred or original sin continued to have its presence in the human psyche and the reconstitution of the soul required further moral and spiritual adjustments. As a result, the religious identification of believers continued to be fleshed out within the theological boundaries of nature and grace and the radical act of inward reorientation transcribed onto the soul in justification, moreover, occurred with explicit implications that were fully realized only in sanctification.[249] Stated in a more positive fashion, the presence of the Holy Spirit in the life of the soul lured the human subject into an intimate relationship with God and the experience of God's love. In this way, the disciple who becomes cognizant of the atonement of Christ is enabled to respond to God's love with love. In short, love is a self-multiplying gift.[250] This was an important distinction for Wesley who understood sanctification as the underpinning of the work of the Holy Spirit that was "rectifying our wills and affections."[251]

Throughout the 1760s, Wesley carried on various conversations about his understanding of spiritual perfection. As mentioned previously, a fraction of the disputes revolved around the etymological misunderstanding of the word. At another level, as with the Calvinists, who were opposed to Wesley's understanding of the function of sin in human nature as well as his notion that entire sanctification was able to rectify sin's power in human life, Wesley was adamant that spiritual perfection was the answer to the Calvinist's thorny enigma. Furthermore, he entertained the idea that complete perfection or entire sanctification, as it was sometimes called, was attainable in the present life. In his homily on Jesus's Sermon on the Mount, Wesley ridiculed the Calvinists and asserted his fundamental belief in the priority of sanctification:

Figure 7. Samuel Robert: Prayer and the Devil. Courtesy of John Walsh

We must cry aloud to every penitent sinner, "Believe in the Lord Jesus Christ, and thou shalt be saved." But at the same time we must take care to let all men know we esteem no faith but that which worketh by love"; and that we are not "saved by faith" unless so far as we are delivered from the power as well as the guilt of sin. And when we say, "Believe, and thou shalt be saved," we do not mean, "Believe, and thou shalt step from sin to heaven, without any holiness coming between, faith supplying the place of holiness;" but, believe and thou shalt be holy; believe in the Lord Jesus, and thou shalt have peace and power together.[252]

However, it was the Calvinists who began to press the point with Wesley and he in turn formulated a theological rationale for his teaching about sanctification. Samuel Robert, a Methodist with Calvinistic leanings, in his unpublished manuscript notebook drew a picture of a demonic apparition that appeared to him concerning his prayers.[253] Robert opened his comments about Wesley at the beginning of his notebook with the declaration: "I really believe that Mr. John Westlay [sic] himself is quite a Stranger to the Saving Knowledge of Jesus; In so much that he is nothing but a blind man."[254] In the 1758 conference, the preachers were warned to treat the topic circumspectly and then, following the London conference of 1759, Wesley published his *Thoughts on Christian Perfection*.[255] Wesley's essay was published in a question and answer format, which gave him the opportunity to summarize his beliefs about perfection succinctly. Question twenty-eight asked: "Is this death to sin and renewal in love gradual or instantaneous?" John Wesley's response was affirmative but elusive: "The change wrought when the soul dies to sin is of a different kind and infinitely greater than any before, and than any one can conceive till he experiences it."[256] The answer opened the door for both British and American Methodists to consider the possibility and priority of instantaneous sanctification. Of course, such experiences already had occurred, as Wesley's meeting with Gibson indicated. What Wesley did not count on, however, was that the Methodists that had been under his watchful care would start to move in directions that he had not directed and this eventually caused him to sever relationships with preachers that he had once considered dear to his evangelical programe. But, in the 1760s, those who claimed extraordinary experiences multiplied and demanded his immediate attention. The question Wesley had to consider was whether instantaneous experiences would become woven into the fabric of his understanding of religious experience and therefore characterize the religious identification of Methodists altogether.

Central to this phase of development in Methodist history were Thomas Maxfield and George Bell. Thomas Maxfield, a native of Bristol had been converted by John Wesley when he first visited there in 1739.[257] After two years of travelling with Charles Wesley, Bell returned to Bristol in 1741. Maxfield was a powerful preacher during the Evangelical Revival and in the nineteenth century, Luke Tyerman who sided with Wesley in the controversy nevertheless took note of Maxfield's preaching ability: "His sermons being accompanied with such power, that numbers were made penitent and were converted."[258] However, Wesley had been disturbed by the irregularity of the conversions which occurred under Maxfield's preaching, and he rushed to London so that the Methodist societies would be restored to order. Wesley's intentions was prevented by his mother, Susanna, who had been living next door to the Foundery, and advised

Figure 8. "The Reverend Mr Thomas Maxfield, Assistant Chaplain to the Right Honourable the Countess of Huntingdon." Methodist Archives. University of Manchester.

her son that Maxfield was as qualified to preach as Wesley himself, and told John: "Take care what you do with respect to that young man, for he is as surely called of God to preach as you are."[259] Maxfield's disciple, George Bell, less astute was an opportunist who found in the Methodists a means of securing a place for himself among the fringe of the movement. Despite current research, little is known about Bell's life outside of his involvement in the controversies of the 1760s.[260] He had been born in county Durham, but when is not known, and he died in Paddington sometime in 1807. Bell had served as a corporal in the King's life guards until he had a religious experience around 1758.[261] Both Maxfield and Bell interpreted the New Testament admonition of being filled with the Holy Spirit. After their own conversion experiences, they began preaching and teaching in London to various Methodist societies and insisted that the same Spirit which had operated through Christ was also present and speaking through them too. Moreover, they embraced the idea that sanctification explicitly entailed the idea of "sinless perfection" where a believer who had experienced a "second birth" was incapable of error or sin in his or her life. As a consequence, there emerged various types of issues over doctrine and order that both frustrated and burdened Wesley during the decade.

John Wesley, at the conclusion of his sermon on Christian perfection, had firmly asserted, "if *any* unrighteousness remain in the soul it is not cleansed from *all* unrighteousness . . . It remains, then, that Christians are saved in this world from all sin, from all unrighteousness; that they are now in such a sense perfect as not to commit sin, and to be freed from evil thoughts and evil tempers."[262] A crisis emerged when several Methodist followers took this idea to heart along with Wesley's conviction that "perfect love" and justification were gifts instantaneously granted. The end result was a distorted perfectionism that insisted on illusionist epiphanies and a coterie of followers that elevated their personal experiences above reasonable practices or expectations.

At the centre of the controversy were several groups who were meeting in London during the early 1760s. In a letter of 3 April 1761, which Wesley included in the *Arminian Magazine,* a Mrs. Jay claimed after being perturbed by wandering thoughts she experienced an ecstatic vision of a third heaven, where her soul was visibly prostrated before the Lord's feet. It was then that she was overwhelmed with a peace that enabled her to focus on Jesus Christ. In a moment God replaced her drifting thoughts with a focused consciousness which set her mind and heart on Christ.[263] Others underwent this type of experience too and eventually it became known as a "second blessing."[264] Despite Wesley's sermon on wandering thoughts, published in 1762, where he noted that human beings continued to struggle with thoughts that distracted their focus, several interpreted these "blessings" as a deposit of sanctifying grace which brought their souls into a deeper awareness of God.[265] Initially Wesley was not disconcerted by these expressions of religious fervour. On 14 February 1761, for example, Wesley expressed his approval of the London situation: "The work of God goes on mightily here both in conviction and conversion . . . I believe within five weeks six in one class have received remission of sins and five in one band received a second blessing."[266] He was happy for news of them to be published and on 9 August 1772, he wrote to Jane Salkeld (1755-1812), a school mistress in Weardale: "Exhort all the little ones that believe to make haste and not delay the time of receiving the second blessing; and be not backward to declare what God has done for your soul to any that truly fear him."[267]

Unlike John, however, Charles Wesley believed that entire sanctification was not attainable before death, and was usually reserved for death-bed conversions.[268] Often more sceptical than his brother, Charles Wesley not only insisted that the idea of instantaneous holiness underestimated the reality of sin in the human, which he repeatedly saw demonstrated in various enthusiastic groups that exhibited *theosis* to a fault. In an account of his encounter with Prophetess Mary Lavington, a French Prophet, who many Methodists in London during the 1760s heard with eager anticipation, Charles Wesley observed:

> As that she can call the Angels & Archangels & command Christ himself to her in whatever shape she pleases, that GOD appears to her sometimes as a Dove and sometimes as an Eagle. That in prayers she sees a little Angel on a Ladder with a Cap & Feather denoting the Swiftness of his Motion . . . That the Sacnt [sic; sacrament] was a Beggarly Element & God would shortly destroy all outward things, Means, Ordinances & Churches.[269]

An interesting commentary on the Methodists in London during the 1760s, which is substantiated by this document, indicates that despite the rhetoric that John and Charles Wesley produced against the French Prophets several of the Methodists were intrigued by Lavington's ministry, which indicates that the French Prophets had penetrated Methodism more significantly than has previously been admitted. From John Wesley's viewpoint, however, fervent prayer meetings and ecstatic experiences were all elements of the revival which were endorsed by divine presence. Even though there were incidents that he could not condone, Wesley was convinced that they could not be discounted altogether because of their irregularity or issues relating to possible psychological deception. On the eve of the 1760s controversy, he recorded in his journal for 25 November 1759: "The shadow is no disparagement of the substance, nor the counterfeit of the real diamond. We may farther suppose that Satan will make these visions an occasion of pride . . . But still, to slight or censure visions in general would be both irrational and unchristian."[270] Wesley attributed the experience of the "second blessing" and its favourable reception among Methodists in London to the fervent prayers of members in attendance at the meetings, among which George Bell was included.[271] Without resolving the situation in London, however, John Wesley left on Monday, 9 March and did not return until 31 October. While Wesley was away, Thomas Maxfield and George Bell emerged and gave leadership to an extreme group of perfectionists. As a consequence, upon Wesley's return, things were heightened and the architect of the Methodists found himself in the middle of an intense battle for both his movement of renewal and adherence of a balanced belief in the doctrine of perfection.

With John Wesley absent from London, there developed a leadership vacuum among those who claimed to have received demonstrative manifestations of love and holiness. As the perfectionist revival progressed, there was not only an upsurge of zeal for the experience of sinless perfection but also a mounting dislike by enthusiastic adherents against Wesley's caution of those who were claiming perfection for themselves. At the 1761 Leeds conference, Wesley discussed the idea of perfection at great length and everyone seemed to be satisfied. But later that year, William Grimshaw (1708-63) told Wesley that some of his preachers were dissatisfied with his restraint on the subject and mocked Wesley as "a child of the devil."[272] As a consequence, the affair became extremely damaging not only to Wesley's explicit leadership but his teaching on Christian perfection which caused the movement towards "entire sanctification" to lose much of its attractiveness.

The damage that the London societies suffered can be seen in an extraordinary letter composed by the Irish Methodist, John Walsh (1745-99). Walsh, a deist had been converted under the preaching ministry of John Wesley on one of his preaching tours. At the insistence of Charles Wesley, he wrote an account of the society which Maxfield and Bell were involved with during the 1760s. The letter included poetry, letters, and personal reflections, at the centre that were comments on his own pursuit of perfection.[273] The document indicates that, like many Methodists of the day, Walsh's own sinful condition was revealed to him in dreams and stood in tandem with a wide circle of Methodists in the eighteenth century which saw no contradiction between visions of supernatural splendour and the experience of justification and sanctification. A Mrs. Burroughs, for example, "saw daily, sometime before & ever since, the Air full of Spirits."[274] John Walsh had recorded his own dreams in the context of his pursuit of perfection and had recollected the arrogance of those who claimed to have received absolute and total perfection.[275] Nevertheless, his visions and dreams of salvation indicated that there was in his mind a coherent line that moved from the visible to the invisible worlds.

Walsh's letter also demonstrated that George Bell had a significant influence on the life of the London societies. Despite Walsh's continual experiences of ecstasy and rapture, Bell doubted his perfection. Their relationship was taxed and Walsh wrote to Bell: "My own Ears having heard you say that you was perfect: then that you could not fall from your perfect State, unless GOD himself could fall from his Throne."[276] George Bell claimed to have experienced sanctification in 1761 with a vision that John Wesley later included in the *Arminian Magazine*. In the vision, Bell confessed: "I seemed as if my spirit was just ready to force its way out of my body."[277] However, on 12 January 1762, Walsh

brought Bell to converse with John Berridge (1716-93), an evangelical Anglican.[278] There Bell revealed his passion and focus:

> What he now chiefly said was, that GOD had given him the Gift of healing,
> which he had already practiced & or raising the Dead, which he should perform
> in GOD's time. That the Milennium was begun, & he should never die. That he
> & several other Men had seen Satan bound & cast into the bottomless Pit, & the
> Angel had set a Seal upon him that he should not come out to deceive the Na-
> tions.[279]

When Wesley returned to London and visited the societies again on 1 November 1761, he found them in disarray. A description by a G. C. entitled
"Thoughts on the Work of Sanctification," included in the *Arminian Magazine*
in 1790, portrayed the London disturbances in sensational terms: "They . . . pro-
fessing to have gifts of healing, and in London did really attempt to heal the
blind, and raise the dead."[280] The disputes in London were burdensome for Wesley. In correspondence with his brother in 1762, John expressed his concern to
Charles: "The meeting in Beech Lane, before I came to town, was like a bear-
garden; full of noise, brawling, cursing, swearing, blasphemy, and confusion."[281]
As he had done earlier, with his field preaching experiences in Bristol, John
Wesley noticed that there were many who exhibited genuine signs of justification and sanctification. He recorded in his journal for 14 November 1762: "I
spent an hour with a little company near Grosvenor Square. For many years this
has been the darkest, driest spot of all in or near London. But God has now wa-
tered the barren wilderness, and it is become a fruitful field."[282]

The challenge posed by Maxfield and Bell required resolution, and it became
evident that their continued membership in the Methodist society was problematic for Wesley. Soon after Wesley returned from his preaching tour, he had
sought to bring about reconciliation between himself and the two self-
proclaimed leaders of the London societies—Maxfield and Bell. Wesley had not
only established his commitment to the doctrine of perfection through his own
preaching but on 21 December 1761, he began to write his "Farther Thoughts on
Christian Perfection," which was published later in 1763.[283]

At the conference of 1761, Maxfield had been charged with a minor offence
but Wesley had come to his defence and cooler heads prevailed. By the end of
1761, however, on 29 December, Wesley called another meeting with the intention of clearing the air but Maxfield was conspicuously absent. Wesley recorded
his frustration in a journal entry for that day: "In order to remove some understandings, I desired all the parties concerned to meet me. They did so; all but
T[homas] M[axfield], who flatly refused to come. Is this only the first step toward a separation? Alas for the man! Alas for the people!"[284]

Even though Maxfield would join Wesley to serve over two thousand communicants at Spitalfields on 1 January 1762, nearly a year had passed into the
controversy and the confusion of matters in the London societies became increasingly divisive. On 2 January, 1762, Wesley left London again and did not
return until 30 October. With Wesley's second absence matters descended further, as George Bell waxed more hysterical in his prayer meetings which culminated in his predicting the world would reach a cataclysmic end on 28 February

1763. Upon his return, an alarmed Wesley visited Bell and attempted to convince him of grotesque errors. All was futile, however, and Wesley observed that Bell "was as unmoved as a rock."[285] A month later, on 5 February 1763, Bell turned in his class ticket. On the same day, Maxfield followed suit and ceased to meet in class meeting. It was an anguished time for Wesley and in correspondence with Charles, he wrote: "The frightful stories wrote from London had made all our preachers in the North afraid even to mutter about perfection; and, of course, the people on all sides were grown good Calvinists in that point. . . . No man was more profitable to me than George Bell while he was simple of heart. Oh for heat and light united!"[286] A couple of years on the other side of the controversy, he wrote to Charles again and expressed his frustration and despair. In a letter of 27 June 1766, John Wesley referred to himself as an "honest heathen," and "a proselyte of the Temple." Then, he revealed the heaviness of his heart over the issue of perfection: "[I have no] direct witness, I do not say that [I am a child of God], but of anything invisible or eternal. And yet I dare not preach otherwise than I do, either concerning faith, or love, or justification, or perfection . . . I want all the world to come to ὂυ οὐκ οἶδα."[287] John Wesley's depression was pronounced because Thomas Maxfield had been one of his first preachers who he referred to as a "son in the gospel." Henry Rack has underscored this relationship and suggested that it was because of Wesley's support and encouragement that Maxfield enjoyed his status as a respected Methodist preacher.[288] The division that ensued between father and son, however, not only indicated a separation of personalities but a division within the movement itself which threatened the very unity that Wesley sought for his Methodist people.

The secession that Maxfield and Bell caused was both intense and important. The damage inflicted over sinless perfection was a major one and Wesley distanced himself from the London disturbances. Immediately after his confrontation with George Bell it became apparent, for Wesley at least, that he must maintain his status as leader of the Methodists. As a consequence, Wesley issued a letter to the *London Chronicle* and publicly withheld his endorsement of Bell.[289] A month later, and five days after Bell turned in his class ticket, John Wesley wrote to the editor of the *London Chronicle* with a more final denunciation.[290] For Maxfield, however, the issue was not so transpicuous. In his *A Vindication of the Rev. Mr. Maxfield's Conduct, In Not Continuing with the Rev. Mr. John Wesley: And of his Behaviour Since That Time,* Maxfield outlined his recollection of the course of events.[291] On the title page was the New Testament citation Acts 26.2: "I think myself happy, King Agrippa, because today I shall answer for myself before you concerning all the things which I am accused by the Jews." The core of the matter for Maxfield was the manner in which he believed Wesley had jockeyed for political position after the separation occurred between Bell and himself. Wesley had, in Maxfield's judgment, demonized his opponents without regard to their erstwhile value to the evangelical cause. "While I was with Mr. Wesley's, and preached with them, my Life, Character, and Doctrine were entirely approved of," wrote Maxfield, "but upon my not continuing with them, I was greatly approached both as to my Life and Doctrine."[292] Additionally, Maxfield highlighted the association of Bell and Wesley and recounted Wesley's repeated support of Bell. Why, reasoned Maxfield, the sudden change of mind which defaced him publicly in the *London Chronicle*. George Bell, contended Maxfield, did not leave for the reasons that Wesley had stipulated, "but for his double Dealings and unfaithful proceedings."[293]

It would appear that Maxfield's claim had more merit than Wesley allowed. The evidence in Wesley's journals and letter correspondence reveal a leader of a movement that was finding it difficult to control a faction that was moving quickly towards independence. Additionally, it is a note of contradiction why Wesley was so critical of Bell's prediction about the end of the world when he too had approvingly utilized others who had interest in eschatological predictions. Certainly such accounts were not uncommon in the eighteenth century. Johann Bengel (1687-1752), pietist scholar of the New Testament and well respected by John Wesley, had predicted the consummation of the world would occur in 1836 and Charles Wesley himself predicted the world would end in 1794.[294] In a letter written to an unknown correspondent in the spring of 1754, Charles Wesley declared an exact date for the calamitous end of the world: "GOD has been pleased to lead me this winter, as it were by the hand, thro the labyrinth of the scripture Prophecies relative to the latter times . . . . It will appear a Paradox to affirm that all these events will be accomplished in FORTY years time counted from this present year 1754."[295] Charles Wesley's letter showed that he had been interested in eschatological prophecies for about eight years prior to his writing of the letter.[296] What is more, there was indication that Charles Wesley entertained the idea of writing a book on end-time prophecies.[297] Though there is no documentation that would suggest that John Wesley was aware of this specific letter of his younger brother, it is hard to imagine that he would have been unaware of his younger brother's interests in eschatology or predictions about the end of the world. One may wonder, then, in all the Wesleyan corpus, why there is no strict warning from John Wesley about the errors involved in such speculations. Furthermore, with Charles Wesley's own reserved attitudes about the London societies in the 1760s, it would be logically consistent that Bell's prediction of the cataclysmic end of the world was an issue that carried more political collateral than either he or his older brother were willing to admit. This contention, Gareth Lloyd maintains, was a dark feature where John Wesley cannot be seen in a good light. Lloyd writes: "The activities of George Bell, encouraged by John Wesley, came very close to destroying Methodism within the capital and certainly drove a nail into the coffin of Anglican-Methodist relations."[298] Contrary to predications in the eighteenth century that announced the end of the world, Bell's was strongly associated with an incautious view of the apocalypse that would have incited alarm among his hearers. It was this from which John Wesley felt it necessary to separate himself.

Seeing All Things Clearly:
The Place of Visionary Experiences

H. Ray Dunning wrote some time ago in his *Grace, Faith, and Holiness: A Wesleyan Systematic Theology* that human experience is always simultaneously subjective and objective.[299] Nothing could have been more clear to John Wesley as he increasingly became more conscious of the experiences of people who embraced his view of salvation. Both traditional and counter-cultural, the experiences of the Methodists in eighteenth-century England and North America saw their encounters with God something that not only defined their piety but an important part of their self-understanding. This was true in a controversial way when it came to the affirmation of dreams and visions. The length of the discussion offered in this chapter already gives evidence that the experience of visionary experiences among Methodists during the Enlightenment was an important one and should not be sidelined too quickly in a discussion of popular religion during the period.

What this indicates above all else is that the experience of God was important to John Wesley and his followers because it was an energy and force that transformed their lives in conscious and unconscious ways. Ever the empiricist, Wesley was adamant that an observation of human nature would reveal certain and distinct categories which one could reasonably outline specific features about both God and human nature. Describing the religion he preached Wesley wrote in *An Earnest Appeal to Men of Reason and Religion*: "A religion evidently founded on, and every way agreeable to, eternal reason, to the essential nature of things. Its foundation stands on the nature of God and the nature of man, together with their mutual relations."[300] In human experience Wesley found data that could not be regulated to one sector but spoke to the project of religious epistemology on several different levels. The experience of the divine was not to be neatly compartmentalized but viewed in a polyvalent spectrum. This, no doubt, caused Wesley continual problems as he attempted to sort out the authentic from fabricated experiences of his adherents. There were some who fabricated experiences or, at the very least, were self-deceived about their so-called days of "judgment." One instance came from Margaret Barlow who some Methodists, including John Wesley, believed to be given over to "strong delusion." She claimed to have a word from God about the final judgment that did not materialize at her forecasted time. Wesley sarcastically asked in his journal how she reconciled matters:

> Easily enough. "Moses, said she, could not see the face of God till he had fasted forty days and forty nights. We must do the same." So for three weeks they too no sustenance but three gills of water per day, and three weeks more they took each three gills of water-gruel per day. What a mercy that half of them did not die in making the experiment![301]

The problems associated with discernment did not eclipse the truth of experience altogether. For Wesley, the avalanche of experiences that emerged in his preaching and others like him on several continents spoke to the validity of religious experience in the Evangelical Revival in general and the experiences of Methodists in particular.

What became an interesting feature of eighteenth-century Methodism, however, was the insistence that visions and dreams be located as a confirmation of the theological doctrines of justification and sanctification. The occurrence of dreams among Methodists in the modern world not only served to give validity to the idea that the doctrine of justification and sanctification which was being preached by Methodists in England but also by those trans-Atlantic preachers who were finding followers with increasing intensity.[302] Additionally, however, and what is more important to the argument presented here, is that the visions and dreams of these early converts was a indicator that the ideas and theology of grace which the Methodists were promoting in their proclamations enabled individuals to see more clearly into an invisible world. And what they saw was remarkable. Not only were there visions of the Trinity and the movement of redemption throughout human history but also portraits of splendour that awaited them if they could continue to the end. The function of visionary experiences were many but first and foremost they enabled individuals to make sense of their plight and to coherently see their lives within a matrix that was held together by love, compassion, and grace.

Notes

1. Mary Fletcher, *The Life of Mrs. Mary Fletcher Consort and Relict of the Rev. John Fletcher Vicar of Madeley, Salop. Compiled from Her Journal, and Other Authentic Documents,* ed., Henry Moore (1817; repr., Salem, OH: Schmul Publishing Co., 1997), 115. Mary Bosanquet later married John Fletcher, vicar of Madeley in 1777. Throughout the discussion here she will be referred to as Mary Bosanquet in the text and footnoted as Mary Fletcher.

2. 12 April 1784. *BEW* 23: 302.

3. Fletcher, *The Life of Mrs. Mary Fletcher,* 108-10.

4. From the Judeo-Christian Scriptures, the tithe was ten percent of one's income given to God as an offering. See Malachi 3. 10-20.

5. Fletcher, *The Life of Mrs. Mary Fletcher,* 108.

6. Fletcher, *The Life of Mrs. Mary Fletcher,* 109.

7. "Dreams are visual experiences that are necessarily transformed into words in order to turn them into meaningful communication, not just among individuals, but also between the dreaming individual and her/himself. Their presence in culture is thus characterized by a semiotic complexity of levels in which the seen and the heard, the spoken and the shown, are intensely interrelated, but also marked in their difference . . . Thus they resemble other states in which numinous and supernatural experiences occur." Galit Hasan-Rokem, "Communication with the Dead in Jewish Dream Culture," in David Shulman and Guy Stroumsa, eds., *Dream Cultures: Explorations in the Comparative History of Dreaming* (Oxford: Oxford University Press, 1999), 213. While there is much debate on the definition of dreams, especially in relation to visions, I shall adopt for my analysis the above quotation by Hasan-Rokem.

8. Artemidorus, *Artemidorus' Oneirocritica: Text, Translation, & Commentary,* trans. and ed., Daniel E. Harris-McCoy (Oxford: Oxford University Press, 2012).

9. Justin Martyr, *First Apology,* xviii in *ANF* 1: 169.

10. Tertullian, *A Treatise on the Soul*, iii in *ANF* 47: 225.

11. "Dreams believed to be a divine means of communication to worshippers or the work of evil spirits, became terrifying experiences, the subject of minute investigations." W. H. C. Frend, *The Rise of Christianity* (Philadelphia, PA: Fortress Press, 1984), 168.

12. See for example, Max Voigt, *Beiträge zur Geschichte der Visionenliteratur im Mittelalter* (Leipzig: Mayer and Müller, 1924). More focused are the essays in Carolyn Muessig and Ad Putter, eds., *Envisaging Heaven in the Middle Ages* (London: Routledge, 2007) and Bernard McGinn, "Visions and Visualizations in the Here and Hereafter," *Harvard Theological Review* 98 (2005): 227-46.

13. B. C. Barker-Benfield, The *Manuscripts of Macrobius Commentary on the Somnium Scipionis* (D. Phil. thesis, Oxford University, 1975).

14. Steven Kruger, "Medical and Moral Authority in the Late Medieval Dream," in Peter Brown, ed., *Reading Dreams: The Interpretation of Dreams from Chaucer to Shakespeare* (Oxford: Oxford University Press, 1999), 62. See also Steven Kruger, *Dreaming in the Middle Ages* (Cambridge: Cambridge University Press, 1992), 83-122.

15. René Descartes, "Olymica," in C. Adam and P. Tannery, ed., *Oeuvres de Descartes*, Nouvelle Ed.,11 vols. (Paris: J. Vrin, 1996), 10:180-88. On Descartes dream see Richard A. Watson, ed., *The Dream of Descartes* (Carbondale, IL: Southern Illinois University Press, 1987), Michael Keevak, "Descartes Dream and Their Address for Philosophy," *Journal for the History of Ideas* 53 (1992): 373-96, and Alan Gabbey and Robert E. Hall, "The Melon and the Dictionary: Reflections on Descartes Dreams," *Journal for the History of Ideas* 59 (1998): 651-58.

16. John Bunyan, *The Pilgrim's Progress: from this world to that which is to come: delivered under the Similitude of a Dream; wherein is discovered the manner of his setting out his dangerous journey, and safe arrival at the desired countrey* (London: Printed for Nathan Ponder, 1678). "These allegorical dreams told a story in which a man received in sleep an insight into divine truth, either through direct instruction by a symbolic or supernatural guide, or by participation in a symbolic action." Mabel Schneider, *John Bunyan's The Pilgrim Progress in the Tradition of Medieval Dream Visions* (Ph. D. thesis, University of Nebraska, 1969), 3.

17. John Locke, *An Essay Concerning Human Understanding*, 2.1.16. "Various parcels of visible ideas, not joined in nature, start up together in the fancy, contiguous to each other, we often see monsters, chimeras, and combinations, which have never been actually presented." David Hartley's *Observations on Man, His Frame, His Duty, and His Expectations.* 2nd ed., 2 vols. (London: Printed by Richard Cutwell, 1791), 1: 73, where Hartley offered an analysis of human nature and dreams.

18. François-Marie Arouet (Voltaire), *Philosophical Dictionary*, ed. and introduction, John R. Iverson (1764; repr., New York: Barnes and Noble, 2006), 391. For discussion of the life of Voltaire, Roger Pearson, *Voltaire Almighty: A Life in Pursuit of Freedom* (London: Bloomsbury, 2005).

19. Thomas Tyron, *A Treatise of Dreams & Visions, Wherein the Causes Natures and Uses of Nocturnal Representations, and the Communications both of Good and Evil Angels as also Departed Souls, to Mankinde, are Theosophically Unfolded; that is, According to the Word of God, and the Harmony of Created Beings.* 2nd ed. (London: n.p., 1700), 31-32. Also a Mr. Squire's "The Case of Henry Axford, who recovered the use of his tongue, after having been four years dumb, by means of a frightful dream," *Royal Society of London Philosophical Transactions General Index*, 142.

20. Andrew Baxter, *An Enquiry into the Nature of the Human Soul; wherein the Immateriality of the Soul is Evinced from the Principles of Reason and Philosophy* (London: Printed by James Bettenham, 1740).

21. Baxter, *An Enquiry into the Nature of the Human Soul*, 270-71.

22. David Hall's *Worlds of Wonder, Days of Judgment: Popular Religious Belief in Early New England* (1989; repr., Cambridge, MA: Harvard University Press, 1990) and Peter Williams, *Popular Religion in America: Symbolic Change and the Modernization Process in Historical Perspective* (1980; repr., Urbana, IL: University of Illinois Press, 1989), provide introductions to this facet of American history.

23. Mechal Sobel, *Teach Me Dreams: The Search for Self in the Revolutionary Era* (Princeton: Princeton University Press, 2000), 30.

24. See, Freeborn Garrettson, *The Experience and Travels of Freeborn Garrettson, Minister of the Methodist-Episcopal Church in North America* (Philadelphia, PA: n.p., n.d.; repr., Dublin: R. Jackson, 1778); Chloe Russell, *The Complete Fortune Teller and Dream Book* (Boston, MA: n. p., 1800); and John Woolman, *A Journal of the Life, Gospel Labours, and Christian Experiences of that Faithful Minister of Jesus Christ, John Woolman* (Philadelphia, PA: Printed by Joseph Crukshank, 1774).

25. John Wigger, *Taking Heaven by Storm: Methodism and the Rise of Popular Religion in America* (New York: Oxford University Press, 1998), 106. See also, Donald Byrne, *No Foot of Land: Folklore of American Methodist Itinerants* (Metuchen, NJ: Scarecrow Press, 1975); and Lester Ruth, *A Little Heaven Below: Worship at Early Methodist Quarterly Meetings* (Nashville, TN: Kingswood Books, 2000).

26. One such instance was a well known occurrence west of Penzance in Cornwall which described a "large fleet of ships . . . and the scene was changed to an army or armies, seeming to be smartly engaged in battle," *Gentleman's Magazine* 24 (1752): 482. John Wesley also commented on the story, 7 September 1755. *BEW* 21: 28.

27. Nat Turner, for example, lead a violent slave rebellion, based on a dream. See, Kenneth S. Greenberg, ed., *Nat Turner: A Slave Rebellion in History and Memory* (Oxford: Oxford University Press, 2003).

28. 19 November 1738. *BEW* 19: 21. See also John Wesley's *Works* (Bristol: William Pine, 1774), 4: 99, where this section of Wesley's journal was marked by an asterisk which accentuated the seriousness that Wesley placed on it.

29. Haxey Carr located southwest of Epworth in South Yorkshire.

30. 24 July 1757. *BEW* 21: 116-117, where Wesley related a narrative of a woman who had a premonition in a dream of drowning at Haxey Carr. She was ridiculed for her dream and reluctantly made the journey to market only to fall off her horse while passing through the drains where she drowned. Also, John Wesley to Mary Wesley, 7 May 1756. *LJW* 3: 177, where Wesley wrote of a dream of his own death to his wife.

31. Throughout this chapter dreams and visionary experiences are used interchangeably as many writers of the period, especially the Methodists, made little distinction between the two in their own experiences.

32. John Tillotson, *The Works of Dr. John Tillotson, Lord Archbishop of Canterbury*, 3 vols. (London: Printed for J. and R. Tonson, et. al., 1752), 1: 76. Also, Isabel Rivers, "Grace, Holiness and the Pursuit of Happiness: Bunyan and Restoration Latitudinarianism," in N. H. Keeble, ed., *John Bunyan: Coventicle and Parnassus* (Oxford: Clarendon Press, 1988), 75-89. Rivers, *Reason, Grace, and Sentiment*, 1: 250-52.

33. John Wesley, "On a Single Eye," *BEW* 4: 124. This sermon was written while Wesley was spending time in western England in the Autumn of 1789. It was later, included in his *Arminian Magazine* 13 (1790): 569-75, 626-30.

34. Wesley, "On a Single Eye," *BEW* 4: 125. "They [heaven and earth] also proclaim that they made not themselves; 'therefore we are, because we have been made; we were not therefore before we were, so that we could have made ourselves.' And the voice of those that speak is in itself an evidence." Augustine, *Confessions*, 11.4 in *NPNF*, 1: 165. Note, in Wesley's translation of Augustine, the personal pronoun was italicized, which was always a sign of soteriological significance. See also: "O turn unto your rest! Turn to

him in whom are hid all the treasures of happiness!" Wesley, "Spiritual Worship," *BEW* 3:101, where he admonished after quoting the passage from Augustine.

35. Wesley, "Spiritual Worship," *BEW* 3: 99; John Wesley, "Dives and Lazarus," *BEW 4*: 3-18.

36. 3 March 1748. *BEW* 20: 211.

37. Laurence Willard Wood, *The Meaning of Pentecost in Early Methodism: Rediscovering John Fletcher as John Wesley's Vindicator and Designated Successor* (Lanham, MD: The Scarecrow Press, Inc., 2002), 209-222.

38. See my "Seeing Salvation: The Place of Dreams and Visions in John Wesley's *Arminian Magazine,*" in Kate Cooper and Jeremy Gregory, eds., *Miracles: Representations of Divine Power in the Life of the Church,* 376-88.

39. John Wesley, 1 December 1782 to 31 December 1786. *BEW* 23: 432-582 and 1 January 1787 to 23 February 1791. *BEW* 24: 196-348 respectively. Unfortunately the *Diaries* for the period at the beginning of the publication of the *Arminian Magazine* have been lost.

40. See Samuel Rogel, "John Wesley's Arminian Magazine," *Andrews University Seminary Studies* 22 (1984): 231-47. Also helpful, George Williams, *"'The Word came with Power': Print, Oratory, and Methodism in Eighteenth-Century Britain"* (Ph.D. thesis, University of Maryland, 2002), 142-86.

41. John Wesley, ed., *Arminian Magazine* 7(1784): np.

42. "Book Inventory," MARC, np. See, Vicki Tolar Burton, "'Something for the People to Read': John Wesley's book inventory (1791)," *Bulletin of the John Ryland University Library of Manchester* 85 (2003): 227-49.

43. Burton, *Spiritual Literacy,* 233-65.

44. John Wesley to George Holder, 8 November 1790. *LJW,* 8: 247.

45. Reinhard Wittmann, "Was there a Reading Revolution at the End of the Eighteenth Century?" in Gugliemo Cavallo and Roger Charter, eds., *A History of Reading in the West,* trans. Lydia Cochrane (Cambridge and Oxford: Polity Press and Blackwell Publishing Ltd., 2003), 288.

46. John Wesley, ed., *Arminian Magazine* 4 (1781): 26.

47. John Wesley, ed., *Arminian Magazine* 6 (1783): 322.

48. John Wesley, ed., *Arminian Magazine* 6 (1783): 578-79.

49. John Wesley, ed., *Arminian Magazine* 9 (1773): 79-80.

50. See Collen Shantz's groundbreaking *Paul in Ecstasy: The Neurobiology of the Apostle's Life and Thought* (Cambridge: Cambridge University Press, 2009), esp. 131-33, who explores the role of altered states of consciousness in Paul's statements about ecstasy in the New Testament. Particular insightful is her examination of the effect of suffering on the brain.

51. John Cennick, *The Beatific Vision; or, Beholding Jesus Crucified. Being the Substance of a Discourse Preached in Ballymenagh, in Ireland, in the Year 1755,* 3rd ed. (London: Printed by H. Trapp, 1786), 19.

52. "And, for the third time, this worthless woman went to the hymeneal altar, and was actually married to a third husband, though the other two, to whom she had been already married, were still alive." So, Tyerman, *The Life and Times of John Wesley,* 2: 285, contemptuously outlined Ryan's three marriages. See also, Rack, *Reasonable Enthusiast,* 268.

53. "The autobiography of Sarah Ryan became a canonical text for Methodists because of the extremity of her sinfulness and the totality of her self-mastery." Mack, "Religious Dissenters in Enlightenment England," 11.

54. John Wesley, ed., *Arminian Magazine* 2 (1779): 301. It is also significant that before going to the church Ryan emphasized the personal pronoun in her declaration, "My soul is on thy promise cast: 'The promise is for *me!*'"

55. Wesley, ed., *Arminian Magazine* 2 (1779): 302.

56. Henry D. Rack, "Early Methodist Visions of the Trinity," *Proceedings of the Wesley Historical Society* 46 (1987): 38-44, 57-69.

57. Rack, "Early Methodist Visions of the Trinity," 43.

58. John Wesley to Hester Ann Roe, 11 February 1777. *LJW* 6: 253. See John Wesley, ed., *Arminian Magazine* 2 (1779): 203-04.

59. John Wesley, ed., *Arminian Magazine* 2 (1779): 203-04. "I beheld the beauty of the Trinity, shining on my soul as the sun in his strength! The Lamb of God embraced me as a son of his love! And the Holy Spirit moved prolific on my spirit, as it did once on the confused waters in the creation! My barren bosom flamed as the altar when the bright rays of the Sun of righteousness shined upon me." John Cennick to John Wesley, 29 March 1739. *BEW* 25: 617-18.

60. For an interesting analysis of Methodist membership in eighteenth-century England see Clive D. Field, "The Social Composition of English Methodism to 1830; a Membership Analysis," *Bulletin of the John Rylands Library of Manchester* 76 (1994): 153-69. Compare also G. M. Ditchfield, *The Evangelical Revival* (London: UCL Press, 1998), 65 and David Luker, *Cornish Methodism, Revivalism, and Popular Belief, c. 1780-1870* (D. Phil. thesis, Oxford University, 1987), 136. For analysis of female Methodists and their dreaming in the eighteenth century, Mack, *Heart Religion in the British Enlightenment*, 219-60.

61. Little is known of this early Methodist woman. Paul Chilcote, *Her Own Story: Autobiographical Portraits of Early Methodist Women* (Nashville, TN: Kingswood Books, 2001), 102, places her after a brief stay at the London Foundery in her home town of Bristol where she married her husband, John Hall—also unknown. Her diary extended from 12 December 1765 to 24 April 1775. John Wesley preached at her funeral on 1 October 1780. "About two, I preached a funeral sermon at Kingswood for that blessed saint, Bathsheba Hall, a pattern for many years of zealously doing and patiently suffering the will of God." John Wesley, 1 October 1780. *BEW* 23: 187.

62. John Wesley, ed., *Arminian Magazine* 4 (1781): 196.

63. Wesley, ed., *Arminian Magazine* 4 (1781): 197.

64. John Wesley, ed., *Arminian Magazine* 3 (1780): 598.

65. Phyllis Mack, *Visionary Women: Ecstatic Prophecy in Seventeenth-Century England* (Berkley, CA: University of California Press, 1992), 15-44.

66. Mack, "Religious Dissent in Enlightenment England," 5.

67. G. J. Barker-Benfield: *Sex and Society in Eighteenth-Century Britain* (Chicago: University of Chicago Press, 1992), 269-273.

68. Rack, "Early Methodist Visions of the Trinity,"66.

69. Rack, *Reasonable Enthusiast*, 338. *Pace* Rack, Mack, *Heart Religion in the British Enlightenment*, 227-32, sees the primary importance of dreams to be emotive.

70. Thomas Church, *Remarks on the Reverend Mr. Wesley's Last Journal in a Letter* (London: Printed for M. Cooper, 1745), 61; Thomas Church, *Some Farther Remarks on the Rev. Mr. John Wesley's Last Journal, together with a few Considerations of his FARTHER APPEAL; Shewing the Inconsistency of his Conduct and Sentiments, with the Constitution and Doctrine of the Church of England, and explaing the ARTICLES elating to JUSTIFICATION. To which is annexed, A VINDICATION of the REMARKS, Being a REPLY to Mr. Wesley's ANSWER, in a second LETTER to that Genleman* (London: Printed and Sold by M. Cooper, 1746).

71. John Wesley, "The Principles of a Methodist Farther Explained," *BEW* 9: 200. Wesley also responded to attacks from Edmund Gibson, George Lavington, and William Warburton and their opposition to his view of the supernatural and claim of having received divine messages in dreams and visions. See Wesley's letters to these three Bishops in *BEW* 11: 335-51, 361-436, and 467-538.

72. See John W hitehead, *The Life of the Rev. Wesley, M. A. Some Time Fellow of Lincoln-College, Oxford. Collected from his Private Papers and Printed Works; and Written at the Request of his Executors. To which is Prefixed, Some Account of his Ancestors and Relations: with the Life of the Rev. Charles Wesley, M. A. Collected from his Private Journal, and never before Published. The whole forming a History of Methodism, in which the Principles and Economy of the Methodists are Unfolded*, 2 vols. (London: Stephen Couchman, 1793), 2: 104-16.

73. Mrs. John Hutton to Samuel Wesley, junior, 1738. Priestly, ed., *Original Letters by the Rev. John Wesley*, 70.

74. "God deliver us from visions that shall make the law of God vain." Samuel Wesley to Mrs John Hutton, 1738. Priestly, ed., *Original Letters by the Rev. John Wesley*, 74.

75. Samuel Wesley, junior to John Wesley. *BEW* 25: 579. "I am afraid Ahab's lying spirits may be but too pertinent." Samuel Wesley, junior, to John Wesley, 13 December 1738, *BEW* 25: 598, that revealed much scepticism over the topic among the brothers.

76. "Dreams offer the closest observable parallels to the waking phenomenon of visions and hallucinations, for the visual wealth of dreams suggests that such images are always available but blocked from our attention during normal consciousness." Shantz, *Paul in Ecstasy*, 114.

77. John Wesley to Samuel Wesley , junior, 4 April 1739. *BEW* 25: 622-23. This response was also inserted in Wesley's journal. See John Wesley , 20 May 1739. *BEW* 19: 59-60. Additionally, John Wesley used it in response to William Warburton in his open letter to the Bishop. See Wesley, "A Letter to the Right Rev erend The Lord B ishop of Glouchester. Occasioned by his Tract, On the Office and Operations of the Holy Spirit," in "The Appeals to Men of Reason and Religion and Certain Related Open Letters," *BEW 9:* 496. Compare also: "I have seen very many persons changed in a moment, fr om the spirit of fear, horror, despair, to the spirit of love, joy, and peace . . . In several of them this change was wrought in a dream, or during a strong representation to their mind of Christ, either on the cross, or in glory." John Wesley , *A Short History of the People Called Methodists, BEW* 9: 471.

78. John Wesley to Samuel Wesley, junior, 3 February 1739. *BEW* 25: 600. In this same letter, John Wesley had faulted Bishop G eorge Bull (163 4-1710) for the belittlement of Article XI. "Quae si ita sint, actum est de fundamentali Ecclesiae Anglicanae per fidem solam." John Wesley, "Hypocrisy in Oxford (Latin Text)," *BEW* 4: 412. On Article XI, see E. J. Bicknell, *The Thirty-Nine Articles*, 3rd rev. ed. by H. J. Carpenter (London: Longmans, Green and Co., 1955), 199-207.

79. "Charles has at last told me in plain terms—he believes no more of dreams and visions than I do." Samuel Wesley, junior, to John Wesley, 26 March 1739. *BEW* 25: 613:

80. John Wesley to Samuel Wesley, junior, 27 October 1739. *BEW* 25: 695.

81. On the death of Samuel Wesley junior, see Tyerman, *The Life and Times of John Wesley*, 1: 286-87.

82. Josiah Pratt, ed., *Eclectic Notes; or, Notes of Discussions on Religious Topics at the Meetings of The Eclectic Society, London. During the Years 1798-1814*, 2nd ed. (London: James Nisbet & Co., 1865), 84. "Such manifestations being altogether of an extraordinary nature, and having long since ceased, should any person in these later ages profess to be favoured with new revelations from God, he would either be deceived himself, or

be attempting to deceive others." Josiah Pratt's, *Forty Family Sermons* (London: J. Hatchard and Son, 1830), 94.

83. Cornelius Cayley, *The Riches of God's Free Grace, Display'd in the Conversion of Cornelius Cayley. Late Clerk in the Princess Dowager of Wale's Treasury. To the Faith of Jesus Christ, his Lord and God. Being a Faithful Account of the Lord's Remarkable Dealings with him from Seven Years of Age; the Trials and Temptations He Met with in a Course of Several Years. As also how He hath met in a Course of Several Years. As also how He was called to Preach the Glorious Gospel of Jesus Christ; and what he hath met with Particular in the Exercise thereof, in many Parts of England and Wales* (Norwich: n. p., 1757), 59.

84. Luker, *Cornish Methodism, Revivalism, and Popular Belief, c. 1780-1870*; David Luker, "Revivalism in Theory and Practice: The Case of Cornish Methodism." *The Journal of Ecclesiastical History* 37 (1986): 603-19; C. D. Little, "Early Methodism in Manchester," *Proceedings of the Wesley Historical Society* 25 (1945-1946): 116-22; Henry Rack, "Between Church and Sect: The Origins of Methodism in Manchester," *Bulletin of the John Rylands University Library of Manchester* 80 (1988): 65-87.

85. John Rule, "Methodism, Popular Beliefs and Village Culture in Cornwall, 1800-50," in Robert Storch, ed., *Popular Culture and Custom in Nineteenth-Century England* (London: Croom Helm, 1982), 48.

86. For treatments of dreams and their influence in nineteenth-century culture see Maureen Perkins, "The Meaning of Dream Books," *History Workshop Journal* 48 (1999): 102-12 and Rhodri Hayward, "Policing Dreams: History and the Moral Use of the Unconscious," *History Workshop Journal* 49 (2000): 142-60.

87. It is interesting that Alister McGrath's *Justitia Dei: A History of the Christian Doctrine of Justification*, 2nd ed. (Cambridge: Cambridge University Press, 2002), 239, only mentions Wesley's significance in passing though he notes on 467n50: "In England, the doctrine is particularly associated with Wesley, who expressed it in his concept of 'entire sanctification.'"

88. See, for example, Eric von Eicken, *Rechtfertigung und Heiligung bei John Wesley* (Ph.D. thesis; University of Heidelberg, 1939); Harald Lindström, *Wesley and Sanctification: A Study in the Doctine of Salvation* (1950; repr., London: The Epworth Press, 1956); Herbert Boyd McGonigle, *Sufficient Saving Grace: John Wesley's Evangelical Arminianism* (Carlisle, PA: Paternoster Publishing 2001); Randy Madddox, *Responsible Grace: John Wesley's Practical Theology* (Nashville, TN: Kingswood Books, 1994), 94-229; and Lucurgus Starkey, Jr., *The Work of the Holy Spirit: A Study of Wesleyan Theology* (New York: Abingdon Press, 1962).

89. Fletcher, *The Life of Mrs. Mary Fletcher,* 38.

90. John Wesley, "The New Birth," *BEW* 2: 187. See, Albert Outler, "The New Birth: An Introductory Comment," *BEW* 2: 186, who noted that Wesley preached on the Johannine passage more than sixty times during his life. Also: "Faith in general is a divine, supernatural ἔλεγχος, 'evidence' or conviction 'of things not seen,' not discoverable by our bodily senses as being either past, future, or spiritual. Justifying faith implies, not only a divine evidence or conviction that 'God was in Christ, reconciling the world unto himself,' but a sure trust and confidence that Christ died for *my* sins, that he loved *me*, and gave himself for *me*." John Wesley, "Justification by Faith," *BEW* 1: 194.

91. John Wesley, "Human Life A Dream," *BEW* 4: 108-19.

92. Wesley, "Human Life A Dream," *BEW* 4: 111; Furthermore, Wesley's assertion: "For does not the soul see, in the clearest manner, when the eye is of no use, namely in dreams?" John Wesley, "The Good Steward," *BEW* 2: 289.

93. Wesley, "Human Life A Dream," *BEW* 4: 112.

94. Wesley, "Human Life A Dream," *BEW* 4: 117-18.

95. Jean-Pierre van Noppen, *Transforming Words: The Early Methodist Revival from a Discourse Perspective* (Bern: Peter Lang, 1999), 105-08.

96. Rupert Davies, "General Rules and Rules of the Band Societies: An Introductory Comment," *BEW* 9: 67.

97. John Wesley, 24 February 1741. *BEW* 19: 183-84, that Wesley met with the bands at Bristol where forty individuals were separated from the Methodists. See also Watson, *The Early Class Meeting*, 104-08.

98. John Wesley, *The Nature, Design, and General Rules, of the United Societies, in London, Bristol, King's-wood, and Newcastle upon Tyne*, 3rd ed. (Newcastle upon Tyne: Printed by Felix Farley, 1743). This document is also found in *BEW* 9: 70-79.

99. John Wesley, *The Nature, Design, and General Rules of the United Societies, in London, Bristol, King's-wood, and Newcastle upon Tyne, WJW*, 9: 70.

100. John Wesley, "Manuscript Account of Two Remarkable Stories—1756, 1758," in "Wesley's Sermon Box III-IV," MARC. Compare also, Daniel Flores and Thelma Herrera-Flores, "Two Remarkable Stories: Lost Entries of John Wesley's Journals," *Methodist History* 38 (2000): 251-57, where the document is transcribed with brief introductory comments. Also, John Wesley, "Dives and Lazarus," *BEW* 4: 4-18. Compare also Richard Sault's *The Second Spira, being a Fearful Example of an Atheist, who had Apostatised from the Christian Religion, and Died in Despair at Westminster, Dec., 8, 1692*, 4th ed. (London: Printed for John Dunton, 1693) and Wesley's extract of it in his *Arminian Magazine* 6 (1783): 24-28, 79-83, 132-133.

101. Wesley, "Two Remarkable Stories," np. See also, D. Dunn Wilson, "The Importance of Hell for John Wesley," *Proceedings of the Wesley Historical Society* 34 (1963): 12-16. Compare this account to Wesley's denouncing Baron Swedenborg's view of hell in his journal entry in 1779. 22 April 1779. *BEW* 23: 126-128.

102. Wesley, "Dives and Lazarus," *BEW* 4: 15.

103. "Our main doctrines, which include all the rest, are three, that of repentance, of faith, and of holiness. The first of these we account, as it were, the porch of religion; the next, the door; the third is religion itself." John Wesley, "The Principles of a Methodist Farther Explained," *BEW* 9: 227.

104. Wesley, "Dives and Lazarus," *BEW* 2: 166.

105. Harald Lindström, *Wesley and Sanctification: A Study in the Doctrine of Salvation*, 30-34. See Colin Williams, *John Wesley's Theology Today* (New York: Abingdon Press, 1960), 59-61.

106. Ann Taves, "Knowing through the Body: Dissociative Religious Experience in the African- and British-American Methodist Traditions," *Journal of Religion* 73 (1993): 200-22.

107. David Hempton, *Methodism: Empire of the Spirit* (New Haven: Yale University Press, 2005), 56.

108. Taves, "Knowing through the Body," 206.

109. George Whitefield, *George Whitefield's Journals* (1960; repr., Carlisle, PA: Banner of Truth Trust, 1992), 263.

110. See, for example, Lori Anne Ferrell and Peter McCullough, eds., *The English Sermon Revised: Religion, Literature and History 1600-1750* (Manchester: Manchester University Press, 2000), who have strangely omitted Methodist preaching in their analysis of the period.

111. Leigh Eric Schmidt, *Hearing Things: Religion, Illusion, and the American Enlightenment* (Cambridge, MA: Harvard Universty Press, 2000), 65.

112. *Gentleman's Magazine* 14 (1747): 504. Note the imagery of "endangering the peace."

113. Frank Lambert, *Inventing the "Great Awakening"* (Princeton: Princeton University Press, 1999), 43.

114. For John Cennick, see John Cennick, "An Account of the Most Remarkable Occurrences in the Awakenings at Bristol and Kingswood till the Brethren's Labours Began There in 1746," 108-109; for George Whitefield, see George Whitefield to John Wesley, 25 June 1739. *BEW* 25: 661-62; for Charles Wesley, see Charles Wesley, *The Journal of the Rev. Charles Wesley, M. A. Sometime Student of Christ Church, Oxford. To Which are Appended Selections From His Corresponance & Poetry,* 2 vols. (London: Wesleyan Methodist Book Room, 1811), 1: 243, 247, 314, 316.

115. William Sargent, *Battle for the Mind* (London: Heinemann, 1957), 91-122.

116. Evelyn Gen Jenson, *John Wesley's Use of Three Types of Classical Oratory—Forensic, Epideictic, and Deliberative—In His Journal* (Ed.D. thesis; Ball State University, 1980), 128-75.

117. See Frederick Masser, "Problem in Preaching: An Analysis of the Preaching Power of John Wesley," *The London Quarterly and Holborn Review* 2 (1933): 309-22 and Paul Scott Wilson, "Wesley's Homiletic: Law and Gospel for Preaching," *Tornto Journal of Theology* 10 (1994): 215-55. See also Henry Abelove, *The Evangelist of Desire: John Wesley and the Methodists* (Stanford: Stanford University Press, 1990), 40-48.

118. Thomas Jackson, ed., *The Lives of Early Methodist Preachers,* 6 vols. (London: Wesleyan Conference Office, 1865-66), 1: 37. See Abelove, *The Evangelist of Desire,* 25.

119. Heitzenrater, *Mirror and Memory: Reflections on Early Methodism,* 163.

120. Wesley, "A Farther Appeal to Men of Reason and Religion," *WJW* 11: 177-82.

121. "Many are represented as falling suddenly to the ground, in horror and agony not to be conceived, and rising again with equal expressions of peace and consolation. Their conversions were usually attended with these violent symptoms; and, for several years, few meetings occurred, where Mr Wesley presided, without one or more instances of the same kind." John Hampson, *Memoirs of the Late Rev. John Wesley, A. M. with a Review of His Life and Writings, and a History of Methodism, from it's Commencement in 1729, to the Present Time,* 3 vols. (London: Printed for the author by James Graham, 1791), 1: 212.

122. 30 December, 1742. *BEW* 19: 308.

123. See, John Wesley, "Journals and Diaries IV (1755-1765)," *WJW,* 21: 195-200; idem., "The Methodist Societies: History, Nature, and Design," *WJW* 9: 470-72.

124. 30 May 1759. *BEW* 21: 195.

125. 30 May 1759. *BEW* 21: 196.

126. 30 May 1759. *BEW* 21: 196. "I preached on those words in the Second Lesson, 'We know that we are of God [I John 5.19].' One sunk down, and another, and another. Some cried aloud in agony of prayer . . . I was obliged to conclude the service, leaving many in the church crying and praying, but unable either to walk or stand." 30 May 1759. *BEW* 21: 196.

127. Hampson, *Memoirs of the Late Rev. John Wesley,* 2: 83.

128. E. P. Thompson, *The Making of the English Working Class* (1963; repr., London: Penguin Books,1991), 411-40. See the informative essay by John Walsh and David Hempton, "E. P. Thompson and Methodism," in Mark Noll, ed., *God and Mammon: Protestants, Money, and the Market, 1790-1860* (Oxford: Oxford University Press, 2001), 99-120.

129. Thompson, *The Making of the English Working Class,* 419. "A more appalling system of religious terrorism, one more fitted to unhinge a tottering intellect and to darken and embitter a sensitive nature, has seldom existed." W. E. H. Lecky, *A History of*

England in the Eighteenth Century (1892; repr., London: Longmans, Green, and Co., 1910), 3: 77:

130. Thompson, *The Making of the English Working Class*, 405.

131. 25 November 1759. *BEW* 21: 234.

132. 25 November 1759. *BEW* 21: 234-35.

133. 25 November 1759. *BEW* 21: 235.

134. For a treatment of this thesis in a broad scope, see Ward, *Early Evangelicalism.*

135. Hempton, *Religion and Political Culture in Britain and Ireland*, 30.

136. Jonathan Clark, *English Society 1660-1832: Religion, Ideology and Politics During the Ancien Regime*, 2nd ed. (Cambridge: Cambridge University Press, 2000), 284-300.

137. Francis MacNutt, a Roman Catholic, in his book *Overcome by the Spirit: The Extraordinary Phenomenon That is Happening to Ordinary People* (Grand Rapids, MI: Chosen Books, 1990), 14, refers to the experience as "a demonstration of God's power." Also, in this regard, Jean-Jacques Suurmound's *Word & Spirit at Play: Towards a Charismatic Theology*, trans. John Bowden (Grand Rapids, MI: William B. Eerdmans Publishing Company, 1994). Interestingly, Harvey Cox's *Fire From Heaven: The Rise of Pentecostal Spirituality and the Reshaping of Religion in the Twenty-first Century* (New York: Addison-Wesley Publishing Company, 1995), 144-57, finds striking resemblances between the history of jazz and its emphasis on improvisation and charismatic experiences.

138. "Wesley . . . did not make a rigorous distinction between primary and secondary causation nor privilege one over the other in the context of narrative." Taves, *Fits, Trances, & Visions*, 56.

139. 30 June 1739. *BEW* 19: 76; Wesley, "A Farther Appeal," *BEW* 11: 123.

140. Jane March to Mary Fletcher, 13 June, 1792. MARC, MAM F1 5.2.2.

141. Martin Schmidt, *John Wesley: A Theological Biography*, trans. Norman Goldhawk (New York: Abingdon Press, 1962), 1: 124-212.

142. At the beginning of the Enlightenment there were those who often mingled portent and providence into their sea narratives. "I am as ready to believe there are yet in Nature some *Terra Incognita* both as to Cause and Consequences too." Daniel Defoe's *The Storm*, 5, for example.

143. 17 January 1736. (Manuscript Voyage Journal) *BEW* 18: 341. See Kenneth Collins, "John Wesley and the Fear of Death as a Standard of Conversion," in Kenneth Collins and John Tyson, eds., *Conversion in the Wesleyan Tradition* (Nashville, TN: Abingdon Press, 2001), 56-68.

144. 17 January 1736. (Manuscript Voyage Journal) *BEW* 18: 345.

145. 17 January 1736. (Manuscript Voyage Journal) *BEW* 18: 345.

146. Rack, *Reasonable Enthusiast*, 123-33.

147. Heizenrater, *Wesley and the People Called Methodists*, 69-71. For Wesley's part, however, the account of his social and legal problems was highlighted by a sense of providence. See, for example, 26 August 1737 to 16 December. (Manuscript Voyage Journal) *BEW* 18: 559-71. "I again consulted with my friends, who agreed with me that the time we looked for was now come. And the next morning [Nov. 23], calling on Mr. Causton, I told him I designed to set out for England immediately." 3 November 1737. *BEW* 18: 194-95 in Wesley's first published extract of the journals for the period.

148. For a different view, see Geordan Hammond, "John Wesley in Georgia: Success or Failure?" *Proceedings of the Wesley Historical Society* 56 (2008): 297-305.

149. 2 December 1737. *BEW* 18: 204.

150. "I began to read and explain some passages of the Bible to the young Negro. The next morning another Negro who was on board desired to be a hearer too. From them I went to the poor Frenchman, who understanding no English, had none else in the ship

with whom he could converse. And from this time I read and explained to him a chapter in the Testament every morning." 7 January 1737. *BEW* 18: 208.

151. 28 December 1737. BEW 18: 207.

152. 29 January 1738. *BEW* 18: 214.

153. A. Skevington Wood, *The Burning Heart: John Wesley, Evangelist* (Grand Rapids, MI: William B. Eerdmans Publishing Company, 1967), 60. Compare also David Bebbington, *Evangelicalism in Modern Britain: A History from the 1730s to the 1980s* (1989; repr., London: Routledge, 2002), 40, who asserts that Peter Böhler was John Wesley's "chief guide" during this part of Wesley's life. See also Colin Podmore's *The Moravian Church in England 1728-1760* (Oxford: Clarendon Press, 1998), 72-96.

154. Clifford Towlson, *Moravian and Methodist: Relationships and Influences in the Eighteenth Century* (London: Epworth Press, 1957), 47.

155. "I now renewed and wrote down my former resolutions." 28 February 1738. *BEW* 18:227-28. The resolutions were fourfold: 1) Openness and unreserved attitude to those he conversed with; 2) Continual seriousness and eschewing levity; 3) Using speech that only glorifies God; and 4) Taking no pleasure that does not promote the glory of God.

156. See F. Ernest Stoeffler, "The Wesleyan Concept of Religious Certainty—Its Pre-History and Significance," The *London Quarterly and Holborn Review* 33 (1964): 128-39.

157. "Faith is a species of belief, and belief is defined, an assent to a proposition upon rational grounds. Without rational grounds there is therefore no belief, and consequently no faith." John Wesley to Susanna Wesley, 29 July 1725. *BEW* 25: 175.

158. John Wesley to Susanna Wesley, 29 July 1725. *BEW* 25: 179. "I am . . . at length come over entirely to your opinion, that saving faith (including practice) is an assent to what God has revealed, because he has revealed it, and not because the truth of it may be evinced by reason." John Wesley to Susanna Wesley, 22 November 1725. *BEW* 25: 188, for Wesley's agreement with his mother's view of faith.

159. 18 February 1738. *BEW* 18: 226. "Everything which is not directed to this end [the teachings of the revealed Word] among individual mystics nor which does not fit this rule, cast aside!" Jacob Spener, *On Hindrances to Theological Studies*, in *Pietists: Selected Writings*, ed., Peter Erb (New York: Paulsit Press, 1983), 70.

160. 4 March, 1738. *BEW* 18: 228.

161. Robert Moore, *John Wesley and Authority: A Psychological Perspective* (Missoula, MT: Scholars Press, 1979), 98. Compare, John P. Lockwood, ed., *Memoirs of the Life of Peter Böhler* (London: Wesleyan Conference Office, 1868), 70-74.

162. 24 May 1738. *BEW* 18: 242-43.

163. 24 May 1738. *BEW* 18: 243.

164. Donald Spaeth, *The Church in an Age of Danger: Parsons and Parishoners, 1660-1740* (Cambridge: Cambridge University Press, 2000), 186-87.

165. James W. Fowler, "John Wesley's Development in Faith," in *The Future of the Methodist Theological Traditions*, ed., M. Douglas Meeks (Nashville, TN: Kingswood Books, 1985), 172-192.

166. John Wesley, *The Journal of John Wesley*, ed., Nehemiah Curnock, 8 vols. (1909; repr., London: Epworth Press, 1938), 1: 475-76n1, where it was pointed out by Curnock that this was a Moravian society which meet in Nettington Court, on Aldersgate street and led by James Hutton.

167. 24 May 1738. *BEW* 18: 250. The preface was not Luther's commentary but his *A Methodicall Preface Prefixed before the Epistle of S. Paul to the Romanes, Very Necessary and Profitable for the Better Understanding of it. Made by the Right Reverend Father and Faithful Servant of Christ Jesus, Martin Luther, Now Newly Translated out of*

Latin into English by William Wilkenson (London: np, 1594), as Ward pointed out in n76 to this section of Wesley's journal. See also, John McNeill, "Luther at Aldersgate," *The London Quarterly and Holborn Review* 164 (1939): 200-17 and Martin Schmidt, "Die Bedeutung Luthers für John Wesleys Bekehrung," *Lutherjahrbuch* 20 (1938): 125-59; Schmidt, *John Wesley: A Theological Biography*, 1: 213-309.

168. Elmer Clark, ed., *What Happened at Aldersgate: Addresses in Commemoration of the Bicentennial of the Spiritual Awakening of John Wesley in Aldersgate Street, London, May 24, 1738* (Nashville, TN: Methodist Publishing House, 1938) and Randy Maddox, ed., *Aldersgate Reconsidered* (Nashville, TN: Kingswood Books, 1990), for representative views.

169. 24 May 1738. *Works of John Wesley*, 32 vols. (Bristol: William Pine, 1771-74), 1: 200-01. For more on this aspect of Wesley's journals see Randy Maddox, "Aldersgate: A Tradition History," in *Aldersgate Reconsidered*, 133-46, esp. 133-35.

170. 20 July 1740. *BEW* 19: 162.

171. John Wesley, "On Faith," *BEW* 4: 188.

172. John Wesley, *Explanatory Notes*, 4: 587 (Hebrews 11.1).

173. "Concerning the spiritual world? It seems it will not be possible for us to discern them at all till we are furnished with senses of a different nature, which are not yet opened in our souls." Wesley, "On Faith," *BEW* 4: 192.

174. Gunter, *The Limits of 'Love Divine,'* 79.

175. Anthony Ashley Cooper, *Characteristics of Men, Manners, Opinions, and Times,* (ed.), Lawrence Klein (1711; repr., Cambridge: Cambridge University Press, 1999), 294.

176. Matthew Tindal, *Christianity as Old as the Creation: or, The Gospel, A Republication of the Religion of Nature* (London: T. Warner, 1730), 162. However, see Joseph Butler, *The Analogy of Religion, Natural and Revealed, to the Constitution and Course of Nature* (London: Printed by J. Jones, 1736), who argued against the Deists.

177. 21 February and 28 February 1739. *BEW* 19: 377-78. The exercise of collecting notes from his readings was a discipline which Wesley practiced throughout his life.

178. John Wesley, ed., *The Doctrine of Salvation, Faith, and Good Works. Extracted from the Homilies of the Church of England* (London: Printed for James Hutton, 1739); John Wesley, ed., *On Justification by Faith Only, According to the Doctrine of the Eleventh Article of the Church of England* (London: Printed for James Hutton, 1739).

179. John Wesley, "Justification by Faith." *BEW* 1: 182-99.

180. 28 May 1738. *BEW* 18: 252.

181. 28 May 1738. *BEW* 18: 253.

182. Albert Outler, "Justification By Faith: An Introductory Comment," in *BEW* 1: 181. "Therefore God's affirming of Abraham, that faith was imputed to him for righteousness, plainly shows that he worked not; or, in other words, that he was not justified by works, but by faith only." John Wesley, *Explanatory Notes*, 4: 371 (Romans 4.5), where Wesley noted about Abraham and his commitment to justification by faith.

183. Wesley, "Justification by Faith," *BEW* 1: 184.

184. John Deschner, *Wesley's Christology: An Interpretation* (Dallas: Southern Methodist University Press, 1960), 70-71.

185. John Wesley, "Justification by Faith," *BEW* 1: 189.

186. Wesley, "Justification by Faith," BEW 1:193. "For Luther, the gospel destroys all human righteousness." McGrath, *Iustitia Dei: A History of the Christian Doctrine of Justification*, 199.

187. John Wesley, "Justification by Faith," *BEW* 1: 194.

188. 2 May 1739. *BEW* 19: 54.

189. "A bystander, one John Haydon, was quite enraged at this, and being unable to deny something supernatural in it, laboured beyond measure to convince all his acquaintance that it was a delusion of the devil." John Wesley's to Samuel Wesley Junior, 10 May 1739. *BEW* 25: 646.

190. "Falling to the ground or floor as if dead, although often accompanied by other dissociative phenomena, was common among British Methodists in the early years . . . . In articulating the experiences of his early followers, Wesley cast their experiences into an 'idiom' that rendered them meaningful." Taves, "Knowing through the Body," 203-204. Often, as Taves also remarks, Wesley would label such experiences like Haydon's as "sunk down," "dropped down," or "fell prostrate." Other times he simply described the occurrences apart from the idiomatic phrases. See 17 April 1739 to 26 April 1739. *BEW* 19: 49-52; ibid., "Journal and Diaries IV (1755-1765)," *WJW* 21: 171, 384; John Wesley, 9 November 1758. *BEW* 22: 129-130; John Wesley, 25 March 1780. *BEW* 23: 162.

191. 2 May 1739. *BEW* 19: 54.

192. 2 May 1739. *BEW* 19: 54.

193. John Wesley, "On Faith." *BEW* 4: 188.

194. Robert Cushman, *John Wesley's Experimental Divinity: Studies in Methodist Doctrinal Standards* (Nashville, TN: Kingswood Books, 1989), 58. See also, J. Ernest Rattenbury, *The Evangelical Doctrines of Charles Wesley's Hymns* (London: Epworth Press, 1941), 243-77.

195. "The Methodist movement became a conscious and deliberate challenge to the rationalistic attitude towards religion characteristic of the churchmanship of the age." Norman Sykes, *Church and State in England in the XVIIIth Century* (Cambridge: Cambridge University Press, 1934), 391.

196. John Bennett, *Manuscipt 1745 Minutes*, MARC, np. See, *Methodist Minutes of the Methodist Conferences* (London: John Mason, 1862), 1: 9.

197. Bennet, *Mirror of the Soul,* 22.

198. Bennet, *Mirror of the Soul*, 23.

199. Bennet, *Mirror of the Soul*, 23.

200. Bennet, *Mirror of the Soul*, 23.

201. See Figures 4-6. "The Tree of Life." For information on Haggerty see Abel Stevens, *History of the Methodist Episcopal Church in the United States of America*, 2 vols. (New York: Carleton and Porter, 1864-67), 2: 66-67.

202. Jane March to Mary Fletcher, 10 November 1812. MARC, MAM 5.2.11

203. "For in the evening I received a letter from Oxford which threw me into much perplexity. It was asserted therein that no doubting could consist with the least degree of true faith; that whoever at any time felt any doubt or fear was not *weak in faith,* but had *no faith* at all; and that none hath any faith till the law of the Spirit of life has made him *wholly* free from the law of sin and death. Begging God to direct me, I opened my Testament on 1 Cor. 3, verse 1, etc., . . . Surely, then these men had *some degree* of faith, though it is plain their faith was but *weak.*" John Wesley, 6 June 1738." *BEW*, 18: 254, shortly after his Aldersgate experience of 24 May 1738. Also, John Wesley to Revd. George Stonehouse, 27 November 1750. *BEW*, 26: 441-48, which was also included in 28 November 1750. *BEW* 20: 366-72.

204. Herbert McGonigle, *Sufficient Saving Grace: John Wesley's Evangelical Arminianism* (Carlisle: Paternoster Press, 2001), 179-216, has a brief historical background to pertinent issues of the Calvinist-Arminian debates in eighteenth-century England.

205. John Wesley, "Predestination Calmly Considered," *JWJW* 10: 229-30.

206. See pp. 49-59.

207. On the other hand, John Calvin, *Institutes of the Christian Religion*, ed., John McNeill, trans. Ford Lewis Battles, 2 vols. (Philadelphia, PA: The Westminster Press, 1960), III.17.xiii.

208. Wesley, "Predestination Calmly Considered," *JWJW* 10: 230. See also, Kenneth Collins, *John Wesley: A Theological Journey* (Nashville, TN: Abingdon Press, 2003), 169-71.

209. John Wesley, "On Working Out Our Own Salvation," *BEW* 3: 203.

210. Maddox, *Responsible Grace*, 147-48.

211. See John Wesley, "The Lord our Righteousness," *BEW* 1: 450-51. See Albert Outler's footnote to this sermon, 450-51n15, for a brief but useful history of the teaching. Also, Eberhard Jüngel, *Justification: The Heart of the Christian Faith*, trans. Jeffrey Cayzer with an Introduction by John Webster (Edinburgh: T & T Clark, 2001), 15-50.

212. Robert Newton Flew, *The Idea of Perfection in Christian Theology: An Historical Study of the Christian Ideal for the Present Life* (London: Oxford University Press, 1934), vii. The three writers and their works that Flew cited were William Burt Pope, *Compendium of Christian Theology*, rev. ed. 3 vols. (London: np, 1879), 3: 28-99; Harold William Perkins, *The Doctrine of Christian Perfection* (London: Epworth Press, 1927); and F. Platt, "Perfection (Christian)," *Encyclopedia of Religion and Ethics*, 9: 728-37.

213. "There can be no doubt of the importance of the doctrine of perfection in the history of Methodism." Williams, *John Wesley's Theology Today*, 167.

214. John Wesley, "Large Minutes," *JWJW* 8: 299.

215. For a succinct overview of this growth, Hempton, *Methodism: Empire of Spirit*; Hempton, *The Religion of the People*, 3-28; David Hempton, "Methodist Growth in Transatlantic Perspective, ca. 1770-1850," in Nathan Hatch and John Wigger, eds., *Methodism and the Shaping of American Culture* (Nashville, TN: Kingswood Books, 2001), 41-85.

216. Hempton, *The Religion of the People*, 7.

217. Leonard W. Cowie, *Hanoverian England 1714-1837* (New York: Humanities Press, 1967), 77.

218. James Logan, "The Evangelical Imperative: A Wesleyan Perspective," in James Logan, ed., *Theology and Evangelism in the Wesleyan Heritage* (Nashville, TN: Kingswood Books, 1994), 15-33.

219. *Minutes of Several Conversations, Between the Rev. John Wesley, M. A., and the preachers in connection with him* (London: Printed for George Whitfield, 1779 [sic]), 1.

220. "Indeed I wanted a little rest, having rode in seven months above four and twenty hundred miles." 7 August 1759. *BEW* 21: 224.

221. George Eliot, *Adam Bede* (1799; repr., Oxford: Oxford University Press, 2000), 38.

222. "Wesley . . . was an itinerant, but not a wandering, evangelist, and, . . . there is no doubt at all that his rounds were a highly organised affair, in every way like the circuit plans that his assistants had to organise all the time, and every superintendent must still publish quarterly." W. R. Ward, *Faith and Faction* (London: Epworth Presss, 1993), 251.

223. Hempton, *Methodism: Empire of The Spirit*, 6, 32-54. See also T. C. W. Blanning, *The Culture of Power and the Power of Culture: Old Regime Europe 1660-1789* (Oxford: Oxford University Press, 2002), 289.

224. Richard Carwardine, "Methodist Ministers and the Second Party System," in Russell Richey, Kenneth Rowe, and Jean Miller Schmidt, eds., *Perspectives on American Methodism: Interpretative Essays* (Nashville, TN: Kingswood Books, 1993), 159.

225. "Middle Atlantic Methodists came from a wide array of social ranks: not only women of all classes and blacks—in itself an unusual diversity—but also poor men, middling farmers, greater merchants, and planters. In the Middle Atlantic city societies in

particular, the movement attracted labouring men, artisans, *and* the 'new men' of late-eighteenth-century capitalist expansion: commercial, industrial, and professional entrepreneurs." Dee Andrews, *The Methodists and Revolutionary America, 1760-1800: The Shaping of an Evangelical Culture* (Princeton: Princeton University Press, 2000), 155.

226. Nathan Hatch, *The Democratization of American Christianity* (New Haven: Yale University Press, 1989), 125-61; Wigger, *Taking Heaven By Storm*, 48-79; John Wigger, "Fighting Bees: Methodist Itinerants and the Dynamics of Methodist Growth, 1770-1820," in Hatch and Wigger, eds., *Methodism and the Shaping of American Culture*, 87-133.

227. Peter Cartwright, *Autobiography of Peter Cartwright* (1856; repr., Nashville: Abingdon Press, 1984), 192.

228. Cartwright, *Autobiography of Peter Cartwright*, 192.

229. Francis Asbury, *The Journal and Letters of Francis Asbury*. Ed., Elmer Clark. 3 vols. (Nashville, TN: Abingdon Press, 1958), 1: 379. See also E. Brooks Holifield, *Theology in America: Christian Theology in America* (New Haven, CT: Yale University Press, 2003), 256-72.

230. Howard Watkin-Jones, *The Holy Spirit from Arminus to Wesley* (London: Epworth Press, 1929), 71.

231. John Wesley, "Appendix B: Wesley's Interview with Bishop Butler, August 16 and 18 1739." *BEW* 19: 471. For a historical background of this meeting, see Frank Baker, "John Wesley and Bishop Joseph Butler: A Fragment of John Wesley's Manuscript Journal 16th to 24th August 1739," *Proceedings of the Wesley Historical Society*, 42 (1980): 93-100.

232. Wesley, "Appendix B: Wesley Interview with Bishop Butler," *BEW* 19: 471.

233. Gunter, *The Limits of 'Love Divine,'* 118-55. Also, Mathias Kürschner, "The Enthusiasm of the Rev. John Wesley," *Wesleyan Theological Journal* 35 (2000): 114-37.

234. John Wesley, "The Nature of Enthusiasm," *BEW* 2: 49-50.

235. Wesley, "The Nature of Enthusiasm," *BEW* 2: 50.

236. See Geoffrey Wainwright, "John Wesley's Trinitarian Hermeneutics," *Wesleyan Theological Journal* 36 (2001): 7-30

237. John Wesley, "On the Trinity," *BEW* 2: 385.

238. John Wesley to a Roman Catholic, 18 July 1749. *LJW* 3: 9. For an examination of this letter see Geoffrey Wainwright's "Trinitarian Theology and Wesleyan Holiness," in ST Kimbrough. ed., *Orthodoxy and Wesleyan Spirituality* (Crestwood, NY: St Vladimir's Seminary Press, 2002), 59-80.

239. John Pearson, *An Exposition of the Creed*, rev. ed. (1659; repr., New York: D. Appleton and Company, 1880), 459-99.

240. "The importance of the idea of perfection to Wesley is indicated by his frequent mention of it: in his sermons and other writings, in his journals and letters, and in the hymn books he published with his brother Charles. He never abandoned the general position with regard to Christian perfection which derives from his introduction to practical mysticism in 1725 and was then first expressed; it is a continuous theme in his sermons and books." Harald Lindström, *Wesley and Santification: A Study in the Doctrine of Salvation* (London: Epworth Press, 1950), 126.

241. Jeremy Taylor, *Rule and Exercise of Holy Living: The Means and Instruments of Obtaining Every Virtue, and the Remedies against Every Vice, and Considerations Serving to the Resisting All Temptations, Together with Prayers Containing the Whole Duty of a Christian* (London: Printed for John Meredith and J. Heptnstoll, 1650).

242. Frank Baker, "The Birth of John Wesley's Journal," *Methodist History* 8 (1970): 25-32.

243. "Our end in leaving our native country was not to avoid want (God having given us plenty of temporal blessings), nor to gain the dung or dross of riches or honour; but singly this—to save our souls, to live wholly to the glory of God." 14 October 1735. *BEW* 18: 136-37.

244. Kenneth Collins, *The Scripture Way of Salvation: The Heart of John Wesley's Salvation* (Nashville, TN: Abingdon Press, 1997), 153.

245. "In this he has been consistently misunderstood by all who would understand the English word 'perfect' as a translation of the Latin *perfectio*. In medieval Latin *perfectus* meant 'faultless'—unimprovable! That any human state can be perfect in *this* sense had rightly been denied by Aquinas, and had been reserved by the Westminster Divines 'for the state of glory only.'" Albert Outler, ed., *John Wesley*, 30-31.

246. John Wesley, "Christian Perfection," *BEW* 2: 104.

247. Wesley, "Christian Perfection," BEW 2: 106.

248. Wesley, "Christian Perfection," *BEW* 2: 110.

249. "Indeed this grand point, that there are two contrary principles in believers, nature and grace, the flesh and the spirit—runs through all the epistles of St. Paul, yea, through all the Holy Scriptures." John Wesley, "On Sin in Believers," *BEW* 1: 322.

250. "But love as a positive virtue has no limits. It can increase infinitely." Theodore Runyon, *The New Creation: John Wesley's Theology Today* (Nashville, TN: Abingdon Press, 1998), 89.

251. John Wesley to a Roman Catholic, 18 July 1749. *LJW* 3: 9.

252. John Wesley, "Sermon on the Mount V," *BEW* 1: 559-60.

253. See Figure 7: "Samuel Robert's Prayer and the Devil." I am grateful for John Walsh in letting me use his copy of this valuable document.

254. Samuel Robert. *Mss. Notebook*, np.

255. John Wesley, *Thoughts on Christian Perfection*, in Albert Outler, ed., *John Wesley*, 283-98.

256. John Wesley, *Thoughts on Christian Perfection*, in Albert Outler, ed., *John Wesley*, 294.

257. See Figure 8: "The Reverend Mr Thomas Maxfield, Assistant Chaplain to the Right Honourable the Countess of Huntingdon."

258. Tyerman, *The Life and Times of Rev. John Wesley*, 1: 369.

259. Tyerman, *The Life and Times of Rev. John Wesley*, 1: 369. Gunter, *The Limits of 'Love Divine,'* 162-63, correctly notes that the tracing of this story to oral tradition probably was first recorded by Henry Moore and Thomas Coke. "The right hand of the Lord bringeth mighty things to pass. Not the least of them is that my wife cordially loves T. Maxfield." John Wesley to Charles Wesley, 8 September 1761. *LJW* 4:162, certainly a curious notation by John Wesley.

260. Kenneth G. C. Newport, "George Bell, Prophet and Enthusiast," *Methodist History*, 35 (1997): 95-105; Kenneth G. C. Newport, *Apocalypse & Millennium: Studies in Bibilical Eisegesis* (Cambridge: Cambridge University Press, 2000), 97-100; Kenneth G. C. Newport and Gareth Lloyd, "George Bell and Early Methodist Enthusiasm: A New Manuscript Source from the Manuscript Archives," *Bulletin of the John Rylands University Library of Manchester* 80 (1998): 89-101.

261. John Wesley, ed., *Arminian Magazine*, 3 (1780): 674-76.

262. John Wesley, "Christian Perfection," *BEW* 2: 120.

263. John Wesley. ed., *Arminian Magazine* 4 (1781): 442. All in all, John Wesley published no fewer than sixty letters from fifteen correspondents who had experienced liberation from wandering thoughts in 1761. See, Charles Goodwin's "Setting Perfection Too High: John Wesley's Changing Attitudes Toward the 'London Blessing,'" *Methodist History* 36 (1998): 86-96.

264. John Wesley, ed., *Arminian Magazine* 4 (1781): 278.

265. Albert Outler, "Appendix A: Wesley's Text: Editions, Transmission, Presentation, and Variant Readings," in *Sermons IV (115-141)*, *BEW* 4: 469, provided a publishing history of the sermon. For the sermon see, John Wesley, "Wandering Thoughts," *BEW* 2: 126-37.

266. John Wesley to Sarah Crosby, 14 February 1761. *LJW* 4:133.

267. John Wesley to Jane Salkeld, 9 August 1772. *LJW* 5: 333. See also, 5 June 1772. *BEW* 22: 334-35; 12 June 1774. *BEW* 22: 414; 10 June 1784. *BEW* 23: 316, for references to Jane Salkeld (later Jane Nattrass) and her work.

268. On this, see also William Beveridge's, *Private Thoughts. Part II. Private Thoughts Upon a Christian Life: or, Necessary Devotion for its Beginning and Progress Upon Earth, in Order to its Final Perfection in the Beatific Vision*, 11th ed. (1712; London: T. Longman, 1724).

269. Charles Wesley, *Lavington's Case*, MARC, DDCW 8/12, 25.

270. 25 November 1759. *BEW* 21: 235.

271. Charles Goodwin, "Setting Perfection Too High," 89.

272. Whitehead, *Life of Wesley*, 2: 297. See Rack, *Reasonable Enthusiast*, 337.

273. John Walsh to Charles Wesley, 11-15 August, 1762. MARC, EMV-134. For the complete letter see "Appendix 2: John Walsh's Letter to Charles Wesley, 1762."

274. John Walsh to Charles Wesley, 2a.

275. John Walsh to Charles Wesley, 3b.

276. John Walsh to Charles Wesley, 4a.

277. John Wesley, ed., *Arminian Magazine* 3 (1780): 674. "He [George Bell] was converted in the year 1758, and pretended to be sanctified in the month of March, 1761." Tyerman, *The Life and Times of John Wesley*, 2: 433.

278. *DNB*, "Berridige, John (1716-1793)."

279. John Walsh, *Letter to Charles Wesley*, 4b. It should be noted that Wesley related several incidents where by the hands and prayers of George Bell miraculous events transpired. One such happening was the healing of Mary Special, who suffered from lumps in her breast. At the end of the day, Wesley concluded that it was authentic. See, 26 December 1761. *BEW* 21: 345-46, here 346: "Now here are plain facts: (1) She *was* ill; (2) she *is* well; (3) she became so in a moment. Which of these can, with any modesty, be denied?"

280. John Wesley, ed., *Arminian Magazine* 13 (1790): 42.

281. John Wesley to Charles Wesley, 11 December. 1762. *LJW* 4: 196. "There can however be no doubt that the desire of many London Methodists to be perfect was reaching epidemic, and in some instances, unhealthy proportions." Gareth Lloyd, "John Wesley and the London Disturbances 1760-1763," *Asbury Theological Journal* 56 (2002):122.

282. 14 November 1762. *BEW* 21: 343. "A few (very few compared to the whole number) first gave way to enthusiasm, then to pride, next to prejudice and offence, and at last separated from their brethren. But although this laid a huge stumbling-block in the way, still the work of God went on." 18 November 1763. *BEW* 21: 439.

283. John Wesley, *Farther Thoughts on Christian Perfection* (London: n. p., 1763).

284. 29 December 1761. *BEW* 21: 346.

285. 7 January 1763. *BEW* 21: 402.

286. John Wesley to Charles Wesley, 25 May 1765. *LJW* 4: 245.

287. John Wesley to Charles Wesley, 27 June 1766. *LJW* 5:16.

288. "He [John Wesley] had indeed given him [Thomas Maxfield] leave to preach, obtained ordination for him, used him as an assistant and defended him when in trouble." Rack, *Reasonable Enthusiast*, 338.

289. John Wesley to the Editor of the *London Chronicle*, 7 January 1763. *LJW* 4: 200.

290. "Sir, I take this opportunity of informing all whom it may concern (1) that Mr. Bell is not a member of our Society; (2) that I do not believe either the end of the world or any signal calamity will be on the 28th instant; and (3) that not one in fifty, perhaps not one in five hundred, of the people called Methodists believe any more than I do either this or any other of his prophecies." John Wesley to the Editor of the *London Chroncile*, 9 February 1763. *LJW* 4: 202.

291. Thomas Maxfield, *A Vindication of the Rev. Mr. Maxfield's Conduct, In Not Continuing with the Rev. Mr. John Wesley: And of His Behaviour Since That Time. With an Introductory Letter, to the Rev. George Whitefield* (London: Printed and Sold by J. Keith, 1767).

292. Maxfield, *A Vindication of the Rev. Mr. Maxfield's Conduct*, 13.

293. Maxfield, *A Vindication of the Rev. Mr. Maxfield's Conduct*, 23.

294. Johann Albrecht Bengel, *Sechzig erbauliche Reden über die Offenbarung Johannis, oder vielmehr Jesus Christi*, 3rd ed. (Stuttgart: Johann Christop Erhard, 1758). For Bengel's fascination with calculating the end of the word see Gerhard Sauter, "Die Zahl als Schlüssel zur Welt: Johann Albrecht Bengels 'prophetische Zeitrechnung' im Zusammenhang seiner Theologie," *Evangelische Theologie* 26 (1966): 1-36 and David Brady, *The Contribution of British Writers Between 1560 and 1830 to the Interpretation of Revelation 13.16-18 (the number of the Beast): A Study in the History of Exegesis* (Tübingen: Mohr, 1983), 218-24. For Charles Wesley's eschatological hermeneutics, see Newport, *Apocalypse & Millennium*, 119-44. On Bengel's influence on John Wesley, see Ward, *Early Evangelicalism*, 135-39.

295. Charles Wesley to an Unknown Correspondent, 25 April 1754. Newport, *Apocalypse and Millennium*, 145.

296. "The first time I began to attempt the scripture calculations relating to the conversion of the Jews, the fall of the Antichrist and the introduction of the fullness of the Gentiles was in the year 1746." Charles Wesley to an Unknown Correspondent, 147.

297. "What I have now hinted is only a small part of the scripture-evidences relating to the subject, which you must be content with till the book comes out." Charles Wesley to an Unknown Correspondent, 148.

298. Lloyd, "John Wesley and the London Disturbances 1760-1763," 130.

299. "Experience has both a subjective and an objective aspect. It is always 'of' something, even if only our own emotional states. There is a shaping influence that each pole has on the form or content of the experience resulting from the encounter between these poles." H. Ray Dunning, *Grace, Faith, and Holiness: A Wesleyan Systematic Theology* (Kansas City: Beacon Hill Press, 1988), 398.

300. John Wesley, "The Appeals to Men of Reason and Religion and Certain Related Open Letters," *BEW* 11: 55.

301. 14 June 1790. *BEW* 24: 180. A gill was a measurement of a quarter to half pint of liquid.

302. Lambert, *Inventing the "Great Awakening,"* 87-124.

Chapter 5

Balsamic Virtue:
Supernatural Healing in John Wesley

Therefore expect from Him, not what you deserve, but what you want—health of soul and health of body: ask, and you shall receive; seek, and you shall find; not for your worthiness, but because "worthy is the Lamb."[1]

Shall we forget His power to heal
Or doubt as unbelievers still?[2]

Upon their return from the American colonies in 1736 and 1737, John and Charles Wesley found themselves confused and dejected.[3] The Wesley brothers returned to their British homeland with their bodies spent, their morale low, and their souls restless. The missionary venture that led them to America was met with various problems and the difficulties they faced while abroad baffled their understanding of the order of salvation and the means of God's grace.

On 21 May 1738, Charles Wesley was bedridden with pleurisy and imagined that a Mrs. Musgrave had entered the house and uttered peculiar words which only troubled him: "In the name of Jesus of Nazareth, arise, and believe, and thou shalt be healed of all thy infirmities." The full account of the incident for that Whitsunday was recorded in his journal:

The words struck me to the heart. I sighed, and said within myself, "O that Christ would but speak thus to me!" I lay musing and trembling: then thought, "But

165

what if it should be Him? I will send at least to see." I rang, and Mrs. Turner coming, I desired her to send up Mrs. Musgrave. She went down and returning, said, "Mrs. Musgrave had not been here." My heart sunk within me at the word, and I hoped it might be Christ indeed. However, I sent her down again to inquire, and felt in the meantime a strange palpitation of heart. I said, yet feared to say, "I believe, I believe!" She came up again and said, "It was I, a weak, and sinful creature, spoke; but the words were Christ's: he commanded me to say them, and so constrained me that I could not forebear."[4]

For other Methodists in the eighteenth century, including John Wesley, healing was a category layered with different meanings. Like Charles Wesley in the above quotation, many Methodists in the Enlightenment believed that the presence of healing was a support and corroboration for their belief in the supernatural; an indication that God's new created order had broken into a sinful world. Physical and spiritual healing often dovetailed in Methodist narratives in the era as supernatural intervention was underscored in the warp and woof of human existence. John Pawson's (1737-1806) encounter with a man who experienced a death bed conversion followed by a remarkable physical healing was like those of other Methodists during the period. Pawson, an "Assistant" of John Wesley who was ordained for ministry in Scotland, was requested at the bedside of a dying man who had experienced neither justifying nor sanctifying grace.[5] In the account that Wesley included in the *Arminian Magazine,* Pawson admitted that he had "little hopes of doing him good." However, after some conversation and prayer, Pawson told the man that he was near the point of death and that there was an urgent need for his reliance on the atonement of Christ. The results were extraordinary for both body and soul: "He then was something distressed; and began to pray as well as he could . . . till, either that night or the following, the Lord spoke peace to his soul and what was very remarkable, his body was healed at the same time; so that he got up the next morning and went and told his neighbours what the Lord had done for him."[6] Theodore Runyon, writing of the priority of grace in Wesley's thought, highlights the theological rationale for Pawson's experience. "In Wesley's doctrine of prevenient grace," Runyon states, "he makes clear, on the one hand, the impossibility of fallen humanity saving itself apart from the action of the re-creative Spirit and, on the other, his conviction that God does indeed intervene in the human situation to open up new possibilities for us."[7]

Following Wesley, the Methodists attributed significance to the healing of the body, as well as the soul, in God's plan of redemption. Always interested in the advancement of science and its implications for society, Wesley saw the physical body as constitutively associated with the four primal elements of the natural order; earth, water, air, and fire.[8] His writings on healing, therefore, was framed within the doctrine of creation where he also outlined the significance of both body and soul. In his first university sermon preached at St. Mary's on 15 November 1730, for example, Wesley effectively related the consumption of forbidden fruit by Adam and Eve with the later notions of low-density lipoproteins and atherosclerosis.[9] In like manner, Wesley fit his view snugly into a vitalist view of human nature. In her illuminating essay on vitalist philosophy and medicine, Roseylne Rey notes that physicians in the modern era maintained the belief in the unity of humanity with both physical and moral categories.[10]

Though Wesley was not a physician in the strict sense of the term, he easily moved back and forth in his writings between empirical and moral categories when he discussed the human body.[11] On 24 July 1761, for example, he summarized the content of a recent sermon in which he expounded Christian perfection:

> I observed: (1) As long as we live our soul is connected with the body. (2) As long as it is thus connected, it cannot think but by the help of bodily organs. (3) As long as these organs are imperfect, we are liable to mistakes, both speculative and practical. (4) Yea, and a mistake may occasion my loving a good man less than I ought, which is defective, that is, a wrong temper. (5) For all these we need the atoning blood, as indeed for every defect of omission. Therefore, (6) all men have need to say daily, "Forgive us our trespasses."[12]

In this chapter, I will argue that John Wesley embraced a coherent position for understanding the relationship between the human body and the experience of the supernatural. The analysis of the Wesleyan corpus offered here will indicate that, first as a figure of the Enlightenment and the Evangelical Revival, John Wesley was sensitive to scientific developments while he maintained a fundamental belief in the healing nature of a supernatural deity. As such, this chapter is closely linked to some of the issues already discussed in Chapter Three. As discussed there, exorcism was a type of healing that restored the human subject from malevolent evil.

One of Wesley's inspirational sources on the topic of exorcism was the non-juror physician and theologian, Dr. Thomas Deacon. Deacon performed exorcisms as therapeutic exercises in northern England, especially Manchester, in the early part of the eighteenth century. Additionally, contrary to some prevailing medical theories of the Enlightenment, as Deborah Madden has argued, Wesley maintained that supernatural healing should be embraced by enlightened society; and, far from being a type of quackery left over from antiquity, the healing ministry of the church was in line with the movement of science for the restoration of individuals to a balanced plan of health and wholeness.[13]

The Healing Ministry of the Church: Its Place and Priority

Before a perlustration of John Wesley's idea of healing is considered it will be helpful to appreciate the broader significance of therapeutic ministry in the history of the Christian church. The healing narratives of Jesus were crucial to the church's self-understanding in primitive Christianity. Indeed, as John Meir shows in his study of the life of Jesus: "In its narratives, the Christian sources of the first and second generation remembered Jesus even more clearly as a healer of bodily ills than as an exorcist."[14] In this, contemporary biblical scholarship is in agreement with Meir. Stevan Davies, for one, argues that Jesus might have viewed himself as a physician. "It is entirely possible," writes Davies, "that Jesus thought of himself as a physician. Three times he is reported to have used the term physician self-referentially, in each case by citing a proverb."[15] The healing narratives of these first accounts carried powerful connotations which were multidimensional; providing a network for which the life of Jesus's self-identification was understood while also marking an underpinning paradigm for comprehending the early church's ongoing mission and ministry.

In the medieval church, however, healing miracles assumed dimensions that broadened the religious imagination of people living in a different time. [16] Though the narratives of the early Christian world proved significant for the religious context of the ecclesiastical communities of the first century, healing miracles in the medieval church provided a hermeneutic with wider social and political contextualities. Moreover, miraculous healings at various shrines suggested that amazing powers were available for pilgrims.[17] Alongside the healing narratives that were utilized in the medieval church there also grew popular secular guides for healthy living. Together they formed a network which reminded the votary of healing techniques which could be utilized in both natural and supernatural dimensions. Of the former, the *regimen sanitatis*, were documents which prescribed various aspects of holistic health and various remedies for healthy living.[18] However, despite the value of such advice literature, there was an overwhelming sense of the power and presence of the invisible world which relics and shrines referenced for the medieval mind, evidencing a rationale for the belief in the supernatural dimension of human existence.[19] The popularity of Jacobus de Voragine's *Golden Legend* in the twelfth century, for example, was filled with numerous stories of saints who experienced supernatural healings of one sort and another.[20] A legend collected about Saint Benedict, for instance, described a young monk whose body was mortally crushed by a falling stone and was miraculously brought back to life by the saint's prayers.[21]

Less fantastic, Thomas Aquinas explained the need for the sacrament of Extreme Unction in his *Summa Theologica*, when he contended that the sacrament "causes a bodily healing, not by a natural property of matter, but by the Divine power which works reasonably."[22] For many believers the healing of the body was connected to the resurrection of Christ—rhetorically and theologically. Caroline Bynum writes: "When persecuting clergy accused heretics of denigrating the body, of identifying it with rot, of denying that it can be healed or glorified, they had powerful weapons . . . . Images found in art, theology, and hagiography all suggest that salvation is reassemblage or regurgitation of exactly the bodies we have on earth; heaven is changelessness."[23] Eternity, then, was immanent and transcendent, fragile and powerful in the religious imagination of individuals living in this era of intellectual history.

At the dawn of the Reformation, despite the attacks on Roman superstition, belief in the power of God's healing mercies continued in the intellectual climate of the day.[24] Diarmaid MacCulloch in his survey of the era has documented that this period of history was marked by an "enthusiasm" that was confident that God was fundamentally interested in working out redemption within a typology of the human heart.[25] Not only did debates continue among Catholics and Protestants about the monarchy and the ability to rid people of scrofula and similar diseases but there were other indications that people were unwilling to abandon the belief in divine intervention and especially the possibility of heal-ing.[26]

Notwithstanding Martin Luther's (1483-1546) opposition to Catholic abuses, there continued to be scepticism about Copernician cosmology among those who followed his first rebellion in 1517.[27] More particularly, even with Luther's own opposition to the Zwickau prophets in Wittenberg in 1522, he embraced the idea of supernatural healing and its continued presence in the life of the church.[28] Initially Luther had viewed supernatural healing as a gift for the primi-tive Church and believed, like the other charismata, it had eventually played out its role and faded away. At the end of his life, however, Luther opposed his early scepticism. In 1540, for example, it was through his own prayers that Philip Me-lanchthon (1497-1560) was spared from a serious illness.[29] On another instance in 1545, a year before his death, Luther was asked what advice he would give for a mentally ill man. In response Luther wrote instructions for a healing ser-vice, a practice which he accepted and encouraged. "This is what we do," de-clared Luther, "and that we have been accustomed to do, for a cabinetmaker here was similarly afflicted with madness and we cured him by prayer in Christ's name."[30]

John Calvin (1509-64) too, despite his own disagreement with the Catholic teaching of Extreme Unction, saw healing as a valid sign of God's grace. Like Luther, Calvin noted in his *Institutes of the Christian Religion* that charismata (χάρίσματα) had ceased after the apostolic era and were no longer present among modern Christians. Nevertheless, the Swiss reformer asserted that "the Lord is indeed present with his people in every age; and he heals their weakness as often as necessary, no less than of old; still he does not put forth these mani-fest powers, nor dispense miracles through the apostles hands."[31]

In the seventeenth and eighteenth centuries, however, there emerged a very different approach to medicine and healing in *l'historie des mentalités*.[32] As new ideas about remedies and personal health began to appear, the category of "im-provement" surfaced throughout a vast amount of literature that permeated the period. Adrian Wilson suggested in his essay on medicine in Hanoverian Lon-don that the concept of "improvement" and its corollary "progress" were the anvils on which medicine and healing were formulated in the Enlightenment. "It was the concept of improvement," he claimed, "which permitted the eighteenth-century projector or reformer to couch his (or, rarely, her) scheme in a language of potentially universal appeal. 'Improvement' seized the moral high ground: opponents could appear as the obstructors of progress."[33] Wilson's argument appears well documented. John Bellers (1654-1725), a Quaker, wrote and pub-lished his ideas for the improvement of physic in 1714 and maintained, *inter alia*, that the College of Physicians and Surgeons "should draw up a Summary of Advice, in both of their Faculties, in the plainest manner, of what common Errors should be avoided in Practice, as well as what is fit to be done; for a gen-eral Information to all the Practicioners in PHYSICK and CHIRURGERY through the Nation, that they may be the more successful to their Patients."[34]

The emphasis on progress in the Enlightenment, however, did not eclipse the idea of supernatural intervention in the curative process. In modern England both religious and secular forms of healing enjoyed a co-habitation in the minds of many patients and physicians and, as Lucienda Beier has argued, it was rare for a patient to be treated by "one approach to the exclusion of the other."[35]

Certainly there were a variety of physicians, like the controversial George Forman (1552-1611), who relied on unscientific techniques and mingled astrology, magic, and medical knowledge in his medical practice.[36] At the same time there were scientists, physicians, and surgeons, who embraced the belief in supernatural healing. Robert Boyle (1627-91), for example, commented on the healing ministry of Jesus in Mark 1.1 in the second part of his *The Usefulness of Natural Philosophy* and highlighted Christ's miraculous powers. "When I consider," wrote Boyle, "the character given of our great master and exemplar, . . . I cannot but think such an imployment worthy of the very noblest of his disciples."[37] However, it was the Scottish physician George Cheyne (1671-1743), who incorporated Newton's concept of "aether theory" into a system that demonstrated the direct and active role that God played in the physicality of the natural world.[38] The Scottish physician consistently asserted the physical world could be identified in terms of both natural and supernatural categories. Anita Guerrini, explaining the logic of Cheyne's reasoning comments: "Body and spirit occupied opposite ends of the chain of being, but both were extended and therefore capable of changing into each other."[39]

Still, among the panorama of popular and elite viewpoints, there existed a telluric appraisal of the supernatural and its efficacy for men and women living in society. This may have been in part, because modern medical science was in its fledgling stages. It was also, however, a commentary on the unwillingness of the human spirit to isolate scientific and spiritual knowledge into neat and detached compartments. But, that being said, when John Wesley contributed to the discussions about the possibility of healing in the modern world he was convinced that there were occurrences and circumstances in the human enterprise where a knowledge of temporal agency would be insufficient to account for the magnitude of religious experiences and their value for evaluating a transcendental view of reality. In the next portion of this chapter I will maintain that Wesley was both familiar with developments in medicine and saw within these scientific advancements a confirmation of the Christian faith and its affirmation of the healing nature of a supernatural God.[40]

The Fearful Physician: John Wesley and the Possibility of Healing Grace

One of the striking elements in evaluating John Wesley's writings is how much he made of medical imagery in spreading his evangelical message.[41] His considerable knowledge of medical theory has been substantiated by Wesleyan and non-Wesleyan scholars alike.[42] The images that Wesley incorporated into his writings had multiple uses as they did for other Protestants during the modern period. In addition to emphasizing the restorative value of the love of God, Wesley's religious message was often couched in terminology that reflected the medical language of his day. Words like "physician," "illness," and "healing," served a dual function. On one hand, they signified concepts that linked primitive and contemporary views of health and wholeness; a continuum that has endured throughout history. On the other hand, the language that Wesley utilized in his letters, sermons, journals, and tracts pointed, at least in part, to what it meant to be a Methodist.[43] To exemplify, it was a required obligation for those who would call themselves "Methodists" to visit and provide for the needs of the sick. A lengthy letter to Vincent Perronet (1693-1785) in 1748 illustrated Wesley's thinking on this employment. "Upon reflection," wrote Wesley to Perronet, "I saw how exactly in this we had copied after the primitive Church. What were the ancient deacons? What was Phebe the deaconess but such a visitor of the sick."[44] Because the Class leaders and Stewards could not care for all the ill in London, Wesley systematically divided the city into twenty-three districts and selected forty-six additional "Visitors of the Sick," who would make contact with the infirm three times every week. The "Visitors" had a fourfold task: "To inquire into the state of their souls, and to advise them as occasion may require. To relieve them, if they are in want. To do anything for them which he (or she) can do. To bring in his accounts weekly to the Stewards."[45] This was a practice that Wesley followed himself while he made house to house visitations and when he encountered those stricken with illness or disease in hospitals.[46]

From these early encounters, John Wesley published a seventeen page twopenny tract in 1745 entitled *A Collection of Receipts for the Use of the Poor* which was the precursor to his popular *Primitive Physic: or An Easy and Natural Method of Curing Most Diseases,* that followed two years later.[47] The latter, became a standard in Methodist circles so that G. S. Rousseau observed: "It was found in almost every English household, especially in those of the poor, usually beside the Bible . . . and somehow it sold more copies than any other medical handbook of the age."[48] The little book which became popular for Methodist piety and practice was interesting not only for the selection of remedies and cures that could be acquired and administered by almost anyone but also for the ways in which Wesley intermingled natural and supernatural categories and perceived their joint role in the restoration of the individual to health and wholeness.

The body of the *Primitive Physic* was filled with advice derived from various popular medical authors and from Wesley's own personal experience. His prefatory remarks, however, set his enterprise into a theological and pastoral framework that was unique.[49] In it, Wesley stated his view of disease and healing remedies. The *Primitive Physic,* it should be stressed, highlighted minor ailments which the individual could be treated by the reader. In his studious review of normal medical practices from ancient times, Wesley concluded: "Tis probable, physic, as well as religion, was in the first ages chiefly traditional: every father delivering down to his sons, what he had himself in like manner received, concerning the manner of healing both outwards hurts and the diseases incident to each climate, and the medicines which were of the greatest efficacy for the cure of each disorder."[50] Accordingly, he endorsed for his readers a classic example of "traditional" physic that had been handed down through various generations; namely, the combination of proper diet along with a regimented exercise programme which might, Wesley held, prevent the development of cancers, gout, and asthmatic coughs, among many other ailments and diseases that could harm the body.

John Wesley maintained throughout his life a belief in the restorative power of diet and exercise. His chief mentor, in this regard, was George Cheyne who at one time lost two-hundred and eighteen pounds by a strict regimented program.[51] In 1724 Cheyne published his influential *An Essay of Health and Long Life,* which went through four editions in its first year and nine total editions in his lifetime. In it, the noted physician conceived of the body and soul intricately connected where one could not harm one without affecting the other. "The infinitely wise Author of Nature," wrote Cheyne, "has so contrived Things, that the most remarkable RULES of preserving LIFE and HEALTH are moral Duties commanded us, so true it is, that Godliness has the Promise of this Life, as well as that to come."[52] John Wesley enthusiastically adopted George Cheyne's regimen for healthy living, and recommended his works to the Methodist societies and for the children who attended the Kingswood school.[53]

In addition to his belief in dietary regulation and physical exercise Wesley was also excited by the discovery of electricity.[54] In her history of electricity during the Enlightenment, Patricia Fara has aptly noted the importance of its discovery for modern intellectual development was firmly grounded in the idea of empirical science. "Electricity," writes Fara, "was the greatest scientific invention of the Enlightenment . . . by the middle of the eighteenth century, electrical experiments were being performed all over Europe with new, powerful instruments that could produce, store and discharge static electricity."[55] Wesley envisioned enormous benefits from the use of electricity among the Methodists and read voraciously about its discovery and applications.[56] At one point he referred to it as a "surprising medicine" and on another asserted that it was a "thousand medicines in one."[57] In 1747 Wesley recorded that he, along with some friends, had attended some "electrical experiments,"[58] and in 1756, he obtained an electrical apparatus for healing various types of sicknesses and diseases.[59] Later that year, he reported that he had "ordered several persons to be electrified, who were ill of various disorders, some of whom found an immediate, some, a gradual cure."[60] Excited by this new found resource, Wesley proceeded to electrify thousands, carrying his portable electrical machine with him as he preached around the country. A entry for his journal on 9 November 1756, claimed remarkable and beneficent results for the treatment:

> From this time I appointed, first some hours in every week and afterward hours in every day, wherein any that desired it might try the virtue of this surprising medicine. Two or three years after, our patients were so numerous that we were obliged to divide them; so part were electrified in Southwark, part at the Foundery, others near St. Paul's, and the rest near the Seven Dials. The same method we have taken ever since. And to this day, while hundreds, perhaps thousands, have received unspeakable good, I have not known one man, woman, or child, who has received any hurt thereby. So that when I hear any talk of the danger of being electrified (especially if they are medical men who talk so), I cannot but impute it to great want either of sense or honesty.[61]

A careful review of Wesley's own documentation reveals his fascination for electric current and his belief that its therapeutic benefits for treating various ailments. On Sunday and Monday, 31 October and 1 November 1759, Wesley had revised his own work on electricity, and published it a few months later in 1760 under the title *The Desideratum: Or, Electricity made plain and useful. By a Lover of Mankind, and of Common Sense.*[62] At the conclusion of the essay, Wesley urged any doubter: "Let him for two or three Weeks (at least) try it himself in the above-named Disorders. And then his own Senses will shew him, whether it is a mere Play-Thing, or the noblest Medicine yet known in the World."[63] In the same year Wesley revised his *Primitive Physic* to include

Figure 9: "John Wesley's Electrifying Machine." Author's Personal Copy.

fifty afflictions that could be remedied by the proper application of electricity.[64] The preface of the *Desideratum*, as well, was full of personal testimonies to the benefits of this resource in curtailing sickness and restoring health to the human body. Twenty-two years later on 19 October 1781, the mature Wesley advised one of his preachers, John Bredlin (1737-1819), what he and other field preachers had repeatedly experienced. "I do not know," conferred Wesley to Bredlin, "any remedy under heaven that is likely to do you so much good as the being constantly electrified. But it will not avail unless you persevere therein for some time."[65] From Wesley's perspective, the importance of the discovery of electricity lay not in the speculative advancement of science but in the practical utilization of knowledge which would assist the distressed.

Yet John Wesley was not naïve about either the power or the limitations of natural science. He knew that human diseases often demanded more serious resolutions than home-spun remedies or electric shock treatments could provide. In various editions of the *Primitive Physic*, he emphasized that the remedies contained in his little book were for simple disorders. Despite those who misunderstood him, like William Hawes (1736-1808), founder of the Royal Humane Society, who criticized Wesley and the *Primitive Physic*, John Wesley reiterated that his work contained remedies for minor cases and extreme illnesses required more serious measures.[66] In the preface to the 1780 edition, Wesley repeated what he had said many times before: "But I still advise, 'in complicated cases, or where life is in immediate danger, let every one apply without delay, to a physician that fears God.' From one who does not, be his name ever so great, I should expect a curse rather than a blessing."[67]

At the core of Wesley's understanding of healing, however, was the love and grace of God. This he saw manifested not only in the progress of knowledge in the modern world but also in supernatural healings which transcended natural philosophy and science.[68] Because sin was a violent assault on the pristine condition of the human self, God's love was a vital component in the *ordo salutis* which remedied the damage that sin had inflicted. John Bowmer has argued that "Wesley held that God was ever working His beneficent will, which was to be discerned even in suffering, so that in God alone was all cure ultimately to be found."[69] In this regard, Wesley's commentary on Job 5.4 in his *Explanatory Notes* is instructive. In his analysis of Job, whom Wesley saw within a Christological typology, the agony of the protagonist's suffering was interpreted in light of all human suffering: "*In array*—They are like a numerous army, who invade me on every side. This was the sorest part of his calamity, wherein he was an eminent type of Christ, who complained most of the sufferings of his soul."[70] When healing occurred—especially supernatural healing—the act of God's grace was, in Wesley's estimation, more than the privation of pain or the erasure of scars. Healing was a realization of a new reference point for understanding human existence.[71]

In this light, therefore, the transforming power of supernatural healing was intended to complement the natural forms of healing that were often realized in less spectacular ways.[72] At this juncture, then, John Wesley stood apart from those sceptics in the Enlightenment who bifurcated natural and supernatural elements of religion. Thomas Woolston (1670-1733) is a case in point. In his *Six Discourses on the Miracles of Our Saviour*, Woolston contended that the miracles of Jesus were both untenable and undesirable for the Christian.[73] In that work, Woolston had questioned the miracles of Jesus and suggested that the healing miracles in particular were historically unreliable events which, at best, could only be considered parabolic. In his analysis of the blind man at the pool of Bethsaida, Mark 8. 22-26, the freethinker conjectured in his third *Discourse*:

> This whole story is what our Savour calls a *Camel* of a monstrous Size for Absurdities, Improbabilities and Incredibilities, which our *Divines*, and their implicit Followers of these last Ages have swallowed without chewing; whilst they have been straining at *Knats* in Theology, and hesitating at frivolous and indifferent Things of the Church, of no Consequence. As to *Jesus's* Miracle in this Story, which consisted in his healing a Man, of no body knows what *Infirmity*, there neither is nor can be proved any Thing supernatural in it, or there had been an express Description of the Disease, without which it is impossible to say, there was a miraculous Cure wrought.[74]

While there was no indication that John Wesley read Thomas Woolston's essays on miracles, there is little doubt that he was familiar with the tenets of Deism. Throughout his lifetime, as the overseer of the Methodist movement in Britain, he considered the Deists and their idea of natural religion to be a threat to his understanding of the supernatural and the foundation of Christianity. In a entry for his journal on 12 May 1746, for example, Wesley related how he had had dinner with a gentleman who regarded humanity selfish and "truly miserable." The gentleman's assessment elicited an attack against Deism by Wesley: "I should not wonder if every rational deist were of the same mind. Nay, they must, if consistent with themselves. For it is sure all men are both miserable and selfish, whatever show they may make who have not faith, even that 'evidence of things not seen,' the very being whereof they question."[75] Obversely, the pages of Methodist narratives were showcased with individuals who sometimes experienced extraordinary demonstrations of healing grace which exuded happiness and holiness.[76] Illustrative of this facet of spirituality in eighteenth-century England was the testimony of the dissenter Susannah Arch who curiously used the same biblical narrative that Woolston had lampooned in his third *Discourse*.[77] John Wesley, who would collect a variety of sources for his readers published this one in the fifth volume of the *Arminian Magazine* under the title of "A Narrative of the Cure of Susannah Arch":

> Soon after this [the removal of a distemper that she normally had every November], hearing people talk of a miraculous cure of one that was lame, I asked one that sat by me concerning it. She told me, a maid that had been lame seventeen years was miraculously cured. I told her, I was waiting at the pool, believing that I should be made whole. From that time my heart was drawn out to wrestle more earnestly with God, crying out, Lord! Why not I? Why not I a poor Leper?[78]

In the journals too, which were published and read by thousands—Methodists and non-Methodists alike, there were stories of supernatural miracles. The long term success of these two documents suggests that the appeal of John Wesley's belief in supernatural healing struck a chord within the consciousness of his readers.[79] The space which Wesley attached to such narratives throughout his lifetime also corroborates that the apprehension of an invisible world was an important and integral component of the Methodists and their self-understanding in the eighteenth century. Henry Rack has aptly asserted that to dismiss this stitch from the Methodist fabric is to misread Methodist history.[80] Not only was Wesley aware of the medical dimensions of illness in his day but was familiar with the rhetorical significance of healing and its history in the Christian tradition.[81] This was so, at least in Wesley's mind, because sin was viewed as a serious transgression against God's order for humanity and the presence of healing in both its natural and supernatural dimensions served both rhetorical and theological functions in his thoughts about the restorative nature of grace.

In large measure, Wesley embraced the image of sin as a disease, which enabled him to address both body and soul as he conceptualized the importance of healing for his evangelical agenda. But sin did not have the final word for the believer in his thought and narratives of good deaths were found in Methodist literature during the eighteenth century, which displayed for the reader the consummation of a life lived according to the dictates of piety.[82] However, there were times of healing that could only be attributed by reason to the existence of miraculous causes.[83]

John Wesley was often quick to admit his confidence in the healing mercies of God. An example of Wesley's resolution is found in a letter he sent to his ailing brother Charles on 21 September 1760:

> I care not a rush for ordinary means; only that it is our duty to try them. All our lives and all God's dealings with us have been extraordinary from the beginning. We have all reason, therefore, to expect that what has been will be again. I have been preternaturally restored more than ten times. I suppose you will be thus restored for the journey, and that by the journey as a natural means your health will be re-established, provided you determine to spend all the strength which God shall give you in His work.[84]

One of the reasons why Wesley exhibited reliance in supernatural healing was because he experienced it in his own life. As I noted earlier, Wesley was interested in collecting narratives that exhibited a simple, though not always clear, affirmation of supernatural realities and their intersection with human subjects. Though, he was reluctant to record his own experiences, when it came to supernatural healing, Wesley willingly related in detail his own personal encounters and observations.

Wesley's journals and letters were highlighted with examples of personal illnesses and recoveries. A memorable case occurred in Ireland in 1775.[85] Wesley's preaching tour there had started during Holy Week. The travelling had been rough and the preaching in the open air had finally got the better of the elderly Wesley. On 13 June he wrote in his journal: "I now found a deep obstruction in my breast; my pulse[s] were exceedingly weak and low. I shivered with cold, though the air was sultry hot, only now and then burning for a few minutes."[86] Although he continued to preach in the open at Derryaghy, he found his "nature sunk, and I took my bed, but I could no more turn myself therein than a new-born child. My memory failed as well as my strength, and well-nigh my understanding."[87] His throat became extremely sore, his tongue went black as he convulsed repeatedly. Fervent prayer was offered for Wesley by a small group who claimed Hezekiah and his fifteen year reprieve from death (II Kings 20.6), as a model of their petition for their beloved Methodist leader. At the same time, one of Wesley's well known preachers, Alexander Mather (1733-1800) read an erroneous newspaper report that Wesley had died; nevertheless, he opened his Bible *sortes biblicae* and his eyes fell on Isaiah 38.5: "Behold, I will add unto thy days fifteen years," a reading Mather interpreted prophetically for Wesley.[88] Other agreed, believing his deliverance would be miraculous. Several of their letters were gathered into the *Arminian Magazine* in 1787, which indicated that Wesley himself considered this a signal event in his experience of grace. A certain Mrs. J. T., for example, wrote to John Wesley on 8 July 1775: "O Sir, what a week of suspense and anguish had I! You will not surely blame me that I could not give you up; that my prayers helped to detain you in the vale below. Forgive your weeping friends if they have brought you back from the skies: surely in the end you will be amply recompensed!"[89] On the same day, a Mrs. P. B. related in correspondence: "Every one mourned as if they had lost their great earthly good; and yet it did not seem a selfish sorrow: 'We mourned for millions': for souls yet unconverted; for children yet unborn."[90] Interestingly, like Hezekiah of the Old Testament, John Wesley lived another fifteen years and eight months, passing away on 2 March 1791!

The Old Unfashionable Medicine: Prayer

The first pamphlet that John Wesley wrote was *A Collection of Forms of Prayer for Every Day in the Week,* published in 1738.[91] The work consisted of morning prayers along with reflective questions that were meant for examination by the reader during the evening. Throughout the Evangelical Revival, John Wesley's followers were known by their disciplined commitment to prayer. The more zealous of his preachers rose at four o'clock in the morning, spending hours in prayer before preaching in the marketplace to people on their way to work. When John Fletcher (1729-85) was asked for a definition of a Methodist, he informed his implied interlocutor: "Why, the Methodists are a people that do nothing but pray. They are praying all day and all night."[92] In a sermon entitled *The More Excellent Way,* Wesley described the inseparability of works of piety and mercy and made an emphatic call to Methodists to become people of prayer:

In what *manner* do you transact your worldly business? I trust with *diligence,* whatever your hand findeth to do, doing it with your might; in justice, rendering to all their due, in every circumstance of life; yea, and in mercy, doing unto every man what you would he should do unto you. This is well; but a Christian is called to go still farther—to add piety to justice; to intermix prayer, especially the prayer of the heart, with all the labour of his hands. Without this all his diligence and justice only show him to be an honest heathen—and many there are who profess the Christian religion that go no farther than honest heathenism.[93]

Throughout his lifetime Wesley viewed intercessory prayer as a discipline which should be inculcated by the Methodist societies and bands. In his popular essay on Christian Perfection, published during the London disturbances of the 1760s, Wesley emphasized: "God does nothing but in answer to prayer . . . Every new victory which a soul gains is the effect of a new prayer."[94] This statement was not only central to Wesley's theology of sanctification but central for his entire evangelical agenda. With prayer, the Methodists envisioned a whole unconverted world on the horizons and the possibility of touching men, women, and children with God's love. To Joseph Benson (1748-1821), John Wesley wrote in the winter of 1772: "I love prayer-meetings, and wish they were set up in every corner of the town."[95] Certainly Leslie Church was not far off the mark when he described the rationale of these gatherings for eighteenth-century Methodists:

The first Methodists did not become so humbly yet surprisingly confident because they discovered John Wesley was a great man! Not was it because they evolved a successful ecclesiastical system—but they waxed valiant in their fight against evil in their own hearts and in the world, because they believed they were in vital and direct contact with God.[96]

On a social level, however, Wesley saw within prayer meetings an ability to network Methodists into a convivial community that was cloaked with a divine strategy that would aid their evangelical cause. On several occasions he attributed the prayer meetings as a key component for the revival which was occurring throughout Britain; viewing them, furthermore, as the impetus behind the awakening of souls.

The Sheffield conversions in the 1780s were a case in point. Wesley reflected on the renewal that had taken place which included extraordinary experiences and additions to societies. He was certain that the experience of converts was due in large measure to the strategic operation of prayer meetings among the Methodists in the region. In a letter written to the assistant Edward Jackson in the autumn of 1788, he wrote: "But the grand means of the revival of the work of God in Sheffield was the prayer-meetings. There were then twelve of them in various parts of the town every Sunday night. Keep up these, and you will keep up the flame."[97] It excited Wesley to know that in many cases the leadership of these prayer meetings came not from itinerant preachers but local laity who had embraced the evangelical message. In other instances, such as the Yorkshire revival in the 1790s, the prayers of laity were instrumental for the revival altogether.[98]

At a different level, however, Wesley confidently professed that prayer was a means which made the supernatural accessible for the individual believer, as well as for the transformation of larger groups. In this regard, the healing which Methodists demonstrated was dramatically portrayed as a quality that was externally and internally conditioned. In the preface to the *Primitive Physic* Wesley had admonished: "Above all, add to the rest, (for it is not labour lost) that old unfashionable medicine prayer. And have faith in God who *'killeth and maketh alive, who bringeth down to the grave, and bringeth up.'"*[99] Sometimes prayer served alongside natural remedies in the process of healing but at other times prayer Wesley viewed prayer as sufficient medicine in itself. Such was the case of a Mr. Kingsford who had entirely lost the use of one his legs and contemplated the need of a physician only to reason with himself: "But God can do more for me than any physician."[100] Immediately he sensed strength in his leg and began to walk. On other occasions, the result of prayer was extraordinary and the mention of medicine and science was omitted in Wesley's narrative accounts. The healing function of prayer was portrayed throughout the writings of Wesley and other Methodists throughout the eighteenth century with unapologetic fervour and in the societies Methodist members were trained from a very early stage that their life of faithfulness was grounded in the exercise of a devoted prayer life. The rising in the morning at four o'clock for prayer became an identification of the disciples who incorporated this means of grace in their life of faith.

Alongside the presence of prayer in the Methodist societies was also the discipline of fasting.[101] From the early days of the Holy Club at Oxford until his last days in London, John Wesley embraced fasting as a necessary component of the Christian life. In Wesley's later writings there is indication that he had abandoned the idea of stationary fasts. Nevertheless, there is an overwhelming amount of evidence that suggests that he continued to associate the discipline of fasting with the idea of spiritual renewal in the life of the societies. In his *Short*

History of the People Called Methodists, Wesley recounted the amazing revival of a lethargic society in Durham. Wesley wrote:

> There is something remarkable in the manner wherein God revived his work in this place. A few months ago the generality of the people in this circuit were exceedingly lifeless. Samuel Meggot (now with God) perceiving this, advised the society in Barnard Castle to observe every Friday as a day of fasting and prayer. The very first Friday they met together God broke in upon them in a marvellous manner. And his work has been increasing among them ever since. The neighboring societies heard of this, agreed to follow the same rule, and soon experienced the same blessing. Is not the neglect of this plain duty (I mean fasting, ranked by our Lord with thanksgiving and prayer) one general occasion of deadness among Christians? Can anyone willingly neglect it and be guiltless.[102]

On another occasion, to his younger brother Charles, John Wesley spoke of his commitment and his brother's negligence in the matter of enforcing fasting among the Methodist preachers. In a letter, he wrote to Charles Wesley on 8 August 1752, demanding an immediate account: "Some of our Preachers here have peremptorily affirmed that you are not so *strict* as me . . . I suppose they mean those which condemn 'needless self-indulgence,' and recommend the means of grace, fasting in particular—which is well nigh forgotten throughout this nation. I think it would be of use if you wrote without delay and explain yourself at large."[103]

It had been in 1733, when John Wesley made the acquaintance of Thomas Deacon, the nonjuror and physician, that Wesley was encouraged to undertake a serious examination of the place and priority of fasting in primitive Christianity. Later, Deacon enlisted Wesley as a contributor in his *A Compleate Collections of Devotions both Publick and Private: Taken from the Apostolical Consititutions, the Ancient Liturgies, and Common Prayer Book of the Church of England.*[104] Frank Baker wrote of the importance of this encounter between Deacon and Wesley: "Wesley returned from this visit thoroughly fired with zeal both for the ancient Church and for the 'stations,' which he continually urged upon his friends and pupils, from time to time exultantly recording in his diary that one or the other of them was 'convinced of Stations.'"[105]

What remained clear throughout Wesley's life was that fasting enabled the disciple to wait on the appearance of God, which at times occurred in mundane fashion and at other moments was revealed in spectacular ways. In a sermon on fasting, for example, there was little doubt in the mind of the evangelical leader that it was supernatural assistance that enabled Moses, Elijah, and Jesus to fast for forty days.[106] In addition to a commitment to individual and communal holiness, Wesley also encouraged the Methodists to observe fast days in the eighteenth century. However, a "more weighty reason for fasting is that it is an help to prayer; particularly when we set apart larger portions of time for private prayer. Then especially it is that God is often pleased to lift up the souls of his servants above all things in earth, and sometimes to rap them up, as it were, into the third heaven."[107] Throughout his writings, Wesley was quick to give evidence of the power of fasting for healing and wholeness. At the end of the *Primitive Physic,* for example, Wesley listed fasting-spittle, as a possible cure for various ailments and diseases.[108] Contrary to others during Wesley's day who degraded healing into an enterprise, Wesley was not interested in healing for itself but set himself apart from cultic followings of the day like Bridget Bostock (1678-1749), a healer in Cheshire who gathered a following in the 1740s and 1750s and used fasting spittle in her healing techniques.[109] For Wesley, however, the correlation of medicine and miracles provided a compatible and verifiable source of God's healing grace.[110]

However much John Wesley was committed to the discipline of prayer and fasting, there emerged tensions over these pious exercises and a determinate resolution was required inside Methodist circles. The "enthusiasm" of George Bell found expression in claims to supernatural healing which caused embarrassment to the movement. In various issues of the *Arminian Magazine*, Wesley sympathetically included accounts of some miraculous healings that had occurred by the hands of Bell. One came from the life of Mary Spread, who claimed she was healed of breast cancer by the prayers and touch of Bell. She had been told that her situation was hopeless but after Bell decided that she had sufficient faith to be healed, he touched her breast and the haemorrhage immediately stopped. The pain returned the following day, but after prayers, ceased again and her breast was healed of its cancerous scars.[111] In a lengthy letter to Charles Wesley, John Walsh reported of a meeting of Bell and Whitefield on January 12, 1762, at Tot'nam Court Road. Bell boldly declared that "GOD had given him the gift of healing, which he had already practiced & or raising the Dead, which he should perform in GOD's time."[112] George Bell and his sectators in the London societies saw this form of healing both as a miraculous cure and a sign of the restoration of the gifts of the Holy Spirit in the life of the believers, and consequently, a prolepsis to the immanent end of the world because the gift, according to Bell, was peculiar to those who manifested spiritual perfection in the latter days. This, claimed Wesley, was a distortion of the concept of healing because it bifurcated the alliance of nature and grace in God's plan of redemption. When a Methodist woman asserted that healing had come to her loved one at the hands of Wesley himself, he related the event but stopped short of claiming credit for the incident, commenting: "If so, give God the glory."[113]

Wesley never thought, however, that prayer accompanied by fasting was a technique that could manipulate the hand of God. In a published sermon he declared: "Not that there is any natural or necessary connection between fasting and the blessings God conveys thereby. But he will have mercy . . . and he hath in all ages appointed this to be a means of averting his wrath, and obtaining whatever blessings we from time to time stand in need of."[114] Furthermore, he never stipulated that healing was a mark of sanctification nor did he locate healing of the physical body as an essential or even verification of the authenticity of the Revival. Rather, he continued to record such occurrences as evidence for his belief in the supernatural.

The Eucharist and Healing in Early Methodism

The Methodist belief that prayer and fasting had therapeutic power was not surprising. In the rise of Methodism in the eighteenth century, prayer played a significant role which spoke to the Methodist sense of identity and the struggles that contributed to that self-understanding. Additionally, the activities of prayer and fasting demonstrated the fundamental belief in supernatural realities for Methodists and their confidence in the intersection of visible and invisible worlds was not a vain one. For the Methodists living in the modern world, both in Britain and North America, the belief that a deity interacted in the daily occurrences of human beings was both desired and expected.[115] What has been passed over by historians of the Methodist movement, however, is the role of healings which occurred when the Eucharist was celebrated.

From early Christian history the supernatural power present in Eucharist celebrations has been expressed in a variety of ways. Eamon Duffy in his *The Stripping of the Altars*, observes that the miracle stories surrounding the host in medieval society revealed devotional and polemical themes which more times than not addressed the threat of doubters and their unbelief.[116] Duffy's comment that in the medieval church "power 'leaked' from the host and blood," carried a rhetorical significance that encompassed theological truth and also offered implications for the socio-political realm as well.[117] During the Middle Ages, there emerged intricate speculations about the healing efficacy of the host which was consumed by the votary. People read and discussed various theories which conjectured about the healing effect of the body and blood of Christ as the elements of the meal were chewed, swallowed, digested, and even excreted by communicants. One scholar of the period explains that "ingesting the host put the Christian into contact with the ineffable through a mysterious food that brought both salvation and health, both signified by many late medieval writers with the same word, *salus*."[118] Despite Renaissance humanists, like Desiderius Erasmus (1466-1536), who avidly used satire to poke at the superstition of the medieval churchmen, there continued to be a belief that the Eucharist meal had miraculous potential which might endow the restoration of body and soul.[119]

In the eighteenth century among Protestants, though, few emphasized the healing nature of the Lord's Supper as the Methodists did. The celebration of both the Eucharist and love feasts for Methodists, writes Lester Ruth, were "staggered by the graciousness of God they experienced in the sacrament and by the overwhelming sense of God's presence."[120] The high place of the Eucharist in the faith of eighteenth-century Methodists was controversial, however. The issues that Wesley confronted over lay presidency and administration of the Lord's Supper evidenced problems that delved into the deeper issues of order and control in the Methodist societies. Another facet that must not be overshadowed, moreover, was Methodists' incorporation of their sacramental understanding of divine presence into the wider fabric of affirmations about miraculous and supernatural manifestations of grace.[121]

Fundamental to the idea of divine power for both John and Charles Wesley was the image of the crucified Jesus. Throughout various narratives of the period Methodists unabashedly avowed visions of the horrific nature of Christ's death which, they contended, brought relief and healing to the visionary and at times to those listening to the tale of their testimonies.[122] A sermon which Wesley wrote during the Holy Club period at Oxford in 1733, and was published over a half-century later, summarized his sentiments about the death of Christ and its remembrance in the Eucharist. In the first point of the published sermon, Wesley underscored his dedication to the idea of constant communion and the power of the crucified Saviour to heal both body and soul:

> Whatever way of life we are in, whatever our condition be, whether we are sick or well, in trouble or at ease, the enemies of our souls are watching to lead us into sin. And too often they prevail over us. Now when we are convinced of having sinned against God, what surer way have we of procuring pardon from him than the "showing forth the Lord's death," and beseeching him, for the sake of his Son's sufferings, to blot out all our sins?[123]

Wesley himself received communion weekly and during special times in the Christian calendar, like Holy Week, he communicated daily. For the Methodists, the presence of the crucified Christ in the Lord's Supper was tantamount to the fullness of a divine love that was offered to all humanity.[124] John Wesley repeatedly reminded Methodists that the power of the Eucharist lay in the idea of the sacred meal as a "converting ordinance." On 27 June 1740, he preached on the idea of constant communion and in support of the idea of the Eucharist as a *converting* ordinance, declared: "For many now present know, the very beginning of your *conversion* to God (perhaps, in some, the first deep *conviction*) was wrought at the Lord's Supper."[125] However, the idea of conversion was just the beginning of Wesley's understanding of the power of the sacred meal.

Central to both the Wesley brothers' understanding of the Eucharist was the universal nature of the atonement of Christ. "To them," wrote John Bowmer, "the Atonement and the Eucharist were inseparably linked."[126] In the collection of hymns, *Hymns on the Lord's Supper*, which was first published in 1745 and went through nine editions during the eighteenth century, there was a section devoted to the Eucharist and the idea of Christian sacrifice.[127] Hymn 119 rehearsed the active power of Christ's blood:

> Hear his Blood's prevailing Cry,
> Let thy Bowels then reply,
> Then thro' Him the Sinner see,
> Then in Jesus look on Me.[128]

The atoning significance of the crucified Christ incorporated the believer into God's power which had cancelled sin. The Eucharist, then, demonstrated for Wesley a bridge between the life of Christ in its human dimensions and a reality that lay beyond the finitude of human limitations. It was not uncommon in Methodist narratives during the period for communicants receiving the host to have visions of the crucified Saviour and experience the healing efficacy of the wounds of Christ.[129] In other contexts too, the Lord's Supper was central to demonstrable displays of devotion that was followed by ecstasy and spiritual expectation. At Cambuslang, in Scotland, for instance, George Whitefield and other Kirk ministers preached over seventeen sermons and attracted in excess of 80,000 communicants within the span of thirty days.[130] The intensity and fervour of the revival lead the Scottish evangelical, John Erskine (1721-1803) to publish a popular tract where he confidently asserted that a millennial future was evidenced by various revival occurrences in New England and Scotland.[131]

In North America too, the Eucharist became important for communicants and their realization of the supernatural dimension of their religiosity. Thus, John Wesley could agree with the fervour of James Haw, a Kentucky Methodist, and included his comments about the experience of the Lord's Supper during a 1788 camp meeting in the *Arminian Magazine*. Haw wrote of the experiences of communicants, in Kentucky, with Pentecost imagery: "The work of sanctification amongst the believers broke out at the Lord's Table; and the spirit of the Lord went through the assembly like a mighty rushing wind."[132] In Wesley's published journals, too, there were preternatural events that were directly linked to the Eucharist. On his Georgia missionary journey in 1736, for example, Wesley recounted how a pregnant woman contracted a fever and desired to receive communion before she died. "At the hour of her receiving," recorded the young Wesley, "she began to recover, and in a few days was entirely out of danger."[133] Eighteen months later, in May of 1738, John connected the Eucharist to the healing of his brother Charles, who suffered from pleurisy. After praying for the health of his brother on Saturday evening, John Wesley recorded the miraculous events on Whitsunday just before his brother's own "palpitation of heart" experience, which was quoted at the opening of this chapter:

> The next day, being Whitsunday, after hearing Dr. Heylyn preach a truly Christian sermon (on "They were all filled with the Holy Ghost"—and so, said he, may *all you* be, if it is not your fault), and assisting him at the Holy Communion (his curate being taken ill in the church), I received the surprising news that my brother had found rest to his soul. His bodily strength returned also from that hour. "Who is so great a God as our God?"[134]

There was little doubt among Methodists in the eighteenth century that the Eucharist drew them into a presence that though in this world was not of this world.

Wesley's Commitment: Healing and Wholeness

John Wesley's commitment to the idea of natural and supernatural forms of healing was considerable. Throughout his travels, he was constantly being approached by individuals who were in need of physical, emotional, and spiritual healing. His compassion was not merely a response to his theological sensibilities; rather, it was a theological coherence for which Wesley found validity in the daily experiences of those he encountered. The empirical and pastoral dimensions of Wesley's training found its deepest expression in his care for people of various walks of life as he travelled throughout towns and villages. In the preface to the 1747 *Primitive Physic*, Wesley underscored his commitment to aiding individuals with the dispensation of medicines and remedies. Wesley recorded in his journal for 4 December 1746, his design for the first free public dispensary in London, which was set up the next year. The passage recorded not only the success of his venture but also a holistic approach to healing. "I mentioned to the society," he wrote, "my design of giving physic to the poor. About thirty came the next day, and in three weeks about three hundred. This we continued for several years, till, the number of patients still increasing, the expense was greater than we could bear. Meantime, through the blessing of God, many who had been ill for months or years were restored to perfect health."[135] In Wesley's mind, neither natural nor supernatural dimensions of healing were to be overshadowed.

At the root of his concern about illness in the eighteenth century was the problem of distress and relief. James Donat has pointed out that in the eighteenth century the universities that were graduating physicians were few. In Oxford, Cambridge, and Edinburgh there were scarcely above two dozen students graduated every year that could treat a population of five to nine million people.[136] From Wesley's perspective, the handing out of physic to the poor and needy was both socially and ethically mandated. Of the former, the distribution of needed medications was necessary because of the overwhelming odds that faced qualified physicians in his time. Of the latter, the distributions of pills and other medications was practiced as a significant part of the Methodist mission and ministry. Additionally, there were an increasing amount of physicians who were practicing the trade as a means to increase their personal wealth and not to serve and aid the people who were in need of healthcare. In the preface to his 1747 edition of the *Primitive Physic* Wesley wrote of his disdain for a majority of the physicians coming out of universities at this time. "They," Wesley barbed, "fill'd their Writings with abundance of Technical Terms, utterly unintelligible to plain Men. They affected to deliver their Rules, and to reason upon them, in an abstruse, and philosophical manner."[137] In short, John Wesley believed that the practicing of medicine should reach as many as possible.

For similar reasons, Wesley was committed to an understanding of God's healing grace which he believed accessible in the lives of all individuals. Obviously he saw the development of scientific knowledge as a gift to be utilized for the benefit of humanity. As demonstrated previously, Wesley was not only interested in setting up and maintaining dispensaries throughout his connexion but as we have seen he also became interested in electricity and other advancements in the art of healing.[138] However, there were occasions and circumstances when human ingenuity and intelligence could not meet the need of the individual. One example was the case of a Mr. Kingford, who Wesley described in his journal in the autumn of 1787 as a man of substance and piety. Kingsford had lost the use of his ankles and knees in 1780 and for six years he had sought the advice and remedies of various physicians. While he was in Bath on a business trip he again sent for a physician as he had done many times before. But this time he had a change of heart and strategy. Wesley approvingly quotes his testimony:

> At Bath, I sent for a physician. But before he came, as I sat reading the Bible, I thought, "Asa sought to the physicians and not to God," but God can do more for me than any physician. Soon after, I heard a noise in the street and, rising up,

found I could stand. Being much surprised, I walked several times about the room. Then I walked into the square and afterwards on the Bristol road. And from that time, I have been perfectly well, having as full a use of all my limbs as I had seven years ago.[139]

Healings came through prayers, dreams, and impressions of the mind merely by uttering the name of Christ. One came from Wesley's own experience. In 1756 Wesley had been struggling against various ailments which was hindering his effectiveness on preaching tours. On Sunday, 3 October 1756, he had occasion to celebrate Eucharist and recorded his strategy:

> My disorder returned as violent as ever. But I regarded it not while I was performing the service at Snowfields in the morning or afterward at Spitelfields, till I went to the Lord's Table in order to administer. A thought then came into my mind. "Why do I not apply to God in the beginning, rather than the end of an illness?" I did so and found immediate relief, so that I needed no farther medicines.[140]

The pivotal point that Wesley repeatedly emphasized in ordinary and remarkable demonstrations of healing, however, was the love of God that reaches out to all men, women, and children.

Notes

1. John Wesley to Alexander Knox, 26 August 1778. *LJW* 6: 318.

2. Charles Wesley, "Hymns on the Four Gospels." *The Poetical Works of John and Charles Wesley*, ed., George Osbourn, 13 vols. (London: Wesleyan-Methodist Conference Office, 1868-72), 10: 340.

3. "When the Wesleys returned from America their spiritual state was peculiar, and far from being satisfactory to themselves." Thomas Jackson, *The Life of the Rev. Charles Wesley, M. A.: Some Time Student of Christ-Church, Oxford: Comprising A Review of His Poetry; Sketches of The Rise and Progress of Methodism; with Notices of Contemporary Events and Characters* (New York: G. Lane and P. P. Sandford, 1844), 99.

4. Charles Wesley, *The Journal of the Rev. Charles Wesley, M. A. Sometime Student of Christ Church, Oxford. To Which are Appended Selections From His Correspondance and Poetry*, 2 vols. (London: Wesleyan Methodist Book Room, 1811), 1: 90-91. Charles Wesley related in his journal account how Mrs. Turner had a dream where Jesus was knocking at the door of the house the night that Charles Wesley had been stricken with illness. At Friday evening prayers the word of God came to her again commanding her to go speak the healing message to Charles Wesley. Initially she ignored these promptings but after her brother reminded her of the repercussions of Jonah she visited Charles Wesley on Whitsunday and spoke the words that brought "a strange palpitation of heart." For commentary on this experience see Jackson, *The Life of the Rev. Charles Wesley*, 99-127.

5. For Pawson's life, see John Pawson, *A Short Account of the Lord's Gracious Dealings with J. Pawson* (Leeds: Edward Baines, 1801) and *Wesley's Veterans*, 4: 1-121.

6. John Wesley, ed., *Arminian Magazine* 5 (1781): 243. For other spiritual healing occurrences in Manchester see John Pawson's "Some account of the life of Mr John Pawson," MARC, Diaries Box, 27. See also, Rack's "Between Church and Sect," 84.

7. Runyon, *The New Creation*, 27-28.

8. John Wesley, "God's Approbation of His Works," *BEW* 2: 388.

9. John Wesley, "The Image of God," *BEW* 4: 297.

10. "The vitalists' primary thesis was an affirmation of the unity of man, a being which must always be studied as a whole, and whose physical and moral aspects are closely conjoined." Roselyne Rey, "Psyche, Soma, and the Vitalist Philosophy of Medicine," in John P. Wright and Paul Potter, eds., *Psyche and Soma: Physicians and Metaphysicians on the Mind-Body Problem From Antiquity to Enlightenment* (Oxford: Clarendon Press, 2000), 255-65, esp. 256. See also, Roselyne Rey, *Naissance et development du vitalisme en France, de la deuxième moitié du XVIIIe siècle à la fin du Premier Empire* (Oxford: Voltaire Foundation, 2000).

11. For examination of Wesley's interaction with eighteenth-century medical techniques and theories, see Deborah Madden, *Pristine Purity: Primitivism and Practcal Piety in John Wesley's Art of Physic* (D. Phil. thesis, Oxford University, 2003). Also Deborah Madden, *A Cheap, Safe, and Natural Medicine: Religion, Medicine and Culure in John Wesley's Primitive Physic* (Amsterdam: Rodopi, 2007).

12. 24 July 1761. *BEW* 21: 337.

13. See Deborah Madden, "Experience and the Common Interest of Mankind: The Enlightened Empiricism of John Wesley's Primitive Physic," *British Journal of Eighteenth-Century Studies* 26 (2003): 41-53 and "Medicine and Moral Reform: The Place of Practical Piety in John Wesley's Art of Physic," *Church History* 73 (2004): 741-58. For an overview of quackery in the modern world see Roy Porter, *Quacks: Fakers & Charlatans in English Medicine* (1989; repr., Stroud: Tempus Publishing Ltd., 2000).

14. John Meir, *A Marginal Jew: Rethinking the Historical Jesus*, 4 vols. (New York: Doubleday, 1994), 2: 679. "The synoptic authors chose to present Jesus of Nazareth as a healer *par excellence*." Lousie Well's *The Greek language of healing from Homer to New Testament Times* (Berlin: Walter de Gruyter, 1998), 120.

15. Stevan Davies, *Jesus the Healer: Possession, Trance, and the Origins of Christianity* (New York: Continuum, 1995), 67. Additionally, compare Evelyn Frost, *Christian Healing: A Consideration of the Place of Spiritual Healing in the Church of To-Day in the Light of the Doctrine and Practice of the Ante-Nicene Church* (London: A. R. Mowbray,1940); Morton Kelsey, *Healing and Christianity: In Ancient Thought and Modern Times* (New York: Harper and Row Publishers, 1973), 52-128; Meir, *A Marginal Jew*, 2: 678-772; Amanda Porterfield, *Healing in the History of Christianity* (Oxford: Oxford University Press, 2005), 21-41; John Pilch, *Healing in the New Testament: Insights from Medical and Mediterranean Anthropology* (Minneapolis, MN: Fortress Press, 2000); John Pilch, "Sickness and Healing in Luke-Acts," in Jerome Neyrey, ed., *The Social World of Luke-Acts* (Peabody, MA: 1991), 181-209; Harold Remus, *Jesus as Healer* (Cambridge: Cambridge University Press, 1997); and Graham Twelftree, *Jesus the Miracle Worker: A Historical & Theological Study* (Downers Grove, IL: InterVarsity Press, 1999), 281-330.

16. Ronald C. Finucane, *Miracles & Pilgrims: Popular Beliefs in Medieval England* (London: Book Club Association, 1977), 59-188.

17. G. J. C. Snoek, *Medieval Piety from Relics to the Eucharist: A Process of Mutual Interaction* (Leiden: E. J. Brill, 1995), 338-41. See also the more recent study on miracles in the medieval church from Robert Barlett, *The Natural and the Supernatural in the Middle Ages* (Cambridge: Cambridge University Press, 2008) and Carl S. Watkins, *History and the Supernatural in Medieval England* (Cambridge: Cambridge University Press, 2009).

18. Carole Rawcliffe, *Medicine & Society in Later Medieval England*, 2nd ed. (London: Sandpiper Books, 1999), 36-57, provides a discussion of the *regimen sanitatis* and

its place in medieval culture. For the fine line between natural and supernatural healing in the medieval world, see Finucane, *Miracles & Pilgrims*, 59-99

19. "The theoretical debates failed to put off the people, who knew that they had contact with an unworldly reality through the relics." Snoek, *Medieval Piety from Relics to the Eucharist*, 357.

20. "The popularity of the *Legend* was such that some one thousand manuscripts have survived, and, with the advent of printing in the 1450s, editions both in the original Latin and in every Western European language multiplied into the hundreds. It has been said that in the late Middle Ages the only book more widely read was the Bible." William Granger Ryan, "Introduction," in Jacobus de Voragine, *The Golden Legend: Readings on the Saints*, trans. William Granger Ryan (Princeton: Princeton University Press, 1993), 1: xiii.

21. Voragine, *Golden Legend*, 1: 189.

22. Aquinas, *Summa Theologica*, Supplement, 30.2.

23. Caroline Walker Bynum, *The Resurrection of the Body in Western Christianity, 200-1336* (New York: Columbia University Press, 1995), 220, 223-24.

24. See Euan Cameron, "The Power of the Word: Renaissance and Reformation," ed., Euan Cameron, *Early Modern Europe: An Oxford History* (Oxford: Oxford University Press, 1999), 63-101. For an examination of the Protestant Reformation and its view of medieval Catholicism see Eamon Duffy's *The Stripping of the Altars: Traditional Religion in England 1400-1580* (New Haven: Yale University Press, 1992), 478-593 and *The Voices of Morebath: Reformation & Rebellion in an English Village* (New Haven: Yale University Press, 2001), 84-110.

25. "The Reformation would not have happened if ordinary people had not convinced themselves that they were actors in a cosmic drama plotted by God, that in the Bible he had left them a record of his plans and directions as to how to carry them out. Their revolution was not simply a search for personal salvation. They changed the way that their world worked because they were convinced that this visible world was the least important part of the divine plan." Diarmaid MacCulloch, *The Reformation: A History* (New York: Viking, 2003), 532.

26. Marc Bloch, *The Royal Touch: Sacred Monarchy and Scrofula in England and France*, trans. J. E. Anderson (London: Routledge & Kegan Paul, 1973). See also James Turrell, "The Ritual of Royal Healing: Scrofula, Liturgy, and Politics," *Anglican and Episcopal History* 68 (1999): 3-36.

27. Brooke, *Science and Religion*, 82-99. For Luther's rebellion, Richard Marius, *Martin Luther: The Christian Between God and Death* (Cambridge, MA: Harvard University Press, 1999), 190-218.

28. The literature on Martin Luther and the Zwickau prophets is extensive. See Martin Brecht, *Luther: Shaping and Defining the Reformation 1521-1532*, trans. James Schaaf (Minneapolis, MN: Fortress Press, 1990), 137-195 and Karl Gerhard Steck, *Luther und die Schwärmer* (Zollikon-Zürich: Evangelischer Verlag, 1955). For a general and brief discussion of Martin Luther's view of miracles, see Paul Althaus, *The Theology of Martin Luther*, trans. Robert Schultz (Philadelphia, PA: Fortress Press, 1966), 429-45.

29. For accounts of this episode see George Cubitt's *The Life of Martin Luther* (New York: Carlton & Phillips, 1853), 311-12 and Robert Bruce Mullin's *Miracles & the Modern Religious Imagination* (New Haven: Yale University Press, 1996), 84.

30. Martin Luther, *Letters of Spiritual Counsel*, trans. and ed., Theodore Tappert (1955; repr., Philadelphia, PA: Westminister John Knox Press, 2006), 51-52. For a provocative account of Luther's idea of miracles see Philip M. Soergel's *Miracles and the Protestant Imagination: The Evangelical Wonder Book in Reformation Germany* (Oxford: Oxford University Press, 2012), 33-66.

31. John Calvin, *Institutes of the Christian Religion,* trans. and ed., John McNeill and Ford Lewis Battle (Philadelphia, PA: The Westminster Press, 1960), 4.18. See also Colin Brown, *Miracles and the Critical Mind* (Grand Rapids, MI: William B. Eerdmans Publishing Company, 1984), 15-18.

32. For the idea of the history of mentalities, see Peter Burke, "Strengths and Weaknesses of the history of Mentalities," *History of European Ideas* 7 (1986): 439-51 and Gaskill, *Crime and Mentalities in Early Modern England,* 3-29.

33. Adrian Wilson, "The Politics of Medical Improvement in Early Hanoverian London," in Andrew Cunningham and Roger French, eds., *The Medical Enlightenment of the Eighteenth Century* (1990; repr., Cambridge: Cambridge University Press, 2004), 8.

34. John Bellers, *An Essay Towards the Improvement of Physick. In Twelve Proposals. By Which the Lives of many Thousands of the Rich, as Well as of the Poor, may be Saved Yearly* (London: J. Sowle, 1714), 5-6.

35. Lucinda McCray Beier, *Suffers & Healers: The experience of illness in Seventeenth-Century England* (London: Routledge & Kegan Paul, 1987), 154.

36. See Barbara Howard Taylor, *The Notorious Astrological Physician of London: Works and Days of Simon Forman* (Chicago: University of Chicago Press, 2001).

37. Robert Boyle, *Some Considerations Touching the Usefulness of Natural Philosophy: Proposed in Familiar Discourses to a Friend, by Way of Invitation to the Study of it* in *The Works of the Honourable Robert Boyle,* 6 vols. (London: Printed for J. and F. Rivington, et.al., 1744), 138-39.

38. George Cheyne, *The Philosophical Principles of Religion, Natural and Revealed,* 2 vols. (London: Printed for George Strahan, 1715), 1: 42.

39. Anita Guerrini, "Newtonianism, Medicine and Religion," in Ole Peter Grell and Andrew Cunningham, eds., *Religio Medici: Medicine and Religion in Seventeenth-Century England* (Aldershot: Scolar Press, 1996), 302.

40. For more on Wesley's knowledge and influence of these aspects of healing and wholeness see the essays in Deborah Madden, ed., *"Inward & Outward Health": John Wesley's Holistic Concept of Medical Science, the Environment and Holy Living* (London: Epworth Press, 2008).

41. R. Jeffrey Hiatt, "John Wesley & Healing: Developing a Wesleyan Missiology," *The Asbury Theological Journal* 20 (2004): 89-109; Phillip Ott, "John Wesley on Health as Wholeness," *Journal of Religious History* 30 (1991): 43-57; Phillip Ott, "Medicine as Metaphor: John Wesley on Therapy of the Soul," *Methodist History* 33 (1995): 178-191.

42. Wesley Hill, *John Wesley Among the Physicians: A Study of Eighteenth Century Medicine* (London: Epworth Press, 1953); E. Brooks Holifield, *Health and Medicine in the Methodist Tradition* (Nashville, TN: Abingdon Press, 1986), 3-60; John Cule, "The Rev. John Wesley, M. A. (Oxon.), 1703-1791: 'The Naked Empiricist' and Orthodox Medicine," *The Journal of the History of Medicine and Allied Sciences* 45 (1990): 41-63; Madden, *A Cheap, Safe, and Natural Medicine*; Madden, "Medicine and Moral Reform," 741-58; Samuel Rogal, "Pills for the Poor: John Wesley's Primitive Physic," *The Yale Journal of Biology and Medicine* 51 (1978): 81-90.

43. "And are not they partakers of the same guilt, though in a lower degree, whether surgeons, apothecaries, or physicians, who play with the lives or health of men to enlarge their own gain?" John Wesley, "The Use of Money," *BEW 2:* 272, where a negative image of physicians was highlighted in his sermon to accentuate the idea that Methodists are not to be greedy.

44. John Wesley to Vincent Perronet, 1748. *LJW* 2: 306. "Begin, my dear brethren, begin now: else the impression which you now feel will wear off; and possibly it may never return! What then will be the consequence? Instead of hearing that word, 'Come, ye blessed . . . . For I was sick and ye visited me,' you must hear that awful sentence,

'Depart, ye cursed! . . . For I was sick, and ye visited me not!'" John Wesley's sermon on this topic, "On Visiting the Sick," *BEW* 3: 385-97, where after citing Phobe again concluded his homily with a stern warning.

45. John Wesley to Vincent Perronet, 1748. *LJW* 2: 306.

46. "O what a harvest might there be, if any lover of souls who has time upon his hands would constantly attend these places of distress, and with tenderness and meekness of wisdom instruct and exhort those on whom God has laid his hands, to know and improve the day of their visitation!" 7 September 1741. *BEW* 19: 226.

47. John Wesley, *A Collection of Receipts for the Use of the Poor*, 3rd ed. (Bristol: Felix Farley, 1746); John Wesley, *Primitive Physic: or, An Easy and Natural Method of Curing Most Diseases* (London: Thomas Trye, 1747).

48. George S. Rousseau, "John Wesley's Primitive Physic (1747)," *Harvard Library Bulletin* 16 (1968): 242. See also, John Tuck, "'Primitive Physic': An Interesting Association Copy," *Proceedings of the Wesley Historical Society*, 45 (1985): 1-7 and Clair D. Wilcoxon, "The Whole Man: A Study of John Wesley's Healing Ministry," *Religion in Life* 28 (1959): 580-86.

49. "Wesley's preface would make an excellent study in itself." Rousseau, "John Wesley's Primitive Physic (1747)," 242n2.

50. Wesley, *Primitive Physic*, v.

51. "Cheyne's contemporaries were no doubt amazed by his weight reduction from 448 pounds to 130. The further fact that he practiced what he preached about the relation of weight and diet also lent him credibility lacked by many eighteenth-century physicians." George S. Rousseau, "Mysticism and Millenarianism: 'Immortal Dr. Cheyne,'" in Ingrid Merkel and Allen Debus, eds., *Hermeticism and the Renaissance: Intellectual History and the Occult in Early Modern Europe* (Washington, DC: Folger Shakespeare Library, 1988), 197.

52. George Cheyne, *An Essay of Health and Long Life*, 4th ed. (Dublin: Printed for George Ewing, 1725), 3. "His account made clear the parallel between spiritual and bodily healing." Anita Guerrini, *Obesity & Depression in the Enlightenment: The Life and Times of George Cheyne* (Norman, OK: University of Oklahoma Press, 2000), 9.

53. See Randy Maddox, "Kingswood School Library Holdings (CA. 1775)," *Methodist History* 41 (2002): 342-370. "I cannot but observe it is one of the most ingenious books which I ever saw." 12 March 1742. *BEW 19:* 256, for John Wesley's endorsement of Cheyne's *Natural Method of Curing Diseases*.

54. Walter J. Turrell, *John Wesley: Physician & Electrotherapist* (Oxford: Blackwell, 1938).

55. Patricia Fara, *An Entertainment for Angels: Electricity in the Enlightenment* (Cambridge: Icon Books, 2003), 2; Patricia Fara, *Science: A Four Thousand Year History* (Oxford: Oxford University Press, 2009), 164-69. See also Michael Brian Schiffer's, *Draw the Lightning Down: Benjamin Franklin and Electrical Technology in the Age of Enlightenment* (Berkley, CA: University of California Press, 2003), 67-106. Also helpful is Paoli Bertucci's *Sparks of Life: Medical electricity and natural philosophy in England, c. 1746-1792* (D. Phil. thesis, Oxford University, 2001); Paoli Bertucci, "Revealing Sparks: John Wesley and the Religious Utility of Electrical Healing," *British Journal for the History of Science* 39 (2006): 341-62.

56. Among the works that John Wesley read on electrotherapy were Benjamin Martin's *Essay on Electricity: Being an enquiry into the nature, cause and properties thereof, on the principle of Sir Isaac Newton's theory of vibrating motion, light, and fire; and the various phaenomena of fourty-two capital experiments* (Bath: Printed for the author and et. al., 1746); John Freke, *An Essay to Shew the Cause of Electricity* (London: Printed for W. Innys, 1746); Benjamin Wilson's, *An Essay on towards an Explication of the Phae-*

nomena of Electricity, contained in three papers (London: Printed for C. Davis and M. Cooper, 1746); *A Short View of Electricity* (London: C. Nourse, 1780); Benjamin Hoadley, Junior, *Observations on a Series of Electrical Experiments by Dr. Hoadly and Mr. Wilson* (London: Printed for T. Payne, 1756); Richard Lovett's, *The Subtle Medium prov'd . . . Qualities ascribed to Aether or elementary Fire of the Ancient Philosophers are to found in Electrical Fire* (London: Printed for J. Hinton, W. Sandby, and R. Lovett, 1756); Richard Lovett, *An Appendix on Electricity rendered Useful in Medical Intentions* (London: np, 1760); Richard Lovett, *The Electrical Philosopher, containing a new System of Physics founded upon the Principle of an Universal Plenum of Elementary Fire* (Worcester: Printed by the author and R. Lewis, 1774); Joseph Priestly's, *History and Present State of Electricity with Original Experiments*, 2nd ed. (London: Printed for J. Dodsley, J. Johnson, J. Payne, and T. Cadell, 1769) and Benjamin Franklin's, *Experiments and Observations on Electricity, Made at Philadelphia in America by Mr. Benjamin Franklin, and Communicated in Several Letters to Mr. Collinson, of London, F.R.S.* (London: Printed by E. Cave, 1751).

57. 9 November 1756. *BEW* 21: 81; 4 January 1768. *BEW* 22: 117.

58. 16 October 1747. *BEW* 20: 195.

59. See Figure 9: "John Wesley's Electrifying Machine."

60. 9 November 1756. *BEW* 21: 81.

61. 9 November 1756. *BEW* 21: 81.

62. John Wesley, *The Desideratum: or, Electricity made plain and useful. By a Lover of Mankind, and of Common Sense* (London: W. Flexney, E. Cabe, George Clark, George Keith, and T. Smith, 1760).

63. Wesley, *Desideratum*, 72. "It [electricity] cures abundance of Diseases, even the most stubborn . . . So that this is not only one of the greatest Curiosities in the World, but one of the noblest Medicines that God ever gave to Man." Wesley, *Survey of the Wisdom of God*, 2: 118.

64. Samuel Rogal, "Electricity: John Wesley's 'Curious and Important Subject.'" *Eighteenth-Century Life* 13 (1989): 83.

65. John Wesley to John Bredlin, 19 October 1781. *LJW* 7: 86.

66. William Hawes, *An Examination of Mr. John Wesley's Primitive Physic*, 2nd ed. (London: Printed for the author, 1780).

67. Wesley, *Primitive Physic*, v.

68. "The love of God, as it is the sovereign remedy of all miseries, so in particular it effectually prevents all the bodily disorders the passions introduce, by keeping the passions themselves within due bounds. And by the unspeakable joy and perfect calm, serenity, and tranquillity it gives the mind, it becomes the most powerful of all the means of health and long life." Wesley, *Primitive Physic*, xii-xiii, where Wesley identified the love of God in terms of preventive medicine.

69. John Bowmer, "John Wesley's Philosophy of Suffering," *The London Quarterly and Holborn Review* 184 (1959): 62.

70. Wesley, *Explanatory Notes*, 2: 1533 (Job 5.4).

71. Andrew Sung Park, "Holiness and Healing: An Asian American Voice Shaping the Methodist Traditions," in Joerg Rieger and John J. Vincent, eds., *Methodist and Radical: Rejuvenating a Tradition* (Nashville, TN: Kingswood Books, 2003), 95-106.

72. "Healing, in Wesley's view, could be either natural or supernatural, and it could occur through both medication and prayer." E. Brooks Holifield, *Health and Medicine in the Methodist Tradition*, 28.

73. Thomas Woolston, *Six Discourses on the Miracles of Our Savior in view of the Present Controversy between Infidels and Apostates*, 2nd ed. (London: Printed for the Author, 1727). Woolston's *Discourses*, were published with instalments between 1727 to

1729 and went through a total of six editions during his lifetime. After their publication he was tried and convicted of four counts of blasphemy on 4 March 1729. See *DNB*, "Woolston, Thomas." Also, James A. Herrick's *The Radical Rhetoric of English Deists: The Discourse of Scepticism*, 1680-1750 (Columbia, SC: University of South Carolina Press, 1997), 77-102.

74. Woolston, *Discourse on the Miracles of our Saviour*, 34.

75. 12 May 1746. *BEW* 20: 120-21.

76. "It is easy to track down numerous Methodist accounts of healing miracles (even supposed or promised resurrections from the dead) and visions." Kenneth G. C. Newport, "Early Methodism and The French Prophets: Some New Evidence," *Proceedings of the Wesley Historical Society* 50 (1996): 136.

77. For a discussion of Susannah Arch, see Shaw, *Miracles in Enlightenment England*, 120-25.

78. John Wesley, ed., *Arminian Magazine* 5 (1782): 314-15.

79. It should also be noted in Wesley's often overlooked *A Concise Ecclesiastical History from the Birth of Christ to the Beginning of the Present Century*, 4 vols. (London: J. Parramore, 1781), 1: 117, supernatural healings and providential miracles were portrayed as constitutive events for the growth of Christianity in its earliest period.

80. "It is a mistake to dismiss this as peripheral to Wesley's teaching and mission." Rack, *Reasonable Enthusiast*, 350.

81. For an contemporary treatment of these issues see Porterfield, *Healing in the History of Christianity* and David Harley, "Rhetoric and the Social Construction of Sickness and Healing," *The Social History of Medicine* 12 (1999): 407-35.

82. See my chapter, "'Inward and Outward Health': The Supernatural Dimensions of Healing in John Wesley," in Madden, ed., *"Inward & Outward Health*," 213-32. Also, Hindmarsh, *The Evangelical Conversion Narrative*, 256-59 and Henry D. Rack, "Evangelical Endings: Death-Beds in Evangelical Biography," *Bulletin of the John Rylands University Library of Manchester* 74 (1992): 39-56.

83. "After his death in 1791 class leaders continued to pray for the sick, and Methodists continued to hope for supernatural cures . . . Within four decades of Wesley's death . . . some of his successors were insisting that Methodism should promote spiritual healing." Holifield, *Health and Medicine in the Methodist Tradition*, 38.

84. John Wesley to Charles Wesley, 28 September 1760. *LJW* 4: 108.

85. Tyerman, *The Life and Times of the Rev. John Wesley*, 3: 203.

86. 13 June 1775. *BEW* 22: 455.

87. 17 June 1775. *BEW* 22: 456.

88. "The sceptic will sneer; but the Christian will exercise an unfaltering faith in the glorious text, which, in the history of the church, has been confirmed in instances without number: 'The effectual fervent prayer of a righteous man availeth much.'" Tyerman, *The Life and Times of the Rev. John Wesley*, 3: 203-04. Tyerman's account was based on a York society book.

89. "Letter 436," in John Wesley, ed., *Arminian Magazine* 10 (1787): 553.

90. "Letter 437," in John Wesley, ed., *Arminian Magazine* 10 (1787): 554.

91. John Wesley, *A Collection of Forms of Prayer For Every Day in the Week*, 3rd ed. (London: William Strahan, 1738); 14 May 1765. *BEW* 21: 510-11. According to Richard Green's *The Works of John and Charles Wesley: A Bibliography* (London: C. H. Kelly, 1896), 9, the work went through six editions during John Wesley's lifetime.

92. John Wesley, "On the Death of John Fletcher," *BEW* 3: 615.

93. John Wesley, "The More Excellent Way," *BEW* 3: 269.

94. John Wesley, "A Plain Account of Christian Perfection," in *JWJW* 11: 437. For an analysis of Wesley's statement, see Marjorie Suchocki's "The Perfection of Prayer,"

in Randy Maddox, ed., *Rethinking Wesley's Theology for Contemporary Methodism* (Nashville, TN: Kingswood Books, 1998), 49-63.

95. John Wesley to Joseph Benson, 11 December 1772. *LJW* 6: 3.

96. Leslie E. Church, *More about the Early Methodist People* (London: Epworth Press, 1949), 245.

97. John Wesley to Edward Jackson, 24 October 1788. *LJW* 8: 99.

98. For the Yorkshire revival see John Baxter, "The Great Yorkshire Revival 1792-96," in Michael Hill, ed., *Sociological Yearbook of Religion in Britain*, 8 vols. (London: SCM Press, 1968-75), 7: 46-76.

99. Wesley, *Primitive Physic*, vii-viii.

100. 25 October 1787. *BEW* 24: 63.

101. For a treatment of fasting and miracles in eighteenth century British religion consult Jane Shaw's *The Miraculous Body and other Rational Wonders: Religion in Enlightenment England* (Ph. D. thesis, University of California at Berekley, 1994), 61-102; Jane Shaw, "Fasting women: the significance of gender and bodies in radical religion and politics, 1650-1813," in Timothy Morton and Nigel Smith, eds., *Radicalism in British Literary Culture, 1650-1830: From Revolution to Revolution* (Cambridge: Cambridge University Press, 2002), 101-15. For analysis of John Wesley's idea of fasting see my article "The Value of Self-Denial: John Wesley's Multidimensional View of Fasting," *Toronto Journal of Theology* 19 (2003): 25-40.

102. Wesley, *A Short History of the People Called Methodists, BEW* 9: 483-84. "I am glad to hear that the work of God is so prosperous at Newry. Continue to seek Him by fasting, and you shall see still greater things than these." John Wesley to James Macdonald, 18 January 1791. *LJW* 8: 256, a correspondence Wesley penned just six weeks before his death.

103. John Wesley to Charles Wesley, 8 August 1752. *BEW* 26: 498.

104. Thomas Deacon, ed., *A Compleate Collections of Devotions both Publick and Private: Taken from the Apostolical Consititutions, the Ancient Liturgies, and Common Prayer Book of the Church of England*, 2 vols. (London: np, 1734), 2: 72-73.

105. Frank Baker, *John Wesley and The Church of England* (London: Epworth Press, 1970), 31. Also, Campbell's *John Wesley and Christian Antiquity*, 121, has noted that Wesley bought a series of blank books with the intention of writing a "Genesis on Fasting," which has been lost in completed form.

106. John Wesley, "Upon our Lord's Sermon on the Mount: Discourse the Seventh," *BEW* 1: 595.

107. Wesley, "Upon our Lord's Sermon on the Mount: Discourse the Seventh," 600.

108. Wesley, *Primitive Physic*, 126-27. The cures listed there were blindness, contracted sinews, corns, cuts, deafness inflamed eye-lids, scorbutic tetters, sore legs, warts, asthmas, cancers falling sickness, gout, gravel, kings evil, leprosy, palsy, rheumatism, scurvy, stone, and swelled liver.

109. *ODNB*, "Bostock, Bridget." See also, Owen Davis, "Charmers and Charming in England and Wales from the Eighteenth Century to the Twentieth Century," *Folklore* 109 (1998): 41-52.

110. Rack, "Doctors, Demons and Early Methodist Healing," 137-52.

111. John Wesley, ed., *Arminian Magazine*, 13 (1790): 42.

112. John Walsh to Charles Wesley, 134, 4b.

113. 31 May 1785. *BEW* 23: 363.

114. John Wesley, "Upon our Lord's Sermon on the Mount: Discourse the Seventh," 600-01.

115. Ruth, *A Little Heaven Below*, 83-93. See also Karen Westerfield-Tucker's *American Methodist Worship* (Oxford: Oxford University Press, 2001), 118-55.

116. Eamon Duffy, *The Stripping of the Altars: Traditional Religion in England 1400-1580* (New Haven: Yale University Press, 1992), 102-07.

117. Duffy, *Stripping of the Altars*, 110.

118. Edward Muir, *Ritual in Early Modern Europe* (Cambridge: Cambridge University Press, 1997), 160. See also Michael Witmore, *Culture of Accidents: Unexpected Knowledges in Early Modern England* (Stanford, CA: Stanford University Press, 2001), 22.

119. For an example of the satire see Desiderius Erasmus's *Praise of Folly*, trans. Betty Radice (1511; London: Penguin Books, 1993), 131-32.

120. Ruth, *A Little Heaven Below*, 135.

121. "They went to the table because John and Charles Wesley led them there. They continued to go, not because John and Charles Wesley were great men, but because they experienced vital and direct contact with God in the sacrament." Steven Hoskins, "Eucharist and Eschatology in the Writings of the Wesleys," *Wesleyan Theological Journal* 29 (1994): 70.

122. Hindmarsh, *The Evangelical Conversion Narrative*, 179. See also Marilyn McCord Adams, *Christ and Horrors: The Coherence of Christology* (Cambridge: Cambridge University Press, 2006).

123. John Wesley, "The Duty of Constant Communion," *BEW* 3: 429. The sermon and its idea of constant communion had a long history which relied on the nonjuror Robert Nelson, *Companion for the Festivals and Fasts of the Church of England* (London,: W. Bower, 1705) and Arthur Bury, *The Constant Communicant* (Oxford: np, 1681). See also John Wesley's extract of Nelson's *Great Duty* and the published sermon in his *Arminian Magazine* 10 (1787): 229-36 and 290-95.

124. "Everlasting love and free grace undergird a universal gospel. These convictions lay at the very heart of the Wesleyan understanding of the revival." James Gordon, "'Impassive He Suffers; Immortal He Dies': Rhetoric and Polemic in Charles Wesley's Portrayal of the Atonement," *Scottish Bulletin of Evangelical Theology* 18 (2000): 64.

125. 27 June 1740. *BEW* 19: 158. Susannah Wesley, the mother of the Wesley brothers, also gave witness to this aspect of the Lord's Supper in her own life too. See, Arnold Dallimore, *Susanna Wesley: The Mother of John & Charles Wesley* (Grand Rapids, MI: Baker Book House, 1993), 162.

126. John C. Bowmer, *The Sacrament of the Lord's Supper in Early Methodism* (London: Dacre Press, 1951), 180.

127. John and Charles Wesley, *Hymns on the Lord's Supper with a Preface concerning The Christian Sacrament and Sacrifice Extracted from Doctor Brevint* (Bristol: Felix Farley, 1745).

128. Wesley, *Hymns on the Lord's Supper*, 101. "The main Intention of CHRIST herein, was not, the bare *Remembrance* of his Passion; but over and above, to invite us to his Sacrifice, not as done and gone many Years since, but, as to Grace and Mercy, still lasting, still *new*, still the same as when it was first offer'd for us." Wesley's extract of Brevint's *The Christian Sacrament and Sacrifice*, 6.

129. Rack, *Reasonable Enthusiast*, 406.

130. Hindmarsh, *The Evangelical Conversion Narrative*, 193-225.

131. John Erskine, *The Signs of the Times Considered, or the high Probability that the present Appearances in New England, and the West of Scotland, are a Prelude of the Glorious Things promised to the church in the latter Ages* (Edinburgh: Printed by T. Lumisden and J. Robertson, 1742). For John Erskine's life and significance see Jonathan M. Yeager, *Enlightened Evangelicalism: The Life and Thought of John Erskine* (Oxford: Oxford University Press, 2011). For the Cambuslang revival see Duncan Macfarlan, *The Revivals of the Eighteenth Century, Particularly at Cambuslang* (Edinburgh: John John-

stone, 1847) and Mark Noll, *The Rise of Evangelicalism: The Age of Edwards, Whitefield and the Wesleys* (Downers Grove, IL: InterVarsity Press, 2003), 108-115.

132. James Haw, "An extract of a letter from James Haw, elder of the Methodist Epicopal church in America, to Bishop Asbury: written from Cumberland near Kentucke, about the beginning of the year 1789," in John Wesley, ed., *Arminian Magazine* 13 (1790): 203.

133. 2 December 1735. *BEW* 18: 141.

134. 2 December 1735. *BEW* 18: 141.

135. 4 December 1746. *BEW* 20: 150-51.

136. James G. Donat, "Empirical Medicine in the 18th Century: The Rev. John Wesley's Search for Remedies that Work," *Methodist History* 44 (2006): 217. See also Hill, *John Wesley Among the Physicians*, 2-3

137. Wesley, *Primitive Physic*, iii.

138. In addition to his *Primitive Physic* and *Desideraturm* Wesley wrote about the effects of tea drinking, gout, and nervous disorders. See, James Donat, "Empirical Medicine in the 18th Century," 216n1.

139. 25 October 1787. *BEW* 24: 63.

140. 3 October 1756. *BEW* 21: 78. See also 6 April 1756. *BEW* 21: 49; 16 November 1775. *BEW* 23: 110; and 12 April 1784. *BEW* 23: 302, for other examples.

Chapter 6

The Reluctant Death of Spirits in the Nineteenth Century

> After preaching, I rode on to Newcastle. Certainly, if I did not believe there was another world, I should spend all my summers here, as I know no place in Great Britain comparable to it for pleasantness. But I seek another country, and therefore am content to be a wanderer upon the earth.[1]

> Fanaticism is the child of false zeal and of superstition, the father of intolerance, and of persecution; it is therefore very different from piety, though some persons are pleased to confuse them.[2]

At the conclusion of his recent study of nineteenth century responses to eighteenth-century history, Brian W. Young utilizes what he terms an "archeology of the haunting."[3] What is obvious as one considers the Methodists in the eighteenth and nineteenth centuries is that the rudiments of an invisible world were not quickly extinguished in the religious imagination of people living during the *fin de siècle*. Instead, the fascination of the supernatural was translated into a vast assortment of ideas which viewed human nature as an open textbook for spiritual and psychical research and at the beginning of the Victorian era the ideas of preternatural and supernatural occurrences was far from eclipsed in the identities of believers and non-believers alike. From an interest in the gifts of the Holy Spirit mentioned in the New Testament epistles (Romans 12; I Corinthians

12; and Ephesians 4) to pronouncements of extraordinary events in the lives of men and women, individuals and groups continued to grapple with the idea of transcendental elements experienced in the context of human history.

The emergence of proto-Pentecostal experiences among believers in Scotland and England suggested to some believers that God's presence could still be experienced in supernatural and miraculous dimensions and indeed was not extinct or dormant in the world. Edward Irving (1792-1834) and Alexander Scott (1805-66), who were ministers in Scotland, contended that it was only because the faith of Christians had waxed cold that there was an absence of supernatural demonstrations in the faith of the contemporary church. When Scott became absorbed by the New Testament teaching of charismata or gifts of the Holy Spirit, and Irving permitted the teaching of the Pauline doctrine within the contours of religious services in 1829, a renewed fascination with the idea of supernatural intervention was the result.[4] Scott's sermons on the subject in Port Glasgow were instrumental in eliciting a demonstration of the gift of tongues among congregants in the area and by 1831, David Bebbington claims, similar experiences accompanied by prophecies and divine healings were occurring in London.[5]

In the eighteenth century, female experiences of the supernatural played a significant role both in England and North America.[6] The increased subjection of women to men in the nineteenth century religious discourse, however, did not obscure female apprehensions of the divine. Gareth Lloyd has shown that Methodist women in the modern world, both in the eighteenth and nineteenth centuries, were living out their understanding of Wesleyan holiness and continued to identify with the concept of a supernatural God in their daily religious experiences. Commenting on the life of Mary Bosanquet, Lloyd writes that "throughout her life she was regarded an expert in the interpretation of supernatural phenomena."[7] But Bosanquet was not alone among female Methodists at the turn of the century. Gathered together with her were Sarah Crosby, Sarah Ryan, Mary Tooth and a host of other women who affirmed the validity of healings, dreams, visions, exorcisms, and other types of supernatural phenomena, all of which was underscored by the idea of particular providence. John Wesley had important associations throughout the eighteenth century with women and the coterie of contacts he made with the opposite sex attested to the trust and value he placed on individual women for spiritual leadership in the Methodist movement. For Wesley, then, the receptivity that his message by women gave evidence of their desire to know God more intimately. Sarah Crosby wrote in her diaries for 23 April 1778:

> While praying alone, my spirit was overpowered with the Divine presence. My soul melted within me with love to my Lord, and very fervent desires for the salvation of precious souls, especially the souls I had lately been called to speak to in five or six places. Sure I am that prayer, and those tears, cannot remain unanswered. It seemed as though I could not live if Jesus did not save sinners.[8]

In the nineteenth century, however, women offered various testimonies about their spiritual experiences. An important and integral part of those testimonies was the process of their reception of divine knowledge which were often acquired through unusual means. Mary Barritt (1772-1851), later Mary Taft, became one of the leading female evangelists in the Methodist connexion during the century. No stranger to controversy she faced considerable opposition to her preaching ministry but remained faithful to her calling. Barritt's resolution to continue her proclamation ministry was confirmed as she received invitations to preach from Methodist pioneers like John Pawson, Alexander Mather, Thomas Vasey (1814-71), William Bramwell (1759-1818), and Thomas Shaw (d. 1801). Barritt's ministry became so successful that she returned home to visit her parents only annually. Her autobiography recorded her evangelistic zeal and promise:

> The great business of our life is to be daily preparing for eternity. This, to us, as accountable and immortal creatures, is of the utmost moment. Herein is involved *our all*, our present peace, and our future and endless well-being. In comparison with this, our weightiest temporal matters are lighter than vanity. May the Spirit of the Almighty so give us to feel the solemn weight of eternal things.[9]

A predominant concern both by those inside and outside the fold, however, was the Methodists and their commitment to the supernatural. John Whitehead (1740?-1804), John Wesley's personal physician and biographer, noted in his biography of Wesley that he was too eager to believe stories about the supernatural—even to his detriment. Whitehead wrote: "Mr. Wesley's chief weakness was a too great readiness to credit the testimony of others, when he believed them sincere, without duly considering whether they had sufficient ability and caution to form a true judgment of the things concerning which they bore testimony."[10] Nineteenth-century Methodism was constrained to resolve that "true judgment."

James Crawfoot and the Magic Methodists

By the time Hugh Bourne (1772-1852) and William Clowes (1780-1851) heard James Crawfoot (1759?-1839) preach at Mow Cop on 31 May 1807, the noted leader of the Forest Methodists or Magic Methodists as they were sometimes called, were well established.[11] Sometime after his conversion in 1783, Crawfoot joined the Methodist society at Duddon Heath where he was soon to be a class leader in 1796. At the beginning of the nineteenth century, Crawfoot moved from Duddon to the Delamere Forest in Northern England where those attracted by his preaching were experiencing extraordinary manifestations of religious fervour, primarily with trances and visions.

Crawfoot and the group of Magic Methodists gathered around him made the belief in the supernatural a central feature of their religious expressions. In Bourne's manuscript journals, there were short descriptions of his encounter with Crawfoot. On 18 June 1807, for instance, Bourne recorded his fascination with the content of Crawfoot's preaching and declared that the rustic mystic proclaimed the "deep parts of Religion."[12] Crawfoot's topic was the "Bride of Christ" and Bourne further noted that in elaborating the biblical imagery Crawfoot proclaimed that "the wife had great power with her husband."[13] During this period, however, Crawfoot had experienced difficulties. His wife had died and other Methodists became more than concerned about the activities that were occurring in the forest with Crawfoot and those who were enraptured by his charisma. John Tomlinson highlights in his essay that camp meetings were an opportunity for individuals who were looking for a social space to practice their religion. Tomlinson maintains: "Camp meetings were a show of strength, and expression of collective faith, and an opportunity to display the 'power.'"[14] Indeed the Primitive Methodists, a group of Wesleyans who emerged in the early nineteenth century with the intention of living out John Wesley's passion for historical Christianity, considered open-air preaching, prayer meetings, and experiences of conversion a model of biblical Christianity which Wesley and Whitefield had captured during their lifetimes. James Obelkevich in his study of nineteenth-century religion in south Lindsey observed that the Primitive Methodists were expected to have a "spiritual career."[15]

This "spiritual career" of the Primitive Methodists was most often fleshed out in the context of camp meetings where they could feel the ramifications of grace in demonstrative measures. When the first volume of the Primitive Methodist church magazine entitled *A Methodist Magazine, Conducted by the Camp-Meeting Methodists Known by the Name of Ranters, Called Also Primitive Methodists* was released in 1819 it had, among other divisions, a section on camp meetings which was designed to "shew the effects of pious exertions, conducted by the opening of providence, and supported by the word and Spirit of God."[16] And Jeremiah Gilbert (1789-1852), a pioneer in the Primitive Methodist connexion who suffered various persecutions in Sheffield where he instigated a work,[17] wrote an article on the significance of camp meetings and described the fervent tone of the camp meetings:

> Many hundreds were assembled, and during the forenoon, there were, it was thought, as many as nine praying souls, to one prayerless soul. The loud Amens were like claps of thunder; and the bursting joys from different Christians, were like the voice of many waters. There was at one time, I believe, about sixteen praying companies: and every praying company was engaged in the noble work of wrestling with God for the salvation of immortal souls.[18]

Crawfoot used this type of atmosphere to his advantage and promoted a particular type of religiosity that was inclusive of people who did not fit into traditional forms of religious expression in the early nineteenth century. However, the hierarchy of leadership among Methodists were less than pleased as the denomination which was growing in numbers began to consider at what extent they could embrace expressions of the divine which retracted, or at least resisted, from a proper understanding of reason. At a quarterly meeting at the end of 1807 Crawfoot was questioned as to whether he had taken liberties and ignored the *Discipline* of Methodists by preaching at a Quaker meeting. He replied with honesty and asserted that in so doing he had not transgressed what it meant to be a Primitive Methodist.[19]

The influence of Crawfoot's life on young Bourne was deeply significant. On Thursday, 3 November 1808, Bourne wrote of Crawfoot's influence:

I sat talking with Crawfoot and others [sic] they were talking and I breathed my Soul to God for the Holy Ghost to come upon that church. I turned my Head and J. Crawfoot was looking at me [sic] his face shone. I could not bear it but was near fainting away. I felt as if my inside were rising out of one and going to God. My Soul breathed Lord Jesus receive my Spirit but I did not go down nevertheless the Lord made great discoveries to one and I felt resolute to feel after this thing.[20]

Especially impressed on Bourne's mind was the spiritual power that Crawfoot displayed. At one meeting, Bourne confessed on 12 November 1808: "J. Crawfoot came in a little time and we fell into conversation. The Lord opened my Heart to receive his testimony and his speech dropped upon me."[21]

The field-preaching of the Methodists provided an open theatre that was given to irregular experiences of the divine and Crawfoot was no exception to the tendency of emotion in these contexts. The Primitve Methodists who gathered in the Delamere Forest experienced visions of Christ and ecstasies of one sort and another to the extent that they became known as "Magic Methodists." Similar experiences occurred in camp meetings in North America too where visionary experiences caused extreme "happiness" and led to shouts of joy and exultation so that groups of Methodist votaries came to be called "shouting Methodists."[22] Unique to the Magic Methodists, however, were visions and trances that made commentary on the leadership of the church. Common to the ones which Bourne recorded were female Methodists and their apprehensions that portrayed a hierarchical scale that indicated Methodist preachers that were preferred over less respected ones.[23] The visions often positioned preachers on a ladder with the most respected ones at the top and lesser ones located in descending order. In more cases than not, Crawfoot was catalogued at the top ring of the ladder in these visions followed by the American preacher Lorenzo Dow (1777-1834), and then Bourne himself.[24]

Crawfoot's authority among Magic Methodists was based on a conviction that the Holy Spirit which worked through him was identical to the one that worked through the primitive church. While at a prayer meeting in Crawfoot's home in 1809, Bourne learned of the success of the Magic Methodists. Bourne recorded in his journal:

I was praying for the Lord to bring that Church up in the power, and prayed till the Spirit witnessed. He [Crawfoot] instructed me to watch and wait for the accomplishment saying that it was the same spirit which wrote the Scriptures and therefore the testimony was as firm as the Scripture and that much depended upon my holding faith. That I might get through as much work with half as much praying if I minded this point. This observation made me very happy.[25]

However, Bourne was not "very happy" with Crawfoot and the Magic Methodists for long. For some unknown reason, Bourne separated from Crawfoot. Michael Sheard conjectures that Crawfoot's visionary experiences were at the hub of the division.[26] Certainly dreams and visions continued among Primitive Methodists throughout much of the nineteenth century.[27] However, the Primitive Methodists and their revivalist techniques eventually moved to more traditional forms of worship.[28] John Petty in his history of the Primitive Methodist Church wrote in his conclusion of the obstacles that confronted the church, especially in large industrialized communities: "But yet in many of them its societies are few and feeble, its Sabbath-schools far from numerous, its chapels small and uninviting, compares with the amount of population."[29] In the end, the connexion could not match its spiritual resources to the growing trends of industrialization in the modern world.

Jabez Bunting: A Break from Strange Occurrences

What James Crawfoot never came to terms with in an explicit way Jabez Bunting (1779-1858) hit head on. Bunting had been converted in 1794 and became President of the Methodist Conference for the first time in 1820.[30] Born in Manchester, Bunting's father had been a tailor and committed to the Methodists. Exposed at a very young age to radical revivalists in northern England, Bunting saw early on how revivalists mixed religion and emotion in order to achieve a desired evangelical result. However, as a young man, Bunting had been educated to appreciate the classics, as Wesley had himself. More importantly, he had a keen eye for the various theological controversies that emerged in a variety of connexional disputes.[31] Thus, a tension emerged in Bunting's life between the practice of his religiosity and its expression of a heart religion that focused on the renewal in the church and a life of the mind that maintained intellectual integrity which endeavoured to make the Christian faith relevant in a progressive and modern world.

For Bunting, the manifestations of the revivals at the opening of the nineteenth century rested too much on the side of "enthusiasm." He looked at the revivals in some detail and judged them excessively divisive and believed they rested too much on emotion instead of thought and reason. In a letter he wrote of a religious revival that demonstrated a spirit of division to a fault: "The people in this town are tired of parties & divisions: & in general equally tired of the rant and extravagancies of what is called revivalism."[32] At times, Bunting could be vitriolic and condescending in his assessment, as when he characterized revivalists in Sheffield, a place where Wesley had experienced renewal in the 1780s. Bunting wrote in correspondence to James Wood that he was surprised to see people in that area liberated from "the follies of enthusiasm." Then, he went on to explain: "So few of them have attained to any considerable degree of mental improvement, or possess much general intelligence."[33]

Bunting's arguments were not merely *ad hominem* attacks, however. At the core of Bunting's discontent with revivalism in the nineteenth century was its predilection towards instantaneous fixes to deep seated spiritual problems and the reluctance to resolve issues with intellectual integrity. Far too many of the revivalists seemingly refused to engage themselves in the intellectual issues that were required for a thoughtful adjustment of Christianity in a new age and time.[34] In a letter Bunting received from Abraham Farrar (1788-1849), an itinerant preacher who served the King Street circuit in Bristol from 1839-47, a Mr. Griffith developed a following that was proving detrimental to other Methodist churches in the area. Farrar wrote to Bunting: "After Conference, a strong party spirit unfolded itself in favour of noisy and late meetings, which made our young colleague Mr. Griffiths its center, who became at once outrageously popular. Since then, all other congregational prayer meetings, etc. etc. than those where he has presided, have been comparatively small . . . In fact we have been almost revived into ruin."[35]

Such was the case with Methodists who were attending meetings which promoted millennialism. In Exeter, Joanna Southcott (1750-1814) caused considerable problems.[36] Bunting looked upon her activities with disdain, primarily because he believed she eschewed a life of reason and promoted her own particular brand of self-aggrandizement. That she was an ex-Methodist certainly also added insult to injury. Upon receiving word from a friend that she had developed a following in Leeds, Bunting wrote of the perils of being lured by her prognostications: "She says that she is the bride, the Lamb's wife mentioned in the Revelation; and such as believe her testimony, she seals, by means of red wax, to the day of Redemption. Some hundreds in Leeds have thus been sealed of late."[37] Instead, the strength of Methodism, in Bunting's view, was the systematic and patient discipline of renewal in the local parish. Its validation was being realized as the Methodists became more sensitive to the intellectual integrity of their faith and work.

The Meaning of the Supernatural: John Wesley's Views Transformed

In the flow of nineteenth century Methodism, John Wesley's commitment to the supernatural became transformed. In many respects, Methodism found itself at the turn of the century in a position that required a re-examination of its commitments and strategy as it moved into a new age. Henry Rack describes this challenge succinctly: "For some years after the death of Wesley (1791), Methodism had to grapple with problems which may broadly be described as those of a missionary society growing into a Church."[38] Travelling preachers soon took on the role of ordained clergy and the place of laity was hammered out in context of what it meant to be a part of an organized church.

All the organizational changes that Methodists were working through during the nineteenth century was insignificant, however, compared to the theological issues which required major adjustments in the movement that had started out as a renewal movement among some young scholars at Oxford University at the beginning of the eighteenth century. Liberalism increasingly emerged as a force to be dealt with during the period, challenging cherished beliefs of historical and orthodox Christianity.[39]

Rationality was at a crossroads too, however, and the attraction of extraordinary experiences was running into various roadblocks with a scientific canon that increasingly had smaller regions reserved for the miraculous. In 1841, Charles MacKay (1814-1889) wrote his influential *Extraordinary Popular Delusions and the Madness of Crowds*.[40] In it he gave warnings about prophecies, fortune-telling, witchcraft, haunted houses, and relics.[41] There, however, is an irony to Mackay's work. If the attraction of the crowds was, as McKay suggested in his preface, at the level of a "moral epidemic," then what exactly was the features of the "delusions" that Mackay treated in his book that kept attracting the masses in light of the advancements of science and rationality.

At the foundation of Wesley's understanding of his Methodist movement had been a supernatural identification of the religious self. As has been demonstrated, his commitment to an empirical observation of human nature caused him to consider seriously the testimonies and claims of transcendental experiences of people inside and outside the Methodist movement. John Wesley was honest enough to admit that in some cases there was psychological manipulation and deception but in others there was no reasonable cause, he thought, to deny the existence of non-material forces and realities which must be acknowledged and reckoned with. For Wesley, the Methodist belief in an invisible world fit into a broader spectrum of the Christian faith and he found many evidences of authentic faith and the existence of miraculous occurrences in the faith and life of individuals in both plebeian and elite populations.

Nineteenth-century Methodists, however, eventually became uneasy about Wesley's commitment to such an invisible world and continued to grapple with issues that would preserve the status of their venerable leader while moving beyond his affirmations of the supernatural which they judged increasingly unsustainable. This surfaced in a variety of ways but generally either was manifested as a dislodging of belief in the supernatural altogether or, at the very least, reserved for a metaphorical status.[42] Bourne's and Primitive Methodism's separation from the Magic Methodists in this regard was a statement which loomed large, even though Bourne probably did not realize it at the time. Though the Primitive Methodists would continue to make room for the miraculous in their religiosity, a modification in its emphasis eventually emerged.[43]

Despite the continued gravitation toward more modern understandings of transcendental themes, however, there continued to be a reluctance to let go of Methodism's founder and his commitment to an invisible world. An anonymous print of the nineteenth century which portrayed the elderly Wesley ascending to heaven escorted by two angels, was an affirmation not only of Wesley's commitment to the significance of the supernatural but also an identification that went beyond the man to a movement that he founded and sustained throughout his lifetime.[44]

The belief in an invisible world, then, whether interpreted literally or metaphorically continued to have a significant impact on the religious identification of Methodists, as it had been for others. The reasons for this were multiple but at its core was the idea that the Enlightenment and its method of a radical empiricism that opened up a revolutionary programmatic and went beyond mere temporal understandings of human nature. Louis Dupré in his book on the Enlightenment poignantly comments: "The science of the person was to provide the foundation for all others."[45] For Wesley, the study of human nature continued to reveal aspects of the human psyche that indicated that there was more to life than what could fit into neat and controlled compartments. The surfacing of preternatural and supernatural realities was an invitation to study the self that revealed old and new possibilities.

Figure Ten. "John Wesley, that Excellent Minister of the Gospel, carried by Angels into Abraham's Bosom, March, 1791." Methodist Archives, University of Manchester."

Notes

1. 4 June 1759. *BEW* 21: 201.

2. John Fletcher, *The Works of John Fletcher*, 4 vols. (1825; repr., Salem, OH: Schmul Publishers, 1974) 4: 233.

3. Brian W. Young, *The Victorian Eighteenth Century: An Intellectual History* (Oxford: Oxford University Press, 2007), 149.

4. *DNB*, "Scott, Alexander John."

5. "In one year forty-six spiritual cures were reported among the Irvingites of England alone." Bebbington, *Evangelicalism in Modern Britain*, 91.

6. Two fascinating studies are Mack, *Heart Religion in the British Enlightenment* and Heather D. Curtis, *Faith in the Great Physician: Suffering and Divine Healing in American Culture*, 1860-1900 (Baltimore, MD: The John Hopkins University Press, 2007).

7. Gareth Lloyd, "Repression and Resistance: Wesleyan Female Public Ministry in the Generation after 1791," *Proceedings of the Wesley Historical Society* 55 (2005): 112. See also Deborah Valenze, *Prophetic Sons and Daughters: Female Preaching and Popular Religion in Industrial England* (Princeton: Princeton University Press, 1985).

8. Sarah Crosby, *The Diaries of Sarah Crosby* in Paul Wesley Chilcote, ed., *Her Own Story: Autobiographical Portraits of Early Methodist Women* (Nashville, TN: Kingswood Books, 2001), 83.

9. Mary Taft, *Memoirs of the Life of Mrs. Mary Taft: Compiled from Her Journals, and Other Authentic Documents*, 2nd ed., 2 vols. (Devon: S. Thorpe, 1831), 1: 169.

10. Whitehead, *The Life of the Rev. John Wesley*, 2: 307.

11. Little is known about James Crawfoot's life. For treatment of his life and significance see Henry Rack, *James Crawfoot and the Magic Methodists* (Englesea Brook: Englesea Brook Primitive Methodist Museum Committee, 2003), 1-13; Henry D. Rack, *How Primitive was Primitive Methodism?* (Englesea Brook: Englesea Brook Primitive Methodist Museum Committee, 1996), 13-19; Edward Langton, "James Crawfoot: the Forest Mystic," *Proceedings of the Wesley Historical Society*, 30 (1955): 12-15; John W. B. Tomlinson, "The Magic Methodists and their Influence on the Early Primitive Methodist Movement," in Cooper and Gregory, eds., *Signs, Wonders, Miracles*, 389-99. Also, George Herod, *Biographical Sketches of those Preachers whose Labours Contributed to the Organization and Early Extension of Primitive Methodism* (London: T. King, 1855), 241-71.

12. Hugh Bourne, *Manuscript Journals*, MARC, DDHB 3.3, 17.

13. The biblical imagery of the Bride of Christ comes from the New Testament passage in Ephesians 5.21-33.

14. Tomlinson, "The Magic Methodists." 391.

15. James Obelkevich, *Religion and Rural Society: South Lindsey 1825-1875* (Oxford: Clarendon Press, 1976), 230.

16. *A Methodist Magazine, for the Year 1819, Conducted by the Camp-Meeting Methodists Known by the Name of Ranters, Called Also Primitive Methodists* (Leichester: J. Fowler, 1819), np.

17. *DEB*, "Gilbert, Jeremiah."

18. Jeremiah Gilbert, "On Camp-Meetings, &c, in 1821," *A Methodist Magazine* 4 (1822): 9.

19. Herod, *Biographical Sketches*, 252-254. See also, Rack, *James Crawfoot and the Magic Methodists*, 2.

20. Bourne, *Manuscript Journals*, MARC, DDHB 3.4, 50-51.

21. Bourne, *Manuscript Journals*, MARC, DDHB 3.4, 55-56.

22. See Winthrop Hudson, "Shouting Methodists," *Encounter* 29 (1968): 73-84. Also, Taves, "Knowing through the Body," 209-222 develops her idea of "the shout complex." Lester Ruth, ed., *Early Methodist Life and Spirituality* (Nashville, TN: Kingswood Books, 2005), 161-87 offers some primary source documentation.

23. Bourne, *Manuscript Journals*, MARC, DDHB 3.5, 58-61

24. Rack, *How Primitive was Primitive Methodism?*, 16.

25. Bourne, *Manuscript Journals*, MARC, DDHB, 3.5, 15.

26. "In contrast with the *Methodist Magazine*, the *Primitive Methodist Magazine* had a 'Providence Department' until as late as 1860." Michael Sheard, *The Origins and Early Development of Primitive Methodism in Cheshire and South Lancashire, 1800-1860* (Ph. D. thesis, University of Manchester, 1980), 74.

27. Rack, *How Primitive was Primitive Methodism?*, 15.

28. See, for example, Esther Lenton, "Primitive Methodist Camp Meetings in Shropshire," *Proceedings of the Wesley Historical Society* 52 (1999): 1-14 and Jeremy Morris, "The Origins and Growth of Primitive Methodism in East Surrey," *Proceedings of the Wesley Historical Society* 48 (1992): 133-49.

29. John Petty, *The History of the Primitive Methodist Connexion, from its Origin to the Conference of 1860, The First Jubilee Year of the Connexion* (1860; rev. edn., London: John Dickenson, 1880), 579.

30. *DMBI*, "Bunting, Dr. Jabez;" see also Hempton, *The Religion of the People*, 91-108, for more on Jabez's life and ministry.

31. James H. Rigg, *Jabez Bunting, a Great Methodist Leader* (New York: The Methodist Book Concern, 1905).

32. Jabez Bunting, *The Early Correspondence of Jabez Bunting, 1820-1829*, ed., W. R. Ward (London: Offices of the Royal Historical Society, 1972), 112-13.

33. Bunting, *The Early Correspondence of Jabez Bunting*, 166.

34. See, for example, Geoffrey Rowell, *Hell and the Victorians: A Study of the Nineteenth-Century Theological Controversies concerning Eternal Punishment and the Future Life* (Oxford, 1974; repr., Oxford: Clarendon Press, 2000).

35. W. R. Ward, ed., *Victorian Methodism: The Correspondence of Jabez Bunting* (Oxford: Oxford University Press, 1976).

36. On Joanna Southcott, see Susan Juster's *Doomsayers: Anglo-American Prophecy in the Age of Revolution* (Philadelphia, PA: University of Pennsylvania Press, 2003), 239-59.

37. Thomas Percival Bunting, *The Life of Jabez Bunting, D. D., with Notices of Contemporary Persons and Events,* 2 vols. (New York: Harper & Brothers, Publishers, 1859), 1: 189.

38. Henry D. Rack, *The Future of John Wesley's Methodism* (London: Lutterworth Press, 1965), 19.

39. Martin Wellings, *Evangelicals Embattled: Responses to Evangelicals in the Church of England to Ritualism, Darwinism and Theological Liberalism 1890-1930* (Carlisle: Paternoster Press, 2003), gives a succinct analysis of the theological trends in this period of ecclesiastical history. See also Timothy Larsen's *Crisis of Doubt: Honest Faith in Nineteenth-Century England* (Oxford: Oxford University Press, 2006).

40. Charles Mackay, *Extraordinary Popular Delusions and the Madness of Crowds* (1841; repr., New York: Barnes & Noble, 2004).

41. Charles Mackay, *Extraordinary Popular Delusions*, 209-28, 229-47, 374-457, 481-501, and 563-69.

42. For more on the romantic side of the supernatural, Robert Nighall's *A Geography of Victorian Gothic Fiction: Mapping History's Nightmares* (Oxford: Oxford University Press, 1999).

43. Geoffrey Milburn, *Primitive Methodism* (Peterborough: Epworth Press, 2002), 54-62.

44. See Figure Ten: "John Wesley, that Excellent Minister of the Gospel, carried by Angels into Abraham's Bosom," March, 1791.

45. Louis Dupré, *The Enlightenment & the Intellectual Foundations of Modern Culture* (New Haven: Yale University Press, 2004), 45.

Appendix 1

"John Wesley's Summing Up the Matter of Old Jeffrey, 1726"

1. Presently after any noise was heard, the Wind commonly rose, and which whistled very loud round the house, and increased with it.
2. The signal was given which my Father likens to the turning round of a Windmill when the wind changes; Mr. Hoole, the Rector of Haxey to planing of dead boards; my Sisters to the swift winding up of a Jack. It commonly began at the corner of the Top of the Nursery.
3. Before it came into any room, the latches were frequently lifted up, the windows clattered, and whatever Iron or Brass was about the chambers rung and jarred exceedingly.
4. When it was in any room let them make what noise they would, as they sometimes did on purpose its dead hollow notes would be clearly heard above them all.
5. It constantly knocked while the prayers for the King and Prince were repeating and was plainly heard by all in the room but my Father, and sometimes by Him: as were also the thundering knocks at the Amen.
6. The sound very often seemed in the air in the midst of a room, nor could they, ever make any like it themselves by any contrivance.
7. Tho' it seemed to rattle down the pewter, to clap the doors, draw the curtains, kick the man's shoes up and down, yet it never moved anything except the latches, otherwise than by making it tremble, unless once when it threw upon the nursery door.
8. The mastiff tho' he barked violently at it the first day he came, yet whenever it came afterwards, nay sometime before the Family perceived it, he ran whining or quite silent, to shelter himself behind some of the Company.
9. It never came by day, till my Mother ordered the Horn to be blown.
10. After that time scarce anyone could go from one room to another but the latches of the doors they went to were lifted up before they touched them.
11. It never came into my Father's Study, till he talked to it sharply, called it deaf and dumb Devil and bid it cease to disturb innocent children, and come to him in his study, if it had any thing to say to him.
12. From the time of my mother's desiring it might not disturb her from 5 to 6, it was never again heard once in her chambers from 5 till she came downstairs nor at any other time when she was in employ'd in devotion.
13. Whether our clock went right or wrong it always came near as could be grist when by the night it wanted a quarter of ten.

Appendix 2

John Walsh's Letter to Charles Wesley, 1762[1]

(1)

Walsh's Ranters
August 11 1762.

To the Reverend Charles Wesley. London. August 11, 1762

 Sir/.

  The Account You desire me to write of my own Experience & Remarks on others, requiring much haste, You will be sure to find it both irregular & inelegant, as well as extremely short for such a subject. I can write nothing well, unless I take time to compose, correct, & alter, with such a degree of slowness & diffidence, that an Account of the Lord's Dealings with me, which I begun almost three years ago, will probably be not finish'd in 3 or 4 more. but as in the present case, You desire only Truth and Intelligence, I shall be contents with making myself understood, & thus hurry over the matter, without any farther Apology.

  At the Age of six Years I was much given to Swearing, Drunkenness, & other Sins. At Seven the Lord strongly drew me by the Cords of Love, & I delighted in his presence, abhorred Sin, & thirsted after Righteousness. I then suffer'd great Persecution, especially from other Boys. The Lord soon after hid his Face, & I forgat him a considerable time. he return'd again convincing me not of actual, but original Sin. I know this horrors a lone while, sought his Face & was hated by all or most about me. At Ten I was justified, declared it, & pray'd publickly. great my Pride thereupon that I would scarce acknowledge GOD my superior, sinn'd against him by desire of the Creature, which is yet my besetting Sin & besetting Temptation, made several vain attempts to gratify that sensual Desire, & lost the Knowledge of GOD. I was alarm'd soon after by a Dream, sought him earnestly, was persecuted vehemently, & found his favour again: which I lost [Black mark] & found, lov'd & hated Sin, from time to time, till I was fourteen Years old: when I was ashamed of all my past Religion, went

---

1. The numbers inside parenthesis are the original paginations of Walsh's letter. A previous version of this letter was transcribed in my thesis, "*Methodism and the Miraculous: John Wesley's Contribution to the Historia Miraculorum.*" (D. Phil.Thesis, Oxford University, 2006).

to Sea, & inspite of innumerable Visitations & Providences, no Weapon that was
formed against me being ever able to prosper, I sinn'd against my GOD with a
high hand I counted my past Experience Foolish[scribble marks]ness, & hated
the Remembrance there[scribble marks]of till I totally forgat it. I fell into such a
State in the Year 1747. as may be call'd indeed Scepticism, but consisted more
of Atheism than either Deism, or Pythagoreanism; which were the only two
Systems I could ever adopt in those Days, beside Atheism. I then made a great
mock of true Religion, laughing at the glorious Trinity, challenging the GOD
who dies to save me, while arguing against [h]is Divinity, once especially upon
Constitution Hill, to strike me [d]ead with Thunder & Lightning if he were a
GOD. & that being not done, I insisted on having gain'd my Point with my
Antagonist. but, strange to tell, I was yet favour'd, & visited Night & Day, by
the unknown GOD: Take the following Instance, which I copy verbatim from
the Description of a Tour I made in Hampshire: "September 17, 1755. My
Companion   stay'd   at   Petersfield,   which   I   [v]isited   Stonard   Hill.
_____   this Prospect entertain'd me above two Hours; &
methought the Solitude gave a keener enjoyment of this Vision; the Weather
being the finest of the whole Year, & all things gilded by the clear Sunshine:

> Delightful Solitude! O bright Abode,
> To think of Nature & of Nature's GOD!
> Now sacred Temples, Altars, I despise;
> And hail my GOD; & view the Azure Skies.
> Then down to Earth I turn my curious Eye [small scribble mark].
> And still his Footsteps all around me spy.
> No Objects strike me but his glory teach;
> No Sounds are utter'd but tho Godhead preach.
> I'll in the chorus join my humble Voice,
> And like the little buzzing Flies rejoice.

Thus, from the Scenes of unadulterated Nature, my Contemplation took wing to
the great Architec[scribble mark]t: no reasonable Soul arriving, to take a proud
offence at my lowly Rapsody:

> While eager Wors their feeble Aid impart,
> Mix'd with the sighing Language of the heart,
> GOD of all Worlds! Thy Glory to rehearse:
> Musing the vastness of the Universe:
> How vast your flaming Sun! That glowing Sky!
> How vast this Earth! & what an Atom I

Before the end of September 1755 my Sister Leadbetter, whose turning
Methodist about a year before, made me wish her dead & think her mad,
venturing to give me some kind advice, I proudly gainsaid [scribble marks] till
her unaffected Piety beginning to touch me, & GOD being pleas'd to make her
tho Instrument of my Conversion, the strong Chain of Atheism began to loosen

about me, so that I went with her to hear your Brother; whose Words I thought incomprehensible, but felt the   sweet presence of my unknown GOD; who girded me then, as oft before, while I knew him not.

I was justified November 24, 1756. Before & after which, Mr. Swain often told me what difference of Opinion subsisted among Christians. wherefore I besought the Lord, both frequently & earnestly, to defend me from all opinions, be my only Teacher, & keep me from all error: at which times he would dart those Words into my Mind, "Cease ye from Man whose Breath is in his Nostrils, for wherein is he to be accounted of."

About the beginning of the Year 1757. Mr. Swain surprised me with the first Tidings of the strange Doctrine of Perfection in the Flesh: wherefore I begged of the Lord to shew me whether it was right or wrong; who giving me no Answer, but continuing to bless me as usual, I was contested with seeking him alone as formerly, and thought withine myself, of Perfection, "Do you stand on one hand while Predestination keeps on the other; & I will go strait forward, between the two, to the GOD of my Salvation." but the Preaching of Thomas Walsh at last brought me over to the belief of Perfection. I then sought *it* with extreme earnestness, counting my knowledge of GOD a small thing, because I had not found him out unto Perfection: but generally when I pray'd to be made perfect, he would cause an Idea of the Room wherein I was justified to rise before me, & a sweet repetition of those Words to pass through me, "There he gave the Blessing, & Life for evermore." Yet would I not desist from seeking Perfection: as so Sanctification, a very great & astonishing degree of it was given me about 6 Weeks before my Justification. perhaps there is no Sin so strong as that which beset me; & yet in a single Moment, the Mighty GOD, in answer to my Request, so fully destroy'd its power, that for above [Page is cut off here] Years, I confidently believ'd it would subsist no more.

It seems needful in this place to break the thread of my Narrative, & insert a L^r: which I wrote to Mr. Berridge several years after; because that L^r. Contains an account of Experience which I had about this time. That Gentn::, who had always pro-tested against Perfection, having sent me a L^r: in its behalf, I wrote this answer verbatim.

"Edgware. May 28, 1761."

"Dear Sir./

Seeing You give me permission to write "without reserve, & have never taken offence at the freedoms I use, my intention is now to set before You the chief Observations I have made concerning such of the Methodists as call themselves perfect. I have had free conversation with 8 of them, & shall say something of each, I trust without partiality, when I have told you a little of my own Experience therein.

About ½ a Year after my Justification, I began to seek Perfection [scribble mark] with great desire; & expected it from time to time, till I receiv'd the Gift so call'd: which I take for a kind of healing, or doubling the Faith that preceeded it. You may read in Mr. Wesley's German Travels, of several at Hernhuth receiving the same. but, how are the mighty fallen! My great mistake about it was, That after being so blest, I should sin no more; because the propensity to Sin would be taken away, so as never to return. but surely the Promises of GOD are still conditional, & he yet says to every Saint of his, "Be thou faithful unto Death, & I will give thee a Crown of Life." I felt Sin again in my heart at the end of 27 Hours; & spoke as freely thereof in Band, as I did of the perfect Gift. but the first Person call'd perfect, who heard me talk of Sin being yet in my heart, w^d have had me count it only Temptation. I have often since that time, felt the perfect Love of GOD, I suppose more than 1,00 times, casting out all Fear, & not seldom the whole propensity to sin. I believe also, this to be the common Experience of all real Xtians; but have long suspected, that many Professors of Justification had it not, or have surely lost it: & when the Lord mani-fests his Love to any of those, it is no wonder they should mistake it for Perfection. As to such whose Experience resembles mine, I believe they are ashamed

(2)

to retract their first Declaration. Whether I am right or wrong in these Thoughts, it seems to me certain, that your Preaching was not wrong at all in the Year 1759. for the Lord own'd it altogether: nor could I perceive any differnce when You was at London, except an increase of his Talents. The good GOD increase them to You more & more.

I come now to the Persons intended.

M^{rs}.. Burroughs of Deptford told me, she rejoic'd so much when made perfect as to shed many Tears; & saw daily, some time before & ever since, the Air full of Spirits; the good resembling Stars, or pieces of Silver Coin, & fewer in number than the evil; which resembled Seels [Eeels?] or Serpents, & enter;d the Mouth, Nose & Ears of every Person, or almost all she met with, & would frequently lay themselves cross their Eyes; but the good were far swifter in operation. The shadows of the evil appear'd to her also in the Water, when passing the Thames, & I think the good with them. I could see nothing amiss in her Life; but a boisterousness attended her Soul for GOD, whim I believe she really loves.

I meet in band at Deptford with M^r. Joyce, a zealous loving Person, who has long counted himself perfect. he said, Satan brought the figure of a naked Woman to tempt him every Night; but on his praying, it disappear'd; & a round Light, above a foot Diamerter, then appear'd till he fell asleep. I have seen no evil in him, except it were his desiring me to make interest with Lady Huntingdon, get him the Place of Master Sailmaker in Deptford Yard; because of the great good a perfect Man might do with such a Salary.

The remaining six are in London.

M^{rs}. Crosby was desired to talk with me, on account of her eminence among the Perfect, when I had experien'd & lost what is call'd Perfection: but being unable to speak of any thing above what I knew, she fled from me soon after in the Chapel, & refus'd to visit my Sister Leadbetter any more; lest I sh^d: bring her to a 2^d Interview.

I think it improper to name the next young Woman; who had not long declared herself perfect, when she desired me to give 2Shil^s: on her account to another; for she had no change, & w^d: return it the next time we met. I did so & often saw her afterwards without receiving it: whereupon I said at last, "I gave what you desired me." "No, said she, for I gave it myself." wherefore I went again to the Person in distress; who denying the matter, I return'd to the perfect one; who then said, "if I did not give her 2S:, I am sure I gave one." & so ended this trifling Affair. I made no reply; but co^d: never since think her perf^t:, tho' probably justified.

Mrs.. Clay You are no Stranger to: I bro^t. you her promise, at Everton, to speak no more against the Work of GOD which was carried on thro' your Ministry; but meeting with her afterwards at Bedford, she disputed ½ Hour against it.

M^r. Bell coming to tell his Perfection, the Day after your L^r: which favours that Doctrine came to hand, I credited his assertion, sought the same, & hearing You was at London, wrote a Line to let you know thereof. but have since had sufficient cause to think him less conscien[scribbled mark]cious than I ever found him before. but as he was always ready to imbibe some new notion, I hope his Faith will overcome this, even as it has the rest.

M^r: Wake, of the Life Guards, whom I always tho^t: a well-meaning honest Man, has told me, That his Perfection is compleat with regard to his Body, but his Mind still roves from GOD. & he fear'd it was wrong to speak thus freely to me; lest being weak, I might stumble at his Acknowledgement.

M^r: Langshaw, a Stranger whom I met one Hour in Band, seems fill'd with Love & Zeal, just as John Keeling was, & calls himself perfect: which I dare not gainsay.

I can recollect no more Persons whom I have had any particular knowledge of, while counting *themselves* xxxx (scribble marks) perfect; & I will not relate any thing by hearsay. GOD give you discernment to set me right, if this L^r be wrong. I receiv'd much benefit by yours of March 23^d:; & so have some of my Friends, especially M^r: & M^rs: Swain: but your allowing Perfection, has caus'd me to write all the foregoing Thoughts upon it.

O may GOD give me such Perfection as chiefly consists in the thought of Love, evidently seen in M^rs: Hardwick, & the depth of Humility, evidently seen in M^r. Fletcher! yet these declare themselves poor Sinners; & utterly disclaim Perfection, tho' not the Doctrine. I strive to know the Trees, my dear Friend, by their Fruit: for Discernment is a useful part of Xtianity.

   The Lord guide you by his holy Spirit, & suffer not your thoughts to err."

  "I am your affectionate Brother, in the Hope set before us,"

"J:W:"
This Letter had such an effect on Mr. Berridge, that he has every since opposed the Doctrine of Perfection. alas. alas!

I will now turn back to the year 1757. The fear of GOD prevented me from saying I was perfect, but evil was far away, & GOD continually with me. once indeed I felt, in process of time, upon a great Provocation, that Anger was yet in me, & at the end of 14 Months, perceiv'd the same again: but in respect of my besetting Sin, it seem'd as totally foreign to me as to an Angel of GOD; nor was the Lord ever, that I know of, absent from me or out of my Thoughts, & I wonder'd exceedingly that my Brethren who had known the Lord longer, did not rejoice in him as I did. for none could I find, no not even among the Boasters of Perfection, who knew any thing of my Joy. wherefore I would put them to mind of such Scriptures as this, "Let the Inhabitants of the Rock sing; let them shout for joy from the tops of the Mountains." my talking thus would amaze them, & make them share, as if they thought me distracted. but still I tho^t they might rejoice if they pleas'd even as I because they were also Believers. Nothing more delighted me than the seeming Extirpation of my besetting Sin: a strong Temptation to which, began its Assault in July 1759. The waters roar'd amain, the Fires flamed exceedingly: but none could come near enough to touch me. a little Presumption might have made me say, like our present Perfectionists, "Satan comes indeed, but finds nothing in me." thus I went on to the middle of February, *1760* when all things conspired to case me down from the Mount of GOD. but rather would I have parted from Life itself than my great Blessedness, I never ceased from watching & praying, I was free *to my thinking,* from the very Shadow of Sin, & went about doing good with all my might, even at the frequent hazard of my Life, & to this very Day, the Lord has not shown me that ever I was remiss in following him; yet in effect, he then said unto me, "Go thou down also & profess the Sins of thy Youth. I give thy besetting Sin dominion over thee, & thou shalt desire, but not enjoy it." such has indeed been my lot: for on the 19th., Sin & Temptation, like two mighty Robbers, while I resisted even unto blood, prevail'd agains^t me; & have ever since trampled me under foot; but as I have never committed any willful Sin, I cannot say that I have ever since fallen into any Condemnation. yet has my Warfare been astonishingly great, nothing *of like kind perhaps, being* [scribbled out word] more bitter than my Temptations, & nothing sweeter than by Consolations. Take one Instance of the latter.

August 4, 1760. Being alone in my House at Knightsbridge, I inexpressibly harrass'd with my besetting Temptation this Afternoon, running up Stairs & down as if distracted, & praying in vain to be deliver'd from corrupt Desire, till I fell into a kind of Despair, & could say little more than this, "Lord, if I perish, be it at thy feet." I c^d. hardly reach West Street at the Chapel time; where the Sermon, as customary, proved a dead Letter to me: the Temptation however ended with it; & I wonder'd at my resembling so lately an incarnate Devil. but when the 2 last Lines of the Hymns were sung, at least that I heard, as follows,

> "Thy warfare's past, thy Mourning, o'er,
> Look up, for thou shalt weep no more."

To the best of my remembrance I heard only this, "_____Mourning's o'er,

> "Look up for thou shalt weep no more."

& instantly lifting up my Soul in strong Hope, I wish'd for the repetition of Those Lines; but when sung again, could only hear, "_____Thy Warefare's o'er,

> "Look up, for Thou shalt weep no more."

but O, what joy did I then feel! & what a visionary Scene appear'd to the Eye of my Soul! For it seem'd as if I saw myself lying on a Death Bed, & heard & saw the Almighty speaking to me from a Cloud, & filling my Soul with as strong Assurance, as if he had even sworn by himself to me,

> "
> _____Thy Warfare o'er,
> Look up, for thou shalt weep no more."

The first Impression caus'd me to weep with a small audible Cry: Then I lean'd along, for some Minutes, while the Tears of gladness ran down my face, & I trembled much; for the same gracious Words & Appearance, Tho' lessening by degrees, long visited my Soul: & I co^d: scarce describe it with dry Eyes, till next Day. _____ I then counted it as firm a Promise to me from the Lord, as the following Promise from the *Angel* [above a scratched out section] was to Daniel,: "_____ Thou shalt rest, & stand in Thy lot at the end of the Days." I believe also, from hence, that my Temptations & Trials will not entirely cease, till I am going to expire.

Such being my general Experience, I consider'd it altogether:, even from my Justification, & Wrote these verses thereupon, Sept^r: 1, 3, 1760.

> O, that I now could shew thy peaceful ways,
> And speak the Wonders of Redeeming Grace!
> But Language fails, & utt'rance melts away,
> Before the Blaze of this my Gospel Day.
> O King of Glory, stoopest thou to shine,
> On such a vile Earth, & such a Soul as mine!
> I know, I feel, thy precious Blood apply'd:
> For me the great Jehovah bled & died!
> No guilty Weight my Conscience longer feels:
> I still am sprinkled, & the Blood still heals.
> O, matchless Love, my trembling Soul to save,

And bid me triumph o'er the dreaded Grave!

(3)

If he [big ink spot] re thou lead, along the narrow Way,
And after bring me to the Realms of Day,
I'll sing thy Praises in the Courts above;
The boundless Mansions of eternal Love;
Where thy dear Saints, in blest communion sing
The ceaseless Triumphs of their glorious King;
Beholding & resembling what Thou art;
Thou, from whose Presence I shall not depart,
But all the Heaven of Heavens be round me spread,
And everlasting Joy upon my head, [scratch mark through
bottom of comma to make the punctuation point for the
exclamation]!
Glory to GOD onhigh, my Song shall be,
And, glory to the Lamb, who died for me.

September 18, 1760. I went from Knightsbridge to live at Edgware.
December 31. I dream'd of going round M^r: Whitefield's Gallery at Tot'nam
Court, feeling great love to him & the People, & praying for them with strong
joy. This very Dream I was favour'd with several preceeding Nights. wherefore
I cast away my Prejudice, & heard him the next Day with a good Will. and
indeed it was time I should, tho' I knew it not, as the Preaching at West Street
was much [scratched out word] *much* alter'd, & the Shechinah would would no
more visit me while his Word was preach'd in that Temple, except once while
M^r. John Jones cried out, "O Death, where is thy Sting. &c."
January 14, 1761. I heard that M^r. Berridige was perswaded to believe the
Doctrine of Perfection at last Sunday's Love Feast.
February 25. The Men Bands at West Street were a greater number than usual,
& disputed much about Perfection; which I counted a false Doctrine, founded on
spiritual Pride. They who pleaded for it were many, & shew'd much warmth;
their Opponents were few & cool: only M^r. Bell spoke with vehemence against
it.
March 5. I dream'd of hearing a large Company sing Hymns in the open Air,
unintelligibly, wherefore I went from them, & while I utter'd some other
Ejaculations.
April 24. I rejoic'd in the Lord greatly, while walking thro' Hide Park &
shunning the common Track. I felt a Deliverance from the whole propensity to
Sin, as common in such Visitations, praised the Lord with great thankfulness, &
vehemently besought him to hasten the Day of Judgment; which has been for
some years the most earnest & frequent of all my Petitions.
April 26. I heard 2 Sermons at West Street, maintaining the Doctrine of
Perfection; moreover the generality of the Methodists I convers'd with are of

that opinion; all which co^d: not alter mine, Of a Propensity to Sin being felt by the greatest Saints on earth, at one time or other, when strongly tempted to their old Besetting Sin. Yet have I been long acquainted with the perf^t. love of GOD at intervals; to whome I can truly say,

> "Lord I am Thine; & on thy side thou King of Glory."

July 4, 1761. M^r. Bell who call'd himself perfect, being abroad, I sat in his House meditating; & after desiring the Lord to shew me his true State, open'd a Bible, & cast my Eye first on, 2 Chron: 25,2. "And he did <u>that</u> <u>which</u> <u>was</u> right in the sight of the Lord, but not with a perfect heart." about which time, (on account of my saying, Neither him nor any other call'd perfect, appear'd to have so much of the Mind that was in X^t. as M^{rs}. Hardwick &c.) he went abruptly from me, & when we met again, said, he w^d. have spoke to me no more, if the Lord had not bid him receive me as a Brother.

July 5. While M^r. Neal preach'd at West Street, I tho^t: several justified; especially one who sat next me: but he said, He was justified before, & now made perfect; because he had wept with extreme Joy, as I have done 1,00 Times; tho' without presuming to call myself perfect, or any thing better than a Dog or Swine. I was told by M^r. Bowen & Amos Copeland that their hearts were clean; the former in a Week after Justification. I went this Evening to M^r. Bell's assembly by Grovesnor Square, & felt a strange overcoming power, without any Joy, while he pray'd that GOD w^d. make me perfect.

July 7. Having kept some time from Tot'nam Court, on account of M^r. Whitefield's Illness, & my great dislike to M^r. Davis, I forgot by what means I was induced to go this Evening; where I heard M^r. Davis a full Hour on, "____ Him that comethe to me. I will in no wise cast out." & at the close, while I was in great heaviness, he strongly declared the Faithfulness of GOD; to whom I lifted up this Prayer, "Heaven & Earth, I believe, shall pass away; but not one jot of thy Word. O speak to me! bid me live for every. let me be glad in thy Love to all Eternity, for Jesus' sake." Immediately the Preacher cried out, "Heaven & Earth shall pass away, but not 1 jot of his Word. & can he give thee up? no: for he hath loved thee with an everlastg. Love." all which the Lord applying, I trembled & wept with great joy, & strong Assurance of his everlasting Love. This reconciled me to M^r. Davis, & so fully put an end to my Bigotry, that I have gone ever since with equal readiness, to Tot'nam Court as West Street.

July 9. Out of 8 Men, with whom I met in private Band, 6 declared they had clean hearts; & the chief of them, M^r. Langshaw, to whom I said, "Let him that standeth, take heed lest he fall: & be not high minded but fear." Tho' he seem'd to like these, & most of my Words, call'd me afterwards in his Prayer, <u>An Advocate</u> <u>for</u> <u>the</u> <u>Devil</u>. & likewise bro^t. Accusations against M^r. Vardin, the Leader, who had no otherwise contradicted him than by recommending Caution.

July 12. Rece^d. the Sacr^t. at W:Street, & heard M^r. Maxfield; who confidently said, to me & all such, "O Fools, & slow of heart." I heard M^r. Maddan at the Lock this Afternoon, 58 Min^s: on, "Because thou hast rejected the Word of the Lord, he hath also rejected thee from being King." I rejoic'd in the Lord several times; especially when he said, "He that toucheth You [scribbled mark/possibly God] toucheth the Apple of his Eye."

July 21. M^r. Davis was in his Sermon when I came to Tot'nam Court, on, "My Grace is sufficient for thee." Wherein he sharply preach'd against the Doctrine of Perfection, calling it the greatest Blasphemy that he knew. The Word came with power; &

(4)

I felt the Lord's Presence from first to last, removing from my Soul a great weight of Distrust & Anxiety. my Rejoicings were so frequent, & so many Words applied that it w^d. be tedious to write them. none came with so great energy as these, "Fear not thou Worm Jacob." I then so wept & trembled that several Eyes were upon me.

July 22. I waked with a Headach, probably from last Nights Joy in the Holy Ghost. a Joy which several of my West Street Brethren once villify'd, entilling it a Tremer Framer & Feeling: but now in the Pride of their Wisdom, call even a little degree of it Perfect:.

July 27. With full confidence in my GOD, I went to Reading, as Lieutenant of a Press Gang.

September 27, 1761. I rece^d. a Letter from M^r. Bell, lamenting my Imperfection. wherefore I wrote thus to him the next Day.

"My dear Brother./

You seem jealous for the Salvation of my Soul; & I thank You. "The tokens of Inspiration are in your L^r:; by which I know your Soul must alive to GOD: for whose honour I am jealous on your account: my own Ears having heard You say, first, that you was perfect: then that you c^d.. not fall from your perfect State, unless GOD himself co^d fall from his Throne. whereas I have pass'd thro' that delightful State wherein You now are, & of which You presume to boast, but am safely bro^t.. down, by the mighty Workings of the Holy Ghost, into the deep Vale of Humiliation; where I see distinctly, That You & I, tho' X^t..be formed in us, are no better than dead Dogs by Nature, nor any more holy after the Flesh than the Fish of the Sea or Fowls of Heaven. I surely dwell in a Body of Death & Corruption even as they: nor is your Body better than Dust & Ashes. The Body of X^t..was perfect indeed, & therefore co^d.. not see Corruption: but is your Soul united to such a Body? or do you not lie with a Woman to this Day, because your Flesh lusteth against your Spirit? Even a poor Heathen, Alexander the great, co^d.. tell his Flatters, "I am surely no GOD, because I bled like a mortal Man when wounded; & because I desire Women." You must likewise acknowledge, that You are not changed into the clean, the holy Nature of GOD, whose Dwelling is not with Flesh; or must deny that You desire your Wife when you lie with her. I doubt not but your Body is a Temple of the living GOD, as I know that my own is: & yet we must see Corruption; having dead Bodies already in GOD's account, because of Sin; that original

Leprosy, which is diffused thro' all Creatures under the Sun, so long as they remain embodied. but I doubt not that you & I shall be lean at last, when taken away from the Body, & carried up to the Company of Spirits of just Men made perfect. _____ &c.   &c.   &c.
_____ I doubt not my dear Friend, of our taking sweet council together again, if GOD prolong my Days; which I sometimes think are shortning apace. One Scripture Sign of them that believe, is this, "If they drink any deadly thing it shall not hurt them." why not? "Because underneath us are the everlasting Arms." You have certainly drank a large Draught of spiritual Pride; but the Lord will not let you fall, I verily believe, nor even be hurt when the Temptation is past. You perceive it not now, because rejoicing in your first Love; the time of the Gladness of your heart. My own Espousals to X^t.., or the Celebration of them rather, continued about 3 years, & I had the same power over Sin as You have. O that our Bro^r: Moss, or some other, who has been upon the Moutn like me, & is come down again as I am, had such a zeal for the Truth, if not love to a fellow Disciple, as to glorify GOD by declaring freely, "That there is none good upon Earth but one; that is GOD." Isaiah says, "He will carry the Lambs in his Bosom." & again, "Whom shall he teach Doctrine? Them that are weaned from the Breasts." You are now a Babe in X^t..; & must be wean'd, as I have been, which is a grievous Warfare, before You will understand the true, the lowly Doctrine, Of every Man being abominable by his Nature, & not one being ever made perfect upon Earth."

"The Lord enlighten more & more, both you, & your ever affectionate Brother, in the glorious Gospel," J:W:.

"P.S. My love to our Brethren of the Guards: advise them to rejoice with trembling. I cannot find time to write all I would, & have scribbled over this upon a Common 5 Miles from Reading. You cannot imagine the number & greatness of my Worldly Trials: I have lain all Ni^t.. in a Field; I have had a Town-full of People rise up to destroy me; I have run as great risks in my strange Employment, as some Men run in the service of GOD; I have often gone at the hazard of my Life, in Sickness & bad Weather, to perpetrate what I approve not: & as to the Men I am connected with, it may be truly said, "The best of them is as a Brier." & almost all other Men have declared a kind of civil War against me. Where w^d. your Perfection be in such Temptations as mine? I have Fightings without, & Fears within: but the Grace of GOD has hitereto been sufficient for me, & made me more than Conqueror over the World, the Flesh, & the Devil."
November 30. I return'd to London: having been hurt by nothing but my Besetting Temptation; which continued to increase upon me.
January 12, 1762. By M^r. Berridge's desire, I bro^t.. M^r. Bell to converse with him at M^r. Whitefield's in Tot'nam Court Road: where I said little, for my own part, except the same observation which M^r. Berridge made, That Mr Bell had then something dismal & shocking in his face, which indeed I had observ'd ever since March 27, 1761. when he first told me that he was perfect, whereas he had

a remarkably good look before. what he now chiefly said was, That GOD had given him the Gift of healing, which he had already practiced, & of raising the Dead, which he should perform in GOD's time, That The Milennium was begun, & he sh^d. never die, That he & several other Men had seen Satan bound & cast into the bottomless Pit, & the Angel had set a Seal upon him that he sh^d. not come out to deceive the Nations: & that all M^r. Berridge's excellent Observations did not at all shake his confidence of these things. & indeed his whole Deportment, Calmness & Assurance, wrought so much upon me, that I had tho^{ts}.. of asking him to heal my Mother; who was astmatic; & sh^d.. probably have credited all he said, for I had imbibed the Doctrine of Perfection a few Days before, if the Lord had not bro^t=to my Remembrance

(5)

a tedious & bitter Delusion, shewing me withal, how mightily Satan was permitted in these Days to deceive the truly religious, by appearing as an Angel of Light: wherefore I rejected once more the whole Doctrine of Perfection. as to the Impressions which from time to time, for the space of 5 years, I had believ'd to come from GOD, every one, I think, did really prove to be from him; except the Delusion I have just hinted: which [scribble mark] added much to the Affliction of my Soul.

February 17, 1762. A Man at West Street Bands declared, he had been made perfect by M^r. Bell's laying his hand upon him. & on the 23^d.. much the same thing befell me: wherefore on the 26th.. your Brother had S.S. put on my Ticket.

February 27. I made little doubt of my being perfect till this Afternoon, when I co^d.. not tell whether I felt Anger or no at the ignorance of another perfect Man.

March 4. After dreaming of idolatrous Temptations, the Dream concluded with my praying to GOD, & I rejoic'd in him so greatly that I awoke, upon repeating these Words,

> "Repos'd in those Elysian Seats,
> Where Jonathan his David meets:"
> "There, where no Frosts our Spring annoy,
> Shalt thou alone my love enjoy."

March 20. I rejoic'd before the Lord a considerable time, in a Dream, with this & other triumphant Expressions, "Thou givest me here thy hidden Manna: wilt Thou not give me hereafter the Morning Star."

March 23. I wrote the following L^r. to Mr. Beveridge.

"Dear Sir/."

Being sorely distrest in spirit, the 22^d.. of last Month, I wrote the following Verses:

> Where, O almighty GOD, shall I find rest,

If there no longer wilt inspire my Breast?
Faithful & true, where is thy Spirit flown?
And thy rich Mercy, oft to me made known?
Why can I now no more prevail with thee?
Ah, why this Hiding of Thy face from me?
How, from the daz'ling height of Happiness,
How am I fallen into deep distress?
O raise me up again, my Soul restore,
Let Soul & Body feel Thy quick'ning Power!
Now as of old thy Goodness let me see:
Come Holy Ghost, Thou well-known GOD, to me!
Still condescend my longing Soul to meet:
Come Holy Ghost, eternal <u>Paraclete</u>:
Still to my heart the <u>Blood</u> of <u>Jesus</u> bring;
Thy precious Blood, O <u>Salem's</u> peaceful King!
Ransom'd by thee from all the guilt of Sin,
But still defil'd & longing to be clean,"
"Come that I may from all its power be freed:
Come, O my GOD, & make me free indeed!

M^r. Bell came the next Evening unexpectedly, & said, "Well, now let us pray together; & neither of You (for my Mother was present) resist the Spirit of the Lord." he then pray'd, & I when he had done, but all seem'd unaffected: we then stood up & *he* sung several Verses; which I remember not, Tho' some were significant of my Name being written in the Lamb's Book of Life: & on hearing those, I felt a Palpitation at the bottom of my Stomach, & a small giddiness in my Head; the Lord also gave me his peace at the same-time & M^r. Bell after singing, ask'd my Mother how she found herself; who reply'd, with Tears of joy in her Eyes, "Ah, M^r., it w^d.. be a happy thing if one co^d.. be always thus." he then left us; & in a few Min^s.., the Spirit of the Lord so abundantly fill'd me, that I sat down in an Elbow chair, pray'd silently for an entire deliverance from the power of Sin, breath'd short, & panted in the multitude of Peace from 7 o'clock till ¼ past 8. when I seem'd going to die suddenly, & that I might resist it is I w^d.: but the presence of the Lord being delightful, I said, "Let me fear only thee." and casting my care upon him, I felt as if Lightning, or a slower ethereal Flame, had been penetrating & rolling thro' every Atom of my Body: which being past, I did not breathe so short as before; but found a sweet Composure, & ineffable Calmness of spirit. I then walk'd about the Room rejoicing, & seem'd to feel my Body so light, that I might choose whether to walk or fly. Such has been my unaccountable Experience; neither know I whether I have felt any Sin or not, either spiritual or bodily, from that Hour to This, only in Dreams. but think I have more than once; & w^d. rather call myself the chief of Sinners than a perfect Xtian. How great is the Mystery of Godliness! O that You and I may continually be taught of GOD, and rejoice in his Highness World without end!"

"I am your affectionate Bro^r., in X^t..,"

J:W:.

"P.S. On hearing M^r. Bell ano^r. Ni^t.., sing the Verses he sung Feb^y.. 23^d:., I co^d. recollect that the chief Lines which the Lord then applied to my Soul were these,

> "Sing, O my Soul, for thou hast cause,
> "Thine enemy is slain:
> "Thy Sin that late thy Burden was,
> "No more may rule again:
> "The holy Child the Virgin bore,
> "Delights in thee to dwell:
> "Sing, O my Soul, for thou no more
> "Shall be afraid of Hell.
> "Its Sting, they Sin, he takes away,
> "The Law is disannull'd;
> "Thy Pardon seal'd in endless Day,
> "And there thy Name enroll'd."

March 25. I rejoic'd before the Lord in a Dream, while desiring & expecting his great Day: some of my Words then were, "I know that thou lovest me with an everlasting Love."

March 30, 1762. I took M^r. Bell & M^r. Bowen to see a Widow at Highgate; who was near Death, & almost despairing of Mercy. M^r. Bell ask'd her a few Questions, & bid her speak a few Words *after him*; she did so & was justified: The Holy Ghost coming at the same instant upon us all, & with such power that I cried for joy a considerable time.

April 10. After a mixture of Deliverance & Uncertainty for 46 Days, I now clearly perceiv'd my besetting Sin to remain where it foremerly was, even in me. several other Persons call'd perfect, tho' not M^r. Bell, from time to time acknowledg'd themselves to be in some degree as I was: but what I call'd Sin, they counted Temptation.

April 20. I dream'd of Lewdness, & of abhorring it; whereupon I rejoic'd immediately in the Lord, while uttering these unscriptural Words, "I turn to thee, O Lord, as the lov'd Flower to the Sun."

May 14. One Woman roar'd, & another cried out at W:Street Sacrament. but only once did I *ever* feel the Lord present at these Friday Meetings of the S.S. where often, according to my Judgment, I have heard flat Blasphemy; tho' I forget the particulars.

May 16. My Soul being distrest above measure, by my besetting Temptation, I heard M^r. Davis at Tot'nam Court, 52 Min^s: on Micah 6, 5. I wept & shook several times, with full assurance & joy in the Lord, especially while these or like Words were spoken: "The Lord is thy Refuge." "There is no Enchantment against Jacob, nor Divination against Israel." "I know thou art ready sometimes to conclude, That a Curse is come upon Thee, & that Thy GOD will not visit thee any more. but thou wilt always find him a Covenant-keeping GOD, whose

Love is everlasting. Satan may tell thee otherwise; but believe him not, for he is the Father of Lies. Recollect the past Favours of the Lord: knowest thou not that he who deliver'd thee out of the Paw of the Lion, will deliver the likewise from every accursed Philistine?"

May 19. Being distrest again, I heard M^r. Madden, 55 Min^s.., on Job 19.25,26,27. I rejoic'd in the Lord with great Sweetness, Tears, & shaking, while these Words were utter'd concerning the beatifick Vision," And the Tears shall be wiped away from every Eye."

May 23. I dream'd of saying with a loud Voice, to a tempting Devil, "I am Christ's, & Christ is GOD's." To which he relied, "I know it well."

May 26. In W:Street Bands M^r. Jackson, who is call'd perfect said, X^t.. cut himself open with a Knife, & put him into his Breast. M^r. John Jones disliked the Expression.

May 31. After 6 Hours disorder of Body, & sadness of Soul, I heard M^r. Davis at Tot'-nam Court, 42 Min^s.., on Romans 8,11. I rejoic'd a little most of the time with deep Humilty; & once with great extacy, strong Assurance, Tears, & Shaking, while he utter'd these & like Words, "Fear not; march, go on; thy GOD shall go with thee thro' Fire & water." so ended my Heaviness.

June 22. I sweetly rejoic'd in the Lord, while hearing M^r. Dyer at Tot'nam Court, 36 M^s.., on Philip^s.. 1,23. towards the Conclusion, especially, when these & like Words were utter'd, "Believer, the Day of thine Espousals draw nigh. _____ And in that Day, GOD shall wipe all Tears from thine Eyes."

July 1. I wrote the following Letter to M^r. Berridge.

"Dear Sir/.

I hope you receiv'd my L^r. of March 23^d..; in which [corner missing with partial words] the Deliverance GOD gave me from present Distress, after M^r.. Bell had "sung a few Verses: that Deliverance was not one Day compleat; & yet like Elijah's Cake, it proved a means of strength'ning my Soul above 40 Days; at the end of which I became weak as aforetime, & have ever since lusted as usual in my heart, with frequent Murmurings against GOD.

You have receiv'd in a former L^r.., some account of a much greater & more durable Blessing, tho' of the very same kind as that which I found after M^r. Bell's singing. & I co^d. mention several other Visitations of GOD extremely different from either of these, & exceeding them in point of Sanctification as well as Joy in the Holy Ghost. but it w^d.. be tedious to rehearse them, & impossible to recollect them all. one of the first was on Sunday, May 22, 1757. in the Fields of Risley in Derbyshire: so great & sweet for about an Hour was my Joy in the Lord, that I co^d. then compare my State to none but that of S^t. Paul when caught up into the 3^d. Heavens. O, how much did I then desire to be dissolv'd & see my GOD without a Veil! but he gave me to understand, that his Grace w^d. be sufficient for me while upon the earth: & tho' I heard no Voice, nor saw any thing, I was well contented to wait for my appointed time; being fully assured that he spake such a Promise to me. & why did I not after this, & 1,00 of the like unutterably joyful Communions with GOD, cry out <u>He has made</u>

me <u>perfect</u>! The reason is plain: A Messenger of Satan was then, or about the same time, first sent to buffet me, 2 or 3 Years, chiefly with Suicide; & afterwards a Thorn in the Flesh_____ which remains to this Day, & makes me seem to myself, a perfect Beast, as the former did a meer Devil. Thus are the Favours of GOD always guarded to me, & from time to time he breaks the Pride of my heart in pieces.

Now I will tell you what I think of all who count themselves perfect. They   have tasted something of divine Joy; but neither been used to it, nor fell it a 10th..part so strongly or ineffably as I have. They are neither buffeted by Satan, nor have a Thorn in their Flesh like me; but are absolutely at ease in Sion. Pleasing as that State is, I believe it lays the Soul open to the greatest Snare of Satan, which is spiritual Pride. Alas for me! That very State would be my choice, if I did not fear GOD: who has led me thro' many a terrible fiery Furnace, into none of which am I ever willing to enter. and of all the Gospel Ministers, none has been a means of such blessing to my weary Soul as the Rev^d. Davis; who speaks most of them all to the real Saints that are Tempted, & afflicted, tossed with Tempests, & not comforted." _____ &c &c &c _____"

J:W:.

July 11th... I felt evil Desire at the Table, just before M^r. Dyer & Green gave me the Sacrament; which was the first I ever rece^d. at Tot'nam Court Chapel. I look'd up to GOD, & took it with these Words, "Yet will I cast my Soul on Thee." I rejoic'd in the Lord after it for 10 Minutes, with shaking & wat'ry Eyes. July 16. I rece^d. a L^r. from M^r. Berridge. a small part of which follows.

"Dear Sir/.

I rece^d. your L^r. of July 1. & a former of March [letter page cut off at the bottom right where a numeral is missing]

(6)

"which I return'd no Answer, because I know not how to speak or write "to perfect People, & therefore avoid Correspondence with them. Many "things I saw in them, when at London, which griev'd me much; & "many things here in the Country which have griev'd me more: Such "Pride! Such Boasting! Such Censoriousness! Such Contempt of others! "_____ But what is mighty strange, these perfect People still "talk of growing. If they are really perfect, what can be lacking, "except to continue in that State? As far as I can discern, they are "unwillingly growing or grown out of X^t... They apply to the Lord for Grace "by Prayer & Faith, & Grace is obtain'd: with this Stock they set up, & "trade against the Redeemer; not seeking, as Paul says, to be presented "perfect in X^t, Colos: 1,28. but to be presented perfect in themselves." &c &c.

J:B:.

July 29. M^r. Bell & Bowen spake, & pray'd, as if I had not been justified.

July 30. I dream'd of triumphing in the Favour of GOD; & remember to have repeated these Words in my Dream, "Let the Saints shout for joy; let them sing aloud upon their Beds."

Now, Sir, if You desire to know the present & general [corner of middle page torn away but may be "State" by looking at bottom part of letters] of my Soul, it is my Judgment, "<u>Suffering</u> <u>&</u> <u>Temptations</u>." if the Opinion I have now, & at most times, of myself, I cannot express it more truly than by these few, which are my favourite Words to GOD & Man,

"<u>Behold</u>, <u>I</u> <u>am</u> <u>vile</u>.

As to the Papers, treat them as you please: you have the free consent of your affectionate Brother, in Christ,

John Walsh.

August [scratched out word] 15, 1762

Bibliography

Primary Sources

Unpublished Manuscripts

Book Inventory. Manchester Methodist Archives.

A True and Impartial Relation of a Wonderful Apparition that Happen'd in the Royal Camp in Flanders, The Beginning of this Instant September 1692. Concerning King William. In a Letter to a Gentleman in London, from his Friend, a Captain in the King's Camp. London: Printed for Randall Taylor, 1692.

The Wesleyan Army At War With The Devil (Broadsheet). Bodleian Library, Oxford University, B 20 (186).

Bennet, John. *1745 Minutes*. Manchester Methodist Archives.

Bourne, Hugh. *Manuscript Journals*. Manchester Methodist Archives. DDHB 3.3.

I. JAC.I.C.12, Oxford University, Library of Law.

March, Jane. *Letter to Mary Fletcher*. Manchester Methodist Archives. MAM F1. 5. 2. 2.

_____. *Letter to Mary Fletcher*. Manchester Methodist Archives. MAM F1. 5. 2. 11.

Pawson, John. *Some Account of the Life of Mr John Pawson*. Manchester Methodist Archives. MCA Diaries Box 27.

Robert, Samuel. *Manuscript Notebook*.

Walsh, John. *Letter to Charles Wesley on August 11-15, 1762*. Manchester Methodist Archives. EMV-134.

Wesley, Anne. *Letter to John Wesley*. Manchester Methodist Archives. DDCW 8/15, 37.

Wesley, Charles. *Lavington's Case*. Manchester Methodist Archives. DDCW 8.12.

_____. *Transcriptions of Family Letters Regarding Old Jeffrey*. Manchester Methodist Archives. DDCW 8/15, 8-43.

Wesley, Emily. *Letter to Samuel Wesley, junior*. Manchester Methodist Archives. DDCW 8/15, 17.

Wesley, John. *Summary of the Old Jeffrey Affair.* Manchester Methodist Archives. DDCW 8/15, 43.
Wesley, Susanna. *Letter to Samuel Wesley, junior.* Manchester Methodist Archives. DDCW 8/15, 8.
Wesley, Susanna, junior. *Letter to Samuel Wesley, junior.* Manchester Methodist Archives. DDCW 8/15, 15-16.

Published and Unpublished Engravings and Portraits

John Wesley, that Excellent Minister of the Gospel, Carried by Angels into Abraham's Bosom, March, 1791.
Map of the Garden of Eden Before the Flood. The Gentleman's Magazine, 1738.
Thomas Maxfield.
The Tree of Life. 1780 [?].
Hagerty, John. *"The Tree of Life, 1791."*
The Tree of Life, 1846.
Hogarth, William. *Credulity, Superstition, and Fanaticism.*
Robert, Samuel. *Samuel Robert's: Prayer and the Devil.*

Published Documents

Primary Books, Articles, and Theses

Albani, Giovanni Francesco (Pope Clement XI). *The Famous Bull Unigenitus, in English. With a Short History of its Rise and Progress.* Portsmouth: W. Horton, 1753.
Aldrich, Henry. *Artis Logicae Compendium.* Oxford: Theatro Sheldoniano, 1691.
Alexander, H. G., ed. *The Leibnitz-Clarke Correspondence.* Manchester: University of Manchester Press, 1976.
Almond, Philip C., ed. *Demonic Possession and Exorcism in Early Modern England: Contemporary Texts and their Cultural Contexts.* Cambridge: Cambridge University Press, 2004.
Andrew, Donna, ed. *London Debating Societies, 1776-1799.* London: London Record Society, 1994.
Gentleman's Magazine. 149 vols. London: Edward Cave, 1730-1838.
Glossarium Epicureum. N.p. N.d.
Minutes of Several Conversations, Between the Rev. John Wesley, M. A., and the Preachers in Connection with him. London: Printed for George Whitfield, 1779 [sic].
A Methodist Magazine, for the Year 1819, Conducted by the Camp-Meeting Methodists Known by the Name of Ranters, Called Also Primitive Methodists. Leichester: J. Fowler, 1819.

The Royal Society of London Philosophical Transactions General Index for Volumes 1-70 (1665-1780). 1787. Reprint, New York: Johnson Reprint Corp., 1963.

Sermon or Homilies, Appointed to be read in churches to which are added The Articles of Religion; The Constitutions and Canons Ecclesiastical. London: Society for Promoting Christian Knowledge, 1839.

A True and Impartial Relation of a Wonderful Apparition that Happen'd in the Royal Camp in Flanders, The Beginning of this Instant September 1692. Concerning King William. In a Letter to a Gentleman in London, from his Friend, a Captain in the King's Camp. London: Printed for Randall Taylor, 1692.

Aquinas, Thomas. *The De Mala of Thomas Aquinas*. Translated by Richard Regan. Edited by Brian Davis. Oxford: Oxford University Press, 2001.

_____. *Summa Theologica*. Translated by the Fathers of the English Dominican Province. 5 vols. Allen, TX: Christian Classics, 1948.

_____. *Summa Theologicæ*. Edited by Thomas Gilby, O. P. 61 vols. London: Blackfriars, 1963-81.

Aristotle. *Metaphysics*. The Loeb Classical Library. Translated by Hugh Tredennick. Vols. 271-72. 1933. Reprint, Cambridge, MA: Harvard University Press, 2000.

_____. *On the Soul*. The Loeb Classical Library. Translated by W. S. Hett. Vol. 288 1936. Reprint, Cambridge, MA: Harvard University Press, 2000.

Arouet, François-Marie (Voltaire). *Philosophical Dictionary*. Edited and Translated by Theodore Besterman. London: Penguin, 1972.

Artemidorus. *Artemidorus' Oneirocritica: Text, Translation, & Commentary.* Translated and Edited, Daniel E. Harris-McCoy. Oxford: Oxford University Press, 2012.

Asbury, Francis. *The Journal and Letters of Francis Asbury*. Edited by Elmer Clark. 3 vols. Nashville, TN: Abingdon Press, 1958.

Augustine. *The City of God*. Nicene and Post-Nicene Fathers, First Series. Edited by Philip Schaff. 14 vols. 1887. Reprint, Peabody, MA: Hendrickson Publishers, 1994.

_____. *The Confessions*. Nicene and Post-Nicene Fathers, First Series. Edited by Philip Schaff. 14 vols. 1887. Reprint, Peabody, MA: Hendrickson Publishers, 1994.

_____. *The Divination of Demons*. Translated by Ruth Wentworth Brown. In *The Fathers of the Church: A New Translation,* edited by Roy Deferrari. 67 vols. New York: Fathers of the Church, 1955.

Baxter, Andrew. *An Enquiry into the Nature of the Human Soul, wherein the Immateriality of the Soul is Evinced from the Principles of Reason and Philosophy*. London: James Bettenham, n.d.

Baxter, Richard. *The Certainty of the World of Spirits, Fully Evinced by Unquestionable Histories of APPARITIONS and WITCHCRAFTS, Operations, Voices, &c. Proving the Immortality of Souls, the Malice of the Devils and the Damned, and the Blessedness of the Justified. Written for the Conviction of Sadduccees & Infidels*. London: Printed for T. Parkhurst and J. Salisbury, 1691.

Bedford, Arthur. *The Doctrine of Assurance: OR, The Case of a Weak and Doubting Conscience. A Sermon Preached at St. Lawrence Jewry, in the City of London on Sunday, August 13, 1738 with an Appendix, answering the Objections From the Texts of Scripture*. 2nd ed. London: Printed by Charles Ackers, 1739.

Bekker, Balthasar. *De Betoverde Weereld, Zynde een Grondig Ondersoek Van't Gemeen gevoelen Aangaande de Geesten, Derselver Aart en Vermogen, Bewind en Dedryf: als Ook't Genede Menschen Door Derselver Kraght Gemeenschap Doen*. Deventer: Amsterdam, 1691.

_____. *The World turn'd upside down: or, a Plain Detection of Errors, in the Common Or Vulgar Belief, Relating to Spirits, Spectres or Ghosts, Daemons, Witches &c. In a Due and Serious Examination of their Nature, Power, Administration, and Operation. In What Forms or Shape Incorporeal Spirits Appear to Men, by what Means, and of what Elements they take to Themselves, and form Appearances of Bodies, visible to mortal Eyes; Why They appear, and what Frights and Force of Imagination often delude us into The Apprehensions of supposed Phantasms, through the Intimidation of the Mind, &c. ALSO What evil Tongues have Power to produce of Hurt to Mankind or Irational Creatures; and the Effects Men and Women are able to Produce by their Communication with Good or Evil Spirits, & c*. London: Printed for Elizabeth Harris,1700.

Bellamy, Joseph. *A Letter to the Reverend Author of the Winter-Evening's Conversation on Original Sin*. Boston, MA: Printed by S. Kneeland, 1758.

Bellers, John. *An Essay Towards the Improvement of Physick in Twelve Proposals. By Which the Lives of many Thousands of the Rich, as Well as of the Poor, may be Saved Yearly*. London: J. Sowle, 1714.

Bengel, Johann Albrecht. *Sechzig erbauliche Reden über die Offenbarung Johannis, oder vielmehr Jesus Christi*. 3rd ed. Stuttgart: Johann Christoph Erhard, 1758.

Bennet, John. *Mirror of the Soul: The Diary of an Early Methodist Preacher, John Bennet: 1714-1754*. Edited and an Introduction by Simon R. Valentine. Peterborough: Methodist Publishing House, 2002.

Besse, Joseph. *Modest Remarks upon the Bishop of London's Letter Concerning the Late Earthquakes By One of the People Called Quakers*. London: Printed for T. Howard, 1750.

Beveridge, William. *Private Thoughts. Part II. Private Thoughts Upon a Christian Life: or, Necessary Devotion for its Beginning and Progress Upon Earth, in Order to its Final Perfection in the Beatific Vision*. 11th ed. London: T. Longman, 1724.

Bingham, Joseph. *Origines Ecclesiasticae: Or, The Antiquities of the Christian Church. In Twenty Book in The Works of the Learned Joseph Bingham, M. A. Later Rector of Havant, and Sometime Fellow of University-*

College in Oxford. 2nd ed. 2 vols. London: Printed for Robert Knaplock, 1726.

Boston, Thomas. *Human Nature in its Fourfold State of Primitive Integrity Subsisting in the PARENTS of Mankind in Paradise, ENTIRE DEPRAVATION Subsisting in the Unregenerate, BEGUN RECOVERY Subsisting in the Regenerate, and CONSUMMATE HAPPINESS or MISERY Subsisting in All Mankind in the Future State in SEVERAL PRACTICAL DISCOURSES*. 4th ed. Edinburgh: R. Drummond and Company, 1744.

Boswell, James. *The Life of Samuel Johnson*. 1793. Reprint, London: Everyman's Library, 1992.

Boyle, Robert. *Some Considerations Touching the Usefulness of Experimental Natural Philosophy. Proposed in a familiar DISCOURSE to a FRIEND, by Way of Invitation to the Study of It* in *The Works of the Honourable Robert Boyle*. 6 vols. London: Printed for J. and F. Rivington, et. al., 1744.

Browne, Peter. *The Procedure, Extent, and Limits of Human Understanding*. London: Printed by James Bettenham, 1728.

_____. *Things Divine and Supernatural Conceived By Analogy with Things Natural and Human*. 1733. Reprint, Bristol: Thoemmes Antiquarian Books Ltd., 1990.

Buffon, Georges Louis Leclerc. *Histoire Naturelle*. 44 vols. Paris: De l' Imprimerie Royal, 1749-66.

Bull, George. *Some Important Points of Primitive Christianity Maintained and Defended; in Several Sermons and Other Discourses*. 2 vols. London: n.p., 1713.

Bunting, Jabez. *The Early Correspondence of Jabez Bunting, 1820-1829*. Edited by W. R. Ward. London: Offices of the Royal Historical Society, 1972.

_____. *Early Victorian Methodism: The Correspondence of Jabez Bunting 1830-1858*. Edited by W. R. Ward. Oxford: Oxford University Press, 1976.

Bunting, Thomas. *The Life of Jabez Bunting, D. D., with Notices of Contemporary Persons and Events*. 2 vols. New York: Harper & Brothers, Publishers, 1859.

Bunyan, John. *The Pilgrim's Progress: from this World to that which is to come: Delivered under the Similitude of a Dream, wherein is Discovered the manner of his Setting out his Dangerous Journey, and Safe Arrival at the Desired Countrey*. London: Printed for Nathan Ponder, 1678.

Burnet, Thomas. *The Sacred Theory of the Earth: Containing an Account of the Original of the Earth, and of all the General Changes which it hath Already Undergone, or is to Undergo, till the Consummation of all Things with a Review of the Theory, and of its Proofs; Especially in Reference to Scripture and The Author's Defence of the Work, from the Exceptions of Mr. Warren & An Ode to the Author Mr. Addison*. 4th ed. 2 vols. London: Printed for John Hooke, 1719.

Bury, Arthur. *The Constant Communicant*. London: n.p., 1681.

Butler, Joseph. *The Analogy of Religion, Natural and Revealed, to the Constitution and Course of Nature*. London: Printed for James, John, and Paul Knapton, 1736.

Calvin, John. *Institutes of the Christian Religion*. Translated by Ford Lewis Battles. Edited by John McNeill. 2 vols. Philadelphia, PA: The Westminster Press, 1960.

Campbell, George. *A Dissertation on Miracles: Containing an Examination of the Principles Advanced by David Hume, Esq; in an Essay on Miracles*. Philadelphia, PA: Printed by Thomas Dobson at the Stone House, 1790.

Cartwright, Peter. *Autobiography of Peter Cartwright*. 1856. Reprint, Nashville, TN: Abingdon Press, 1984.

Cave, William. *Primitive Christianity: Or, The Religion of the Ancient Christians in the First Ages Of the Gospel. In Three Parts*. 3 vols. London: Printed for Richard Chiswell, 1673.

Cayley, Cornelius. *The Riches of God's Free Grace, Display'd in the Conversion of Cornelius Cayley. Late Clerk in the Princess Dowager of Wale's Treasury. To the Faith of Jesus Christ, his Lord and God. Being a Faithful Account of the Lord's Remarkable Dealings with him from Seven Years of Age; the Trials and Temptations He Met with in a Course of Several Years. As also how He hath met called to Preach the Glorious Gospel of Jesus Christ; and what he hath met with Particular in the Exercise thereof, in many Parts of England and Wales*. Norwich: n.p., 1757.

Cennick, John. "*An Account of the Most Remarkable Occurrences in the Awakenings at Bristol and Kingswood till the Brethern's Labours Began There in 1746: Written by John Cennick in April, 1750, for the Archives of Bristol and Kingswood*." *Proceedings of the Wesley Historical Society* 6 (1907): 101-10.

———. *The Beatific Vision; or, Beholding Jesus Crucified. Being the Substance of a Discourse Preached in Ballymenagh, in Ireland, in the Year 1755*. 3rd ed. London: Printed by H. Trapp, 1786.

Chambers, Ephraim. *CYCLOPAEDIA: OR, and UNIVERSAL DICTIONARY of ARTS AND SCIENCES; Containing An Explication of the Terms, and an Account of the Things Signified Thereby, in the SEVERAL ARTS, BOTH LIBERAL AND MECHANICAL; And the SEVERAL SCIENCES, HUMAN AND DIVINE: The Figures, Kinds, Properties, Productions, Preparations, and Uses of Things Natural and Artificial: The Rise, Progress, and State of Things ECCLESIASTICAL, CIVIL, MILITARY, AND COMMERCIAL: With the Several Systems, Sects, Opinions, &c. among PHILOSOPHERS, DIVINES, MATHEMATICIANS, PHYSICIANS, ANTIQUARIES, CRITICS, &c. in Several Languages*. 2nd ed. 2 vols. London: Printed for D. Midwinter, 1738.

Chauncy, Charles. *The Opinion of One Who Has Perused the Summer Morning's Conversation*. Boston, MA: Printed by Green and Russell, 1758.

Cheyne, George. *An Essay of Health and Long Life*, 4th ed. Dublin: Printed for George Ewing, 1725.

_____. The *Natural Method of Curing the Diseases of the Body, and the Disorders of the Mind Depending on the Body*. London: Printed for George Strahan and George and Paul Knapton, 1742.

_____. *The Philosophical Principles of Religion, Natural and Revealed*. 2 vols. London: Printed for George Strahan, 1715.

Chilcote, Paul Wesley, ed. *Her Own Story: Autobiographical Portraits of Early Methodist Women*. Nashville, TN: Kingswood Books, 2001.

Chubb, Thomas. *A Discourse on Miracles Considered as Evidence to Prove the Divine Original of Revelation wherein is Shewn, what Kind and Degree of Evidence arises from them, and in which the Various Reasons on Those Questions that Relate to the Subject are Fairly Represented*. London: Printed for T. Cox, 1741.

Church, Thomas. *Remarks on the Reverend Mr. Wesley's Last Journal in a Letter*. London: Printed for M. Cooper, 1745.

Clark, Peter. *Scripture-Doctrine of Original Sin Stated and Defended. A Summer Morning's Conversation between a Minister and a Neighbor, a Reply to a Winter Evening's Conversation*. Boston, MA: Printed by S. Kneeland, 1758.

Clarke, Adam, ed. *Memoirs of the Wesley Family; Collected Principally from Original Documents*. London: Printed by J. and T. Clarke, 1823.

Clarke, Samuel. *A Demonstration of the Being and Attributes of God and Other Writings*. 4th ed. 1738. Reprint, edited by Ezio Vaillati. Cambridge: Cambridge University Press, 1998.

_____. *A Discourse Concerning the Unchangeable Obligations of Natural Religion and the Truth and Certainty of the Christian Religion*. In *A Demonstration of the Being and Attributes of God and Other Writings*, edited by Ezio Vaillati, 147-50. Cambridge: Cambridge University Press, 1998.

_____. *The Works of the Honourable Samuel Clarke*. 4 vols. London: Printed for John and Paul Knapton, 1738.

Cooke, John. *The Preacher's Assistant, (after the manner of Mr. Letsome) containing a Series of Texts of Sermons and Discourses Published Singly, or in Volumes, By Divines of the Church of England, and by the Dissenting Clergy, since the Reformation to the Present Time, Specifying Also the Several Authors Alphabetically Arranged Under Text—With Size, Date, Occasion or Subject-Matter of Each Sermon or Discourse*. 2 vols. Oxford: Printed for John Cooke at the Clarendon Press, 1783.

Cooper, Anthony Ashley. *Characteristics of Men, Manners, Opinions, Times*. Edited by Lawrence E. Klein. 1700. Reprint, Cambridge: Cambridge University Press, 1999.

Crosby, Sarah. *The Diaries of Sarah Crosby*. In *Her Own Story: Autobiographical Portraits of Early Methodist Women*, edited by Paul Wesley Chilcote, 78-84. Nashville, TN:: Kingswood Books, 2001.

D'Alembert, Jean Le Rond and Dennis Diderot, eds. *Encyclopedie, ou, Diction-naire raisonne des Sciences, des Arts, et des metiers, mis en ordre, par une Societe De Gens De Lettres*. 17 vols. Paris: Antoine-Claude Brias-son, 1751-80.

Deacon, Thomas. *A Compleate Collection of Devotions both Publick and Pri-vate: Taken from the Apostolical Constitutions, the Ancient Liturgies, and Common Prayer Book of the Church of England*, 2 vols. London: n.p., 1734.

_____. *A Full, True, and Comprehensive View of Christianity: Containing a Short Historical Account of Religion from the Creation of the World to the Fourth Century After our Lord Jesus Christ. As also the Complete Duty of a Christian in Relation to Faith, Practice, Worship, and Ritu-als, set forth Sincerely, without Regard to any Modern Church, Sect, or Party, as it is taught in the Holy Scriptures, was delivered by the Apos-tles, and received by the Universal Church of Christ during the Four First Centuries. The Whole Succinctly and Fully Laid Down in Two Catechisms, A Shorter and a Longer, each Divided Into Two Parts; Down in Two Catechisms. A Shorter and a Longer, each Divided Into Two Parts; Whereof the one Comprehends the Sacred History, the oth-er The Christian Doctrine. The Shorter Catechism being suited to the meanest Capacity, and calculated for the Use of Children; And the Longer for that of The More Knowing Christian to which is Prefixed A Discourse upon the Design of these Catechisms, and upon the Best Method of Instructing Youth in Them*. London: Printed for S. Newton, 1747.

Defoe, Daniel. *The Storm: Or, A Collection of the Most Remarkable Casualities and Disasters which Happen'd in the Late Dreadful Tempest, Both by Sea and Land*. London: Printed for G. Sawbridge, 1704.

Derham, William, *Astro-Theology: or a Demonstration of the Being and Attrib-utes of God, from a Survey of the Heavens. Illustrated with Copper-Plates*. London: Printed for W. Innys, 1715.

_____. *Physico-Theology: or, a Demonstration of the Being and Attributes of God, from His Work of Creation: Being the Substance of XVI Sermons*. London: Printed for W. Innys, 1713.

Descartes, René. *Olymica*. In *Oeuvres de Descartes,* edited by C. Adam and P. Tannery, 10: 180-88. Nouvelle Edition, 11 vols. Paris: J. Vrin, 1996.

Ditton, Humphrey. *A Discourse Concerning the Resurrection of Jesus Christ. In Three Parts. Wherein I. The Consequences of the Doctrine are Stated Hypothetically. II. The Nature and Obligation of Moral Evidence, are Explain'd at large. III. The Proofs of the Fact of our Saviour's Resur-rection are Propos'd, Examin'd, and fairly Demonstrated to be Con-clusive. Together with an Appendix concerning the Impossible Produc-tion of Thought, from Matter and Motion: The Nature of Human Souls, and of Brutes: The Animal Mundi, and the Hypothesis of the TO ΠAN; as also, concerning Divine Providence, the Origin of Evil, and the Uni-verse in General. 2ⁿᵈ ed.* London: Printed by J. Darby, 1714.

Doddridge, Philip. *The Works of the Rev. Philip Doddridge.* Edited by Job Orton and Edward Williams. 10 vols. Leeds: n.p., 1802-05.

Dodge, Nathaniel. *God's Voice in the Earthquake, or, a Serious Admonition to a Sinful World. A Sermon Preached in the Parish Church of Sheffield, on Sunday December 7, 1755.* York: Printed by Caesar Ward for the Author, 1756.

Easterbrook, Joseph. *An Appeal to the Public Respecting George Lukins (Called the Yatton Demoniac,) Containing an Account of His Affliction and Deliverance; Together with A Variety of Circumstances which Tend to Exculpate him from the Charge of Imposture.* Bristol: Printed for T. Mills, 1788.

Edwards, Jonathan. *A Faithful Narrative of the Surprising Work of God in the Conversion of many hundred Souls in Northhampton, and the Neighboring Towns and Villages of New-Hampshire in New England.* London: Printed for John Oswald, 1737.

———. *The Great Christian Doctrine of Original Sin Defended; Evidences of it's Truth Produced, and Arguments to the Contrary Answered. Containing, in Particular, A reply to the Objections and Arguings of Dr. JOHN TAYLOR, In his Book, Intitled, "The Scripture-Doctrine of Original Sin proposed to, Free and candid Examination, &c.* In *The Works of Jonathan Edwards*, edited by Clyde Holbrooke, 3:103-444. New Haven: Yale University Press, 1970.

———. *Some Thoughts Concerning the Present Revival in New England.* Boston, MA: Printed by S. Kneeland and T. Green, 1743.

Eliot, George. *Adam Bede.* Edited with an introduction and notes by Valentine Cunningham. 1859. Reprint, Oxford: Oxford University Press, 2000.

Erasmus, Desiderius. *Praise of Folly.* Translated by Betty Radice. 1511. Reprint, London: Penguin, 1993.

Erskine, John. *The Signs of the Times Considered, or the high Probability that the Present Appearances in New England, and the West of Scotland, are a Prelude of the Glorious Things Promised to the Church in the Latter Ages.* Edinburgh: Printed by T. Lumisden and J. Robertson, 1742.

Farmer, Hugh. *An Essay on Daemonics in the New Testament.* London: Printed for G. Robinson, 1775.

Fell, John. *Daemonics. An Enquiry into the Heathen and the Scripture Doctrine of Daemons. In Which the Hypothesis of the Rev. Mr. Farmer, and Others on this Subject are Particularly Considered.* London: Printed for Charles Dilly, 1779.

Fieser, James, ed. *Early Responses to Hume*, 2nd rev. ed. 10 vols. Bristol: Thoemmes Press, 1999-2003.

Fletcher, John. *The Works of John Fletcher.* 4 vols. 1825. Reprint, Salem, OH: Schmul Publishers, 1974.

Fletcher, Mary. *The Life of Mrs. Mary Fletcher Consort and Relict of the Rev. John Fletcher Vicar of Madeley, Salop. Compiled from Her Journal, and Other Authentic Documents*. Edited by Henry Moore. 1817. Reprint, Salem, OH: Schmul Publishers, 1997.

Flores, Daniel and Thelma Herrera-Flores. "Two Remarkable Stories: Lost Entries of John Wesley's Journals." *Methodist History* 38 (2000): 251-57.

Franklin, Benjamin. *Experiments and Observations on Electricity, Made at Philadelphia in America by Mr. Benjamin Franklin, and Communicated in Several Letters to Mr. Collinson, of London, F.R.S*. London: Printed by E. Cave, 1751.

Freke, John. *An Essay to Shew the Cause of Electricity*. London: Printed for W. Innys, 1746.

Garrettson, Freeborn. *The Experience and Travels of Freeborn Garrettson, Minister of the Methodist-Episcopal Church in North America*. Philadelphia, PA: n.p., n.d. Reprint, Dublin: R. Jackson, 1778.

Gilbert, Jeremiah. "On Camp-Meetings, &c in 1821." *A Methodist Magazine for the Year 1821* 4 (1822): 8-10.

Glanvill, Joseph. *Saducismus Triumphatus: or, Full and Plain Evidence Concerning Witches and Apparitions. In Two Parts. The First Treating of their Possibility, The Second of their Real Existence*. London: Printed for J. Collins and S. Lownds, 1681.

_____. *Scepsis Scientifica: or, Confest Ignorance, the Way to Science; in an Essay of the Vanity of Dogmatizing, and Confident Opinion*. London: Printed by E. Cotes, 1665.

[Glover, Richard]. *A Serious Expostulation with the Right Reverend the Lord Bishop of London on his Letter to the Clergy and People of London and Westminster*. London: n.p., 1750.

Goldsmith, Oliver. *The Mystery Revealed: Containing a Series of Transactions and Authentic Testimonials, Respecting the Supposed Cock-Lane Ghost; Which have hitherto been Concealed from the Public*. London: Printed for W. Bristow, 1762.

Hammond, William. *Medulla Ecclesiae. The Doctrine of Original Sin, Justification by Faith, and The Holy Spirit, Fairly Stated and Clearly Demonstrated from the Homilies, Articles and Liturgies of the Church of England. Confirmed by Apostolic Texts of Scripture, with Proper Reflexiones, Inferences and Instructions Annexed to each Head. Being the Substance of Several Discourses Preached in Cambridge*. London: Printed for J. Oswald, 1744.

Hartley, David. *Observations on Man, His Frame, His Duty, and His Expectations*. 2nd ed. 2 vols. London: Printed by Richard Cutwell, 1791.

Haw, James. *An extract of a Letter from James Haw, Elder of the Methodist Episcopal Church in America, to Bishop Asbury: Written from Cumberland near Kentucke, about the Beginning of the year 1789*. In *The Arminian Magazine: Consisting of Extracts and Original Treastises on Universal Redemption*, ed., John Wesley, 13: 200-03. London: J. Fry and Company,1790.

Hawes, William. *An Examination of Mr. John Wesley's Primitive Physic*, 2nd ed. London: Printed for the Author, 1780.

Herring, Thomas. *Letters from The Late Most Reverend Dr. Thomas Herring, Lord Archbishop of Canterbury to William Duncombe, Esq., Deceased, from the Year 1728 to 1757. With Notes and an Appendix*. London: Printed for J. Johnson, 1777.

Hoadley, Benjamin, junior. *Observation on a Series of Electrical Experiments by Dr. Hoadley and Mr. Wilson*. London: Printed for T. Payne, 1756.

Hull, Samuel. *The Fluctuating Condition of Human Life, and the Absolute Necessity of a Preparation for the Eternal World, Condiser'd, in a Sermon Occasioned by the Late Shocks of Earthquake, Preached at Lorriners Hall, March 11, 1750: Humbly Recommended to the Serious Perusal of the Inhabitants of London and Westminster*. London: Printed for J. Fuller, 1750.

Hume, David. *An Enquiry Concerning Human Understanding*. 1748. Chicago, IL: Encyclopaedia Brittanica, 1952.

Hutchinson, Francis. *An Historical Essay Concerning Witchcraft. With Observations Upon Matters of Fact; Tending to Clear the Texts of the Sacred Scriptures, and Confute the Vulgar Errors About That Point. And Also Two Sermons: One in Proof of the Christian Religion; The Other Concerning the Good and Evil Angels*. London: Printed for R. Knaplock and D. Midwinter, 1718.

Jackson, Thomas, ed. *The Lives of Early Methodist Preachers*. 6 vols. London: Wesleyan Conference Office, 1865-66.

_____. *Wesley's Veterans: Lives of Early Methodist Preachers Told by Themselves*. Additions and Annotations by John Telford. 7 vols. 1909-14. Reprint, Salem, OH: Schmul Publishers, n. d.

James VI and I. *Daemonologie in the Form of a Dialogue Divided into Three Books*. Edinburgh: Robert Waldegrave, 1597.

Jennings, David. *A Vindication of the Scripture-Doctrine of Original Sin, From Mr TAYLOR's Free and Candid Examination of it*. London: John Oswald, 1740.

Jolley, Thomas. *The Surrey Demoniack: or, an Account of Satan's Strange and Dreadful Actings in and about the Body of Richard Dugdale of Surrey, near Whalley in Lancashire: And how he was Dispossest By Gods Blessing on the Fastings and Prayers of Divers Ministers and People. The Matter of Fact Attested by the Oaths of Several Credible Persons, Before Some of His Majesties Justices of the Peace in the Said County*. London: Printed for Jonathan Robinson, 1697.

Justin Martyr. *First Apology*. In *Ante-Nicene Fathers*, eds., Alexander Roberts and James Donaldson, 1: 159-87. Rev. ed. 10 vols. 1885; Reprint, Peabody, MA: Hendrickson Publishers, 1994.

Kant, Immanuel. *Religion within the Boundaries of Mere Reason*. In *Religion and Rational Theology*, Translated by Allen W. Wood and George Di Giovanni, 39-215. Cambridge: Cambridge University Press, 1996.

Keill, John. *An Examination of Dr. Burnet's Theory of the Earth. Together with some Remarks on Mr. Whiston's New Theory of the Earth*. London: Printed at the Theatre, 1698.

Lactantius. *A Treatise on the Anger of God.* In *Ante-Nicene Fathers*, edited by Alexander Roberts and James Donaldson, 7: 259-80. 1886. Reprint, Peabody, MA: Hendrickson Publishers, 1994.

Lardner, Nathaniel. *The Case of Demoniacs Mentioned in the New Testament: Four Discourses upon Mark v. 19. With an Appendix for Farther Illustrating the Subject.* London: Printed for C. Henderson, 1758.

Lavington, George. *The Enthusiasm of Methodists and Papists Compar'd*, 3 vols. London: Printed for J. and P. Knapton, 1749.

Letsome, Sampson. *The Preacher's Assistant, containing a Series of Texts of Sermons and Discourses Published Singly, or in Volumes, By Divines of the Church of England, and by the Dissenting Clergy, since the Reformation to the Present Time, Specifying Also the Several Authors Alphabetically Arranged Under Text—With Size, Date, Occasion or Subject-Matter of Each Sermon or Discourse.* 2 vols. Oxford: Printed for John Cooke at the Clarendon Press, 1783.

Lindsey, Theophilus. *Sermons, with Appropriate Prayers Annexed.* 2 vols. London: Joseph Johnson & Co., 1810.

Locke, John. *An Essay Concerning Human Understanding.* Edited by Peter H. Nidditch. 1689. Reprint, Oxford: Clarendon Press, 1975.

_____. *Essays on the Law of Nature and Associated Writings.* Edited by W. von Leyden. 1664. Reprint, Oxford: Clarendon Press, 2002.

_____. *The Reasonableness of Christianity as Delivered in the Scriptures.* Edited by John Higgins-Biddle. 1695. Reprint, Oxford: Clarendon Press, 1999.

Lovett, Richard. *An Appendix on Electricity rendered Useful in Medical Intentions.* London: n.p., 1760.

_____. *The Electrical Philosopher, containing a new System of Physics founded upon the Principle of an Universal Plenum of Elementary Fire.* Worchester: Printed for the author and R. Lewis, 1774.

_____. *The Subtle Medium prov'd . . . Qualities Ascribed to Aether or Elementary Fire of the Ancient Philosophers are to found in Electrical Fire.* London: Printed for J. Hinton, W. Sandby, and R. Lovett, 1756.

Luther, Martin. *Letters of Spiritual Counsel.* Translated and Edited by Theodore Tappert. Louisville: Westminster John Knox Press, 1955.

_____. *A Methodicall Preface Prefixed before the Epistle of S. Paul to the Romanes, Very Necessary and Profitable for the Better Understanding of it. Made by the Right Reverend Father and Faithful Servant of Christ Jesus, Martin Luther, Now Newly Translated out of Latin into English by William Wilkenson.* London: n.p., 1594.

Lyndwood, William. *Constitutiones Provinciales.* Oxoniae: Excudebat: H. Hall et. al., 1679.

Macfarquhar, Colin and George Gleig, eds. *Encyclopædia Britannica: or, A Dictionary of Arts and Sciences, Compiled upon a New Plan.* 3rd ed. 18 vols. London: Colin Macfarquhar and George Gleig, 1788-97.

MacKay, Charles. *Extraordinary Popular Delusions and the Madness of Crowds.* 1841. Reprint, New York: Barnes & Noble, 2004.

Malebranche, Nicholas. *Father Malebranche's Treatise Concerning The Search After Truth. The Whole Work Compleate. To Which is Added The Author's Treatise of Nature and Grace. Being a Consequence of the Principles Contain'd in the Search: Together with His Answer to the Animadversions Upon the First Volume: His Defence Against the Accusations of Mr. De La Ville, &c. Relating to the Same Subject*, trans. Richard Sault. London: John Dunton & Steve Manship, 1694.

Martin, Benjamin. *Essay on Electricity: Being an Enquiry into the Nature, Cause and Properties thereof, on the Principle of Sir Isaac Newton's Theory of Vibrating Motion, Light, and Fire; and the Various Phaenomena of Fourty-Two Capital Experiments*. Bath: Printed for the author and et. al., 1746.

Mather, Cotton. *The Christian Philosopher: A Collection of the Best Discoveries of Nature*. London: Printed for Emmanuel Matthews, 1721.

Maxfield, Thomas. *A Vindication of the Rev. Mr. Maxfield's Conduct, In Not Continuing with the Rev. Mr. John Wesley: And of His Behavious Since That Time. With an Introductory Letter, to the Rev. George Whitefield*. London: Printed and Sold by J. Keith, 1767.

Middleton, Conyers, *A Free Inquiry into the Miraculous Powers, which are Supposed to have Subsisted in the Christian Church, from the Earliest Ages through Several Successive Centuries. By Which is Shewn, that we have no Sufficient Reason to believe, upon the Authority of the Primitive Fathers, that any such Powers were Continued to the Church, after the Days of the Apostles*. London: Printed for R. Manby and H. S. Cox, 1749.

_____. *An Introductory Discourse to a Larger Work, Designed Hereafter to be Published, Concerning the Miraculous Powers which are Supposed to have subsisted in the CHRISTIAN CHURCH, from the earliest Ages, through Several Successive Centuries: Tending to Shew, that we have no Sufficient Reason to Believe, upon the Authority of the PRIMITIVE FATHERS, that any such Power were Continued to the CHURCH, after the Days of the Apostles. With a POSTSCRIPT, Containing Some REMARKS on an Archidiaconal Charge. Delivered the last Summer by the Rev. Dr. Chapman, to the Clergy of the Archdeaconery of Sudbury*. London: Printed for R. Manby and H. S. Cox, 1747.

Milton, John. *Paradise Lost*. In *The Riverside Milton*, ed., Roy Flannagan. Boston, MA: Houghton Mifflin Company, 1998.

Montegeron, Carré de. *La Vérité des Miracles Opérés par l'intercession de M. de Paris et autres appellans démontré*. Paris: Chez les Libraires de la Compagnie, 1737.

Naylor, M. J. *The Inantity and Mischief of Vulgar Superstitions. Four Sermons Preached at All-Saints Church, Huntigdon, On the 25th Day of March, in the Years 1792, 1793, 1794, 1795*. Cambridge: Printed for B. Flower, 1795.

Nelson, Robert. *Companion for the Festivals and Fasts of the Church of England*. London: W. Boyer, 1705.

Newton, Isaac. *Isaac Newton: Theological Manuscripts*. Edited by H. McLachlan. Liverpool: Liverpool University Press, 1950.

_____. *Observations on the Prophecies of Daniel and the Apocalypse of St.
John*. London: Printed by J. Darby and T. Browne, 1733.

Niewentyt, Bernhard. *The Religious Philosopher: or, the Right Use of the Contemplation of the World*. Translated by J. Chamberlayne. 3 vols. London: n. p., 1718-19.

Norman, Samuel. *Authentic Anecdotes of George Lukins, The Yatton Demoniac;
with a View of the Controversy, and a Full Refutation of the Imposture*.
Bristol: Printed by G. Routh, 1788.

Outler, Albert, ed. *John Wesley*. 1964. Reprint, New York: Oxford University
Press, 1980.

Pawson, John. *A Short Account of the Lord's Gracious Dealings with J. Pawson*.
Leeds: Edward Baines, 1801.

Pearson, John. *An Exposition of the Creed*, rev. ed. 1691; Reprint, New York:
D. Appleton and Company, 1880.

Peter of Spain (Pope John XXI). *Summa Logicales*. Edited by J. P. Mullaly.
Publications in Medieval Studies 8 (1945): 133-58.

Pratt, Joseph, ed. *Eclectic Notes; or, Notes of Discussions on Religious Topics at
the Meetings of The Eclectic Society, London. During the Years 1798-
1814*. 2nd ed. London: James Nibet, 1865.

_____. *Forty Family Sermons*. London: J. Hatchard and Son, 1830.

Priestley, Joseph. *History and Present State of Electricity with Original Experiments*. 2nd ed. London: Printed for J. Dodsley, J. Johnson, J. Payne, and
R. Lewis, 1769.

Priestly, Joseph, ed. *Original Letters by The Rev. John Wesley, and His Friends,
Illustrative of His Early History, with Other Curious Papers Communicated by The late Rev. S. Badcock. To Which is Prefixed, an Address to
the Methodists*. Birmingham: Printed for Thomas Pearson, 1791.

R. Y. "Account of the Garden of EDEN by the Author of the Account of the Old
World," *Gentleman's Magazine* 8 (1738): 66-69.

Ray, John. *The Wisdom of God in the Works of Creation: in Two Parts, viz.,
Manifested in the Hevenly Bodies, Elements, Metors*, 3rd ed. London:
Printed for Sam Smith and Benjamin Walford, 1701.

Russell, Chloe. *The Complete Fortune Teller and Dream Book*. Boston, MA:
n. p., 1800.

Sanderson, Robert. *Logicae Artis Compendium*, 2nd ed. Oxford: Excudebant
Iohannes Lichfield & Iacobus Short, 1618.

Sault, Richard. *The Second Spira, being a Fearful Example of an Atheist, who
had Apostatised from the Christian Religion, and Died in Despair at
Westminister, Dec., 8, 1692*. London: Printed for John Dunton, 1693.

Scott, Reginald. *The Discourie of Wichcraft, Wherein the Lewde Dealing of
Witches and Witchmongers is Notablie Detected, the Knauerie of Coniurors, the Impietie of Inchantors, the Folliw of Soothsayers, the Impudent Falsehood of Cousenors, the Infidelitie of Atheists, the Pestilent
Practises of Pythonists, the Curiositie of Figurecasters, the Vanitie of*

Dreamers, the Geggerlie Art of Alcumysterie, The Abhomination of Idolatrie, the Horrible Art of Poisoning, the Virtue and Power of Naturall Magike, and all the Conueiances of Legierdemaine and Iuggling are Deciphered: and many other Things Opened, which haue Long Lien Hidden, howbeit Verie Necessarie to be Knowne. Heereunto is Added a not be Doubted of; who instead of Learning and Treatise upon the Nature and Substance of Spirits and Diuels, &c. 1584. Reprint, London: Elliott Stock, 1886.

Sherlock, Thomas. *A Letter from the Lord Bishop of London, to the Clergy and People of London and Westminster, on Occasion of the Late Earthquakes.* London: Printed for John Whiston, 1750.

Spener, Jacob. *On Hindrances to Theological Studies.* In *Pietists: Selected Writings.* Edited by Peter Erb, 65-70. New York: Paulist Press, 1983.

Sprat, Thomas. *The History of the Royal-Society of London, for the Improving of Natural Knowledge.* London: Printed by Thomas Roycrof, 1667.

Sprenger, Jacobus, and Heinrich Kramer. *The Malleus Maleficarum of Heinrich Kramer and James Sprenger.* Translated with an introduction, bibliography and notes by Rev'd Montague Summers. 1928. Reprint, New York: Dover Publications, Inc., 1971.

Squire, Mr. "The Case of Henry Axford, who recovered the use of his tongue, after having been four years dumb, by means of a frightful dream." *The Royal Society of London Philosophical Transactions General Index for Volumes 1-70 (1665-1780),* 143. 1787. Reprint. New York: Johnson Reprint Corp., 1963. 142.

Stukeley, William. *The Philosophy of Earthquakes, Natural and Religious. Or An Inquiry into their Causes, and their Purpose.* London: Printed for C. Corbet, 1750.

[De Sulamar (The Arch Teacher), John Baptist Malaiss]. *A Short Examen of Mr. John Wesley's System, as it Appears in his Publick Proposals Concerning THE DOCTRINE of Original Sin; or The Doctrine of Original Sin Examined at the Living Light of The Doctrine of Truth, In a Letter Publickly Directed to Mr. John Wesley, by John-Baptist, The Arch-Teacher.* London: J. Marshall, 1757.

Swift, Jonathan. *The Story of the St. Alb-ns Ghost, or the Apparition of Mother Haggy.* London: n. p., 1712.

Taft, Mary. *Memoirs of the Life of Mrs. Mary Taft: Formerly Miss Baritt. Compiled from her Journals, and Other Authentic Documents,* 2nd ed. 2 vols. Devon: S. Thorpe, 1831.

Taylor, Jeremy. *Rule of Exercises of Holy Living: The Means and Instruments of Obtaining Every Virtue, and the Remedies against Every Vice, and Considerations Serving to the Resisting All Temptations, Together with Prayers Containing the Whole Duty of a Christian.* London: Printed for John Meredith and J. Heptnsoll, 1650.

Taylor, John. *The Scripture-Doctrine of Original Sin Proposed to Free and Candid Examination.* 2nd ed. London: Printed and Sold by M. Fenner, 1741.

Tertullian, Quintus Septimius Florens. *A Treatise on the Soul.* In *Ante-Nicene Fathers.* Eds., Alexander Roberts and James Donaldson, 3: 181-235. rev. edn., 10 vols. 1885. Reprint, Peabody, MA: Hendrickson, 1994.

Tillotson, John. *The Works of Dr. John Tillotson, Lord Archbishop of Canterbury.* 3 vols. London: Printed for J. and R. Tonson, et. al., 1752.

Tindal, Matthew. *Christianity as Old as the Creation: or, The Gospel, A Republication of the Religion of Nature.* London: T. Warner, 1730.

Toland, John. *Christianity Not Mysterious.* London: Printed for Sam Buckley, 1696.

Tucker, Josiah. *A Brief History of the Principles of Methodism, wherein the Rise and Progress, together with the causes of several variations, divisions, and present inconsistencies of this sect are attempted to be traced out, and accounted for* Oxford: James Fletcher, 1742.

Tyron, Thomas. *A Treatise of Dreams & Visions, Wherein the Causes Natures and Uses of Nocturnal Representations, and the Communications both of Good and Evil Angels as also Departed Souls, in Mankinde, are Theosophically Unfolded, that is, According to the Word of God, and the Harmony of Created Beings.* 2nd ed. London: n. p., 1700.

de Voragine, Jacobus. *The Golden Legend: Readings on the Saints.* Translated by William Granger Ryan. 2 vols. Princeton: Princeton University Press, 1993.

Walpole, Horace. *The Letters of Horace Walpole 4th Earl of Orford* [sic]. Edited by Peter Cunningham. 9 vols. Edinburgh: John Grant, 1906.

Warburton, William. *The Doctrine of Grace: or, The Office and Operations of the Holy Spirit Vindicated From The Insults of Infidelity, and The Abuses of Fanaticism: with Some Thoughts (humbly offered to the consideration of the Established Clergy) Regarding The Right Method Defending Religion Against The Attacks of Either Party. In Three Books.* 3rd ed. London: Printed for A. Millar & T. and R. Ronson, 1763.

Watts, Isaac. *The Ruin and Recovery of MANKIND: Or An ATTEMPT to Vindicate the SCRIPTURAL ACCOUNT of these Great Events upon the Plain Principles of Reason. With an ANSWER to VARIOUS DIFFICULTIES, Relating to ORIGINAL SIN, The Universal DEPRAVATION of NATURE, And the Overspreading CURSE of DEATH; General OFFERS of GRACE to All Men, And the CERTAIN SALVATION of some; The CASE of the HEATHEN NATIONS, And the State of DYING INFANTS. Whereto Are Subjoin'd, THREE SHORT ESSAYS, viz. The Proof of MAN'S Fall By his Misery; The Imputation of Sin and Righteousness; and The Guilt and Defilement of Sin. With a POSTSCRIPT.* 2nd ed. London: Printed for James Brackstone,1742.

Webster, Samuel. *A Winter's Evening's Conversation upon the Doctrine of Original Sin . . . Wherein the Notion of Our Having Sinned in Adam and Being on That Account Only Liable to Eternal Damnation, Is Proved To Be Unscriptural, Emotional, and of Dangerous Tendency.* Boston, MA: Printed and Sold by Green and Russell, 1757.

Wesley, Charles. *The Journal of the Rev. Charles Wesley, M. A. Sometime Student of Christ Church, Oxford. To Which are Appended Selections From His Correspondance and Poetry.* 2 vols. London: Wesleyan Methodist Book Room, 1811.

_____. *The Poetical Works of John and Charles Wesley.* Edited by George Osbourn. 13 vols. London: Wesleyan Methodist Conference Room, 1868-72.

_____. *The Sermons of Charles Wesley: A Critical Edition with Introduction and Notes.* Edited by Kenneth G. C. Newport. Oxford: Oxford University Press, 2002.

_____. Letter to an Unknown Correspondent on April 25, 1754. In *Apocalypse and Millenium: Studies in Biblical Eisegesis.* Edited by Kenneth G. C. Newport, 144-49. Cambridge: Cambridge University Press, 2000.

Wesley, John, ed. *The Arminian Magazine: Consisting of Extracts and Original Treastises on Universal Redemption.* 14 vols. London: J. Fry & Co., 1778-91.

_____. *The Bicentennial Works of John Wesley.* Eds. Richard Heitzenrater, et. al., 18 vols. Oxford and Nashville, TN: Clarendon Press and Abingdon Press, 1980- .

_____. *A Collection of Forms of Prayer For Every Day in the Week*, 3rd ed. London: William Strahan, 1738.

_____. *A Collection of Receipts for the Use of the Poor.* 3rd ed. Bristol: Felix Farley, 1746.

_____. *A Compendium of Logick.* Bristol: Felix Farley, 1750.

_____. ed. *A Concise Ecclesiastical History from the Birth of Christ to the Beginning of the Present Century.* London: J. Paramore, 1781.

_____. *The Desideraturm: or, Electricity made Plain and Useful.* London: W. Flexney, E. Cabe, George Clark, George Keith, T. Smith, 1760.

_____. *The Doctrine of Original Sin: According to Scripture, Reason, and Experience.* Bristol: Felix Farley, 1757.

_____. *The Doctrine of Salvation, Faith, and Good Works. Extracted from the Homilies of the Church of England.* London: Printed for James Hutton, 1739.

_____. *Explanatory Notes on the Old and New Testaments.*1765-66. Salem, OH: Schmul Publishers, 1975.

_____. *Farther Thoughts on Christian Perfection.* London: n. p., 1763.

_____. *The Journal of John Wesley.* Ed., Nehemiah Curnock. 8 vols. 1909. Reprint, London: Epworth Press, 1938.

_____. *On Justification by Faith Only, According to the Doctrine of the Eleventh Article of the Church of England.* London: Printed for James Hutton, 1739.

_____. *The Letters of the Rev. John Wesley, A. M.: Sometimes Fellow of Lincoln College, Oxford.* Edited by John Telford. 7 vols. 1931. Reprint, London: Epworth Press, 1960.

———. *The Nature, Design, and General Rules, of the United Societies, in London, Bristol, King's-wood, and Newcastle upon Tyne.* 3rd ed. Newcastle upon Tyne: Printed by Felix Farley, 1743.

———. *Primitive Physic: or, An Easy and Natural Method of Curing Most Diseases.* London: Thomas Trye, 1747.

———. *Serious Thoughts Occasioned by the Late Earthquake at Lisbon.* Bristol: E. Farley, 1755.

———. *A Survey of the Wisdom of God in the Creation: or A Compendium of Natural Philosophy.* 2 vols. Bristol: William Pine, 1763.

———. *Works of John Wesley.* 32 vols. Bristol: William Pine, 1771-74.

———. *The Works of John Wesley.* Edited by Thomas Jackson. 3rd ed. 14 vols. 1872. Reprint, in 7 vols. Grand Rapids, MI: Baker Books, 2007.

———. *The Works of John Wesley.* Edited by Thomas Jackson, 14 vols, CD-Rom Edition. Franklin, TN: Providence House Publishers, 1994.

Wesley, John and Charles Wesley, ed. *Hymns and Sacred Poems.* 3rd ed. London: William Strahan, 1739.

———. *Hymns on the Lord's Supper with a Preface Concerning The Christian Sacrament and Sacrifice Extracted from Doctor Brevint.* Bristol: Felix Farley, 1745.

Weyer, Johann. *Witches, Devils, and Doctors in the Renaissance: Johann Weyer, De Praestigiis Daemonum.* 1563. Reprint, Binghampton: Medieval & Renaissance Texts & Studies, 1991.

Whiston, William. *The Accomplishment of Scriptural Prophecies.* Cambridge: Printed at the University-Press for Benjamin Tooke, 1708.

———. *An Account of the Daemoniacks, and of the Power of Casting our Demons, Both in the New Testament, and in the Four First Centuries. Occasioned by a Late Pamphlet Intituled, An Enquiry into the Meaning of Daemonics in the New Testament. To which is added, An Appendix, concerning the Tythes and Oblations paid by Christians, during the same Four Centuries.* London: Printed for John Whiston, 1737.

———. *Essay on the Revelation of St. John, so far as concerns the Past and Present Times.* London: Printed for the Author, 1706.

———. *A New Theory of the Earth, From its Original, to the Consummation of all Things. Wherein The Creation of the World in Six Days, The Universal Deluge, and the General Conflagration, as laid down in the Holy Scriptures, are shewn to be perfectly agreeable to Reason and Philosophy. With a large Introductory Discourse Concerning the Genuine Nature, Stile, and Extent of the Mosaick History of the Creation.* London: 1696.

———. *The Eternity of Hell Torments Considered or, A Collection of Texts of Scripture, and Testimonies of the Three first Centuries relating to them. Together with Notes through the Whole, and Observations at the End.* London: Printed for John Whiston and Ben White, 1740.

———. *Mr. Whiston's Account of the Exact Time when Miraculous Gifts Ceas'd in the Church.* London: Printed for the Author, 1749.

Whitefield, George, *George Whitefield's Journals*. 1960. Reprint, Carlisle, PA: Banner of Truth Trust, 1992.

_____. *Whitefield at Lisbon. Being a Detailed Account of the Blasphemy and Idolatry of Popery, as Witnessed By the Late Servant of God, George Whitefield at the City of Lisbon, During His Stay There. Printed Verbatim From His Account Sent to a Friend. Also, A Narrative of the Commencement and Continuation of the Dreadful Earthquake that Totally Destroyed The Above City, with Sixty Thousand Inhabitants, A Few Months After Mr. Whitefield's Visit, on All-Saints Day, Being A Great Festival, and At a Time of High Mass Being Performed at All the Churches. Printed from an Account communicated by an English Merchant residing at that time in Lisbon. With Mr. Whitefield's Remarks Thereon.* London: R. Groombridge & Sons, 1851.

Wilson, Benjamin. *An Essay Towards an Explication of the Phaenomena of Electricity, Contained in Three Papers*. London: Printed for C. Davis and M. Cooper, 1747.

_____. *A Short View of Electricity*. London: C. Nourse, 1780.

Wollaston, William. *The Religion of Nature Delineated* (n. p.: n. p., 1722).

Woodward, John. *An Essay Toward A Natural History of the Earth: and Terrestrial Bodies, Especially Minerals: As Also of the Sea, Rivers, and Springs. With an Account of the Universal Deluge: And of the Effects that it had upon the Earth*. London: Printed for Richard Wilkin, 1695.

Woolman, John. *A Journal of the Life, Gospel Labours, and Christian Experiences of that Faithful Minister of Jesus Christ, John Woolman*. Philadelphia, PA: Printed by Joseph Crukshank, 1774.

Woolston, Thomas. *Discourse on the Miracles of Our Savior in View of the Present Controversy between Infidels and Apostates*. London: Printed for the Author, 1727.

Worthington, William. *An Farther Enquiry into the Case of the Gospel Demoniacks. Occasioned by Mr. Farmer's Letter on the Subject*. London: Printed for J. F. and C. Rivington, T. Payne, and Son, B. White, and H. Payne, 1779.

Warburton, William. *Sermon x: The Fall of Satan*. In *The Works of William Warburton*. 5: 415-35. London: Printed by John Nichols, 1788.

Y. R. "Account of the Garden of EDEN by the Author of the Account of the Old World." *Gentleman's Magazine* 8 (1738): 66-69.

Secondary Sources

Published Documents

Abelove, Henry. *The Evangelist of Desire: John Wesley and the Methodists*. Stanford, CA: Stanford University Press, 1990.

Adams, Marilyn McCord. *Christ and Horrors: The Coherence of Christology.* Cambridge: Cambridge University Press, 2006.

_____. *Horrendous Evils and the Goodness of God.* Ithaca, NY: Cornell University Press, 1999.

Adorno, Theodore W. and Max Horkheimer. *Dialectic of Enlightenment.* Translated by John Cumming. 1972. Reprint, London: Verso, 1999.

Althaus, Paul. *The Theology of Martin Luther.* Translated by Robert Schultz. Philadelphia, PA: Fortress Press, 1966.

Ammicht-Quinn, Regina, *Von Lissabon bis Auschwitz: Zum Paradigmawechsel in der Theodizeefrage.* Freiburg im Breisgau: Herder, 1992.

Andrews, Dee. *The Methodists and Revolutionary America, 1760-1800: The Shaping of an Evangelical Culture.* Princeton: Princeton University Press, 2000.

Ankarloo, Bengt and Stuart Clark, eds. *Witchcraft and Magic in Europe: The Eighteenth and Nineteenth Centuries.* Philadelphia, PA: University of Pennsylvania Press, 1999.

_____, eds. *Witchcraft and Magic in Europe: The Middle Ages.* London: The Athlone Press, 2002.

_____, eds. *Witchcraft and Magic in Europe: The Period of the Witch Trials.* London: The Athlone Press, 2002.

Armogathe, Jean Robert. "A Propos de Miracles de Saint-Médard: les Preuves de Carré de Montgeron et la Positivisme des Lumières." *Revue de L'Historie des Religions* 180 (1971): 135-60.

Ayers, Michael. *Locke: Epistemology and Ontology.* 1991. Reprint, London: Routledge, 2001.

Baker, Derek, ed. *Renaissance and Renewal in Church History.* Oxford: Basil Blackwell, 1977.

Baker, Frank. "The Birth of John Wesley's Journal." *Methodist History* 8 (1970): 25-32.

_____. "Introduction: Wesley as Seen in his Letters." In *Letters I 1721-1739, The Bicentennial Edition of The Works of John Wesley.* Edited by Frank Baker, 25:1-140. Oxford: Clarendon Press, 1980.

_____. *John Wesley and The Church of England.* London: Epworth Press, 1970.

_____. "John Wesley and Bishop Joseph Butler: A Fragment of John Wesley's Manuscript Journal 16th to 24th August 1739." *Proceedings of the Wesley Historical Society* 42 (1980): 93-100.

Barker-Benfield, B. C. *The Manuscripts of Macrobius Commentary on the Somnium Scipionis.* D. Phil. thesis, Oxford University, 1975.

Barker-Benfield, G. J. *The Culture of Sensibility: Sex and Society in Eighteenth-Century Britain.* Chicago, IL: University of Chicago Press, 1992.

Baroja, Julio Caro. *The World of the Witches.* 1961. Reprint, London: Phoenix Press, 2001.

Barry, Jonathan. "Introduction: Keith Thomas and the Problem of Witchcraft." In *Witchcraft in Early Modern Europe: Studies in Culture and Belief.*

Edited by Jonathan Barry, Marianne Hester and Gareth Roberts, 1-45. Cambridge: Cambridge University Press, 1996.

Bartlett, Robert. *The Natural and the Supernatural in the Middle Ages.* Cambridge: Cambridge University Press, 2008.

Baxter, John. "The Great Yorkshire Revival 1792-96." In *Sociological Yearbook of Religion in* Britain. Edited by Michael Hill. 8 vols. 7: 46-76. London: SCM Press, 1974.

Beauregard, Mario and Denyse O'Leary. *The Spiritual Brain: A Neuroscientist's Case for the Existence of the Soul.* New York: Harper Collins Publishers, 2007.

Bebbington, David. *Evangelicalism in Modern Britain: A History from the 1730s to the 1980s.* 1989. Reprint, London: Routledge, 2002.

_____. "Wesley and Science." In *Evangelicals and Science in Historical* Perspective. Edited by David N. Livingston, D. G. Hart, and Mark A. Noll, 120-41. Oxford: Oxford University Press, 1999.

Beier, Lucinda McCray. *Sufferers & Healers: The Experience of Illness in Seventeenth-Century England.* London: Routledge & Kegan Paul, 1987.

Bertucci, Paoli. "Revealing Sparks: John Wesley and the Religious Utility of Electrical Healing." *British Journal for the History of Science* 39 (2006): 341-62.

_____. *Sparks of Life: Medical Electricity and Natural Philosophy in England, c. 1746-1792.* D. Phil. thesis, Oxford University, 2001.

Bicknell, E. J., ed. *The Thirty-Nine Articles*, 3rd rev. ed., By H. J. Carpenter. London: Longmans, Green, and Co., 1955.

Black, C. Clifton and Duane F. Watson, eds. *Words Well Spoken: George Kennedy's Rhetoric of the New Testament.* Waco, TX: Baylor University Press, 2008.

Black, Jeremy and Roy Porter, eds. *A Dictionary of Eighteenth Century History.* London: Penguin Books, 1994.

Blanning, T. C. W. *The Culture of Power and the Power of Culture: Old Regime Europe 1660-1789.* Oxford: Oxford University Press, 2002.

Bloch, Marc. *The Royal Touch: Sacred Monarchy and Scrofula in England and France.* Translated by J. E. Anderson. London: Routledge & Kegan Paul, 1973.

Boas, Marie. "The Establishment of Mechanical Philosophy." *Osiris* 10 (1952): 412-541.

Bodo, Nischan. "The Exorcism Controversy and Baptism in the Late Reformation." In *Lutherans and Calvinists in the Age of Confessionalism.* Edited by Nichan Bodo. 31-51. Aldershot: Ashgate, 1999.

Bostridge, Ian. *Witchcraft and Its Transformations c. 1650-c. 1750.* Oxford: Clarendon Press, 1997.

_____. "Witchcraft Repealed." In *Witchcraft in Early Modern England: Studies in Culture and Belief.* Edited by Barry, Jonathan, Marianne Hester and Gareth Roberts, 309-34. Cambridge: Cambridge University Press, 1996.

Bowmer, John. "John Wesley's Philosophy of Suffering." *The London Quarterly & Holborn Review* 184 (1959): 60-66.

_____. *The Sacrament of the Lord's Supper in Early Methodism.* London: Dacre Press, 1951.

Brady, David. *The Contribution of British Writers Between 1560 and 1830 to the Interpretation of Revelation 13.16-18 (the number of the Beast): A Study in the History of Exegesis.* Tübingen: Mohr, 1983.

Brantley, Richard. *Locke, Wesley, and the Method of English Romanticism.* Gainsville, FL: University of Florida Press, 1984.

Bray, Gerald, ed. *The Anglican Canons 1529-1947.* Woodbridge: Boydell Press, 1998.

Brecht, Martin. *Luther: Shaping and Defining the Reformation 1521-1532.* Trans. James Schaaf. Minneapolis, MN: Fortresss Press, 1990.

Breidert, Wolfgang, ed. *Die Erschütterung der vollkommenen Welt: Die Wirkung des Erdlebens von Lissabon im Spiegel europäischer Zeitgenossen.* Darmstadt: Wissenschaftliche Buchgesellschaft, 1994.

Briggs, Robin. "'Many Reasons Why': Witchcraft and the Problem of Multiple Explanation." In *Witchcraft in Early Modern Europe: Studies in Culture and Belief.* Edited by Barry, Jonathan, Marianne Hester and Gareth Roberts, 49-63. Cambridge: Cambridge University Press, 1996.

_____. *Witches & Neighbours: The Social and Cultural Context of European Witchcraft,* 2nd edn. Oxford: Blackwell Publishers, 2002.

Brooke, John Hedley. *Science and Religion: Some Historical Perspectives.* Cambridge: Cambridge University Press,1991.

_____. *Of Scientists and their Gods: An Inaugural Lecture Delivered before the University of Oxford on 21 November 2000.* Oxford: Oxford University Press, 2001.

Brooks, Peter, ed. *Christian Spirituality: Essays in Honour of Gordon Rupp.* London: SCM Press, 1975.

Brown, Colin. *Miracles and the Critical Mind.* Grand Rapids, MI: William B. Eerdmans Publishing Company, 1984.

Brown, Peter, ed. *Reading Dreams: The Interpretation of Dreams from Chaucer to Shakespeare.* Oxford: Oxford University Press, 1999.

Bryant, Barry. "John Wesley on the Origins of Evil." *Wesleyan Theological Journal* 29 (1994): 120-29.

_____. *John Wesley's Doctrine of Sin.* Ph.D. thesis, University of London, 1992.

Buckle, Stephen. *Hume's Enlightenment Tract: The Unity and Purpose of An Enquiry Concerning Human Understanding.* Oxford: Clarendon Press, 2001.

Buckley, S. J., Michael J. *The Origins of Modern Atheism.* New Haven: Yale University Press, 1987.

Burke, Peter. "Strengths and Weaknesses of the history of Mentalities." *History of European Ideas* 7 (1986): 439-51.

Burns, R. M. *The Great Debate on Miracles: From Joseph Glanville to David Hume.* London: Associated University Presses, 1981.

Burns, William. *An Age of Wonders: Prodigies, Politics, and Providence in England 1657-1727*. Manchester: Manchester University Press, 2002.

Burton, Vicki Tolar. "'Something for the People to Read": John Wesley's Book Inventory (1791)." *Bulletin of the John Rylands University Library of Manchester Journal* 85 (2003): 227-49.

_____. *Spiritual Literacy in John Wesley's Methodism: Reading, Writing & Speaking to Believe*. Waco: Baylor University Press, 2008.

Bynum, Caoline Walker. *The Resurrection of the Body in Western Christianity, 200-1336*. New York: Columbia University Press, 1995.

Byrne, Donald. *No Foot of Land: Folklore of American Methodist Itinerants*. Metuchen, NJ: Scarecrow Press, 1975.

Cameron, Averil. *Christianity and the Rhetoric of Empire: The Development of Christian Discourse*. Berkley, CA: University of California Press, 1994.

Cameron, Euan. "The Power of the Word: Renaissance and Reformation." In *Early Modern Europe: An Oxford History*. Edited by Euan Cameron, 63-101. Oxford: Oxford University Press, 1999.

Campbell, Ted. *John Wesley and Christian Antiquity: Religious Vision and Cultural Change*. Nashville, TN: Kingswood Books, 1991.

_____. "John Wesley and Conyers Middleton on Divine Intervention in History." *Church History* 55 (1986): 39-49.

_____. *The Religion of the Heart: A Study of European Life in the Seventeenth and Eighteenth Centuries*. Charleston, SC: University of South Carolina Press, 1991.

Caparros, E, M. Thériault, and J. Thorn, eds. *Code of Canon Law Annotated*. Montreal: Wilson and LaFleur, 1993.

Card, Claudia. *The Atrocity Paradigm: A Theory of Evil*. New York: Oxford University Press, 2002.

Carwardine, Richard. "Methodist Ministers and the Second Party System." In *Perspectives on American Methodism: Interpretative* Essays. Edited by Russell Richey, Kenneth Rowe, and Jean Miller Schmidt, 159-77. Nashville, TN: Kingswood Books, 1993.

Castle, Terry. *The Female Thermometer: Eighteenth-Century Culture and the Invention of the Uncanny*. New York: Oxford University Press, 1995.

Cavallo, Gugliemo and Roger Charter, eds. *A History of Reading in the West*. Translated by Lydia G. Cochrane. London: Polity, 2003.

Chambers, Paul. *The Cock Lane Ghost: Murder, Sex & Haunting in Dr Johnson's London*. Phoenix Mill: Sutton Publishing Ltd., 2006.

Chappell, Vere, ed. *The Cambridge Companion to Locke*. Cambridge: Cambridge University Press, 1994.

Church, Leslie E. *More About the Early Methodist People*. London: Epworth Press, 1949.

Clark, Elmer, ed. *What Happened at Aldersgate: Addresses in Commemoration of the Bicentennial of Spiritual Awakening of John Wesley in Aldersgate Street, London, May 24, 1738*. Nashville, TN: Methodist Publishing House, 1938.

Clark, J. C. D. *English Society 1660-1832: Religion, Ideology and Politics During the Ancient Regime.* 2nd ed. Cambridge: Cambridge University Press, 2000.

_____. "Providence, Predestination and Progress: or, did the Enlightenment Fail?" *Albion* 35 (2004): 559-89.

Clark, Stuart. "Inversion, Misrule and the Meaning of Witchcraft." *Past and Present* 87 (1980): 118-122.

_____. ed. *Languages of Witchcraft: Narrative, Ideology and Meaning in Early Modern Culture.* Houndmills and New York: Macmillian Press Ltd., and St. Martin's Press, 2001.

_____. *Thinking With Demons: The Idea of Witchcraft in early Modern Europe.* Oxford: Oxford University Press, 1997.

_____. "Witchcraft and Magic in Early Modern Culture." In *Witchcraft and Magic in Europe: The Period of the Witch Trials*, edited by Bengt Ankarloo and Stuart Clark, 97-169. London: The Athlone Press, 2002.

Clark, William, Jan Golinski, and Simon Schaeffer, eds. *The Sciences in Enlightened Europe.* Chicago: University of Chicago Press, 1999.

Clery, E. J. *The Rise of Supernatural Fiction, 1762-1800.* 1995. Reprint, Cambridge: Cambridge University Press, 1996.

Coady, C. A. J. *Testimony: A Philosophical Study.* Oxford: Clarendon Press, 1992.

Collins, Kenneth. *John Wesley: A Theological Journey.* Nashville: Abingdon Press, 2003.

_____. "John Wesley and the Fear of Death as a Standard of Conversion." In *Conversion in the Wesleyan Tradition.* Edited by Kenneth Collins and John Tyson, 56-68. Nashville, TN: Abingdon Press, 2001.

_____. *The Scripture Way of Salvation: The Heart of John Wesley's Salvation.* Nashville, TN: Abingdon Press, 1997.

Compier, Don H. *What is Rhetorical Theology? Textual Practice and Public Discourse.* Harrisburg, PA: Trinity Press International, 1999.

Conner, Stephen. *Dumbstruck: A Cultural History of Ventriloquism.* Oxford: Oxford University Press, 2000.

Cornwall, Robert. "The Search for the Primitive Church: The Use of the Early Church Fathers in High Anglican Church Tradition 1680-1745." *Anglican and Episcopal History* 59 (1990): 303-29.

_____. *Visible and Apostolic: The Constitution of the Church in High Church Anglican and non-Juror Thought.* Newark, DE: University of Delaware Press, 1993.

Cowie, Leonard W. *Hanoverian England 1714-1837.* New York: Humanities Press, 1967.

Cox, John D. *The Devil and the Sacred in English Drama, 1350-1642.* Cambridge: Cambridge University Press, 2000.

Cox, Harvey. *Fire From Heaven: The Rise of Pentecostal Spirituality and the Reshaping of Religion in the Twenty-first Century.* New York: Addison-Wesley Publishing Company, 1995.

Cragg, Gerald R. *From Puritanism to the Age of Reason: A Study of Changes in Religious Thought Within The Church of England 1660 to 1700.* Cambridge: Cambridge University Press, 1966.

Cubitt, George. *The Life of Martin Luther.* New York: Carlton & Phillips, 1853.

Cule, John. "The Rev. John Wesley, M. A. (Oxon.), 1703-1791: 'The Naked Empiricist' and Orthodox Medicine." *The Journal of the History of Medicine and Allied Sciences* 45 (1990): 41-63.

Cunningham, Andrew and Roger French, eds. *The Medical Enlightenment of the Eighteenth Century.* 1990. Reprint, Cambridge: Cambridge University Press, 2004.

Curtis, Heather D. *Suffering and Divine Healing in American Culture, 1860-1900.* Baltimore, MD: The John Hopkins University Press, 2007.

Cushman, Robert. *John Wesley's Experimental Divinity: Studies in Methodist Doctrinal Standards.* Nashville, TN: Kingswood Books, 1989.

Dallimore, Arnold. *Susannah Wesley: The Mother of John & Charles Wesley.* Grand Rapids, MI: Baker Book House, 1993.

Davies, Owen. "Charmers and Charming in England and Wales from the Eighteenth Century to the Twentieth Century." *Folklore* 109 (1998): 41-52.

_____. "Methodism, the Clergy, and the Popular Belief in Witchcraft and Magic." *History* 82 (1997): 252-65.

_____. "Newspapers and the Popular Belief in Witchcraft and Magic in the Modern Period." *Journal of British Studies* 37 (1998): 139-65.

_____. *Witchcraft, Magic and Culture 1736-1951.* Manchester: Manchester University Press, 1999.

Davies, Rupert. "General Rules and Rules of the Band Societies: An Introductory Comment." In *The Methodist Societies: History, Nature, and Design, Works of John Wesley, The Bicentennial Edition of The Works of John Wesley.* Edited by Rupert Davies, 9: 67. Nashville, TN: Abingdon Press, 1989.

Davies, Stevan. *Jesus the Healer: Possession, Trance, and the Origins of Christianity.* New York: Continuum, 1995.

Deconinck-Brossard, Francoise. "Eighteenth-Century Sermons and the Age." In *Crown and Mitre: Religion and Society in Northern Europe Since the Reformation.* Edited by W. M. Jacob and Nigel Yates, 105-21. Maidstone: Kent County Council, Arts, & Library, 1993.

Descher, John. *Wesley's Christology: An Interpretation.* Dallas, TX: Southern Methodist University Press, 1960.

Ditchfield, G. M. *The Evangelical Revival.* London: UCL Press, 1998.

Dobbs, Betty Jo Teeter and Margaret C. Jacobs. *Newton and the Culture of Newtonianism.* Amherst, NY: Humanity Books, 1988.

Dölger, Franz. *Der Exorzimus im Altchristlichen Taufritual.* Paderborn: n. p.,1909.

Donat, James G. "Empirical Medicine in the 18th Century." *Methodist History* 44 (2006): 216-26.

Drees, William, ed. *Is Nature Ever Evil? Religion, Science and Value.* London: Routledge Taylor & Francis Group, 2003.

Dreyer, Frederick. "Faith and Experience in the Thought of John Wesley." *American Historical Review* 88 (1983): 12-30.

Duffy, Eamon. "Primitive Christianity Revived: Religious Renewal in Augustan England." In *Renaissance and Renewal in Church History.* Edited by Derek Baker. 287-300. Oxford: Basil Blackwell, 1977.

_____. *The Stripping of the Altars: Traditional Religion in England 1400-1580.* New Haven: Yale University Press, 1992.

_____. *The Voices of Morebath: Reformation & Rebellion in an English Village.* New Haven: Yale University Press, 2001.

Dunning, H. Ray. *Grace, Faith, and Holiness: A Wesleyan Systematic Theology.* Kansas City, MO: Beacon Hill Press, 1988.

Dupré, Louis. *The Enlightenment & The Intellectual Foundations of Modern Culture.* New Haven: Yale University Press, 2004.

Earman, John. *Hume's Abject Failure: The Argument Against Miracles.* Oxford: Oxford University Press, 2000.

Eddy, Geoffrey T. *Dr Taylor of Norwich: Wesley's Arch-heretic.* Peterborough: Epworth Press, 2003.

_____. "Formica Contra Leonem: An Eighteenth Century Conflict Reassessed." *Methodist History* 38 (2000): 71-81.

_____. "Sartor Resartus: or Taylor New-Tailor'd." *Epworth Review* 26 (1999): 88-98.

_____. "There Goes the Arch-Heretic: The Revd Dr John Taylor of Norwich and Warrington Academy." *Faith and Freedom* 52 (1999): 39-50.

Edwards, Kathryn, ed. *Werewolves, Witches, and Wandering Spirits: Traditional Belief & Folklore in Early Modern Europe.* Kirksville, MO: Truman State University Press, 2002.

Eicken, Eric von. *Rechtfertigung und Heiligung bei John Wesley.* Ph.D. thesis, University of Heidelberg, 1941.

Evans-Pritchard, E. E. *Witchcraft, Oracles, and Magic among the Azande.* 1937. Oxford: Clarendon Press, 1976.

Fara, Patricia. *An Entertainment for Angels: Electricity in the Enlightenment.* Cambridge: Icon Books, 2003.

_____. *Science: A Four Thousand Year History.* Oxford: Oxford University Press, 2009.

Ferber, Sarah. *Demonic Possession and Exorcism in Early Modern France.* London: Routledge Taylor & Francis Group, 2004.

Ferrell, Lori Anne and Peter McCullough, eds. *The English Sermon Revised: Religion, Literature and History 1650-1750.* Manchester: Manchester University Press, 2000.

Festugiere, A. J. *Epicurus and His Gods.* Translated by C. W. Chilton. Oxford: Blackwell, 1955.

Field, Clive D. "The Social Composition of English Methodism to 1830; a Membership Analysis." *Bulletin of the John Rylands University Library of Manchester* 76 (1994): 153-69.

Figge, Horst. "Exorzismus." *Religion in Geschicte und Gegenwart.* Tübingen: Mohr,1828. 2: 790-95.

Finucane, Ronald. *Miracles & Pilgrims: Popular Beliefs in Medieval England.* London: Book Club Associates, 1977.

Fischer, Balthasar. "Baptismal Exorcism in the Catholic Baptismal Rites after Vatican II." *Studia Liturgica* 10 (1974): 48-55.

Flew, Robert Newton. *The Idea of Perfection in Christian Theology: A Historical Study of The Christian Ideal for the Present Life.* London: Oxford University Press, 1934.

Fowler, James W. "John Wesley's Development in Faith." In *The Future of the Methodist Theological Traditions.* Edited by M. Douglas Meeks. 172-92. Nashville, TN: Kingswood Books, 1985.

Frei, Hans. *The Eclipse of Biblical Narrative: A Study in Eighteenth and Nineteenth Century Hermeneutics.* New Haven: Yale University Press, 1974.

Frend, W. H. C. *The Rise of Christianity.* Philadelphia, PA: Fortress Press, 1984.

Frost, Evelyn. *Christian Healing: A Consideration of the Place of Spiritual Healing in the Church of To-Day in the Light of the Doctrine and Practice of the Ante-Nicene Church.* London: A. R. Mowbray, 1940.

Gabbey, Alan and Robert E. Hall. "The Melon and the Dictionary: Reflections on Descartes Dreams." *Journal of the History of Ideas* 59 (1998): 651-58.

Gaskill, Malcolm. *Crime and Mentalities in Early Modern England.* Cambridge: Cambridge University Press, 2000.

_____. "Witches and Witnesses in Old and New England'." In *Languages of Witchcraft: Narrative, Ideology and Meaning in Early Modern Culture.* Edited by Stuart Clark, 55-80. Houndmills: Macmillan Press Ltd., 2001.

Gassmann, Gunther. "Toward a Common Expression of the Apostolic Faith Today." In *What Should Methodists Teach? Wesleyan Tradition and Modern Diversity.* Edited by M. Douglas Meeks, 93-100. Nashville, TN: Kingswood Books, 1990.

Gay, Peter. *The Enlightenment: An Interpretation.* 2 vols. New York: W. W. Norton & Company, 1966.

Gibson, Marion. *Early Modern Witches: Witchcraft Cases in Contemporary Writing.* London: Routledge, 2000.

_____. *Reading Witchcraft: Stories of English Witches.* London: Routledge, 1999.

Gibson, William and Robert G. Ingram, eds. *Religious Identities in Britain, 1660-1832.* Aldershot: Ashgate, 2005.

Gilbert, Jeremiah. "On Camp-Meetings, &c, in 1821." *A Methodist Magazine* 4 (1822): 9-10.

Gill, Frederick. *The Romantic Movement and Methodism: A Study of English Romanticism and the Evangelical Revival.* London: Epworth Press, 1937.

Ginzburg, Carlo. *History, Rhetoric and Proof.* Hanover, NH: University Press of New England, 1999.

_____. *The Night Battles: Witchcraft and Agrarian Cults in the Sixteenth and Seventeenth Centuries*. Translated by John and Anne Tedeschi. Baltimore, MD: The John Hopkins University Press, 1983.

Gijswijt-Hofstra, Marijke. "Witchcraft after the Witch-Trials." In *Witchcraft and Magic in Europe: The Eighteenth and Nineteenth Centuries*. Edited by Bengt Ankarloo and Stuart Clark, 95-189. Philadelphia, PA: University of Pennsylvania Press, 1999.

Golden, James. "John Wesley on Rhetoric and Belles Lettres." *Speech Monographs* 28 (1961): 250-64.

Goldman, Lawrence, ed. *The Oxford Dictionary of National Biography*, 60 vols. Oxford: Oxford University Press, 2001-2004.

Goodman, Felicitas. *How About Demons?* Bloomington, IN: Indiana University Press, 1988.

Goodwin, Charles. "Setting Perfection Too High: John Wesley's Changing Attitudes Toward the 'London Blessing.'" *Methodist History* 36 (1998): 86-96.

_____. "The Terrors of the Thunderstorm: Medieval Popular Cosmology and Methodist Revivalism." *Methodist History* 39 (2001): 101-10.

Gordon, James. "'Impassive He Suffers; Immortal He Dies': Rhetoric and Polemic in Charles Wesley's Portrayal of the Atonement." *Scottish Bulletin of Evangelical Theology* 18 (2000): 56-70.

Grant, Douglas. *The Cock Lane Ghost*. London: Macmillan, 1965.

Green, Richard. *The Works of John and Charles Wesley: A Bibliography*. London: Published for the Author by C. H. Kelly, 1896.

Green, V. H. H. *The Commonwealth of Lincoln College 1427-1977*. Oxford: Oxford University Press, 1979.

_____. *The Young Mr. Wesley*. London: Edward Arnold Publishers Ltd., 1961.

Greenberg, Kenneth S., ed. *Nat Turner: A Slave Rebellion in History and Memory* Oxford: Oxford University Press, 2003.

Gregory, Jeremy. "'In the Church I will live and die': John Wesley, the Church of England, and Methodism." In *Religious Identities in Britain, 1660-1832*. Edited by William Gibson and Robert G. Ingram, 147-78. Hants: Ashgate, 2005.

_____. "The Eighteenth Century Reformation: the Pastoral Task of Anglican Clergy after 1689." In *The Church of England c. 1689—c. 1833: From Toleration to Tractarianism*. Edited by John Walsh, Colin Hayden, and Stephen Taylor, 67-85. Cambridge: Cambridge University Press, 1993.

Gregory, Jeremy and Chamberlain, Jeffrey, eds. *The National Church in Local Perspective: The Church of England and the Regions, 1660-1800*. Woodbridge: The Boydell Press, 2003.

Gross, Alan G. *The Rhetoric of Science*. Cambridge, MA: Harvard University Press, 1996.

Gross, Alan G. and Joseph E. Harmon, and Michael Reidy. *Communicating Science: The Scientific Article from the 17th Century to the Present*. Oxford: Oxford University Press, 2002.

Guerrini, Anita. "Newtonianism, Medicine and Religion." In *Religio Medici: Medicine and Religion in Seventeenth-Century England*. Edited by Ole Peter Grell and Andrew Cunningham, 293-312. Aldershot: Scolar Press, 1996.

_____. *Obesity & Depression in the Enlightenment: The Life and Times of George Cheyne*. Norman, OK: University of Oklahoma Press, 2000.

Gunter, Horst. *Das Erdbeben von Lissabon und die Erschütterung des Aufgeklärten*. Frankfurt im Main: Fischer Taschenbuch Verlag, 2005.

Gunter, W. Stephen. *The Limits of 'Love Divine': John Wesley's Response to Antinominalism and Enthusiasm*. Nashville, TN: Kingswood Books, 1989.

Haas, Jr., J. W. "John Wesley's Views on Science and Christianity: An Examination of the Charge of Antiscience." *Church History* 63 (1994): 378-92.

Habermas, Jürgen. *The Structural Transformation of the Public Sphere: An Inquiry into a Category of Bourgeois Society*. Translated by Thomas Burger with the assistance of Frederick Lawrence. 1992. Reprint, Cambridge: Polity Press, 1999.

Halevy, Elie. *The Birth of Methodism in England*. Translated and Edited by Bernard Semmel. Chicago, IL: University of Chicago Press, 1971.

Hall, David D. *Worlds of Wonder, Days of Judgment: Popular Religious Beliefs in Early New England*. Cambridge, MA: Harvard University Press, 1990.

Hall, Rupert A. *Isaac Newton: Adventure in Thought*. Cambridge: Cambridge University Press, 1992.

Hammond, Geordan. "John Wesley in Georgia: Success or Failure?" *Proceedings of the Wesley Historical Society* 56 (2008): 297-305.

Hampson, John. *Memoirs of the Late Rev. John Wesley, A. M. with a Review of His Life and Writings, and a History of Methodism, from it's Commencement in 1729, to the Present Times*. 3 vols. London: Printed for the Author by James Graham, 1791.

Handley, Sasha. *Ghost Narratives in Modern British Culture*. Ph.D. thesis, University of Birmingham, 2004.

_____. "Reclaiming Ghosts in 1690s England." In *Signs, Wonders, Miracles: Representations of Divine Power in The Life of The Church*. Edited by Kate Cooper and Jeremy Gregory, 345-55. Woodbridge: Boydell Press, 2005.

_____. *Visions of an Unseen World: Ghost Beliefs and Ghost Stories in Eighteenth Century England*. London: Pickering & Chatto, 2007.

Hankins, Thomas. *Science and the Enlightenment*. Cambridge: Cambridge University Press, 1985.

Hansen, Chadwick. *Witchcraft at Salem*. New York: George Braziller, 1969.

Hansen, William. *John Wesley and the Rhetoric of Reform*. Ph.D. thesis, University of Oregon, 1972.

Harden, John. "The Concept of Miracle from St. Augustine to Modern Apologetics." *Theological Studies* 15 (1954): 229-57

Harley, David. "Rhetoric and the Social Construction of Sickness and Healing." *The Social History of Medicine* 12 (1999): 407-35.

Harrison, Peter. "Miracles, Modern Science, and Rational Religion." *Church History* 75 (2006): 493-510.

_____. "Newtonian Science, Miracles, and the Laws of Nature." *Journal of the History of Ideas* 56 (1995): 531-53.

_____. "Original Sin and the Problem of Knowledge in Early Modern Europe." *Journal of the History of Ideas* 63 (2002): 239-59.

Hartman, James. *Providence Tales and the Birth of American Literature*. Baltimore: The John Hopkins University Press, 1999.

Hasan-Rokem, Galit. "Communication with the Dead in Jewish Dream Culture." In *Dream Cultures: Explorations in the Comparative History of Dreaming*. Edited by David Shulman and Guy Stroumsa, 213-32. New York: Oxford University Press, 1999.

Hastings, James, ed. *Encyclopaedia of Religion and Ethics*, 13 vols. London: T & T Clark, 1888.

Hayward, Rhodri. "Policing Dreams: History and the Moral Uses of the Unconscious." *History Workshop Journal* 49 (2000): 142-60.

Headrick, Daniel R. *When Information Came of Age: Technologies of Knowledge in the Age of Reason and Revolution 1700-1850*. Oxford: Oxford University Press, 2000.

Heitzenrater, Richard P. *Mirror and Memory: Reflections on Early Methodism*. Nashville, TN: Kingswood Books, 1989.

_____. *The Poor and the People Called Methodists*. Nashville, TN: Kingswood Books, 2002.

_____. *Wesley and the People Called Methodists*. Nashville, TN: Abingdon Press, 1995.

Hempton, David. *Methodism: Empire of the Spirit*. New Haven, CT: Yale University Press, 2005.

_____. *Methodism and Politics in British Society 1750-1850*. Stanford, CA: Stanford University Press, 1984.

_____. "Methodist Growth in Transatlantic Perspective, ca. 1770-1850." In *Methodism and the Shaping of American Culture*. Edited by Nathan Hatch and John Wigger, 41-85. Nashville, TN: Kingswood Books, 2001.

_____. *The Religion of the People: Methodism and Popular Religion c. 1750-1900*. London: Routledge, 1996.

_____. *Religion and Political Culture in Britain and Ireland: From the glorious Revolution to the Decline of Empire*. Cambridge: Cambridge University Press, 1996.

Herbert, Thomas. *John Wesley as Editor and Author*. Princeton, NJ: Princeton University Press, 1940.

Herrick, James. *The Radical Rhetoric of the English Deists: The Discourse of Skepticism, 1680-1750*. Columbia, SC: University of South Carolina Press, 1970.

Herod, George. *Biographical Sketches of those Preachers whose Labours Contributed to the Organization and Early Extension of Primitive Methodism.* London: T. King, 1855.

Hiatt, R. Jeffrey. "John Wesley & Healing: Developing a Wesleyan Missiology." *The Asbury Theological Journal* 20 (2004): 89-109.

Hill, Christopher. *The Intellectual Origins of the English Revolution Revisited.* 1965. Reprint, Oxford: Clarendon Press, 2001.

Hill, Michael, ed. *Sociological Yearbook of Religion in Britain.* 8 vols. London: SCM Press, 1974.

Hill, Wesley. *John Wesley Among the Physicians: A Study of Eighteenth Century Medicine.* London: Epworth Press, 1953.

Himmelfarb, Gertrude. *The Roads to Modernity: The British, French, and American Enlightenment.* New York: Alfred A. Knopf, 2004.

Hindmarsh, D. Bruce. *The Evangelical Conversion Narrative: Spiritual Autobiography in Early Modern England.* Oxford: Oxford University Press, 2005.

Holbrooke, Clyde A. "'Editor's Introduction to Jonathan Edward's *The Great Christian Doctrine of Original Sin Defended; Evidences of it's Truth Produced, and Arguments to the Contrary Answered. Containing in Particular, A Reply to the Objections and Arguings of Dr. John Taylor, In his Book, Intitled, 'The Scripture-Doctrine of Original Sin proposed to, Free and candid Examination, &c.'"* In *The Works of Jonathan Edwards.* Edited by Clyde A. Holbrooke, 3: 1-17. New Haven: Yale University Press, 1970.

_____. "Original Sin in the Enlightenment." In *The Heritage of Christian Thought: Essays in Honor of Robert Lowry Calhoun.* Edited by John E. Cushman and Egil Grislis, 142-65. New York: Harper and Row Publishers, 1965.

_____, ed. *The Works of Jonathan Edwards,* 25 vols. New Haven: Yale University Press, 1970- .

Holifield, E. Brooks. *Health and Medicine in the Methodist Tradition.* Nashville, TN: Abingdon Press, 1986.

_____. *Theology in America: Christian Theology from the Age of the*
_____. *Puritans to the Civil War.* New Haven: Yale University Press, 2003.

Holland, Bernard. "'A Species of Madness': The Effect of John Wesley's Preaching." *Proceedings of the Wesley Historical Society* 39 (1973): 77-85.

Hood, Bruce M. *Supersense: Why We Believe in the Unbelieveable.* New York: Harper Collins Publishers, 2009.

Hoskins, Steven. "Eucharist and Eschatology in the Writings of the Wesleys." *Wesley Theological Journal* 29 (1994): 64-80.

Houston, J. H. *Reported Miracles.* Cambridge: Cambridge University Press, 1994.

Howson, Colin. *Hume's Problem: Induction and the Justification of Belief.* Oxford: Clarendon Press, 2000.

Hudson, Nicholas. *Samuel Johnson and Eighteenth-Century Thought*. Oxford: Clarendon Press, 1988).

Hudson, Winthrop. "Shouting Methodists." *Encounter* 29 (1968): 73-84.

Hutchison, Keith. "What Happened to Occult Qualities in the Scientific Revolution?" *Isis* 73 (1982): 233-53.

Hutton, Ronald. *The Triumph of the Moon: A History of Modern Pagan Witchcraft*. Oxford: Oxford University Press, 1999.

Israel, Jonathan. "Enlightenment! Which Enlightenment?" *Journal of the History of Ideas* 67 (2006): 523-45.

_____. *Enlightenment Contested: Philosophy, Modernity, and the Emancipation of Man 1670-1752*. Oxford: Oxford University Press, 2006.

_____. *Radical Enlightenment: Philosophy and the Making of Modernity 1650-1750*. Oxford: Oxford University Press, 2001.

Jackson, Thomas. *The Life of the Rev. Charles Wesley, M. A.: Some Time Student of Christ-Church, Oxford: Comprising A Review of His Poetry; Sketches of The Rise and Progress of Methodism; with Notices of Contemporary Events and Characters*. New York: G. Lane and P. P. Sandford, 1844.

Jacob, Margaret C. *Scientific Culture and the Making of the Industrial West*. Oxford: Oxford University Press, 1997.

Jarboe, Betty. *John and Charles Wesley: A Bibliography*. Metuchen, NJ: and London: The American Theological Library Association and The Scarecrow Press, 1987.

Jenson, Evelyn. *John Wesley's Use of Three Types of Classical Oratory— "Forensic," "Epideictic," and "Deliberative"—in his Journal*. EdD thesis, Ball State University, 1980.

Johnson, David. *Hume, Holism, and Miracles* (Ithaca, NY: Cornell University Press, 1999.

Johnston, Nathan. *The Devil and Demonism in Early Modern England*. Cambridge: Cambridge University Press, 2006.

Jonas, Raymond. *France and the Cult of the Sacred Heart. An Epic Tale for Modern Times*. Berkley, CA: University of California Press, 2000.

Jost, Walter and Wendy Olmstead, eds. *Rhetorical Invention & Religious Inquiry: New Perspectives*. New Haven: Yale University Press, 2000.

Jüngel, Eberhard. *Justification: The Heart of the Christian Faith*. Translated by Jeffrey Crayzer. Edinburgh: T & T Clark, 2001.

Juster, Susan. *Doomsayers: Anglo-American Prophecy in the Age of Revolution*. Philadelphia, PA: University of Pennsylvania Press, 2003.

Keeble, N. H., ed. *John Bunyan: Coventicle and Parnassus*. Oxford: Clarendon Press, 1988.

Keevak, Michael. "Descartes Dream and their Address for Philosophy." *Journal for the History of Ideas* 53 (1992): 373-96.

Kelley, Donald R. *The Descent of Ideas: The History of Intellectual History*. Aldershot: Ashgate Publishing Ltd., 2002.

Kelsey, Morton. *Healing and Christianity: In Ancient Thought and Modern Times*. New York: Harper and Row Publishers, 1973.

Kendrick, T. D. *The Lisbon Earthquake.* London: Methuen, 1956.

Kennedy, George. *Classical Rhetoric & its Christian and Secular Tradition from Ancient to Modern Times.* 2nd ed. Chapel Hill, NC: The University of North Carolina Press, 1999.

_____. *New Testament Interpretation Through Rhetorical Criticism.* Chapel Hill, NC: The University of North Carolina Press, 1984.

Kent, John. *Wesley and the Wesleyans: Religion in Eighteenth-Century Britain.* Cambridge: Cambridge University Press, 2002.

Kimbrough, ST, ed. *Orthodoxy and Wesleyan Spirituality.* Crestwood, NY: St Vladimir's Seminary Press, 2002.

Knox, Ronald A. *Enthusiasm: A Chapter in the History of Religion with Special Reference to the xvii and xviii Centuries.* Oxford: Clarendon Press, 1950.

Kruger, Steven. *Dreaming in the Middle Ages.* Cambridge: Cambridge University Press, 1992.

_____. "Medical and Moral Authority in the Late Medieval Dream." In *Reading Dreams: The Interpretation of Dreams from Chaucer to Shakespeare.* Edited by Peter Brown. 51-83. Oxford: Oxford University Press, 1999.

Kürschner, Mathias. "The Enthusiasm of the Rev. John Wesley." *Wesleyan Theological Journal* 35 (2000): 114-37.

Lackey, Jennifer and Ernest Sosa, eds. *The Epistemology of Testimony.* Oxford: Clarendon Press, 2005.

Lambert, Frank. *Inventing the "Great Awakening."* Princeton, NJ: Princeton University Press, 1999.

Langton, Edward. "James Crawfoot: the Forest Mystic." *Proceedings of the Wesley Historical Society* 30 (1955): 12-15.

Lara, Maria Pía, ed. *Rethinking Evil: Contemporary Perspectives.* Berkley, CA: University of California Press, 2001.

Larmer, Robert A. *Water into Wine? An Investigation of the Concept of Miracle.* Kingston: McGill-Queen University Press, 1988.

Larson, Timothy. *Crisis of Doubt: Honest Faith in Nineteenth-Century England.* Oxford: Oxford University Press, 2006.

Lauer, Gerhard and Thorston Unger, eds. *Das Erdbeben von Lissabon und der Katastrophendiskurs im 18. Jahrhundert.* Göttingen: Wallstein Verlag, 2008.

Lawton, George. *John Wesley's English: A Study of his Literary Style.* London: George Allen & Unwin Ltd., 1962.

Lecky, W. E. H. *A History of England in the Eighteenth Century.* 7 vols. London: Longmans, Green and Company, 1910.

_____. *History of the Rise and Influence of the Spirit of Rationalism in Europe.* 2 vols. 2nd ed. London: Longmans, Green and Company, 1865.

Leeper, Elizabeth. "From Alexander to Rome: The Valentinian Connection to the Incorporation of Exorcism as a Prebaptismal Rite." *Vigiliae Christianae* 44 (1990): 6-24.

_____. "The Role of Exorcism in Early Christianity." *Studia Patristica* 26 (1993): 59-62.

Lenton, Esther. "Primitive Methodist Camp Meetings in Shropshire." *Proceedings of the Wesley Historical Society* 52 (1999): 1-14.

Lindström, Harald. *Wesley and Santification: A Study in the Doctrine of Salvation.* 1950. Reprint, London: The Epworth Press, 1956.

Little, C. D. "Early Methodism in Manchester." *Proceedings of the Wesley Historical Society* 25 (1945-1946): 116-22.

Lloyd, Gareth. "John Wesley and the London Disturbances 1760-1763." *The Asbury Theological Journal* 20 (2003): 130-40.

_____. "Repression and Resistance: Wesleyan Female Public Ministry in the Generation after 1791." *Proceedings of the Wesley Historical Society* 55, (2005): 101-14.

Lockwood, John P., ed. *Memoirs of the Life of Peter Böhler.* London: Wesleyan Conference Office, 1868.

Logan, James. "The Evangelical Imperative: A Wesleyan Perspective." In *Theology and Evangelism in the Wesleyan Heritage.* Edited by James Logan, 15-33. Nashville, TN: Kingswood Books, 1994.

Lovejoy, Arthur O. *The Great Chain of Being: A Study of the History of an Idea.* 1936. Reprint, Cambridge, MA: Harvard University Press, 2001.

Luker, David. *Cornish Methodism, Revivalism, and Popular Belief, c. 1780-1870.* D. Phil. thesis, Oxford University, 1987.

_____. "Revivalism in Theory and Practice: The Case of Cornish Methodism," *The Journal of Ecclesiastical History* 37 (1986): 603-19.

MacCulloch, Diarmaid. *The Reformation: A History.* New York: Viking, 2003.

Macfarlane, Alan. *Witchcraft in Tudor and Stuart England: A Regional and Comparative Study.* 2nd ed. London: Routledge, 1999.

Macfarlan, Duncan. *The Revivals of the Eighteenth Century, Particularly at Cambuslang.* Edinburgh: John Johnstone, 1847.

McGinn, Bernard. "Visions and Visualizations in the Here and Hereafter." *Harvard Theological Review* 98 (2005): 227-46.

McGonigle, Herbert Boyd. *Sufficient Saving Grace: John Wesley's Practical Theology.* Carlisle: Paternoster Press, 2001.

McGrath, Alister. *Justitia Dei: A History of the Christian Doctrine of Justification.* 2nd ed. Cambridge: Cambridge University Press, 2002.

Mack, Phyllis. *Heart Religion in the British Enlightenment: Gender and Emotion in Early Methodism.* Cambridge: Cambridge University Press, 2008.

_____. "Methodism and Motherhood." In *Culture and the Nonconformist Tradition.* Edited by Jane Shaw and Alan Kreider. Cardiff: University of Wales Press, 1999.

_____. "Religious Dissenters in Enlightenment England." *History Workshop* 49 (2000): 1-23.

_____. *Visionary Women: Ecstatic Prophecy in Seventeenth-Century England.* Berkley, CA: University of California Press, 1992.

Mackie, J. L. *Problems from Locke.* Oxford: Clarendon Press, 1976.

McManners, John. *Church and Society in Eighteenth Century France.* 2 vols. Oxford: Oxford University Press, 1998.

MacNeill, John. "Luther at Aldersgate." *London Quarterly & Holborn Review* 164 (1939): 200-17.

MacNutt, Francis. *Overcome by the Spirit: The Extraordinary Phenomenon That is Happening to Ordinary People.* Grand Rapids: Chosen Books, 1990.

Madden, Deborah. *A Cheap, Safe, and Natural Medicine: Religion, Medicine and Culture in John Wesley's Primitive Physic.* Amsterdam: Rodopi, 2007.

_____. "Experience and the Common Interest of Mankind: The Enlightened Empiricism of John Wesley's Primitive Physic." *British Journal for Eighteenth-Century Studies* 26 (2003): 41-53.

_____. "Medicine and Moral Reform: The Place of Practical Piety in John Wesley's Art of Physic." *Church History* 73 (2004): 741-58.

_____. *Pristine Purity: Primitivism and Practical Piety in John Wesley's Art of Physic.* D. Phil. thesis, Oxford University, 2003.

_____. ed. *"Inward & Outward Health": John Wesley's Holistic Concept of Medical Science, the Environment and Holy Living.* London: Epworth Press, 2008.

Maddox, Randy. "Aldersgate: A Tradition History." In *Aldersgate Reconsidered*, edited by Randy Maddox, 133-46. Nashville. TN: Abingdon Press, 1990.

_____. "Kingswood School Library Holdings (CA. 1775)." *Methodist History* 41 (2002): 342-70.

_____. *Responsible Grace: John Wesley's Practical Theology.* Nashville, TN: Kingswood Books, 1994.

_____. *Rethinking Wesley's Theology for Contemporary Methodism.* Nashville, TN: Kingswood Books, 1998.

Maggi, Armando. *Satan's Rhetoric: A Study of Renaissance Demonology.* Chicago, IL: University of Chicago Press, 2001.

Marius, Richard. *Martin Luther: The Christian Between God and Death.* Cambridge, MA: Harvard University Press, 1999.

Marshall, Peter. *Beliefs and the Dead in Reformation England.* Oxford: Oxford University Press, 2002.

Martin, Raymond and John Barresi. *Naturalization of the Soul: Self and Personal Identity in the Eighteenth Century.* London: Routledge, 2000.

Masser, Frederick. "Problem in Preaching: An Analysis of the Preaching Power of John Wesley." *The London Quarterly and Holborn Review*, 6th series, 2 (1933): 309-22.

Matthews, Rex *"Religion and Reason Joined": A Study in the Theology of John Wesley.* Ph.D. thesis, Harvard University, 1986.

Mawson, T. W. "Miracles and the Laws of Nature." *Religious Studies* 37 (2001): 33-58.

Mealey, Mark Thomas. *"Taste and See that Lord is Good": John Wesley in the Christian Tradition of Spiritual Sensation.* Ph.D. thesis, University of Toronto, 2006.

Meir, John. *A Marginal Jew: Rethinking the Historical Jesus.* 4 vols. New York: Doubleday, 1994.

Midelfort, Erik. *Exorcism and Enlightenment: Johann Joseph Gassner and the Demons of Eighteenth-Century Germany.* New Haven, CT: Yale University Press, 2005.

_____. *Witch Hunting in Southwestern Germany 1562-1684: The Social and Intellectual Foundations.* Stanford, CA: Stanford University Press, 1972.

Midgley, Mary. *Wickedness: A Philosophical Essay.* 1984. Reprint, London: Routledge Classics, 2001.

Milburn, Geoffrey. *Primitive Methodism.* Peterborough: Epworth Press, 2002.

Millen, Ron. "The Manifestation of Occult Qualities in the Scientific Revolution." In *Religion, Science, and Worldview: Essays in Honour of Richard Westfall.* Edited by M. J. Osler and P. L. Farber, 185-216. Cambridge: Cambridge University Press, 1985.

Mitsuo, Shimizu. *Epistemology in the Thought of John Wesley.* Ph.D. thesis, Drew University, 1980.

Moore, Robert. *John Wesley and Authority: A Psychological Perspective.* Missoula: Scholars Press, 1979.

Morris, Jeremy. "The Origins and Growth of Primitive Methodism in East Surrey." *Proceedings of the Wesley Historical Society* 48 (1992): 133-49.

Mousset, Albert. *L' étrange Histoire des Convulsionnaires de St-Médard.* Paris: Les Edition de Minuit, 1953.

Muessig, Carolyn and Ad Putter, eds. *Envisaging Heaven in the Middle Ages* (London: Routledge, 2007).

Muir, Edward. *Ritual in Early Modern Europe.* Cambridge: Cambridge University Press, 1997.

Mullan, John and Christopher Reid, eds. *Eighteenth-Century Popular Culture: A Selection.* Oxford: Oxford University Press, 2000.

Mullin, Robert Bruce. *Miracles & the Modern Religious Imagination.* New Haven, CT: Yale University Press, 1996.

Newport, Kenneth G. C. *Apocalypse & Millennium: Studies in Biblical Eisegesis.* Cambridge: Cambridge University Press, 2000.

_____. "Early Methodism and The French Prophets: Some New Evidence." *Proceedings of the Wesley Historical Society* 50 (1996): 127-40.

_____. "The French Prophets and Early Methodism: Some New Evidence." *Proceedings of the Wesley Historical Society* 50 (1996): 127-40.

_____. "George Bell, Prophet and Enthusiast." *Methodist History* 35 (1997): 95-105.

Newport, Kenneth G. C. and Gareth Lloyd. "George Bell and Early Methodist Enthusiasm: A New Manuscript Source from the Manuscript Archives." *Bulletin of the John Rylands University Library of Manchester* 80 (1998): 89-101.

Neyrey, Jerome, ed. *The Social World of Luke-Acts.* Peabody, MA: Hendrickson Publishers, 1991.

Nieman, Susan. *Evil in Modern Thought: An Alternative History of Philosophy.* Princeton, NJ: Princeton University Press, 2002.

_____. "What's the Problem with Evil." In *Rethinking Evil: Contmeporary Perspectives.* Edited by Mara Pía Kara, 27-45. Berkley, CA: University of California Press, 2001.

Nighall, Robert. *A Geography of Victorian Gothic Fiction: Mapping History's Nightmare.* Oxford: Oxford University Press, 1999.

Noll, Mark A. *The Rise of Evangelicalism: The Age of Edwards, Whitefield and the Wesleys.* Downers Grove, IL: InterVarsity Press, 2003.

von Noppen, Jean-Pierre. *Transforming Words: The Early Methodist Revival from a Discourse Perspective.* Bern: Peter Lang, 1999.

Noro, Yoship. "Wesley's Theological Epistemology." *Iliff Review* 28 (1971): 59-76.

Obelkevich, James. *Religion and Rural Society: South Lindsey 1825-1875.* Oxford: Clarendon Press, 1976.

Oberman, Heiko. *Masters of the Reformation: The Emergence of a New Intellectual Climate in Europe.* Translated by Dennis Martin. Cambridge: Cambridge University Press, 1981.

Ott, Phillip. "John Wesley on Health as Wholeness." *Journal of Religion and Health* 30 (1991): 43-57.

_____. "Medicine as Metaphor: John Wesley on Therapy of the Soul." *Methodist History* 33 (1995): 178-91.

Outler, Albert. "Appendix A: Wesley's Text: Editions, Transmission, Presentation, and Variant Readings." In *Sermons IV (115-141), The Bicentennial Edition of The Works of John* Wesley. Edited by Albert Outler, 4: 469. Nashville, TN: Abingdon Press, 1989.

_____. "Justification By Faith: An Introductory Comment." In *Sermons I (1-33), The Bicentennial Edition of The Works of John Wesley.* Edited by Albert Outler, 1: 181. Oxford and Nashville, TN: Clarendon Press and Abingdon Press, 1980.

_____. "The New Birth: An Introductory Comment." In *Sermons II (34-73), The Bicentennial Edition of The Works of John* Wesley. Edited by Albert Outler, 2: 186. Nashville, TN: Clarendon Press and Abingdon Press, 1985.

Outram, Dorinda. *The Enlightenment.* 2nd ed. 2005. Reprint, Cambridge: Cambridge University Press, 2006.

Park, Andrew Sung. "Holiness and Healing: An Asian American Voice Shaping in Methodist Traditions." In *Methodist and Radical: Rejuvenating a Tradition.* Edited by Joerg Rieger and John J. Vincent, 95-106. Nashville. TN: Kingswood Books, 2003.

Pearson, Roger. *Voltaire Almighty: A Life in Pursuit of Freedom.* London: Bloomsbury, 2005.

Pelikan, Jaroslav. *Christianity and Classical Culture: The Metamorphosis of Natural Theology in the Christian Encounter with Hellenism.* New Haven, CT: Yale University Press, 1993.

Penelhum, Terrence. *Themes in Hume: The Self, the Will, and Religion.* Oxford: Clarendon Press, 2000.

Perkins, Harald William. *The Doctrine of Christian Perfection.* London: Epworth Press, 1927.

Perkins, Maureen. "The Meaning of Dream Books." *History Workshop Journal* 48 (1999): 102-13.

Peters, Edward. "The Medieval Church and State on Superstition, Magic and Witchcraft: From Augustine to the Sixteenth Century." In *Witchcraft and Magic in Europe: The Middle Ages.* Edited by Bengt Ankarloo and Stuart Clark, 173-245. London: The Atlone Press, 2002.

Petty, John. *The History of the Primitive Methodist Connexion, from its Origins to the Conference of 1860, the First Jubilee Year of the Connexion.* 1860; rev. ed. London, John Dickenson,1880.

Pilch, John. *Healing in the New Testament: Insights from Medical and Mediterranean Anthropology.* Minneapolis, MN: Fortress Press, 2000.

_____. "Sickness and Healing in Luke-Acts." In *The Social World of Luke-Acts.* Edited by Jerome Neyrey, 21-41. Peabody, MA: Hendrickson Publishers, 1991.

Platt, F. "Perfection (Christian)." in *Encyclopedia of Religion and Ethics.* Edited by James Hastings, 10: 728-37. London: T & T Clark, 1888.

Podmore, Colin. *The Moravian Church in England 1728-1760.* Oxford: Clarendon Press, 1998.

Pope, William Burt. *Compendium of Christian Theology.* Rev. Ed. 3 vols. London: n. p., 1879.

Porter, Roy. *Enlightenment: Britain and the Creation of the Modern World.* London: The Penguin Press, 2001.

_____. *The Enlightenment,* 2nd ed. Houndmills: Palgrave, 2001.

_____. *Quacks: Fakers & Charlatans in English Medicine.* Stroud: Tempus Publishing Ltd., 1989, 2000.

_____. "Witchcraft and Magic in Enlightenment, Romantic, and Liberal Thought." In *Witchcraft and Magic in Europe: The Eighteenth and Nineteenth Centuries,* edited by Bengt Ankarloo and Stuart Clark, 191-274. Philadelphia, PA: University of Pennsylvania Press, 1999.

Porterfield, Amanda. *Healing in the History of Christianity.* Oxford: Oxford University Press, 2005.

Prior, Moody. "Joseph Glanvill, Witchcraft, and Seventeenth-Century Science." *Modern Philology* 30 (1933): 180-84.

Quarie, P. "The Christ Church Collection Books." In *The History of the University of Oxford,* 5: *The Eighteenth Century.* 493-511. Oxford: Oxford University Press, 1986.

Rack, Henry D. "Between Church and Sect: The Origins of Methodism in Manchester." *Bulletin of the John Rylands University Library of Manchester* 80 (1998): 65-87.

_____. "Doctors, Demons, and Early Methodist Healing." In *The Church and Healing.* Edited by W. J. Shiels, 137-52. Oxford: Blackwells, 1982.

_____. "Early Methodist Visions of the Trinity." *Proceedings of the Wesley Historical Society* 46 (1987): 38-44, 57-69.

_____. "Evangelical Endings: Death-Beds in Evagelical Biography." *Bulletin of the John Rylands University Library of Manchester* 74 (1992): 39-56.

_____. *The Future of John Wesley's Methodism*. London: Lutterworth Press, 1965.

_____. *How Primitive was Primitive Methodism?* Englesea Brook: Englesea Brook Primitive Methodist Museum Committee, 1996.

_____. *James Crawfoot and the Magic Methodists*. Englesea Brook: Englesea Brook Primitive Methodist Museum Committee, 2003.

_____. *Reasonable Enthusiast: John Wesley and the Rise of Methodism*, 3rd ed. London: Epworth Press, 2002.

Radner, Ephraim. *Spirit and Nature: The Saint-Médard Miracles in 18th-Century Jansenism*. New York: The Crossroad Publishing Company, 2002.

Rattenbury, J. Ernest. *The Evangelical Doctrines of Charles Wesley's Hymns*. London: Epworth Press, 1941.

Rawcliffe, Carole. *Medicine & Society in Later Medieval England*. 2nd ed. London: Sandpiper Books, 1999.

Reiss, Timothy J. *Knowledge, Discovery and Imagination in Early Modern Europe: The Rise of Aesthetic Rationalism*. Cambridge: Cambridge University Press, 1997.

Remus, Harold. *Jesus as Healer*. Cambridge: Cambridge University Press, 1997.

Rey, Roselyne. *Naissance et development du vitalisme en France, de la deuxième moitié du XVIIIe siècle à la fin du Premier Empire*. Oxford: Clarendon Press, 1999.

_____. "Psyche, Soma, and the Vitalist Philosophy of Medicine." In *Psyche and Soma: Physicians and Metaphysicians on the Mind-Body Problem From Antiquity to Enlightenment*. Edited by John P. Wright and Paul Potter, 255-65. Oxford: Clarendon Press, 2000.

Ricoeur, Paul. "'Original Sin': A Study in Meaning." Translated by Peter McCormick. In Paul Ricoeur, *The Conflict of Interpretations: Essays in Hermeneutics*. Edited by Don Ihde, 269-86. Evanston, IL: Northwestern University Press, 1974.

Rieger, Joerg. "Between God and the Poor: Rethinking the Means of Grace in the Wesleyan Tradition." In *The Poor and the People Called* Methodists. Edited by Richard P. Heitzenrater, 83-99. Nashville, TN: Kingswood Books, 2002.

Rieger, Joerg and John J. Vincent, eds. *Methodist and Radical: Rejuvenating a Tradition*. Nashville, TN: Kingswood Books, 2003.

Rigg, J. H. *Jabez Bunting, a Great Methodist Leader*. New York: The Methodist Book Concern, 1905.

Rist, J. M. *Epicurus: An Introduction*. Cambridge: Cambridge University Press, 1972.

Rivers, Isabel. "Grace, Holiness and the Pursuit of Happiness: Bunyan and Restoration Latitudinarianism." In *John Bunyan: Coventicle and Parnassus*. Edited by N. H. Keeble, 75-89. Oxford: Clarendon Press, 1988.

———. *Reason, Grace, and Sentiment: A Study of the Language of Religion and Ethics in England 1660-1780*, 2 vols. Cambridge: Cambridge University Press, 1991-2001.

———. "Responses to Hume on Religion by Anglicans and Dissenters." *The Journal of Ecclesiastical History* 52 (2001): 675-95.

Rogal, Samuel. "Electricity: John Wesley's Curious and Important Subject." *Eighteenth-Century Life* 13 (1989): 79-90.

———. "John Wesley's Arminian Magazine." *Andrews University Seminary Studies* 22 (1984): 231-47.

———. "Pills for the Poor: John Wesley's Primitive Physic." *The Yale Journal of Biology and Medicine* 51 (1978): 81-90.

Roper, Lyndal. *Oedipus & The Devil: Witchcraft, Sexuality and Religion in Early Modern Europe*. 1994. Reprint, London: Routledge, 2002.

———. *Witch Craze: Terror and Fantasy in Baroque Germany*. New Haven, CT: Yale University Press, 2004.

Rose, Bruce Edward. *The Influence of Genre in John Wesley's Journal*. Ph.D. thesis, University of North Carolina at Chapel Hill, 1999.

Rousseau, George S. "John Wesley's Primitive Physic (1747)." *Harvard Library Bulletin* 16 (1968): 242-56.

———. "Mysticism and Millenarianism: 'Immortal Dr. Cheyne.'" In *Hermeticism and the Renaissance: Intellectual History and the Occult in Early Modern Europe*. Edited by Ingrid Merkel and Allen Debus, Washington, DC: Folger Shakespeare Library, 1988.

Rowell, Geoffrey. *Hell and the Victorians: A Study of the Nineteenth-Century Theological Controversies Concerning Eternal Punishment and the Future Life*. 1974. Reprint, Oxford: Clarendon Press, 2000.

Rule, John. "Methodism, Popular Beliefs and Village Culture in Cornwall, 1800-50." In *Popular Culture and Custom in Nineteenth-Century England*. Edited by Robert Storch, 60-79. London: Croom Helm, 1982.

Runyon, Theodore. *The New Creation: John Wesley's Theology Today*. Nashville, TN: Abingdon Press, 1998.

Russell, Jeffrey. *The Devil: Perceptions of Evil from Antiquity to Primitive Christianity* Ithaca, NY: Cornell University Press, 1977.

———. *Lucifer: The Devil in the Middle Ages*. Ithaca, NY: Cornell University Press, 1985.

———. *Mephistopheles: The Devil in the Modern World*. Ithaca, NY: Cornell University Press, 1990.

———. *Satan: The Early Christian Tradition*. Ithaca, NY: Cornell University Press, 1981.

Ruth, Lester, ed. *Early Methodist Life and Spirituality: A Reader*. Nashville, TN: Kingswood Books, 2005.

———. *A Little Heaven Below: Worship at Early Methodist Quarterly Meetings*. Nashville, TN: Kingswood Books, 2000.

Ryan, William Granger. "Introduction." In Jacobus de Voragine, *The Golden Legend: Readings on the Saints*. Translated by William Granger Ryan. 2 vols. 1: xiii-xviii. Princeton, NJ: Princeton University Press, 1993.

Sanides-Kohlrausch, Claudia. "The Lisbon Earthquake, 1755: A Discourse about the 'nature' of nature." In *Is Nature Ever Evil? Religion, Science and Value*. Edited by William Drees, 106-19. London: Routledge Taylor & Francis Group, 2003.

Sargent, William. *Battle for the Mind*. London: Heinmann, 1957.

Sauter, Gerhard. "Die Zahl als Schlüssel zur Welt: Johann Albrecht Bengels 'prophetische Zeitrechnung' im Zusammenhang seiner Theologie." *Evangelische Theologie* 26 (1966): 1-36.

Schaich, Michael. "A War of Words? Old and New Perspectives on the Enlightenment." *German Historical Institute London Bulletin* 24 (2002): 29-56.

Schechner, Sara. *Comets, Popular Culture, and the Birth of Modern Cosmology*. Princeton: Princeton University Press, 1997.

Schiffer, Michael Brian. *Draw the Lightening Down: Benjamin Franklin and Electrical Technology in the Age of Enlightenment*. Berkley, CA: University of California Press, 2003.

Schmidt, Leigh Eric. *Hearing Things: Religion, Illusion, and the American Enlightenment*. Cambridge: Cambridge University Press, 2000.

Schmidt, Martin. "Die Bedeutung Luthers für John Wesleys Bekehrung." *Lutherjahrbuch* 20 (1938): 125-59.

_____. *John Wesley: A Theological Biography*. Translated by Norman Goldhawk. 2 vols. in 3. New York: Abingdon Press, 1962.

Schneider, Mabel. *John Bunyan's The Pigrim Progress in the Tradition of Medieval Dream Visions*. Ph. D. thesis, University of Nebraska, 1969.

Schofield, Robert. "John Wesley and Science in 18th Century England." *Isis* 44 (1953): 331-40.

Schwartz, Hillel. *The French Prophets: The History of a Millenarian Group in Eighteenth-Century England*. Berkley, CA: University of California Press, 1980.

Seigel, Jerrold. *The Idea of the Self: Thought and Experience in Western Europe since the Seventeenth Century*. Cambridge: Cambridge University Press, 2005.

Shantz, Collen. *Paul in Ecstasy: The Neurobiology of the Apostle's Life and Thought*. New York: Cambridge University Press, 2009.

Shapin, Steven. *A Social History of Truth: Civility and Science in Seventeenth-Century England*. Chicago: University of Chicago Press, 1994.

Shapiro, Barbara. *Probability and Certainty in Seventeenth-Century England: A Study of the Relationship Between Natural Science, Religion, History, Law, and Literature*. Princeton: Princeton University Press, 1983.

Sharpe, James. *Instruments of Darkness: Witchcraft in Early Modern England*. Philadelphia, PA: University of Pennsylvania Press, 1997.

Shaw, Jane. "Fasting women: The Significance of Gender and Bodies in Radical Religion and Politics, 1650-1813." In *Radicalism in British Literary*

    Culture, 1650-1830: From Revolution to Revolution. Edited by Timothy Morton and Nigel Smith, 101-15. Cambridge: Cambridge University Press, 2002.

————. "The Late Seventeenth and Eighteenth Centuries." In *Christianity: Two Thousand Years.* Edited by Richard Harries and Henry Mayr-Harting, 162-91. Oxford: Oxford University Press, 2001.

————. *Miracles in Enlightenment England.* New Haven: Yale University Press, 2006.

————. *The Miraculous Body and other Rational Wonders: Religion in Enlightenment England.* Ph.D. thesis, University of California at Berkeley, 1994.

Sheard, Michael. *The Origins and Early Development of Primitive Methodism in Cheshire and South Lancashire, 1800-1860.* Ph.D. thesis, University of Manchester, 1980.

Shepherd, T. B. *Methodism and the Literature of the Eighteenth Century.* London: Epworth Press, 1940.

Skinner, Quentin. *Reason and Rhetoric in the Philosophy of Hobbes.* Cambridge: Cambridge University Press, 1996.

Snape, Michael. "'The Surey Imposter': Demonic Possession and Religious Conflict in Seventeenth-Century Lancashire." *Transactions of the Lancashire and Cheshire Antiquarian Society* 90, (1994): 93-114.

Snoek, G. J. C. *Medieval Piety from Relics to the Eucharist: A Process of Mutual Interaction.* Leiden: E. J. Brill, 1995.

Sobel, Mechal. *Teach Me Dreams: The Search for Self in the Revolutionary Era.* Princeton: Princeton University Press, 2000.

Soergel, Philip M. *Miracles and the Protestant Imagination: The Evangelical Wonder Book in Reformation Germany.* Oxford: Oxford University Press, 2012.

Southey, Robert. *The Life of Wesley and the Rise and Progress of Methodism.* 2 vols. London: Oxford University Press, 1925.

Spaeth, Donald. *The Church in an Age of Danger: Parsons and Parishoners, 1660-1740.* Cambridge: Cambridge University Press, 2000.

Spardafora, David. *The Idea of Progress in Eighteenth-Century Britain.* New Haven: Yale University Press, 1990.

Starkey, Jr., Lucurgus. *The Work of the Holy Spirit: A Study of Wesleyan Theology.* New York: Abingdon Press, 1962.

Steck, Karl Gerhard. *Luther und die Schwärmer.* Zollikon-Zürich: Evangelischer Verlag, 1955.

Stephen, Leslie. *English Thought in the Eighteenth Century.* 2 vols. 1876. Reprint, Bristol: Thoemmes Press, 1991.

Stephen, Leslie and Sidney Lee, eds. *The Dictionary of National Biography.* 22 vols. 1885-1901. Reprint, Oxford: Oxford University Press, 1998.

Stephens, Walter. *Demon Lovers: Witchcraft, Sex, and the Crisis of Belief.* Chicago: University of Chicago Press, 2002.

Stevens, Abel. *History of the Methodist Episcopal Church in the United States of America.* 2 vols. New York: Carleton and Porter, 1864-67.

Stoeffler, F. Ernest. "The Wesleyan Concept of Religious Certainity—Its Pre-History and Significance." *The London Quarterly and Holborn Review* 33 (1964): 128-39.

Strydom, Piet. *Discourse and Knowledge: The Making of Enlightenment Sociology.* Liverpool: Liverpool University Press, 2000.

Suchocki, Marjorie. "The Perfection of Prayer." In *Rethinking Wesley's Theology for Contemporary Methodism.* Edited by Randy Maddox, 49-63. Nashville: Kingswood Books, 1998.

Suurmound, Jean-Jacques. *Word & Spirit at Play: Towards a Charismatic Theology.* Translated by John Bowden. Grand Rapids: William B. Eerdmans Publishing Company, 1994.

Sutherland, Lucy S. "The Curriculum." In *The History of the University of Oxford,* 5: *The Eighteenth Century* edited by Lucy S. Sutherland and L. G. Mitchell, 469-511. Oxford: Oxford University Press, 1986.

Sykes, Norman. *Church and State in England in the XVIIIth Century.* Cambridge: Cambridge University Press, 1934.

Taves, Ann. *Fits, Trances & Visions: Experiencing Religion and Explaining Experience from Wesley to James.* Princeton: Princeton University Press, 1999.

———. "Knowing through the Body: Dissociative Religious Experience in the African- and British-American Methodist Traditions." *Journal of Religion* 73 (1993): 200-22.

Taylor, Barbara Howard. *The Notorious Astrological Physician of London: Works and Days of Simon Forman.* Chicago: University of Chicago Press, 2001.

Thale, Mary. "Deists, Papists and Methodists at London Debating Societies, 1746-1799." *History* 86 (2001): 328-47.

Thomas, Keith. *Religion and the Decline of Magic: Studies in Popular Beliefs in Sixteenth and Seventeenth Century England.* 1971. Reprint, London: Weidenfeld & Nicolson, 1997.

Thompson, E. P. *The Making of the English Working Class.* 1963. Reprint, London: Penguin Books, 1991.

Tomlinson, John W. B. "The Magic Methodists and their Influence on the early Primitive Methodist Movement." In *Signs, Wonders, Miracles: Representations of Divine Power in the Life of the Church.* Edited by Kate Cooper and Jeremy Gregory, 389-99. Woodbridge: The Boydell Press, 2005.

Towlson, Clifford. *Moravian and Methodist: Relationships and Influences in the Eighteenth Century.* London: Epworth Press, 1957.

Tuck, John "'Primitive Physic': An Interesting Association Copy." *Proceedings of the Wesley Historical Society* 45 (1985): 1-7.

Turrell, James. "The Ritual of Royal Healing: Scrofula, Liturgy, and Politics." *Anglican and Episcopal History* 68 (1999): 3-36.

Turrell, Walter J. *John Wesley: Physician & Electrotherapist.* Oxford: Blackwell, 1938.

Twelftree, Graham. *Jesus The Miracle Worker: A Historical and Theological Study*. Downers Grove, IL: InterVarsity Press, 1999.

Tweyman, Stanley, ed. *Hume on Natural Religion*. Bristol: Thoemmes Press, 1996.

———. *Hume on Miracles*. Bristol: Thoemmes Press, 1996.

Tyerman, Luke. *The Life and Times of the Rev. John Wesley, M. A.: Founder of the Methodists*. 3 vols. London: Hodder & Houghton, 1870.

Valenze, Deborah. *Prophetic Sons and Daughters: Female Preaching and Popular Religion in Industrialized England*. Princeton: Princeton University Press, 1985.

Vickers, Brian. *In Defence of Rhetoric*. 1998. Reprint, Oxford: Oxford University Press, 2002.

Vickers, John A., ed. *A Dictionary of Methodism in Britain and Ireland*. London: Epworth Press, 2000.

Voigt, Max. *Beiträge zur Geschichte der Visionenliteratur im Mittelalter*. Leipzig: Mayer and Müller, 1924 .

Wahrman, Dror. *The Making of the Modern Self: Identity and Culture in Eighteenth-Century England*. New Haven: Yale University Press, 2004.

Wainwright, Geoffrey. "John Wesley's Trinitarian Hermeneutics." *Wesleyan Theological Journal* 36 (2001): 7-30.

———. "Methodism and the Apostolic Faith." In *What Should Methodists Teach? Wesleyan Tradition and Modern Diversity*, edited by M. Douglas Meeks, 101-17. Nashville: Kingswood Books, 1990.

———. "Trinitarian Theology and Wesleyan Holiness." In *Orthodoxy and Wesleyan Spirituality*. Edited by ST Kimbrough, 59-80. Crestwood, NY: St. Vladimir's Seminary Press, 2002.

Waldron, Jeremy. *God, Locke, and Equality: Christian Foundations in Locke's Political Thought*. Cambridge: Cambridge University Press, 2002.

Walker, D. P. "The Cessation of Miracles." In *Hermeticism and the Renaissance: Intellectual History and the Occult in Early Modern Europe* edited by Ingrid Merkel and Allen Debus, 101-13. Washington: Folger Shakespeare Library, 1988.

———. *Unclean Spirits: Possession and Exorcism in France and England in the Late Sixteenth and Early Seventeenth Centuries*. London: Scholar Press, 1981.

Walsh, John. "The Cambridge Methodists." In *Christian Spirituality: Essays in Honor of Gordon Rupp*. Edited by Peter Brooks, 249-83. London: SCM Press, 1975.

———. "The Thirty Nine Articles and Anglican Identity in The Eighteenth Century." In *Quand Religions et Confessions se Regardent*. Edited by Christiane d' Haussy, 61-70. Paris: Didier-Erudition 1998.

Walsh, John and Stephen Taylor. "Introduction: the Church and Anglicanism in the 'long eighteenth-century.'" In *The Church of England c. 1689-c. 1833: From Toleration to Tractarianism*. Edited by John Walsh, Colin Hayden, and Stephen Taylor, 1-64. Cambridge: Cambridge University Press, 1993.

Walsh, John and David Hempton. "E. P. Thompson and Methodism." In *God and Mammon: Protestants, Money, and the Market, 1790-1860*. Edited by Mark A. Noll, 99-120. Oxford: Oxford University Press, 2001.

Walsham, Alexandra. *Providence in Early Modern England.* Oxford: Oxford University Press, 1999.

Ward, W. R. *Early Evangelicalism: A Global Intellectual History.* Cambridge: Cambridge University Press, 2006.

_____. *Faith and Faction.* London: Epworth Press, 1993.

_____. "Introduction." in *Journals and Diaries I (1735-1738), The Bicentennial Edition of The Works of John Wesley*. Edited by W. R. Ward and Richard P. Heitzenrater, 18: 1-119. Nashville, TN: Abingdon Press, 1988.

_____. *The Protestant Evangelical Awakening.* Cambridge: Cambridge University Press, 1992.

Watkin-Jones, Howard. *The Holy Spirit from Arminus to Wesley.* London: Epworth Press, 1929.

Watkins, Carl S. *History and the Supernatural in Medieval England.* Cambridge: Cambridge University Press, 2009.

Watson, David Lowes, *The Early Methodist Class Meeting: Its Origins and Significance.* 1985. Reprint, Nashville, TN: Discipleship Resources, 1995.

Watson, Richard A., ed. *The Dream of Descartes.* Carbondale, IL: Southern Illinois, 1987.

Weber, Theodore. *Politics in the Order of Salvation.* Nashville, TN: Kingswood Books, 2001.

Webster, Robert. "Copy of *Compendium of Logick* Found." *Proceedings of the Wesley Historical Society* 53 (2002): 215.

_____. "'Inward & Outward Health': The Supernatural Dimensions of Healing in John Wesley." In *"Inward and Outward Health": John Wesley's Holistic Concept of Medical Science, the Environment and Holy Living*. Edited by Deborah Madden, 213-32. London: Epworth Press, 2008.

_____. "The Lisbon Earthquake: John and Charles Wesley Reconsidered." In *The Lisbon Earthquake of 1755: Representations and Reaction*. Edited by Theodore E. D. Braun and John B. Radner, 116-26. Oxford: Voltaire Foundation, 2005.

_____. "Methodism and the Miraculous: John Wesley's Contribution to the *Historia Miraculorum*." D. Phil. Thesis, Oxford University, 2006.

_____. "Seeing Salvation: The Place of Dreams and Visions in John Wesley's *Arminian Magazine*." In *Signs, Wonders, Miracles: Representations of Divine Power in the Life of the Church*. Edited by Kate Cooper and Jeremy Gregory, 376-88. Woodbridge: The Boydell Press, 2005.

_____. "Sensing the Supernatural: John Wesley's Empirical Epistemology and the Pursuit of Divine Knowledge." *Sewanee Theological Review* 54 (2011): 254-81.

_____. "'Those Distracting Terrors of the Enemy': John Wesley's Rhetoric of Evil." *Bulletin of the John Rylands University Library of Manchester* 85 (2003): 373-85.

_____. "The Value of Self-Denial: John Wesley's Multidimensional View of Fasting." *Toronto Journal of Theology* 19 (2003): 25-40.

Well, Louise. *The Greek language of Healing from Homer to New Testament Times*. New Berlin: Walter de Gruyter, 1998.

Wellbery, David. "The Transformation of Rhetoric." In *The Cambridge History of Literary Criticism*, v: *Romanticism*. Edited by Marshall Brown, 185-202. Cambridge: Cambridge University Press, 2000.

Wellings, Martin. *Evangelicals Embattled: Responses to Evangelicals in the Church of England to Ritualism, Darwinism, and Theological Liberalism 1890-1930*. Carlisle: Paternoster Press, 2003.

Westerfield Tucker. Karen. *American Methodist Worship*. Oxford: Oxford University Press, 2001.

Whitehead, John. *The Life of the Rev. Wesley, M. A. Some Time Fellow of Lincoln-College, Oxford. Collected from his Private Papers and Printed Works; and Written at the Request of his Executors. To which is Prefixed, Some Account of his Ancestors and Relations: with the Life of the Rev. Charles Wesley, M. A. Collected from his Private Journal, and never before Published. The whole forming a History of Methodism, in which the Principles and Economy of the Methodists are Unfolded*, 2 vols. London: Stephen Couchman, 1793.

Wigger, John. "Fighting Bees: Methodist Itinerants and the Dynamics of Methodist Growth, 1770-1820." In *Methodism and the Shaping of American Culture*. Edited by Nathan Hatch and John Wigger, 87-133. Nashville, TN: Kingswood Books, 2001.

_____. *Taking Heaven by Storm: Methodism and the Rise of Popular Religion in America*. New York: Oxford University Press, 1998.

Wilcoxon, Clair D. "The Whole Man: A Study of John Wesley's Healing Ministry." *Religion in Life* 28 (1959): 580-86.

Williams, Colin. *John Wesley's Theology Today*. New York: Abingdon Press, 1960.

Williams, George. *"The Word came with Power": Print, Oratory, and Methodism in Eighteenth-Century Britain*. Ph.D. thesis, University of Maryland, 2002.

Williams, Norman Powell. *The Ideas of the Fall and of Original Sin: A Historical Study*. London: Longmans, Green and Co, 1927.

Williams, Peter. *Popular Religion in America: Symbolic Change and the Modernization Process in Historical Perspective*. Urbana, IL: University of Illinois Press, 1989.

Williams, Sarah. *Religious Belief and Popular Culture in Southward c. 1880-1939*. Oxford: Oxford University Press, 1999.

Wilson, Adrian. "The Politics of Medical Improvement in Early Hanoverian London." In *The Medical Enlightenment of the Eighteenth Century*. Edited by Andrew Cunningham and Roger French, 4-39. 1990. Reprint, Cambridge: Cambridge University Press, 2004.

Wilson, D. Dunn. "The Importance of Hell for John Wesley." *Proceedings of the Wesley Historical Society* 34 (1963): 12-16.

Wilson, Paul Scott. "Wesley's Homiletic: Law and Gospel for Preaching." *Toronto Journal of Theology* 10 (1994): 215-55.

Witherington, Ben. *The Acts of the Apostles: A Socio-Rhetorical Commentary.* Grand Rapids, MI: William B. Eerdmans Publishing, 1998.

Witmore, Michael. *Culture of Accidents: Unexpected Knowledges in Early Modern England.* Stanford, CA: Stanford University Press, 2001.

Wittmann, Reinhard. "Was there a Reading Revolution at the End of the Eighteenth Century?" Translated by Lydia Cochrane. In *A History of Reading in the* West. Edited by Gugliemo Cavallo and Roger Charter, 288-300. London: Polity, 2003.

Wood, A. Skevington. *The Burning Heart: John Wesley, Evangelist.* Grand Rapids, MI: William B. Eerdmans Publishing Company,1967.

Wood, Laurence Willard. *The Meaning of Pentecost in Early Methodism: Rediscovering John Fletcher as John Wesley's Vindicator and Designated Successor.* Lanham, MD: The Scarecrow Press, Inc., 2002.

_____. "Wesley's Epistemology." *Wesleyan Theological Journal* 10 (1975): 48-59.

Yeager, Jonathan. *Enlightened Evangelicalism: The Life and Thought of John Erskine.* Oxford: Oxford University Press, 2011.

Young, Brian W. *Religion and Enlightenment in Eighteentth-Century England: Theological Debate from Locke to Burke.* Oxford: Clarendon Press, 1998.

_____. *The Victorian Eighteenth Century: An Intellectual History.* Oxford: Oxford University Press, 2007.

9 781609 470487